中国人事科学研究院
·学术文库·

# 当代中国的行政改革

中国人事科学研究院　组织编写

余兴安　主编

中国社会科学出版社

图书在版编目（CIP）数据

当代中国的行政改革／中国人事科学研究院组织编写；余兴安主编．—北京：
中国社会科学出版社，2017.5

ISBN 978 - 7 - 5203 - 0102 - 2

Ⅰ.①当…　Ⅱ.①中…　②余…　Ⅲ.①行政管理—政治体制改革—研究—中国
Ⅳ.①D63

中国版本图书馆 CIP 数据核字（2017）第 067693 号

出 版 人　赵剑英
责任编辑　孔继萍
责任校对　沈丁晨
责任印制　李寡寡

出　　　版　中国社会科学出版社
社　　　址　北京鼓楼西大街甲 158 号
邮　　　编　100720
网　　　址　http://www.csspw.cn
发 行 部　010 - 84083685
门 市 部　010 - 84029450
经　　　销　新华书店及其他书店

印刷装订　北京市兴怀印刷厂
版　　次　2017 年 5 月第 1 版
印　　次　2017 年 5 月第 1 次印刷

开　　本　710×1000　1/16
印　　张　24
插　　页　2
字　　数　451 千字
定　　价　98.00 元

# 前　言

2016 年 9 月 19—23 日，国际行政科学学会暨国际行政院校联合会联合大会（以下简称"国际大会"）在成都召开。会议由人力资源和社会保障部、国家行政学院共同主办，中国人事科学研究院、四川大学、成都市人民政府承办，中国行政管理学会、中国行政体制改革研究会、中国机构编制管理研究会协办。

这是国际行政科学领域规格最高、最具学术影响力的盛会，来自 50 多个国家、地区和国际组织的 500 余名专家学者和政府官员共聚一堂，围绕"可持续治理能力建设"这一主题，进行了广泛的交流和研讨。会议期间还举办了洲际行政论坛、中国专场会、金砖国家专场会、联合国专场会、OECD 专场会等数十场专题学术活动，均取得了良好的学术效果。

作为会议的主承办单位，也是国际行政科学学会副主席单位，在会议筹备期间，中国人事科学研究院即邀集国内学者商议，一致认为，一方面要广泛动员我国学者参会，就国际行政科学领域共同感兴趣的问题发出中国声音，贡献中国智慧；另一方面，也要展示我国行政改革的伟大成就，向国际同行介绍我们的成功经验。于是有了编写这本《当代中国的行政改革》的设想及编写工作的展开。

本书旨在全面阐述自改革开放以来特别是近年来我国行政改革的发展历程、主要举措、实际成效和基本经验，内容涉及政府机构改革、职能转变、行政审批制度改革、社会治理创新、政务公开、电子政务、事业单位改革、公共财政改革、人事制度改革、政府绩效管理、行政问责及法制政府建设等，同时对三十余年来我国行政科学研究所取得的成就也进行了回顾与总结。在书稿完成后，请专业人士做了英文翻译，最终形成中英两种文本，在 9 月份的国际大会上印发。

本书的撰著者来自国家行政学院、中国行政管理学会、中国行政体制改革研究会、中国机构编制管理研究会和中国人事科学研究院等单位，他们中既有德高望重的权威学者，如中国行政体制改革研究会会长魏礼群同志，也有长期耕耘于行政科学领域的资深专家和近年来崭露头角的学术新锐。按章节顺序，他们是魏礼群、李利平、陈锋、易丽丽、龚维斌、冯俏彬、李学明、胡仙芝、吴文征、刘小康、尹艳红、胡建淼、华燕、刘杰（所在单位及职务职称在各章文尾有标明，兹不赘述）。

中国人事科学研究院院长、国际大会筹委会秘书长余兴安同志主持了编写工作，提出编写大纲与编写体例，通审文稿。行政学界资深专家高小平、邵景均、顾杰同志参加了文稿的修改讨论，提出了许多有价值的意见。全国政协委员、中国人事科学研究院前任院长吴江同志对编写工作惠予诸多指导，中国人事科学研究院的柳学智、熊缨、乔立娜、王伊、何天纯、郭越君同志协助主编做了组织联络工作和审校工作。

三十余年来中国的行政改革无疑是当代世界行政领域最波澜壮阔的画卷，本书是对这一壮丽画卷所做的一个全景性描绘。在作为会议材料提交去年 9 月的国际大会后，我们又进行了一些修改。现正式交付出版，既是为广大读者提供一份参考文献，同时也藉此在更广泛的范围内听取批评指正的意见。

余兴安

中国人事科学研究院院长

2017 年 4 月

# 目　　录

# 第 一 章

# 中国行政改革的基本历程和经验

行政改革是政治改革的重要内容，是中国改革发展事业的重要组成部分。行政改革包括行政权力结构变革、行政组织机构调整、行政管理制度以及行政手段方式创新等。中国改革开放 40 年来，行政改革取得重大成就，回顾中国行政改革的伟大历程和宝贵经验，研究探讨继续推进改革需要解决的重点问题，对于深刻认识改革开放的伟大成就，继续深化行政体制改革，协调推进"四个全面"战略布局，具有重要意义。

## 一 中国行政改革的背景

行政体制作为国家政治上层建筑的重要组成部分，一个国家的社会经济制度及其发展阶段，决定着一定的行政体制。因此，中国行政改革的发展离不开中国特定的行政传统、经济社会改革的不断深化以及国际行政理论与实践的发展。

### （一）中国行政传统和改革前中国行政体制变迁

1949 年 10 月 1 日，中华人民共和国宣告成立。社会主义制度在中国的确立，为探索建立新型的行政管理创造了条件。1951 年政务院做出《关于调整机构紧缩编制的决定（草案）》，进行了新中国成立后第一次精兵简政工作。1954 年，第一届全国人民代表大会颁布了我国第一部《宪法》，选举了国家主席，成立了国务院，形成了新中国基本的行政框架。从 1954 年年底，用了一年多的时间，对中央和地方各级机关进行了一次较大规模的精简。1956 年又开始重新调整中央与地方的权限关系，这年召开的全国体制会议提出：改进国家行政体制的首要步骤，是先划分中央和各省、自治区、直辖市的行政管理职权，并且对地方的行政管理权予以适当扩大，然后再逐步划分省和县、县和乡的行政管理职权。这次改革一直持续到1960年。20世纪60年代初期，为适应国民经济调整的需要，进行了"精简加集中"的行政体制改革。总的来看，新中国成立后，中国行政体制建设取得了重要进展：一是初步构建了与社会主义国家性质要求相适应的行政管理模式，二是创建了与计划经济体制相适应的行政体制，三是积累了中国行政体制建设的正反两方面经验。可以说，这一历史时期的行政体制发展历程尽管有不少曲折，但探索了中央与地方的权限关系，实施了精兵简政，调整了政府机构设置，建立了社会主义行政体制基本框架，促进了经济社会发展。这一历史时期的行政体制建设为改革开放后的行政体制改革提供了基本前提和重要借鉴，其中最根本的教训就是不能超越经济社会发展水平及相应的客观条件，而一定要从本国国情和实际情况出发，着眼于适应生产力发展的需要，稳步加以调整和变革。

### （二）持续快速的经济社会发展和不断深化的改革开放

1978年以来，中国拉开了伟大的改革开放历史序幕。从农村到城市，从经济领域到其他各个领域，全面改革的进程势不可当。开放从对内到对外，从沿海到沿江沿边，从东部到中西部，对外开放的进程波澜壮阔。这场历史上从未有过的大改革大开放，极大地调动了亿万人民的积极性，极大地解放和发展了社会生产力，推动了社会的全面进步，使中国成功实现了从高度集中的计划经济体制到充满活力的社会主义市场经济体制、从封闭半封闭到全方位开放的伟大历史转折。中国人民的面貌、社会主义中国的面貌、中国共产党的面貌发生了历史性变化，我国综合国力大幅度提升，国际地位和影响显著提高。特别是我国经济以世界上少有的速度持续快速发展起来，从一度濒于崩溃的边缘到总量跃居世界第二，人民生活从温饱不足发展到全面小康，为世界经济发展和人类文明进步做出了重大贡献。持续快速的经济社会发展和不断深化的改革开放事业为中国行政改革提供了动力和基础支撑。

### （三）国际行政改革理论与实践

自 20 世纪 70 年代以来，随着国际形势的变化，国际行政改革理论与实践取得了积极进展，相继出现了以新公共管理运动、公共选择理论和治理理论为代表的政府行政改革理论，并在美国、英国、法国、澳大利亚、新西兰等国家取得了很大的成功。国际行政改革理论和实践的主要内容与措施有：一是政府职能的优化。重新界定政府职能是当代西方发达市场经济国家政府改革的重点之一。在新公共管理运动视野中，政府从大量社会事务中解脱出来，将这些职能交给或归还给社会，由社会经济组织或中介组织去承担，政府则制定法律和规章制度，监督和执行法律法规。二是公共服务的市场化和社会化，即政府充分利用市场和社会的力量，推行公共服务市场化和社会化。三是分权。当代西方国家行政改革的目标之一在于分散政府管理职能，缩小政府行政范围，因而必然要求实行分权与权力下放。四是引入现代化管理技术，即引进现代化管理技术尤其是私营部门的管理技术来"重塑政府"，实现政府管理的现代化，建立一个"市场化""企业化"政府。中国行政改革理论与实践是在借鉴国际最新行政改革理论与实践的基础上进行的，虽然，国家与国家之间的行政体制，由于政治、历史、文化等原因，其改革的路径也不可能相同，我们也不可能照抄照搬国际行政改革的模式，但国际行政改革的理论与实践对于中国开阔眼界，打开思路，具有积极的启迪意义。实际上，中国行政改革正是在借鉴国际行政改革理论与实践有益做法的基础上，不断探索、不断深化，走出了一条中国特色行政改革之路。

## 二　中国行政改革的历程

1978 年年底召开的党的十一届三中全会，开启了我国改革开放和社会主义现代化建设的历史新时期。近 40 年的大改革大开放，使我国成功实现了从高度集中的计划经济体制到充满活力的社会主义市场经济体制、从封闭半封闭到全方位开放的伟大历史转折，经济和社会发展取得了举世瞩目的巨大成就。在这个过程中，按照建设中国特色社会主义的总体目标，根据上层建筑适应经济基础、解放和发展生产力的根本要求，坚持不懈地推进行政改革，并不断取得新突破和重大进展，中国特色社会主义行政体制不断改革与完善。这一时期行政体制变革大体经历了三个阶段。

### （一）冲破高度集中的计划经济体制束缚（1978—1992）

从党的十一届三中全会召开到党的十四大之前，主要是冲破高度集中的计划经济体制和行政管理模式，对完善中国特色社会主义行政体制进行积极探索。这一阶段于 1982 年和 1988 年实施了两次集中的行政体制改革。1982 年进行的国务院机构改革，重点是适应工作重点转移，提高政府工作效率，精简调整机构。国务院部门机构改革完成后，进行了地方机构改革，重点是精简庞大臃肿的机构，克服官僚主义，提高工作效能。1988 年实施了新一轮行政体制改革，改革的任务是进一步转变职能，理顺关系，精简机构和人员，提高行政效率。这次改革首次提出必须抓住转变职能这个关键，紧密地与经济体制改革相结合；按照经济体制改革和政企分开的要求，合并裁减专业管理部门和综合部门内设专业机构；从机构设置的科学性和整体性出发，适当加强决策咨询和调节、监督、审计、信息部门，转变综合部门的工作方式，提高政府对宏观经济的调控能力；贯彻精简、统一、效能原则，清理整顿行政性公司，撤销因人设事的机构，裁减人浮于事的部门和人员；为了巩固机构改革的成果，并使行政管理走上法制化道路，提出用法律手段控制机构设置和人员编制；改革中第一次实行定职能、定机构、定编制的"三定"工作。总体上看，通过这一阶段的改革，初步摆脱了与高度集中的计划经济体制相适应的行政管理模式的羁绊，激发了经济社会活力，促进了生产力的解放和发展。

### （二）适应社会主义市场经济体制（1993—2012）

从党的十四大召开到党的十八大之前，主要是按照发展社会主义市场经济的要求全面推进改革，中国特色社会主义行政体制改革取得重大进展。这一阶段于 1993 年和 1998 年实施了两次集中的行政体制改革。

1993 年国务院机构改革方案的主要内容：一是转变职能，坚持政企分开。要求把属于企业的权力下放给企业，把应该由企业解决的问题交由企业自己去解决，减少具体审批事务和对企业的直接管理。二是理顺关系。理顺国务院部门之间，尤其是综合经济部门之间以及综合经济部门与专业经济部门之间的关系，合理划分职责权限，避免交叉重复。理顺中央与地方关系，合理划分管理权限，使地方在中央方针政策的指导下因地制宜地发展本地区经济和各项社会事业。三是精简机构编制，从1993年开始，地方政府机构改革在全国展开，以转变政府职能为关键，较大幅度地精简了机构和人员，特别是大幅度精简专业经济管理部门。

1998年进行了力度最大的一次行政体制改革。改革的主要内容：一是调整部门职能，按照权责一致的原则，在部门之间划转了100多项职能，相同或相近的职能尽可能交由一个部门承担，过去长期存在而没有解决的职能交叉、多头管理、政出多门、权责不清等问题有了很大改进。二是精简机构编制。主要是大力精简工业经济部门，省、市、县、乡级机构也进行了相应改革。

2002年党的十六大以来，行政改革的主要任务是推进服务型政府和法治政府建设，中国特色社会主义行政体制改革全方位深化。重点围绕构建有利于推动科学发展、促进社会和谐的体制机制，着力进行制度机制创新和管理方式创新。主要包括：更加注重以人为本，促进经济社会全面协调可持续发展和人的全面发展；更加注重发展社会主义民主政治，大力推进科学民主决策，完善决策信息和智力支持系统，增强决策透明度和公众参与度；更加注重转变和全面履行政府职能，强化社会管理和公共服务职能，加快以改善民生和公共服务为重点的社会建设，增强社会创造活力；更加注重规范政府行为，全面推进依法行政，加快建设法治政府；更加注重改进管理方式，大力推进政务公开和电子政务，探索实行行政绩效管理制度。

党的十七届二中全会提出了到2020年建立起中国特色社会主义行政管理体制的改革目标，2008年以后，中国行政改革取得了新突破。政府职能转变取得积极进展，理顺部门关系取得重要突破，在探索实行职能有机统一的大部门体制方面迈出新步伐，集中解决了在宏观调控、资源环境、市场监管、文化卫生等方面70余项部门职责交叉和关系不顺的问题。

### （三）推进政府治理现代化（2013年之后）

这一阶段行政改革的主要任务主要是推进简政放权、放管结合、优化服务等改革，这一时期为行政体制改革向纵深推进的阶段。党的十八大以后，我国进入全面建成小康社会的决胜阶段，十八届三中全会提出了全面深化改革的总目标是发展和完善社会主义制度，推进国家治理体系和治理能力现代化。行政体制改革围绕这一总目标，加快建立中国特色社会主义行政体制。党的十八届三中全会提出，"必须切实转变政府职能，深化行政体制改革，创新行政管理方式，增强政府公信力和执行力，建设法治政府和服务型政府"。主线是深入推进政企分开、政资分开、政事分开、政社分开，持续推进简政放权、放管结合、优化服务等改革，建设职能科学、结构优化、廉洁高效、人民满意的服务型政府，为推进中国经济适应、引领新常态，实现中高速增长，迈入中高端水平提供支撑。

# 三　中国行政改革的主要内容

改革开放后进行的中国行政改革，是在推进经济体制改革、社会体制改革、文化体制改革和政治体制改革的情况下，对行政体制的性质、特点、规律、关系、目标和任务不断深化认识和逐步推进的探索过程，也是对建设中国特色社会主义规律的重大探索过程。实践证明，这个时期的改革和探索取得了很大成功，从根本上摒弃了高度集中的计划经济体制和行政管理模式，基本建立了与发展社会主义市场经济相适应的行政体制。其主要内容是：

## （一）转变政府职能

从传统的计划经济转向社会主义市场经济，必然要求转变政府职能。转变政府职能，不仅是贯穿于改革开放以来近40年的中国行政改革历程中的一条红线，也是中国行政改革的核心。党的十四大提出，转变政府职能的根本途径是政企分开。党的十六大明确提出，政府的职能主要是，经济调节、市场监管、社会管理和公共服务。党的十八大以来，中国行政改革更是紧紧扭住政府职能转变这个"牛鼻子"，以简政放权为突破口，加快转变政府职能，使市场在资源配置中起决定性作用和更好发挥政府作用，切实推进了推动政府职能向创造良好发展环境、提供优质公共服务、维护社会公平正义转变。通过近40年的行政改革，中国政府对微观经济运行的干预明显减少，企业作为市场竞争主体地位得到确立，市场配置资源的决定性作用明显增强，新型宏观调控体系逐步健全，社会管理和公共服务职能不断加强。

### （二）调整行政区划

行政区划的调整与优化是中国行政改革的重要内容。改革开放以来，中国行政改革适应经济社会发展需要、城镇化发展和生产力的变革，中国先后进行了包括建立特区、新建省（直辖市）、撤地建市、县改市、市领导县、县改区等一系列行政区划改革尝试，极大地丰富了中国行政区划的实践内涵。受城镇化进程、中心城市的空间拓展、人口的集聚与增长、交通和通信条件的改善以及政策因素，中国行政区划调整主要有五种主要模式：建制变更、行政区拆分、行政区合并、建制升格以及新设立行政区。其中，撤县设（县级）市的行政区划调整是中国改革开放以来最主要的一种行政区划调整模式。从 1979 年开始到 1997 年暂时结束，实行约 19年。这一期间由于中央两次设市标准的调整，极大地影响了区划变更的整个进程和周期。

### （三）改革政府组织结构

机构是职能的载体，职能配置需要科学的机构设置来履行。改革政府组织机构是中国行政改革的重要内容。改革开放以来，已经先后进行了七次大的政府组织机构改革，总的趋势和要求是根据经济社会发展变化和全面履行政府职能的需要，科学划分、合理界定政府各部门职能，进一步理顺行政组织纵向、横向以及部门之间的关系，健全部门间协调配合机制。通过合理调整机构设置，优化人员结构，既要解决有些部门机构臃肿、人浮于事的问题，又要解决有些部门因职能加强而出现的编制过少、人员不足的问题，做到职能与机构相匹配、任务与人员编制相匹配。2008 年政府机构改革的一个重要特点是积极推进了大部门改革。这次改革，对职能相近、管理分散的机构进行合并，对职责交叉重复、相互推诿、长期难以协调解决的机构进行合并调整。同时，对职能范围过宽、权力过分集中的机构进行适当分设，以改变部门结构失衡和运行中顾此失彼的现象。2013年进行的政府机构改革，进一步优化了部门设置，协调了部门关系，不断完善了决策权、执行权、监督权既相互统一又相互协调的行政运行机制，建立了以宏观调控部门、市场监管部门、社会管理和公共服务部门为主体的政府机构框架，机构设置和职责体系趋于合理。可以说，每次政府组织机构改革都是由经济体制改革推动，以适应发展和完善社会主义市场经济需要为目标，对政府管理体制进行根本性的改造和重塑。

### （四）转变政府管理方式

改革开放以来，中国政府主动适应国内外环境变化和经济社会发展要求，在改进完善已有行政管理方式的同时，坚持以人为本的原则，利用市场机制，采用现代科技成果，简化行政程序，调整管理流程，将政府规制、规划计划、舆论引导、经济激励、信息服务等多种管理方式和手段相结合，使行政管理方式逐步向更加科学化、更加人性化、更加简便化转变：一是创新宏观调控方式。面对经济下行压力较大的情况，积极创新宏观调控方式，明确守住稳增长、保就业的下限和防通胀的上限，保障经济运行在合理区间；集中精力转方式、调结构，适时适度进行预调和微调，提高宏观调控的针对性和协调性。二是将政府管理由事前审批更多地转为事中事后监管，堵塞监管缝隙和漏洞，加大对违法违规者的处罚力度，努力做到"宽进严管"，着力营造公平竞争的市场环境。三是推广政府购买服务，创新政府职能方式。四是加强电子政务建设，着力推进"互联网+政务服务"，利用电子政务平台实施管理和服务，增强了对公众诉求的回应性、提高了行政效率、降低了管理成本、方便了人民群众。

### （五）推进法治政府建设

建设法治政府是改革开放以来，中国行政改革的重大成就，其中一个突出标志是政府逐步实现了从全能政府向有限政府的转变，从管制政府向服务政府、法治政府的目标和要求进一步明确，公民的权利意识和法治观念不断增强，法治政府建设取得了显著进步。法治政府的核心是依法行政，1989年通过的《行政诉讼法》被认为是我国法治建设历程中的一座里程碑。2004年3月，中国政府发布《全面推进依法行政实施纲要》，明确提出了用十年左右的时间，基本实现建设法治政府的目标。此后，法治政府建设步伐加快，《行政许可法》《行政诉讼法》《行政复议法实施条例》等一系列法律法规的颁布实施，我国法治政府的法律制度框架已基本建立，依法行政法律法规体系不断完善，行政立法、执法和监督工作进一步加强，政府建设和行政工作法治化、制度化加快推进，切实用制度管权、管事、管人。通过多年努力，2015 年，法治政府基本建成，行政法规不断健全，行政执法体制改革不断深化，行政执法组织体系更加健全，行政执法程序化、规范化水平明显提高，行政监督制度建设加强，行政权力运行和行政行为实施的法制化、规范化、公开化程度大幅提高。

### （六）加强公务员队伍建设

公务员队伍是政府管理的主体，其素质和能力直接影响政府的执行力和公信力。改革开放以来，中国开始建立现代国家公务员制度。1993 年 4 月国务院通过并颁布了《国家公务员暂行条例》并于同年 10 月起施行，这标志着我国公务员制度的初步形成。此后，全国各地自上而下逐步开始建立和推行国家公务员制度，加强公务员队伍建设。公务员管理法律法规体系逐步健全，包括准入、激励、退出等机制在内的中国特色的国家公务员制度基本建立；政风建设和廉政建设不断推进，公务员队伍整体素质和能力明显提高，形成了一支爱岗敬业、忠于职守、素质优良、作风过硬、勤政廉政的公务员队伍，为进一步建成完善的中国特色社会主义行政体制奠定了坚实基础。

### （七）推进反腐倡廉，建设廉洁政府

廉洁是从政的道德底线，也是政府公信力的基石。改革开放 30 年来尤其是进入 21 世纪以来，中国政府坚持不懈地推进廉洁政府建设，在查办大案要案、惩处腐败分子、加强制度建设、强化对领导干部的监督、治理商业贿赂、纠正损害群众利益的不正之风等方面取得重要进展。国务院每年都召开廉政工作会议，对政府系统的反腐败和廉政建设作出部署。中国各地区各部门都把反腐败和廉政建设纳入经济社会发展总体规划、寓于各项改革和重要政策措施之中。二是制定建设廉洁政府的一系列法律制度，包括制定《中华人民共和国政府采购法》《中华人民共和国反垄断法》《中华人民共和国招标投标法》，规范行政自由裁量权，发挥市场在资源配置中的基础性作用，有效防止腐败行为的发生。三是通过体制机制创新，建设廉洁政府。推进行政审批制度改革，推进干部人事制度改革，

推进司法体制和工作机制改革，推进财政、投资、金融、资源等体制改革，依法查处腐败案例，大力建设廉洁文化，积极开展反腐败国际交流与合作。反对腐败、建设廉洁政治是全人类的共同愿望，也是世界各国政府和政党面临的共同课题。中国将在国际和地区性反腐败交流与合作中发挥积极作用，为建设一个公正廉洁和美好的世界而努力奋斗。

# 四　中国行政改革的基本经验

改革开放以来，中国行政管理体制改革不仅取得了显著成效，而且在实践中积累了宝贵经验，主要有以下六个方面。

## （一）坚持顶层设计，统筹规划

这既是我国行政体制改革的宝贵经验，也是今后一个时期深化行政体制改革的基本遵循。深化行政体制改革需要放到党和国家发展的大局中统筹谋划，在中央统一领导下，与其他方面的改革一起统筹规划部署，整体协调推进。邓小平同志在《党和国家领导制度的改革》一文中指出："改革党和国家领导制度及其他制度，是为了充分发挥社会主义制度优越性，加速现代化建设事业的发展。""我们要不断总结历史经验，深入调查研究，集中正确意见，从中央到地方，积极地、有步骤地继续进行改革。"中国行政体制改革正是在中国共产党的领导下，统筹协调推进的。党的十八大报告指出：要"完善体制改革协调机制，统筹规划和协调重大改革"。这对加强行政体制改革的顶层设计，统筹规划，协调推进各方面改革有着重要意义。中国政府始终把行政改革作为全面深化改革的关键环节，深入研究行政改革与经济改革、政治改革、文化改革、社会改革的相互关系，把握好各方面改革相互适应、相互支撑的规律性和相互制约、相互影响的复杂性，正确处理好改革发展稳定的关系，提高体制改革决策的科学性、权威性，增强各方面改革措施的协调性、配套性、实效性，确保社会主义改革的正确方向和顺利推进。

## （二）坚持渐进式改革策略

中国近40年的改革开放走出一条渐进式改革的成功道路。行政体制改革是深化整个改革的重要环节，是建立和完善社会主义市场经济体制、发展社会主义民主政治的必然要求，因此，中国的行政改革坚持了渐进式改革道路。这一改革道路的基本特点是在坚持中国共产党的政治领导、坚持中国特色社会主义基本制度框架的前提下，所进行的一场有秩序、有探索性、有创新的社会主义行政制度的自我完善和发展革命。有秩序是指中国的行政改革正确处理了改革、发展与稳定的关系，合进协调改革力度、发展速度和国民承受度，是在保持中国基本政治制度和政体基础上对行政运行体制进行的改革。有探索是指中国的行政改革是正确处理了社会主义与市场经济的关系，一切"摸着石头过河"，一切以适应社会主义市场经济的需要所进行的前无古人、无所参照的事业。每一步改革的步伐要踩对、踩准、踩实、踩稳。创新性是指中国行政改革既是对原有行政权力结构和利益格局的重大调整，也是一场深刻的观念变革和思想革命，必须把创新精神贯穿于改革的全过程和每个环节。实践证明，中国行政改革在理论和实践上的每一个进步，都是坚持解放思想、实事求是、与时俱进的结果。推进行政改革，要有长远目标和总体规划，明确改革的路径与方向，又要确定每个时期的重点任务，不可能毕其功于一役；既要充分利用各方面的有利条件，正确把握有利时机，坚决果断地推进改革措施，在一些重要领域迈出较大步伐，又要全面分析面临的矛盾和风险，充分考虑各方面的承受能力，积极稳妥地实施。

### （三）坚持公众参与改革过程

公众是中国改革的主体，中国行政改革亦是如此。全心全意为人民服务是中国共产党和中国政府的根本宗旨，做到一切为了人民、一切依靠人民，是推进各项改革的根本出发点和动力所在。从中国行政改革的价值目标看，改革开放以来的中国行政改革，始终坚持依靠人民、为了人民、服务人民，着眼于适应推进经济和社会发展，不断提高人民群众物质文化生活水平，促进人的全面发展；坚持尊重人民群众的主体地位，维护人民群众的各项权益；充分体现广大人民群众的利益和诉求，使全体人民共享改革发展成果。从中国行政改革的动力机制看，中国行政改革高度重视发挥公众的积极性、主动性和参与性，增强社会经济活力和创造力。实践证明，中国行政改革只有符合人民利益，反映人民呼声，紧紧依靠人民，建设人民满意的政府，才能得到广大人民群众的真心拥护和有力支持。

### （四）坚持围绕发展这一中心任务

中国是一个发展中大国，实现中国经济持续健康快速发展是当代中国的第一要务，也是中国人民为世界发展所做的一大贡献。因此，围绕经济发展，服务经济发展，适应发展始终是中国行政改革的内在驱动力。行政体制是国家体制的基本内容，是中国政治上层建筑的重要组成部分，是经济体制、政治体制、社会体制以及其他体制的结合点，并且有着密切的联系。中国行政改革，尤其是政府机构设置和职能调整，涉及国家经济、政治、文化和社会生活的各个方面，涉及中央与地方、政府与社会、政府与企业、整体利益与局部利益等一系列重要关系。因此，行政体制改革必须放到中国经济社会发展的大局中统筹谋划，服从并服务于促进经济社会发展的需要，做到与完善社会主义市场经济体制进程相适应，与建设社会主义民主政治、完善国家治理体系相协调。

### （五）鼓励创新，勇于实践

中国党和政府的许多重大政策和做法都源于人民群众的创新，源于基层的实践。在深化行政改革中，始终鼓励和支持地方、部门从实际出发，因地制宜，大胆探索，推进创新，为深化改革积累经验。譬如，近年来许多地方和部门围绕政府组织结构、层级体系、管理体制、运行机制、服务方式等方面进行了积极探索，包括推进大部门制改革、探索省直接管理县（市）改革、创新行政管理方式、政务服务标准化、综合执法体制改革，等等。有关部门和地方深入调查研究和客观评估这些改革措施的效果，认真研究解决改革过程中出现的问题，使那些在实践中被证明是行之有效的改革措施得到完善和推广，并体现在顶层统筹和决策部署中来。

### （六）坚持学习借鉴国际经验与符合中国实际相结合

对外开放是中国的基本国策。改革开放以来，中国以更加开放的胸襟，更加积极的心态，更加宽广的视角，大力开展中外行政文化交流，在学习相互借鉴中，为推动人类文明进步做出应有努力。行政改革涉及行政权力关系的调整和政府组织结构的变动，中国行政改革既善于研究借鉴国际上公共治理方面的有益成果，顺应时代发展和变革的潮流，但又不盲目照搬照抄国外模式。同时，中国行政改革又立足于中国地域辽阔、各地情况差异性很大、发展很不平衡、传统行政观念影响深厚等实际，既从全局出发，统一部署，又充分考虑各地特点，分类指导，实现了学习借鉴国际经验与符合中国实际相结合。

**参考文献**

［1］《习近平谈治国理政》，人民出版社 2014 年版。

［2］魏礼群：《行政体制改革论》，人民出版社 2013 年版。

［3］魏礼群：《行政管理体制改革 30 年　回顾与前瞻》，《求是》2009 年第 2 期。

［4］魏礼群主编：《创新政府治理　深化行政改革》，国家行政学院出版社 2015 年版。

（作者：魏礼群　中国行政体制改革研究会会长、国务院研究室原主任、国家行政学院原党委书记、常务副院长）

# 第二章

# 政府机构改革

　　30多年来，中国的行政体制改革全方位、渐进式地展开，内涵丰富，范围广泛，既包括职能和机构的调整，又包括运行机制和管理方式的创新；既包括政府内部的体制改革，又包括外部的协同配套改革。其中，政府机构改革一直是行政体制改革的重要内容。政府机构是政府职能的载体，解决政府职能职责"由谁做"、由谁来承担的问题，因此，政府组织结构的调整、机构体系的变化不仅是行政体制改革的外在表现，也是行政体制改革的核心内容。自1982年以来，中国政府已持续推动了7次集中的政府机构改革。政府机构改革的过程及其特点，完整地展现了中国行政体制改革的大趋势。

## 一　政府机构改革的历程和特点

　　改革开放以来，中国先后于1982年、1988年、1993年、1998年、2003年、2008年和2013年进行了7次集中的政府机构改革。每一次改革都有特定的时代背景，肩负着重要的历史使命。通过改革，有效地回应了不同阶段经济社会发展的客观要求。从改革方式上看，政府机构的每一次改革，基本都是按照部署从国务院机构到省、市、县次第展开、协调推进。

### （一）1982年机构改革：着力精干领导班子和干部队伍

　　1982年的政府机构改革，是在中国全面开创现代化建设新局面的历史条件下提出的。为了适应中国共产党和国家工作中心向经济建设转移的需要，这次重点改革了领导体制，裁并了党政工作机构，精干了领导班子和干部队伍，着力改变机构臃肿、层次繁多、人浮于事的状况。

一是精干领导班子。按照干部"四化"的方针，选拔能够开创局面的干部进入领导班子，减少各级各部门的领导副职。二是废除了实际存在的领导干部职务终身制，建立了干部离退休制度。三是精简机构和人员编制。国务院各部委、直属机构和办公机构从 100 个减为 61 个；人员编制按 25% 精简，国务院各部门从 5.1 万人减为 3 万人左右。

这次改革有特定的历史背景条件，尚未涉及政府职能转变的问题。

**（二）1988 年机构改革：首次提出转变政府职能**

1988 年的机构改革，在转变政府职能、理顺关系、减少政府干预企业经营活动的职能，增强宏观调控职能，改变机构设置不合理和行政效率低下等方面做了努力。

一是紧紧抓住了职能转变这个关键问题，着重理顺政府与企事业单位之间的关系。国务院各部门职能的总体配置做了较大的调整，积极推动政府由微观管理向宏观管理、由直接管理向间接管理、由部门管理向行业管理转变。撤销和裁并了一些专业部门；共有 30 个部门的职能得到了加强。职能转变的具体内容，在部门"三定"方案中进一步明确。二是解决了一批部门之间的职能交叉问题。据统计，经协调解决了部门之间职能交叉问题近 50 个，为明确部门之间的职责分工、减少责任推诿、建立科学的行政体制打下了基础。三是撤销了一批专业经济部门，新组建了几个综合性的行业管理部门，并撤销了大多数部门的专业司局；重点加强了监督、经济调节的部门。根据职能的变化，有些部门减员幅度很大，有些职能加强的部门则增加了编制。四是探索了机构改革、转变职能的途径，为实行公务员制度打下了基础。地方政府的工作部门实行定编定人，并逐步将职能分解到职位，制定了职位说明书，为公务员制度的推行创造了条件。

这次改革的理念有了突破，第一次明确提出了转变政府职能这一核心命题。此后，机构改革开始与国家的宏观发展、与经济体制改革紧密结合起来。

### （三）1993 年机构改革：适应市场经济的需要加快转变政府职能

1992 年，中国共产党十四大明确了建立社会主义市场经济体制的目标，市场在国家宏观调控下对资源配置起到基础性作用。这是 1993 年政府机构改革的时代背景。为适应建立社会主义市场经济体制的需要，必然要相应地调整行政管理体制，加快转变政府职能，进一步改革政府机构。

一是适应社会主义市场经济体制的要求进一步转变政府职能。重点改革了计划、投资、财政、金融管理体制，撤并了一些专业经济部门和职能交叉机构，将综合经济部门的工作重点转到宏观调控上来。二是理顺部门之间的关系。在转变政府职能的基础上，进一步理顺专业部门之间以及专业部门与综合部门之间的关系，明确划分部门的职责权限。三是精简机构和人员。改革后，国务院组成部门由 42 个调整为 41 个。大幅度裁减国务院的非常设机构，由 85 个减少到 26 个。全国精简 200 多万人员编制。

这次改革的主要特点：一是适应社会主义市场经济体制的要求，以转变政府职能为关键，强调加强政府的宏观管理职能，弱化微观管理职能；坚持政企分开，切实落实企业的经营自主权，促进企业经营机制的转换。二是专业经济管理部门的精简力度较大。部分专业经济部门成建制地转为经济实体或服务实体。对一些行政管理职能较多，管理任务重、一时难以转为经济实体的专业经济部门，精简了内设机构和人员，大大减少对企业产、供、销和人、财、物的直接管理。三是较大幅度地精简了机构和人员。四是开始推行国家公务员制度。

### （四）1998 年机构改革：推动政企分开迈出实质性步伐

1998 年 3 月 10 日第九届全国人大一次会议批准了《国务院机构改革方案》，明确了改革目标，即建立办事高效、运转协调、行为规范的行政管理体系，完善国家公务员制度，建设高素质的专业化行政管理干部队伍，逐步建立适应社会主义市场经济体制的有中国特色的行政管理体制。

这次改革，实行党政机关与所办经济实体及直接管理企业的脱钩，在转变职能方面迈出了实质性的步伐。大幅度裁并政府部门，撤销了几乎所有的工业专业经济管理部门，具体包括电力工业部、煤炭工业部、冶金工业部、机械工业部、电子工业部、化学工业部、地质矿产部、林业部、中国轻工业总会和中国纺织总会。这样，政企不分的组织基础得以消除。改革后，国务院组成部门由 40 个精简为 29 个。综合经济部门改组为宏观调控部门，专业经济部门大量减少，移交给企业、社会中介机构和地方的职能有 100 多项。专业经济管理部门都实行政企分开，不再直接管理企业。同时，大幅精简人员编制。这次国务院机构改革提出了行政编制精简 50% 的要求，是历次机构改革人员精简力度最大的一次。改革后，国务院各部门行政编制由 3.23 万名减至 1.67 万名。全国精简行政编制共计 115 万名。

这次机构改革的主要特点：一是机构改革同建立现代企业制度相结合，重点是转变政府职能，实现了政企分开。这次改革中，对政府与国有企业的关系做出了规范，专业经济部门不再直接管理企业。政府经济管理部门基本定型，初步建立起与社会主义市场经济体制相适应的现代政府体制。二是机构改革同国家公务员制度相结合。明确把完善国家公务员制度，建设高素质的专业化行政管理干部队伍作为改革目标的重要组成部分，人员精简分流与优化干部队伍结构、提高公务员队伍素质相结合。三是机构改革同加强行政体系的法制建设相结合。

**（五）2003 年机构改革：注重职能整合和结构调整**

为适应加入世界贸易组织的新要求，2003 年的政府机构改革，着力解决经济社会发展中的突出矛盾和问题。同时，推进健全民主决策机制、强化行政监督等方面的制度建设。

这次改革，政府机构总体格局保持相对稳定，除国务院办公厅外，国务院组成部门为 28 个。改革的重点是集中力量解决行政管理体制中影响改革和发展的突出矛盾和问题，推进政府职能转变。一是深化国有资产监督管理体制改革。设立国资委，把政府的社会经济管理职能和国有资产所有者职能分离，把政府的公共行政管理职能和企业经营者职能分离，实行政企分开。二是完善宏观调控体系，组建国家发展和改革委员会。三是健全金融监管体制，成立银监会。同时，确立了银监会、证监会、保监会分工明确、互相协调的金融分业监管体制。四是建立包括内贸和外贸体制在内的统一的流通管理体制，组建商务部。五是改革食品安全和安全生产监督管理体制。

这次改革的主要特点：一是适应市场经济和加入世界贸易组织的要求，重点强调转变政府职能，强化政府的宏观调控和监督管理职能。二是总体保持了机构格局的稳定，改革的重点放在明确政府职能定位和深化转变上。三是注重职能的整合和职能内部结构调整。四是强调改革是一个循序渐进的过程。并没有对政府机构进行大的调整，而是有针对性地解决当时发展阶段的突出问题。

### （六）2008 年机构改革：积极探索构建大部门制

中国共产党十七届二中全会审议通过了《关于深化行政管理体制改革的意见》，对深化改革的指导思想、基本原则、总体目标和主要任务做出了全面部署。这是关于中国行政管理体制改革的顶层设计。

按照这一部署，这次改革在一些关键领域，包括加快政府职能转变、强化社会管理和公共服务、探索实行职能有机统一的大部门体制、理顺部门职责关系、明确和强化部门责任等方面迈出了重要步伐。一是合理配置宏观调控部门职能。国家发展和改革委员会减少了微观管理事务和具体审批事项，集中精力抓宏观调控。财政部改革完善预算和税政管理，健全中央和地方财力与事权相匹配的体制，完善公共财政体系。中国人民银行进一步健全货币政策体系，加强与金融监管部门的统筹协调，维护国家金融安全。二是加强能源管理机构。设立高层次议事协调机构国家能源委员会。组建国家能源局。三是组建工业和信息化部。将国家发展和改革委员会的工业行业管理有关职责，国防科学技术工业委员会核电管理以外的职责，信息产业部和国务院信息化工作办公室的职责，整合划入工业和信息化部。组建国家国防科技工业局。国家烟草专卖局改由工业和信息化部管理。四是组建交通运输部。将交通部、中国民用航空总局的职责，建设部的指导城市客运职责，整合划入交通运输部。组建中国民用航空局，由交通运输部管理。国家邮政局改由交通运输部管理。保留铁道部，继续推进改革。五是组建人力资源和社会保障部。将人事部、劳动和社会保障部的职责整合划入人力资源和社会保障部。组建国家公务员局。六是组建环境保护部。七是组建住房和城乡建设部。八是国家食品药品监督管理局改由卫生部管理。明确卫生部承担食品安全综合协调、组织查处食品安全重大事故的责任。改革后，除国务院办公厅外，国务院组成部门设置 27 个。

这次改革的主要特点：一是按照政企分开、政资分开、政事分开、政府与市场中介组织分开的要求，取消、下放、转移了政府职能。同时，加强了宏观调控、能源管理、环境保护以及住房、社会保障、安全生产等涉及群众切身利益、关系国计民生的社会管理和公共服务职责。二是在工业和信息化、交通、人力资源和社会保障等领域首次探索实行大部门制。这是中国第一次尝试构建大部门体制，为政府组织架构的调整探索新路径。三是着力理顺部门职责关系。按照一件事情原则上由一个部门负责的原则，进一步明确部门职责分工，解决宏观调控、环境资源、涉外经贸、市场监管、文化卫生等领域多项职责交叉和关系不顺问题。四是强化部门责任。在赋予部门职权的同时，明确了各部门的责任，力求做到有权必有责、权责对等。

### （七）2013 年机构改革：把政府职能转变摆在更加突出的位置

根据中国共产党十八大和十八届二中全会的精神，这次改革是按照建立中国特色社会主义行政体制目标的要求，以职能转变为核心，继续推进机构改革，完善制度机制，提高行政效能。

在国务院层面，围绕转变职能和理顺职责关系，进一步推进大部门制改革，实行铁路政企分开，整合加强卫生和计划生育、食品药品、新闻出版和广播电影电视、海洋、能源管理机构。改革后，国务院正部级机构减少 4 个，除国务院办公厅外，国务院设置组成部门 25 个。

这次改革的主要特点：一是把政府职能转变摆在更加突出的位置。职能转变成为贯穿整个改革过程的灵魂和主线。职能转变与机构改革一起写进了改革方案的题目中。二是把大力简政放权与强化宏观管理和事后监管有机结合起来。在向市场、企业、社会和个人放权的同时，该加强的政府职能必须加强，注重管宏观，强化事后监管。三是在一些老百姓最关心的重要领域的机构调整上迈出关键步伐。实行铁路政企分开，整合加强卫生和计划生育、食品药品、新闻出版和广播电影电视、海洋、能源等领域职责，针对性都很强，解决了一些社会关注度高且长期没有解决的难题。四是在加强事关长远的基础性制度建设上有重大突破。比如建立不动产统一登记制度，建立以公民身份证号码和组织机构代码为基础的统一社会信用代码制度等。这些基础性制度的建立，将对全体公民的行为产生引导力和约束力，对于推动整个行政体制改革、确保政府有效管理具有重要意义。

# 二　政府机构改革的成效

经过 30 多年的努力，中国的政府机构改革取得了明显成效，已初步构建起与社会主义市场经济体制相适应的政府组织体系。从政府建设角度看，改革的成效主要体现在以下几个方面。

## （一）政府的管理理念发生重大变化

与改革开放前相比，现代化的政府角色定位和基本理念已基本形成，适应了当今时代潮流的发展和中国的国情实际。一是确立了责任政府的理念。各级政府及部门的责任逐步得到明确和强化。二是确立了服务政府的理念。各级政府公共服务、社会管理职能不断强化，并在政府职能结构中居于重要位置。能否为公众提供更多更优质更均等化的公共服务，成为衡量政府工作成效的重要标准。三是确立了法治政府的理念。政府及其工作人员必须尊重和维护法律权威、在宪法和法律范围内活动的意识逐步形成。四是确立了廉洁政府理念。勤政廉洁、节俭高效，确保权力在阳光下运行，更好地接受公众的监督，成为政府运行的重要准则。

## （二）政府职能转变取得实质性进展

经过持续的改革，政府职能逐步与社会主义市场经济发展要求相适应，逐步与人民群众不断增长的公共服务需求相适应。一是政府、市场、企业三者之间的关系逐渐理顺，政企分开基本实现。市场在资源配置中的决定性作用得到发挥，以间接手段为主的政府宏观调控体系逐步完善。特别是新一届政府成立以来，简政放权的推进力度前所未有，一大批行政审批事项被取消，能够由市场自我调节和企业自主决定的事项尽量交给市场和企业，有效地释放了市场和社会活力。同时，简政放权并不是一放了之，而是强调放管结合、优化服务，强化政府的事中事后监管职责。二是社会管理和公共服务职能不断加强。着力维护社会稳定和促进社会和谐，社会利益协调机制、矛盾疏导机制和突发事件应急机制等逐步建立；着力发展社会事业和解决民生问题，义务教育、公共卫生和社会保障体系建设等迈出重要步伐。三是社会组织在经济社会事务中的作用逐步增强。各类社会组织蓬勃发展，初步实现了由单纯依靠政府管理向政府与社会协同治理的转型。

### （三） 政府组织机构逐步调整优化

经过改革，与计划经济体制相适应的以计划为龙头、综合部门管理专业部门、专业部门直接管企业的机构框架彻底改变。与社会主义市场经济体制相适应的以宏观调控部门、行业管理部门、市场监管部门、社会管理和公共服务部门为主的机构框架基本建立起来。

### （四） 各级政府和各部门之间的职责关系逐步界定清晰

中央和地方的事权划分趋于合理。不同层级政府的经济社会事务管理权责逐步得到合理界定，各级政府在职能配置上"上下一般粗"的状况得到改善。近两年，中国政府大力推动政府权责清单制度建设，通过"清单"的方式，促使政府照单行权，以刚性的制度管权用权。这一制度设计也为政府间权责划分走向法治化提供了基础。政府各部门之间的职责关系进一步清晰，一些重要领域的部门职责交叉事项逐步划清，部门间协调配合机制逐步建立。

### （五） 政府的制度建设和能力建设逐步加强

政府运行机制和管理方式不断创新，行政效能明显提高。一是科学民主决策机制建设迈出重要步伐，公众参与、专家论证和政府决策相结合的决策机制逐步建立。二是政务公开不断推进，机制逐步健全，范围不断扩大，保障了人民群众的知情权、参与权、监督权。三是政府应急管理体系初步建立，形成了分级响应、属地管理、信息共享、分工协作的应急体系。四是行政监督和问责力度不断加强，包括外部监督、层级监督和监察、审计等专门监督的行政监督体系初步形成，行政问责制在重大事故处置中发挥了重要作用。五是一些关涉人民群众切身利益的基础性制度建设有了实质性进展。

# 三　对政府机构改革的几点认识

中国的政府机构改革，经过30多年的不断探索，改革的思路和目标逐渐明晰，改革方式和手段不断改进，改革领域不断拓宽，已形成了一些符合自身实际的特点，积累了比较丰富的经验，为下一步改革提供了基础。随着经济社会的发展，政府机构改革还将继续深化。政府机构改革不仅对现有权力格局和利益关系进行调整，更是一场深刻的思想革命和观念变革，因此，深化改革需要不断解放思想，推动改革取得更大的突破。

## （一）始终坚持正确的政治方向

改革开放以来，中国的政府机构改革始终是在中国共产党的坚强领导下进行的，始终坚持正确的政治方向。改革始终把维护人民群众的根本利益作为出发点和落脚点，重点关注那些老百姓最关心领域的机构调整，通过机构调整更科学更合理配置职能，为经济社会发展提供保障。因此，对人民负责，为人民服务决定了政府机构改革的方向，也是判断政府机构改革成败的标准。

## （二）围绕经济社会发展大局开展改革

发展是硬道理。中国改革的目的就是解放和发展生产力，促进经济社会全面进步。政府机构改革是全面深化改革的重要内容，必须从全面建成小康社会的大局出发，紧紧围绕经济社会发展大局着力改革，与完善社会主义市场经济体制相适应，与建设社会主义民主政治和法治国家相协调。

## （三）进行一个较长跨度的规划设计

深化政府机构改革是一项长期、系统工程，要循序渐进地推进。改革要坚持精简统一效能的原则，进行一个较长跨度的规划设计，明确改革的优先顺序和重点任务，做到长远目标与阶段性目标相结合。注重处理好政府机构改革与经济、政治、社会、文化等领域改革的关系，处理好政府机构改革内部各项具体改革的关系，协调配套推进改革。充分发挥中央和地方两个积极性，充分发挥社会各方面的积极性，形成推进改革的强大合力。还要正确处理好改革、发展、稳定的关系，综合考虑社会各方面的需求和制约因素，把改革的力度、发展的速度与各方面的可承受程度统一起来。

### （四）更加注重保障和改善民生

保障和改善民生是中国经济社会发展的一项重大任务。政府机构改革要把保障和改善民生放在突出位置，加快推动政府职能转变，更加注重社会管理和公共服务，完善保障和改善民生的制度安排，充分发挥政府在提供公益服务方面的主导作用。

**参考文献**

[1] 李景鹏：《回顾与反思：政府机构改革的经验与教训》，《中国行政管理》2005年第2期。

[2] 王一程：《中国行政管理体制改革的进展与面临的挑战》，《政治学研究》2006年第3期。

[3] 中央机构编制委员会办公室：《在布局中不断推进——我国行政管理体制改革回顾》，《人民日报》2008年12月18日。

[4] 汪玉凯：《中国行政管理体制改革30年：思考与展望》，《党政干部学刊》2008年第1期。

[5] 何颖：《中国政府机构改革30年　回顾与反思》，《中国行政管理》2008年第12期。

[6] 汪玉凯等：《中国行政体制改革30年　回顾与展望》，人民出版社2008年版。

[7] 朱光磊、李利平：《回顾与建议：政府机构改革三十年》，《北京行政学院学报》2009年第1期。

[8] 魏礼群：《建立和完善中国特色社会主义行政管理体制——行政管理体制改革30年回顾与前瞻》，《求是》2009年第2期。

[9] 王澜明：《改革开放以来我国六次集中的行政管理体制改革的回顾与思考》，《中国行政管理》2009年第10期。

[10] 中央机构编制委员会办公室理论学习中心组：《改革开放以来我国行政管理体制改革的光辉历程》，《人民日报》2011年7月25日。

[11] 张志坚：《见证——行政管理体制和劳动人事制度改革》，国家行政学院出版社2012年版。

［12］周志忍、徐艳晴:《基于变革管理视角对三十年来机构改革的审视》,《中国社会科学》2014 年第 7 期。

（作者：李利平  《中国机构改革与管理》杂志社编辑部副主任）

# 第 三 章

# 政府职能转变和行政审批制度改革

政府职能反映了政府活动的基本方向和主要作用，必然随着经济社会发展而不断调整和转变。政府职能转变是中国行政管理体制改革的核心，贯穿于改革开放和现代化建设的全过程。行政审批制度作为政府管理工作的组成部分，是完善社会主义市场经济体制的重要内容，行政审批制度改革是转变政府职能的突破口，也是释放市场活力和社会发展内生动力的重要手段。

## 一 政府职能转变的历史进程和特点

1978 年，中国共产党的十一届三中全会做出决定，把党和国家的工作重点转移到社会主义现代化建设上来，这是在新的历史时期对政府职能转变提出的战略要求。1982 年，中国共产党的十二大提出，必须有系统地完成机构改革和经济体制改革。1982 年至今，我国集中进行了 7 次行政管理体制和机构改革，转变政府职能始终是行政管理体制改革的重要任务。中国共产党的十二届三中全会要求政府机关"实行政企职责分开，正确发挥政府管理经济的职能"。中国共产党的十二届四中全会首次提出了转变政府职能的要求。中国共产党的十三大提出"转变政府职能是机构改革成功的关键"的重要论断。中国共产党的十四大提出建立社会主义市场经济体制的目标，要求加快政府职能转变，并提出转变的根本途径是政企分开。中国共产党的十四届三中全会提出转变政府职能，建立健全宏观调控体系，政府管理经济的职能主要是制定和执行宏观调控政策，搞好基础设施建设，创造良好的经济发展环境。中国共产党的十五大提出，要按照社会主义市场经济的要求转变政府职能，实现政企分开。1998 年的机构改革撤销了大部分专业经济部门，标志着以转变政府经济管理职能、推进政企分开为主要内容的职能转变取得了阶段性成绩。中国共产党的十六大提出深化行政管理体制改革，进一步转变政府职能。中国共产党的十六届三中全会提出加快转变政府职能，深化行政审批制度改革，切实把政府经济管理职能转到主要为市场主体服务和创造良好发展环境上来。中国共产党的十七大提出，加快行政管理体制改革，建设服务型政府，要求"着力转变职能，加快推进政企分开、政资分开、政事分开、政府与市场中介组织分开，减少政府对微观经济运行的干预"。中国共产党的十七届二中全会提出，"实现政府职能向创造良好发展环境、提供优质公共服务、维护社会公平正义的根本转变"。尤其是党中央提出了科学发展观、构建社会主义和谐社会、加强和创新社会管理等一系列重大战略思想，对于新形势下推进政府职能转变有了更高的要求。中国共产党的十八大提出要按照建立中国特色社会主义行政体制目标，深入推进政企分开、政资分开、政事分开、政社分开，建设职能科学、结构优化、廉洁高效、人民满意的服务型政府；深化行政审批制度改革，继续简政放权，推动政府职能向创造良好发展环境、提供优质公共服务、维护社会公平正义转变。中国共产党的十八届三中全会要求，政府要加强发展战略、规划、政策、标准等制定和实施，加强市场活动监管，加强各类公共服务提供；加强中央政府宏观调控职责和能力，加强地方政府公共服务、市场监管、社会管理、环境保护等职责。

通过多年来的持续改革，中国政府职能转变取得了明显进展。政府职能转变的历史进程表现出不断深化的清晰轨迹。

**（一）从适应经济建设和经济体制改革的需要，到适应贯彻落实科学发展观和经济社会协调发展的需要**

中国行政体制改革紧紧围绕党和国家不同时期、不同阶段的中心工作进行，政府职能转变从适应经济体制改革的需要，到适应经济社会发展形势和行政体制改革的要求。政府职能转变按照科学发展观、构建社会主义和谐社会和全面建成小康社会的要求，更加重视以人为本，着力解决经济社会发展不协调、不平衡等问题。从适应经济建设为主转到适应全面推进经济建设、政治建设、社会建设、文化建设和生态环境建设的要求，政府要全面正确地履行职能，要在加强经济调节、市场监管的同时更加注重社会管理和公共服务。

**（二）政府职能的内涵得到丰富和发展，政府职能转变的目标更加明晰**

中国共产党的十六大明确提出了社会主义市场经济条件下政府的四项基本职能，即"经济调节、市场监管、社会管理和公共服务"。中国共产党的十七届二中全会通过的《关于深化行政管理体制改革的意见》，第一次明确提出政府职能转变的目标，即"通过改革，实现政府职能向创造良好发展环境、提供优质公共服务、维护社会公平正义的根本转变"。提出"从制度上更好地发挥市场在资源配置中的基础性作用，更好地发挥公民和社会组织在社会公共事务管理中的作用，更加有效地提供公共产品"，并明确了中央政府和地方政府各自履行职能的重点。中国共产党的十八届三中全会第一次提出了要"处理好政府与市场的关系，使市场在资源配置中起决定性作用和更好发挥政府作用"。由此，政府职能转变的目标逐渐明晰。

**（三）政府职能转变与机构改革紧密结合，赋予政府职能转变新的要求**

科学界定职能和合理设置机构是相互联系、相互依存的关系，政府的职能通过一定的机构来履行，机构以履行一定的职能而存在。回顾7次行政管理体制和机构改革，都是根据当时中心工作和经济社会发展需要对机构进行变动和调整的过程，体现了职能转变的要求，机构改革的任务通过职能的变动和调整来加以落实。中国共产党的十七大提出探索实行职能有机统一的大部门体制，中国共产党的十七届五中全会提出要坚定推进大部门制改革。中国共产党的十八届三中全会提出"转变政府职能必须深化机构改革"，"积极稳妥实施大部门制"，这进一步明确了今后一段时期政府职能转变的方向和重点。

# 二　行政审批制度改革的历史进程和特点

改革开放以来，中国各级地方政府和部门都不同程度地进行了行政审批制度改革。但是，行政审批制度还存在诸多问题，与经济社会发展和法治政府建设的要求不相适应，需要进一步转变政府职能，改革行政审批制度。新一届政府组成以来，深化行政审批制度改革作为转变政府职能的"突破口"和"抓手"，思路不断创新，政府职能转变进入了新的阶段。

## （一）2001 年至 2012 年行政审批制度改革情况

2001 年 9 月，国务院成立行政审批制度改革工作领导小组，将办公室设在监察部。2001 年 10 月，国务院下发《国务院批转关于行政审批制度改革工作实施意见的通知》，对行政审批制度改革提出了总体要求，即不符合政企分开和政事分开原则、妨碍市场开放和公平竞争以及实际上难以发挥有效作用的行政审批，坚决予以取消；可以用市场机制代替的行政审批，通过市场机制运作；对于确需保留的行政审批，要建立健全监督制约机制，做到审批程序严密、审批环节减少、审批效率明显提高，行政审批责任追究制得到严格执行。中国共产党的十六大以后，国务院进一步充实和加强了领导小组及其办公室。中国共产党的十七大以来，为适应国务院机构改革的需要，取消了原国务院行政审批制度改革工作领导小组，成立了由监察部牵头、中央编办、国家发展改革委等 12 个部门组成的行政审批制度改革工作部际联席会议，负责继续深入推进行政审批制度改革。与此同时，各地方都建立了改革工作领导机构，形成了党委、政府统一领导，办事机构组织协调，有关部门各负其责，集中各方面智慧和力量推进审批制度改革的工作格局。

2002 年至 2012 年，国务院先后六批进行了行政审批制度改革。第一批即 2002 年 10 月，取消 789 项行政审批项目；第二批即 2003 年 2 月，取消 406 项行政审批项目，改变 82 项行政审批项目的管理方式；第三批即 2004 年 5 月，取消和调整 495 项行政审批项目，其中取消 409 项，改变管理方式 39 项，下放 47 项；第四批即 2007 年 10 月，取消和调整 186 项行政审批项目，其中取消 128 项，下放 29 项，改变管理方式 8 项，合并 21 项；第五批即 2010 年 7 月，取消和下放行政审批项目 184 项，其中取消 113 项，下放 71 项；第六批即 2012 年 8 月，取消和调整 314 项行政审批项目，其中取消 184 项，下放 117 项，合并 13 项。国务院这六批共取消和调整了 2497 项行政审批项目，占原有总数的 69.3%。

为规范行政审批制度改革，先后制定了《关于行政审批制度改革工作的实施意见》《关于贯彻行政审批制度改革的五项原则需要把握的几个问题》《关于进一步深化行政审批制度改革的意见》等政策规定和文件，明确了改革的指导原则、基本思路、工作目标和方法步骤，使改革工作有章可循。

通过十余年的努力，行政审批制度改革在政治、经济、社会等方面都产生了广泛的积极影响。一是加快了政府职能转变。通过深化行政审批制度改革，把政府不该管的交给企业、社会和市场，逐步理顺政府与市场、政府与社会的关系，权力过分集中的现象有所改变。各级政府在加强和改善宏观调控、强化市场监管的同时，更加注重履行社会管理和公共服务职能，促进经济社会协调发展。二是推进了依法行政。2004 年 7 月《中华人民共和国行政许可法》正式实施，标志着我国行政审批制度改革和行政审批工作走上法制化、规范化轨道。地方和部门按照国务院统一部署，全面清理、废止和修订与法律相违背和不一致的行政法规、规章、规范性文件，新制定了一系列有关行政审批的法规、规章和制度，依法规范政府的权限和履行职能的程序。三是加强了政府管理创新。把推进政府管理创新作为深化行政体制改革的重要内容。行政审批的所有环节，凡不涉及国家秘密、商业秘密和个人隐私的，一律向社会公开，实行"阳光审批"。各地在改革中还积极探索，建立了政务中心或政务大厅，实行一个窗口对外，"一站式"服务；发展电子政务，实行网上申报、网上审批等。这些改革对于减少政府工作流程、优化政府组织结构、提高行政效能，都发挥了重要作用。四是促进了廉政建设。通过深化行政审批制度改革，进一步健全了行政职责体系和问责制度，遏制了权力滥用、以权谋私等违纪违法行为和腐败现象蔓延，推动了政府反腐倡廉建设。

### （二）2013 年以来行政审批制度改革

新一届国务院组成后，把加快转变政府职能、简政放权作为开门第一件大事，把深化行政审批制度改革作为重要抓手和突破口，着力推进简政放权、放管结合和优化服务，"放管服"三管齐下，协同推进。2013 年 6 月，国务院明确行政审批制度改革工作牵头单位由监察部调整为中央编办，国务院审改办设在中央编办。2015 年 4 月，国务院决定将国务院机构职能转变协调小组的名称改为国务院推进职能转变协调小组，作为国务院议事协调机构，并下设了行政审批改革组，负责牵头推进国务院行政审批制度改革。同时，还下设了投资审批改革组、商事制度改革组等专题组和综合组、法制组等功能组。

本届政府成立之初，国务院部门各类审批 1700 多项，投资创业和群众办事门槛多，审批过程手续繁、收费高、周期长、效率低，这不仅严重抑制市场活力、制约经济社会发展，还容易导致权力寻租、滋生腐败，企业和群众对此反映强烈。为此，新一届政府提出要以壮士断腕的决心和勇气向市场和社会放权，郑重承诺本届政府要减少行政审批事项三分之一以上。从 2013 年至 2015 年这三年多来，国务院部门共取消和下放行政审批事项 618 项，占原有审批事项的 36%，本届政府承诺的目标提前超额完成。非行政许可审批彻底终结。连续两次修订政府核准的投资项目目录，中央层面核准的项目数量累计减少约 76%，95% 以上的外商投资项目、98% 以上的境外投资项目改为网上备案管理。推动商事制度改革，工商登记由"先证后照"改为"先照后证"，前置审批精简 85%，注册资本由实缴改为认缴，全面实施"三证合一、一照一码"。个人和企业资质资格认定事项压减 44%。加大减税和普遍性降费力度，先后出台了一系列税收优惠政策，不断扩大营改增试点范围，砍掉了大部分行政审批中介服务事项，取消、停征、减免一大批行政事业性收费和政府性基金。中央政府定价项目减少 80%，中央对地方财政专项转移支付项目减少一半以上。在放权的同时，创新和加强事中事后监管，建立政府部门权责清单制度。针对群众期盼优化公共服务，各地在承接上级下放权限的同时，积极推进本层级的"放管服"改革，多数省份行政审批事项减少 50% 左右，有的达到 70%。

改革有效地激发了市场活力和社会创造力。特别是推动了新动能加快成长，大众创业万众创新热情高涨，新增市场主体持续快速增长，2015 年以来全国平均每天新增 4 万户，其中新登记企业平均每天新增 1.2 万户，企业活跃度保持在 70% 左右。中国营商环境明显改善，市场准入和运行的制度成本大幅降低，全要素生产率稳步提升。

近三年的行政审批制度改革，主要有五个特点：一是既大力取消下放行政审批事项，又注重配套推进制度创新。在分期分批取消下放行政审批事项的同时，推进相关制度创新，如改革工商登记制度，将"先证后照"改为"先照后证"；推进工商注册制度便利化，将注册资本实缴登记制改为认缴登记制，将企业年检制度改为年度报告制度，大幅降低创办企业的门槛；在自贸区探索建立负面清单制度，对市场主体实行"法无禁止即可为"。二是注重运用法治思维和法治方式推进改革。行政审批制度改革的实质是转变政府职能，规范和约束政府行为，实现依法行政。深化行政审批制度改革，从部署到落实，注重运用法治思维、法治方式，严格遵循职权法定、程序合法、公开透明的要求。为依法推进行政审批制度改革和政府职能转变，国务院依照法定程序提请全国人大常委会修订相关法律，对有关行政法规予以废止，对部分行政法规条款进行修改。三是通过公开机制和倒逼机制让改革措施落到实处。新一届政府对简政放权、转变政府职能涉及的具体措施，明确责任单位、参与单位，列出改革完成的时间表，并公开承诺要削减三分之一以上行政审批事项等，表明了全面深化改革的决心和目标。将国务院行政审批事项在各部门网站和中国机构编制网公开，公布权力清单制度，接受群众和社会的监督。同时，针对已经取消下放的行政审批事项引入第三方评估机制，对改革形成倒逼机制，促进改革迈出实质性步伐，使得各项措施落到实处不走空。四是清理存量与严控增量并行，杜绝"边减边增"。在取消和下放行政审批事项的过程中，不仅考虑存量改革，也关注增量控制。国务院先后印发了《关于严格控制新设行政许可的通知》《关于清理国务院部门非行政许可审批事项的通知》，明确要求严格控制新增许可事项，对新增行政审批事项的设立标准和程序做出了严格要求，不允许在清单之外变相设置审批，即使是必要的行政审批也必须规范，防止滋生腐败，做到标准明确、程序严密、运作透明、制约有效和权责分明。同时，清理取消了国务院部门现存的非行政许可审批事项。五是创新政府监管方式。通过完善监管措施，创新监管方式，充分利用市场机制和社会力量，实现政府管理从注重事前审批向重视事中事后监管转变。

# 三　政府职能转变取得的主要成效和基本认识

中国政府在转变政府职能方面取得了积极进展和明显成效，政府的经济调节、市场监管职能得到加强，社会管理和公共服务职能受到重视，政府职能转变不到位、缺位、越位、错位等问题有所改善，这些都为继续全面深化改革奠定了基础。

**一是加强和改善宏观调控。**为适应加快转变经济发展方式的要求，促进科学发展，不断加强和改善宏观调控。遵循社会主义市场经济规律，进一步完善宏观调控体系，更多地运用经济手段和法律手段调节经济活动。加大对经济结构调整的力度，把着力点放到促进经济发展方式转变和推进供给侧结构性改革上，进一步增强宏观调控的预见性、针对性和有效性。

**二是强化和提高市场监管水平。**在市场监管方面，着力解决管理职能分割和监管力度不够的问题，建立和健全统一开放竞争有序的现代市场体系。深化市场监管体制改革，合理界定市场监管范围，逐步形成行政执法、行业自律、舆论监督、群众参与相结合的市场监管体系。规范市场监管行为，改进市场监管方式，依法对市场主体及其行为进行监督和管理，维护公平竞争的市场秩序。努力培育和规范各类市场中介组织和专业服务组织，推动和引导社会力量参与市场监管。

**三是重视社会管理和公共服务。**将各类资源更多地向社会管理和公共服务领域配置。改革财政体制，调整财政收支结构，增加公共产品供给总量，扩大公共服务覆盖面。分类推进事业单位改革，科学合理界定政府与事业单位的关系，强化事业单位提供公益服务的职责，提高公益服务水平。创新公共服务供给方式，通过购买服务等市场化、社会化方式，解决政府在提供公共服务方面的不足。统筹推动行业体制改革，规范和发展社会组织，将协调性职责、服务性职责、技术辅助性职责交给社会组织，发挥社会组织服务社会的作用。

**四是推动层级间和部门间权责关系的进一步明晰，不断提高行政效率。**进一步明晰中央与地方的事权划分和部门间职责划分，政府服务与管理社会的重点更加突出。不同层级政府在职能配置"上下一般粗"的状况有所改善。中央政府对经济社会事务的宏观调控能力进一步提升，地方政府为基层和群众服务的水平得到提高。划清一些重要领域的部门职责交叉事项，逐步建立部门间协调配合机制，明确和强化部门责任。行政执法体系进一步理顺，逐步解决多头执法、多层执法、执法扰民等突出问题。积极推动省直管县体制改革、经济发达镇改革试点，扩大县级政府和发达镇政府的管理权限，增加发展的自主权。

　　从总体上看，中国政府职能转变基本适应经济社会发展要求，推动了行政体制改革的不断深化，促进了服务型政府建设和发展。基本认识有：一是始终以政府职能转变为核心推动行政体制改革，政府职能随着经济社会发展而不断进行调整和转变。二是形成了政企分开、政资分开、政事分开、政府与市场中介组织分开的总体要求，将政府职能转变作为检验行政管理体制成效的主要标准。三是把明确部门职责分工、理顺权责关系、规范中央与地方的关系作为政府职能转变的重点内容。四是把转变政府职能与调整机构设置、创新政府管理方式与行政运行机制等有机结合起来。五是在推进政府职能转变的方法步骤上始终坚持循序渐进、突出重点、不断深化。

**参考文献**

［1］中央机构编制委员会办公室：《在布局中不断推进——我国行政管理体制改革回顾》，《人民日报》2008年12月18日。

［2］朱光磊、于丹：《建设服务型政府是转变政府职能的新阶段——对中国政府转变职能过程的回顾与展望》，《政治学研究》2008年第6期。

［3］中央机构编制委员会办公室理论学习中心组：《改革开放以来我国行政管理体制改革的光辉历程》，《人民日报》2011年7月25日。

［4］应松年：《行政审批制度改革：反思与创新》，《学术前沿》2012年第3期。

［5］王澜明：《深化行政审批制度改革应"减""放""改""管"一起做——对国务院部门深化行政审批制度改革的一点看法和建议》，《中国行政管理》2014年第1期。

［6］唐亚林、朱春：《2001年以来中央政府行政审批制度改革的基本经验与优化路径》，《理论探讨》2014年第5期。

［7］王浦劬：《论转变政府职能的若干理论问题》，《国家行政学院学报》2015年第1期。

［8］冉昊：《我国简政放权和行政审批制度改革的过程、问题与趋势》，《新视野》

2015 年第 5 期。

［9］国务院审改办：《清理规范国务院部门行政审批中介服务工作有关情况》，《中国机构改革与管理》2015 年第 5 期。

［10］国务院审改办：《国务院部门非行政许可审批事项清理工作情况》，《中国机构改革与管理》2015 年第 6 期。

［11］石亚军：《当前推进政府职能根本转变亟需解决的若干深层问题》，《中国行政管理》2015 年第 6 期。

［12］《李章泽同志通报简政放权有关政策情况并答记者问》，《中国机构改革与管理》2015 年第 11 期。

［13］国务院审改办：《行政审批制度改革工作取得新的进展》，《中国机构改革与管理》2016 年第 2 期。

（作者：陈峰　中国机构编制管理研究会副秘书长）

第 四 章

# 事业单位改革

在中国，行政改革的主要内容之一是事业单位改革。自 20 世纪 80 年代开始，事业单位的改革伴随着中国的改革开放，成为与农村改革、国有企业改革、行政体制改革并行的一项重要改革。事业单位是中国独特的公共部门组织形式。事业单位广泛分布在教育、科技、文化、卫生等与民生关系密切的领域，包括各类学校、研究机构、文化团体和医疗机构等，是中国政府提供公益服务的主要载体。目前在法规中，事业单位是指"国家为了社会公益目的，由国家机关举办或者其他组织利用国有资产举办的，从事教育、科技、文化、卫生等活动的社会服务组织"①。虽然事业单位是中国特有的概念，在英文中常翻译为 *public service unit*，在国外，存在着大量职能与中国的事业单位类似的机构，但其名称是各不相同的。根据经合组织（OECD）的统计，典型的组织包括②：独立代理机构（independent agencies）、执行机构（Executive Agencies）、非部门公共实体（non-departmental public bodies）、公法机构（bodies of public law）、半自治机构（semi-autonomous bodies）等。

推进事业单位改革，事关民生改善，科教文卫等事业与老百姓切身利益密切相关，只有深入推进改革，才能满足公众日益增长的公益服务需求。推进事业单位改革，是转变政府职能、建设服务型政府的重要举措。推进事业单位改革，事关经济可持续发展，公益事业是第三产业的重要组成、扩大消费的重要领域，事业单位改革对改善经济增长的动力结构、经

---

① 《事业单位登记管理暂行条例》，国务院令第 411 号，2004 年。

② 《分散化的公共治理：代理机构，权力主体和其他政府实体》，中信出版社 2002 年版。

济转型升级有着重要作用。推进事业单位改革，事关改革开放总体布局。

# 一　事业单位改革回顾

《民法通则》中将法人分为企业法人、机关法人、事业单位法人和社会团体法人四类，事业单位是独立的法人。目前，中国共有事业单位111万个，在职人员3100多万人。事业单位按行业划分有25个大类，100多个小类，人员编制超过40万的行业有10个，超过一半的事业单位在教育领域，共1483万人，其次是卫生、文化领域。事业单位的出现始于中国计划经济时期，在20世纪50年代，中国借鉴苏联的模式，在经济和社会各个领域先后采取了一系列公有化措施，形成了政府包办，由事业单位单一主体供给公共服务的体制。1955年中国政府文件中第一次使用"事业单位"一词，指的是"活动经费由国家财政列为事业项目开支的机关和部门"。

回顾中国事业单位改革，主要经历了以下阶段：

### （一）放权让利，激发活力（1979—1992年）

随着1978年12月中共十一届三中全会召开，确立了以经济建设为中心的工作重点。由于"文化大革命"对经济的破坏，财政对科、教、文、卫事业的投入严重不足，另一方面长期计划思维，政策上限制过严，事业单位活力不足。事业单位改革启动时以适当下放各类事业单位管理权为主。科技领域与经济建设密切相关，科技领域下放权力政策最先启动。紧接着，卫生、教育及艺术表演领域进行行业改革探索。1985年中央出台文件改革了对研究机构的拨款制度，按照不同类型科学技术活动的特点，实行经费的分类管理。扩大了研究机构的自主权，研究所实行所长负责制，明确研究、设计机构和高等学校，可以逐步试行聘任制。在文化领域，随着1985年文化部进行了以承包经营责任制等形式进行艺术表演团体体制改革试验。"以文补文"的有偿业务和经营性活动受到政策鼓励。教育、卫生领域也放权给地方、部门激发活力。比如卫生领域，国家对医院的补助经费，除大修理和大型设备购置外，实行定额包干，补助经费定额确定后，单位有权自行支配使用。在教育领域，1985年，中央明确实行基础教育由地方负责、分级管理的原则，改革高等学校的招生计划和毕业生分配制度，扩大高等学校办学自主权。

经过 1985—1992 年这一时期"放权让利"政策激励，事业单位活力被激发。但事业单位改革处于被动状态，主要推动力来自资金严重不足和事业发展难以为继。所以，事业单位改革焦点主要集中在拓宽事业经费来源上。这一时期，事业单位"创收"模糊了事业单位与企业边界，留下了事业单位功能不清的隐患。

### （二）政事分开，事业单位专项改革（1992—2002 年）

1992 年，随着社会主义市场经济体制改革目标提出后，建立与市场经济体制相适应的政府管理体制是主要任务，事业单位改革开始进入探索建立与社会主义市场经济相配套的事业单位机构和人事管理体制的新阶段。1993 年，事业单位工资制度进行改革，对全额拨款、差额拨款、自收自支三种不同类型的事业单位实行分类管理。改革主要表现为"两个过渡"即全额拨款单位向差额拨款单位过渡，差额拨款单位向自收自支单位过渡，使面向市场的事业单位逐步走向市场。从 1996 年开始，进入事业单位专项改革探索，经济鉴证类社会中介机构脱钩改制，应用型科研机构和工程勘察设计单位转企改制。

这一时期，一方面，政府机构改革，人员精简，政府职能转移出来，事业单位是主要的承接组织。"1998 年政府机构改革，机构减一半，大量的事务需要管理，行政类事业单位数量直线上升。"① 另一方面，随着经济社会发展，政府职能不断扩张，相关行政任务增加，新增了承担行政职能的环境监察、劳动保障监察、文化市场管理等承担行政执法职能的事业单位。新设的行业监管机构，像中国证券监督和管理委员会、中国银行业监督和管理委员会、中国保险业监督与管理委员会、国家电力监管委员会等多为事业单位，出现了一批承担行政职能的事业单位，使得事业单位与行政机关的界限又进一步模糊。

1996 年，《中央机构编制委员会关于事业单位机构改革若干问题的意

---

① 易丽丽：《我国行政类事业单位改革探索——基于对三个试点省（市）的调研思考》，《中国行政管理》2012 年第 9 期。

见》出台，这是第一个针对事业单位共性问题进行规范的文件。事业单位改革从分领域改革向统筹改革方向探索。这一次的基本思路是，"确立科学化的总体布局，坚持社会的发展方向，推行多样化的分类管理，实行制度化的总量控制"①。这一时期，事业单位在人事制度、分配制度、社会保障等方面的改革都取得了进展。1999 年，《事业单位登记管理暂行条例》颁布，在全国范围内统一对事业单位进行登记管理。

2000 年，对国务院部门（单位）所属社会公益类科研机构实行分类改革，将主要从事应用基础研究或向社会提供公共服务，无法得到相应经济回报，国家财政给予经常性经费补助，按非营利性机构运行和管理。事业单位人事制度改革进入密集期，基本思路：一是取消行政级别、实行分类管理、扩大用人自主权、搞活用人机制。二是建立以聘用制为基础的用人制度。三是建立形式多样、自主灵活的分配激励机制。②

这一阶段事业单位改革方向逐渐清晰，事业单位法人登记制度让事业单位作为独立的法人主体，从法律上与行政部门分开；社会化原则改革，与全球新公共管理运动引入市场机制的趋势基本同步；"非营利"概念在文件中出现，被引入了事业单位改革的政策设计。这一阶段确定下来的政事分开原则，使事业单位从行政事业一体化中分离开来，使事业单位成为独立的社会实体，成为接下来事业单位及其管理体制改革的主线。而这一阶段，科学、教育、文化、体育等社会事业市场化导向，朝产业化方向发展，医疗、教育等公共服务领域因减轻财政负担出现追求经济利益，公益性缺乏的不良苗头，一方面，事业单位从大一统的公共部门中分化出来建立新的制度；另一方面，政府机构改革不彻底或新增职能设事业单位承担，模糊了政府和事业单位的边界，"政事不分，政企不分、政社不分"等问题暴露出来，事业单位功能模糊、公益性不足。

### （三）从人事改革入手取得突破，分行业深化改革（2002—2011 年）

在此期间，事业单位人事制度改革以推行聘用制和岗位管理制度为重点在各行业推进，逐步建立适应不同类型事业单位特点区别于行政机关和

---

① 范恒山主编：《中国事业单位改革探索》（上卷），人民出版社 2010 年版。

② 人事部：《关于加快推进事业单位人事制度改革的意见》的通知。

国有企业的人事管理制度。2002 年，由国务院转发人社部文件，事业单位实行全员聘用制，事业单位人员全部签订合同。2002 年事业单位全面推行公开招聘制度，建立和完善绩效考核制度。2006 年事业单位岗位设置管理试行办法下发，事业单位人员从身份管理向岗位管理转变。2006年通过实施绩效工资进行事业单位收入分配制度改革。2008 年，山西、上海、浙江、广东、重庆启动事业单位养老保险试点。

事业单位行业类别复杂，分行业改革不断推进，2003 年，文化事业单位改革力度较大，在全国 9 个地区和 35 个单位进行了文化体制改革试点，试点将文化事业单位分为公益性和经营性两类，公益类以增加投入、转换机制、增强活力、改善服务为重点。2009 年，医药卫生体制改革启动，实行政事分开、管办分开、医药分开、营利性和非营利性分开。公立医院改革开始试点。为破除事业单位管办不分的体制弊端，逐步在广电、文化、新闻出版等领域组建事业集团，与行业主管部门实现管办分离。

这一阶段，事业单位通过人事制度改革激发了活力，收入分配制度、财政制度逐渐深化，养老保险制度改革试点探索。2005 年政府工作报告第一次提出分类推进事业单位改革，2008 年，试点省市开始分类改革试点。事业单位改革从人事制度改革入手，从试点到全面推广，从统一的人事制度改革到事业单位专项改革，从单项改革到综合改革，为事业单位后续改革奠定了基础。

### （四）回归公益，事业单位综合改革阶段（2011 年至今）

2011 年 3 月，《中共中央国务院分类推进事业单位改革的指导意见》正式下发，新一轮事业单位改革启动，这是第一次将事业单位作为一个整体进行改革的顶层设计。本轮事业单位改革总体方案的一个显著特点是：以科学分类为基础，按照社会功能将事业单位分为承担行政职能、提供公益服务、从事生产经营活动三个类别。在科学划分事业单位类别的基础上，根据不同类别事业单位特点有针对性地实施相应政策，推进事业单位改革。公益类事业单位是事业单位的主体部分，是此轮改革的重点与核心。综合性文件下发后，11 个配套文件解决事业单位分类、编制管理、财政有关政策、法人治理结构、收入分配等行业体制改革自身难以解决的共性问题、基础问题和衔接问题。

2011 年开始,以社会功能为分类标准,改革第一步是在清理整顿基础上调整界定事业单位职能。调整职能过程中,将行政职能回归行政机关,将机关技术性、辅助性、服务性职能交给事业单位,将可由社会承担的如评估、鉴定、检验、标准制定等工作交给社会组织和市场。划定职能后再进行科学分类。在此期间,《事业单位人事管理条例》出台,依法进行事业单位管理又迈出一步。养老保险制度实现并轨即机关事业单位工作人员实行和企业职工一样的基本养老保险制度。截至 2015 年,承担行政职能事业单位和从事生产经营活动事业单位类别划分基本完成。随着国务院办公厅下发《关于政府向社会力量购买服务的指导意见》,政府向社会力量购买服务在全国形成趋势,社会力量兴办公益事业的制度环境进一步优化。

## 二 事业单位改革所取得的主要成效

### (一) 回归公益,事业单位改革促进了社会事业的发展

事业单位改革中,一批生产经营型、技术应用型、中介服务型事业单位改制为企业,不再享受事业单位的优惠政策,尊重市场竞争秩序,自主经营、自负盈亏。从事经营活动的事业单位转制为企业,纯化了事业单位公益性的社会功能。

而作为事业单位中比重最大的向社会提供公共产品和公共服务的公益服务组织,30 多年来,教育、卫生、科技、文化等事业单位经过不断的改革,促进社会事业取得了长足的进步。

在教育领域,教育服务的普及程度明显提高,国民受教育机会显著增加,教育公平取得重要进展,城乡、区域、校际、群体教育差距明显缩小,九年义务教育巩固率达到 92.6%,高等教育在学总规模达 3559 万人,位居世界第一。[①]

在卫生领域,全民医保体系基本建立,个人支出占卫生总费用的比重下降到 30%,三大基本医疗保障、保险,即职工基本医保、新农合和城

---

① 袁贵仁:《"十二五"以来特别是十八大以来教育改革发展的成就》,共产党员网,http://news.12371.cn/2015/10/15/ARTI1444846476490108.shtml。

镇居民基本医保，已经超过 13 亿人，参保率达到 95% 以上。医疗服务体系进一步健全，我国医疗卫生机构超过 98 万个，医疗卫生人员总量超过 1000 万人，覆盖城乡的基层医疗卫生服务体系基本建成，基本实现了村村有卫生室、乡乡有卫生院、县县有达标县医院，医疗卫生服务设施条件明显改善。居民 15 分钟内能够到达最近医疗点的比例为 84%，农村达到 80.2%。①

在科技领域，针对科研类事业单位，规定单位主管部门和财政部门不再审批，所有的项目由承担的单位来对科技成果转化，转移转化的收入，全部留归单位。② 同时，结合事业单位分类改革的要求，在国家自主创新示范区、自主创新综合试验区选择若干符合条件的中央级事业单位开展科技成果使用、处置和收益管理改革试点。③

在文化领域，现代公共文化服务体系建设不断推进，初步建成了覆盖国家级、省级、地市级、县级、乡级、村级和城市社区的公共文化服务网络，设立了 4 万个乡镇文化站，60 多万个农家书屋，农民每个月能免费看到一场电影。④

此外，事业单位改革也促进了基本公共服务均等化，推进了服务型政府建设。服务型政府建设着眼于保障和改善民生，建立了相对完善的公共服务体系，大力推进基本公共服务均等化，完善政府公共服务职能体系，优化政府组织机构，改进行政运行机制，加大公共财政投入力度，取得了显著成就。⑤

---

① 李斌：《"十二五"以来特别是十八大以来卫生改革发展的成就》，共产党员网，http://news.12371.cn/2015/10/20/ARTI1445278350425253.shtml。

② 万钢：《"十二五"以来特别是十八大以来我国科技创新发展成就》，共产党员网，http://news.12371.cn/2015/10/22/ARTI1445451095310860.shtml。

③ 财政部、科技部、国家知识产权局：《关于开展深化中央级事业单位科技成果使用、处置和收益管理改革试点的通知》，2014 年。

④ 尹蔚民：《"十二五"以来特别是十八大以来就业和社会保障事业改革发展成就》，共产党员网，http://news.12371.cn/2015/10/21/ARTI1445365460334897.shtml。

⑤ 马宝成：《中国服务型政府建设十年：主要成就和未来展望》，《国家行政学院学报》2012 年第 5 期。

### （二） 政事分开，事业单位功能定位逐渐明确

改革开放后很长一段时间，事业单位是政府的附属，是政府职能的延伸，没有独立的法人地位，出现了许多行政类和企业类的事业单位，承担了过多的行政性和营利性的职能。改革开放前，"一些事业单位功能定位不清，政事不分、事企不分，机制不活"，导致"我国社会事业发展相对滞后，公益服务供给总量不足，供给方式单一，资源配置不合理，质量和效率不高"。①

2011 年新一轮事业单位改革开始后，随着一系列改革措施的出台落实，事业单位被赋予了独立法人资格，政府把不该管、管不好的微观事物交给事业单位，事业单位则以独立法人地位向社会提供公益服务。

在实施政事分开，理顺政府与事业单位的关系的过程中，行政主管部门"减少对事业单位的微观管理和直接管理，强化制定政策法规、行业规划、标准规范和监督指导等职责，进一步落实事业单位法人自主权"，对面向社会提供公益服务的事业单位，"积极探索管办分离的有效实现形式，逐步取消行政级别"。② 事业单位改革进一步强化了政府的公共服务职能，更加明确事业单位是公共服务提供的主要载体，是基本公共服务领域的主体力量，明确的功能定位促使事业单位在完善公共服务方面发挥了更大作用。

### （三） 内部管理体制改革，激发了活力

事业单位改革形成了不同于政府和企业的适应自身发展的内部管理体制，在干部管理、人事制度、绩效管理等方面均有创新。

第一，普遍实行了行政首长负责制，并不断推进法人治理结构建设。自 2012 年起，中央编办牵头组织事业单位法人治理结构试点工作。从全国试点情况看，600 余家事业单位建立了法人治理结构，已取得阶段性成果，试点单位建立了较为健全的法人治理结构和制度。

第二，建立了符合不同类型事业单位特点和不同岗位要求的人事管理

①　中共中央国务院：《关于分类推进事业单位改革的指导意见》，2011 年。

②　同上。

制度，进一步扩大了事业单位的人事管理自主权，引入竞争机制，全面实行岗位聘任制，2014 年年底聘用制度推行率达 93%，公开招聘推行率达 91%。[①]

第三，改革分配制度，根据不同类型事业单位特点建立了不同于行政机关的工资制度，改变了单一的分配方式，尤其激发了专业技术岗位人员的活力。2009 年开始，义务教育学校和公共卫生与基层医疗卫生事业单位全面推行了绩效工资制度，并在其他事业单位实施了绩效工资改革试点，进一步调动了事业单位人员的工作积极性，形成了有效的激励机制，增强了事业单位发展的活力。

### （四）打破垄断，公共服务选择多样性

通过改革，公共服务的提供由政府的大包大揽慢慢转变为由政府、社会组织和企业共同提供公益服务。非公资本通过招标承包、特许经营、非公独资等方式参与营利性公共服务领域。

在教育领域，多种形式的联合办学模式如"公办民助""民办公助""公私联办"等相继出现；社会力量办学如民办小学、民办中学、民办大学等民办学历教育与非学历教育机构等正成为一支重要的办学力量。在科技领域，各种民办科研机构，如民办研发机构、民办科技中介机构、民办科技产业实体等，日渐成为国办科研事业单位的有益补充。在文化领域，社会力量兴办的各类文化事业实体与文化产业实体得到迅速发展，自由职业撰稿人、个体书商、自由职业演员、农村文化个体户、民营书店、民办图书馆、民办文化娱乐场所、社区娱乐组织等纷纷涌现，繁荣了城乡文化市场，促进了文化事业、文化产业的发展。在卫生事业领域，国家制定了鼓励社会办医、全民办医的政策，改变了过去由国家垄断医疗卫生事业领域的状况，允许以社会捐助的形式举办医疗机构、个体医生开办诊所、成立民办医院等，形成了国家、集体、个人等全社会力量办医的局面。

虽然事业单位仍然是占最大比重的公益服务提供主体，但是财政投入方式改革，购买服务制度已经让政府作为直接生产者、安排者和购买者角色分离，政府向事业单位之外的主体购买公共服务，不再直接生产所有公

---

① 刘娟：《推动人事制度改革取得新突破》，《中国组织人事报》2014 年 12 月 24 日。

益服务。政府包办的垄断格局已经打破，公益服务领域市场开始培育，增加了公益服务主体多样性和提供方式的多样化。

# 三　事业单位改革的特点

回顾事业单位 30 年的改革，积累了有价值的经验。概括起来有分类改革、试点改革、渐进改革和系统改革。

## （一）分类改革，注重事业单位差异性

事业单位改革从一开始就特别强调分类，改革对事业单位的多样性和复杂性有清楚的认识。改革的不同时期，分类改革的分类标准不同。自1985 年开始，根据国家的行业标准按行业分类改革，事业单位根据不同行业的特点，随教育、文化、卫生、科技等行业体制改革同步进行，充分调动行业主管部门的积极性。在相当长的一段时间，中国事业单位改革即按此思路进行，在政策上给予行业主管部门更多的空间，避免"一刀切"，这也是国际上的普遍做法。在各行业领域改革中也注重分类，比如医疗、科研等区分营利性和非营利性事业单位。20 世纪 90 年代，事业单位按经费分类改革，即依据经费来源的形式将事业单位分为全额拨款、差额拨款、自收自支三类进行改革。以财政经费为突破口，便于政府对事业单位实施有效的财务管理。近十多年，事业单位分类改革以社会功能为分类标准，以科学分类为基础推进事业单位改革。分类管理是事业单位改革的经验，区分不同类别事业单位的差异性，提高事业单位改革的针对性。

## （二）试点改革，积累经验的基础上全面推开

"摸着石头过河，是富有中国特色、符合中国国情的改革方法，摸着石头过河就是摸规律，从实践中获得真知。"[①] 事业单位改革和中国其他领域改革一样，试点先行，在实践中摸规律。艺术表演团体体制改革于1988 年下半年启动，把国务院确定的进行经济体制综合改革试点的部分

---

① 徐绍史：《改革必须试点先行在实践中摸规律》，《人民日报》2013 年 11 月 19 日。

大中城市，作为艺术表演团体体制改革的试点城市。[①] 1992年深化科研体制改革，就是试点先行。"选择3至5个专业领域的研究机构进行结构调整试点，选择5至10个研究机构进行优化内部结构和运行机制的试点，探索大院大所走企业化道路。"[②] 科研事业单位改革通过试点积累经验，通过试点发现问题，通过试点逐步推开。2000年卫生事业单位人事制度改革，实行产权制度改革的试点单位，经批准探索试行理事会（董事会）决策制、监事会监管制等新型管理制度。2008年事业单位分类改革在山西、上海、浙江、广东、重庆五省市进行试点。重要的改革从试点开始，各试点省结合本地实际情况，研究提出具体的实施方案，按程序报当地党委、政府和编委批准，并向中央编办备案后实施。在实施过程中，与财政、人事和劳动保障等相关职能部门协调合作，总结经验。再比如2010年，公立医院改革试点指导意见下发，要求各省、自治区、直辖市分别选择1—2个城市（城区）作为公立医院改革试点城市，国家在各地试点城市范围内，选出16个有代表性的城市，作为国家联系指导的公立医院改革试点城市。对试点城市出现的问题及时研究解决，不断总结经验，完善改革总体思路和主要政策措施。

事业单位改革试点先行是改革取得的宝贵经验，在推进改革的过程中，从实际出发，因地制宜，下放权力给试点地区和试点单位，调动地方积极性，鼓励不同形式的探索，积累的经验不断汇集，出现的问题及时与相关职能部门沟通协调，正确处理好改革与发展的关系。

### （三）渐进改革，确保平稳过渡

事业单位涉及行业领域多，机构多，人员庞大。先易后难，分步实施，渐进改革是事业单位改革的重要经验。一是不搞"一刀切"，老人老办法，新人新办法。改革是利益重新配置，事关被改革者的切身利益。事业单位改革中涉及人员无论是养老保险、单位转制等，为了减少被改革者的阻力，采取老人老办法、新人新办法，增量改革。二是出台改革过渡期

---

① 国务院：《关于加快和深化艺术表演团体体制改革意见》，1988年。

② 国家科委、国家体改委：《关于分流人才、调整结构、进一步深化科技体制改革的若干意见》，1992年。

政策确保改革平稳。1996 年专门针对事业单位改革的文件就体现了渐进改革的思考。"要推进有条件的全额拨款的事业单位按照有关规定开展有偿服务，逐步向差额补贴过渡；差额补贴的事业单位，要进一步创造条件，向自收自支或企业化管理过渡。"① 改革中要求各地区、各部门要结合实际情况，研究提出可以过渡的事业单位的范围、标准、比例和时间要求。再比如事业单位向企业转制，明确"在过渡期内，原有的正常事业费继续拨付，主要用于解决转制前已离退休人员的社会保障问题"②。比如分类改革，"完全符合某类条件的，直接确定其类别；基本符合某类条件的，先预定其类别，经过相应调整完全符合条件后，再确定其类别"③。渐进改革消化了改革的阻力，将改革对稳定的冲击减小到最少，保护了被改革者的利益。确保中人平稳过渡。三是国家财政兜底。比如在转制过渡期内，按照企业基本养老金计发办法计发的养老金，如低于按照原事业单位退休办法计发的退休金，其差额部分加发补贴，所需费用从基本养老保险统筹基金中支付。用于补贴的基本养老保险基金，由财政部门负担，人力资源和社会保障与财政部共同管理，基金不够了由财政负责补。渐进改革的经验显示缓和了改革矛盾，处理好了改革与稳定的关系。

### （四）　系统改革，专项改革和综合改革"组合拳"

事业单位改革是一个复杂的系统工程。事业单位改革，并不是孤立地进行，一是伴随着行政体制改革，适应社会主义市场经济体制，放权搞活。事业单位改革作为行政体制改革的一部分，或者是行政体制改革的延伸。二是伴随着中国干部人事制度改革强调机关、事业单位、国有企业分类改革。三是事业单位自身的企业化运作和公益性改革。专项的改革和综合改革相结合将改革不断深化。2011 年新一轮事业单位改革，尤其突出改革的系统性，出台新中国成立以来最高规格的文件，解决事业单位共性、衔接性、基础性问题，同时配套了 11 个文件针对分类、机构编制、

---

① 中共中央办公厅：《中央机构编制委员会关于事业单位机构改革若干问题的意见》，1996年。

② 国务院办公厅，《国务院办公厅关于印发分类推进事业单位改革配套文件的通知》，2011年。

③ 中央编制委员会办公室：《关于事业单位分类试点的意见》，2008 年。

法人治理结构、国有资产管理等方面具体改革，"1 + 11"个文件形成了组合拳，系统性推进事业单位改革，改革中处理好事业单位改革与经济体制改革、政府机构改革以及各相关行业体制改革的关系，处理好事业单位改革内部各项具体改革举措的关系，做到改革政策前后衔接，改革措施协调配套。

虽然中国事业单位改革取得了成效也积累了经验。但必须正视的是，中国社会事业发展仍然相对滞后，一些事业单位功能定位不清，政事不分，事企不分，机制不活；公益服务供给总量不足，供给方式单一，资源配置不合理，质量和效率不高；支持公益服务的政策措施还不够完善，监管管理薄弱。这些问题仍然不同程度影响了公益事业的健康发展。截至2015年，事业单位在清理规范基础上完成分类，承担行政职能事业单位和从事生产经营活动事业单位的改革基本完成，公益类事业单位继续留在事业单位序列；而到2020年，则要建立起功能明确、治理完善、运行高效、监管有力的管理体制和运行机制，形成基本服务优先、供给水平适度、布局结构合理、服务公平公正的中国特色公益服务体系。这一改革目标与2020年实现全面建设小康社会目标相衔接。下一步的改革，将以从事公益服务事业单位改革为重点，在教育、卫生、文化、科技等领域继续推进，相关改革措施涉及政事分开、管办分离、法人治理结构、人事制度、收入分配、财政税收、社会保障改革、监督管理等各个领域。

## 参考文献

［1］范恒山：《中国事业单位改革探索》，人民出版社2010年版。

［2］国家教委政策研究室：《教育体制改革文献选编》，教育科学出版社1985年版。

［3］国务院：《事业单位登记管理暂行条例》，2004年。

［4］国务院：《事业单位人事管理条例》，2014年。

［5］OECD：《分散化的公共治理：代理机构，权力主体和其他政府实体》，中信出版社2002年版。

［6］万钢：《"十二五"以来特别是十八大以来我国科技创新发展成就》，共产党员网，http://news.12371.cn/2015/10/22/ARTI1445451095310860.shtml。

［7］徐绍史：《改革必须试点先行在实践中摸规律》，《人民日报》2013年11月19日。

[8] 尹蔚民:《"十二五"以来特别是十八大以来就业和社会保障事业改革发展成就》，共产党员网，http：//news. 12371. cn/2015/10/21/ARTI1445365460334897. shtml。

[9] 易丽丽:《中国行政类事业单位改革探索——基于对三个试点省（市）的调研思考》，《中国行政管理》2012 年第 9 期。

[10] 袁贵仁:《"十二五"以来特别是十八大以来教育改革发展的成就》，共产党员网，http：//news. 12371. cn/2015/10/15/ARTI1444846476490108. shtml。

[11] 中共中央国务院:《中共中央国务院分类推进事业单位改革的指导意见》，2011 年。

（作者：易丽丽    国家行政学院公共管理教研部副教授）

# 第 五 章

# 中国社会治理体制改革与创新

中国自 1978 年实行改革开放政策以来，经济社会政治文化各个方面发生了全方位的巨大变化。在此过程中，社会的组织方式和秩序建构模式也进行了相应的调整和改革，由传统意义的社会管理走向现代意义的社会治理。社会治理体制不断改革创新，主要表现在社会治理理念、社会治理主体、社会治理方式和社会治理重心等几个方面。

## 一 社会治理理念创新

2012 年，中共十八大提出了"国家治理体系和治理能力现代化"这样一个重要思想。作为国家治理体系和治理能力现代化的重要组成部分，"社会治理"在学术界使用多年后正式进入党和国家的理论和政策范畴。社会治理是指，立足公平正义，以维护和实现群众合法权益为核心，协调社会关系，处理社会问题，化解社会矛盾，防范社会风险，促进社会认同，保障公共安全，维护社会和谐稳定。社会治理是一个中国本土化色彩很浓的概念，它与国际上通行的"治理"概念既有相同之处，也有不同。在一定意义上可以把它看作"治理"的一个方面或一个部分。因此，"治理"的理念、原则、方法和手段在很大程度上同样适用于"社会治理"。社会治理是由社会和治理两个词组成的，既可以把"社会"理解为"多种社会力量和社会主体"，即把"社会"作为主语来对待，即社会性力量的治理，也可以把"社会"理解为对象，把"社会"作为宾语来对待，即治理的是社会领域的事情。无论"社会"作为主语还是作为宾语，社会治理都是治理的一个方面，而不是全部。因此，社会治理与治理的不同之处主要在于，治理是一个更大的概念，治理的对象、范围和任务比社会治理要宽泛、复杂和繁重，而社会治理相比于治理则相对简单一些。社会治理是中国特色的理论和概念，是中国历史传统与现实发展的产物，具有很强的"中国特色"，有自己的特点。

### （一）　从社会管理走向社会治理

社会治理是从社会管理发展而来。中国人长期以来习惯于社会管理这一概念，而对治理以及与此相连的社会治理却十分陌生。社会管理是中国土生土长的概念，有人类社会就需要有社会管理，这是天经地义的事情。进入 21 世纪以后，随着中国经济高速发展、城镇化快速推进，经济社会结构以及人们的阶层和需求结构深刻变化，新旧社会问题和社会矛盾交织、频繁发生，迫切需要加强和创新社会管理。2004 年，中共十六届四中全会强调指出，要加强社会建设和管理，推进社会管理体制创新。自此以后，社会管理成为党和政府的一项重要工作，是经济建设和管理之外的另一个重要任务。社会管理也因此受到学术界的重视，成为重要的学术研究领域，产生了一大批有价值的研究成果。但是，当时社会管理主要还是沿用传统的思维模式和手段，把"维护社会稳定"作为唯一目标。一方面是受到治理理论的启发，另一方面是基于对社会管理实践的总结，在中国，党和政府以开放的胸怀和不断创新的理论勇气，提出了社会治理这一新思想。社会治理是对社会管理理论的发展，是顺应时代发展要求、更具人文精神、更加合理的社会管理。

### （二）　立足公平正义

社会治理要求立足公平正义。公平正义既是社会治理的重要原则，也是社会治理方式方法的衡量标准，更是社会治理效果和质量的评判依据。"事不公则心不平，心不平则气不顺，气不顺则难和谐。"不公平、不正义是很多社会问题、社会矛盾、社会冲突产生的根源。近年来，中国政府努力推进权利公平、机会公平和规则公平，致力于改革户籍制度，缩小城乡差距；改革就业、教育和社会保障政策，努力减少不公平现象；深化司法体制改革，规范司法行为，建设公正高效权威的司法制度，努力确保在全社会实现公平和正义。

### （三）坚持以人为本

社会治理要求坚持以人为本，保护公民的合法权益。以人为本就是要求维护人的尊严、满足人的需求、保障人的权利。以人为本是社会治理最重要的原则。实现以人为本，首先要着眼于保护弱势群体，只有弱势群体的权利得到了保护，社会才能真正进步，文明程度才能真正提高。相对于党政干部和专家学者，农民、农民工、贫困人口以及城市就业困难人群是相对的弱势群体，他们的财产财富相对较少，他们的社会地位相对较低，他们的社会影响力相对较弱，他们生产生活中的困难更多一些，但是解决难题的能力却相对较差。近年来，对以上述群体为代表的普通群众的权利保护是党和政府工作的重点。中国一系列公共政策在体现普惠的同时，致力于补齐社会发展的短板，实行倾斜保护和重点保护。中共十八届五中全会提出"十三五"时期要坚持共享发展，让全体人民在改革发展中有更多的获得感，要求大力发展社会事业，着力保障和改善民生，实现"业有所就、劳有所得、学有所教、老有所养、病有所医、住有所居"。只有人民群众的生产生活困难得到了解决，产生社会问题和社会矛盾的空间才会大大压缩。

### （四）追求活力与秩序的统一

社会治理追求秩序和活力的统一，强调既要追求稳定和秩序，更要激发社会活力。追求秩序和活力的统一是社会治理对社会管理理念的重要发展。不能片面强调维护社会秩序而忽视了激发社会活力，要防止出现"一管就死、一放就乱"的局面。新一届中央政府成立以来，一直把"简政放权、放管结合、优化服务"作为深化行政审批制度乃至行政体制改革的中心任务，把政府不该管、管不了、管不好的事情交给市场、交给社会，把该由地方和基层政府去做的事情权力下放，正确处理政府与市场、政府与社会、社会与市场以及中央政府和地方政府的关系，激发市场和社会的活力，鼓励和支持大众创业、万众创新，让一切创造财富的源泉充分涌流，努力做到人尽其才、物尽其用，人人心情舒畅。

### （五）重视源头治理

社会治理要求实行源头治理，而非末端治理，不是坐等问题出来以后再想办法解决，而是要提前预防、事先疏导，不是简单地管控、压制。源头治理要求保障公民权利，着力改善民生，进行社会风险评估，把矛盾、问题、隐患、风险消解在萌芽状态。

# 二　社会治理主体扩大

一般而言，社会治理的主体是多元的，运用多种力量进行治理，实行社会共治。1978 年以前，中国实行高度集中的计划经济体制，政府管理延伸到经济政治和文化等方面。政府（包括党在内的公共权力机构）在一定意义上是国家（国家政权）的代名词，因此，有学者认为，改革开放前中国只有国家，没有市场和社会。"国家—市场—社会"的框架模型中只有强大的国家，国家吞没了市场，也吸纳了社会，既没有市场生存和发展的空间，也没有社会生存和发展的空间。国家（或者说党和政府）几乎是一切公共事务、公共产品、公共服务、社会秩序的唯一提供者。由于没有社会力量，也没有社会空间，因此改革开放以前的社会管（治）理更多的是政治管（治）理。

改革开放以后的 20 年，中国着力打破计划经济体制，建设中国特色社会主义市场经济体制，培育企业家和市场力量，努力发挥市场在资源配置中的决定性作用，国家力量对经济生活的直接干预越来越少，政府与市场的关系逐步向科学合理的方向发展。但是，相比之下，一方面，政府与社会的关系仍不合理，具体表现为政府对社会事务干预过多，干了很多干不了、干不好的事情；另一方面，对于社会成员亟待解决的生活难题，政府往往又缺位，使社会问题和社会矛盾不能得到及时有效解决，群众诉求不能及时有效地得到反映。这种状况不仅造成政府负担过重，还使社会力量得不到发展。建立党政主导下的多元共治社会治理新格局，是中国社会治理体制改革创新的必然选择。

### （一）党政主导

中国特色的社会治理体制要求加强党委领导，发挥政府主导作用，鼓励和支持社会各方面参与，实现政府治理和社会自我调节、居民自治良性互动。社会治理体制是对社会管理体制的继承和发展，它是一种扬弃式的坚持和创新。多元主体参与是在党的领导下和政府主导下进行，因此，创新社会治理首先要加强党的领导，充分发挥政府的主导作用，不是放弃党的领导和政府的主导。但是，党和政府在社会治理中发挥作用的方式又不能简单地沿袭传统的办法，必须与时俱进改革完善。党的领导有利于保证社会治理不走偏方向，沿着正确的轨道前进。中国社会治理不可能照搬别国的经验和做法，需要探索建立与中国历史文化传统、中国特色社会主义市场经济体制相适应的社会治理模式。党的领导有利于团结、组织和动员各方面力量共同参与，因为共产党具有强大的凝聚力和整合力，可以统筹和协调各种力量。新的历史条件下，党对社会治理的领导主要体现在对社会治理形势的判断、重大方针政策的制定上，体现在对社会思潮、价值观念、舆论民意和社会心理的掌握和引导上，体现在对社会治理人才的选拔、使用和培养上。政府对社会治理的主导作用，主要表现为经常性地研判社会发展趋势、编制社会发展专项规划、制定社会政策法规、统筹社会治理方面的制度性设计和全局性事项管理、筹集和合理配置社会治理资源。近年来，各级党委和政府加强了对社会治理宏观政策的研究，加强了社会治理的顶层设计，不断强化社会治理责任制，加强对社会治理的考核，建立更加细化严格的社会治理考核指标体系。

### （二）多元参与

现代社会是复杂社会，人们的社会需求多种多样、千差万别，社会事务纷繁复杂，社会问题和社会矛盾林林总总，党和政府不可能包揽一切，必须动员和运用市场组织、社会组织等多方面力量参与社会治理。中国在构建多元共治的社会治理格局中，一是进一步健全城乡居民自治组织，深入推进居民自治。在这方面，中国党和政府近年来出台了一系列政策和措施。二是改革以共青团、妇联、工会为代表的人民团体，增强其活力，加强其与特定群众的联系，发挥其在社会治理中的重要作用。2015 年 7 月，中央召开党的群团工作会议提出群团工作要以群众为中心，让群众当主角，要大力健全组织特别是基层组织，加快新领域新阶层组织建设，要积极联系和引导相关社会组织。同月，中央出台《关于加强和改进党的群团工作的意见》，指出了工会、妇联、共青团等群团组织改革发展的方向，为焕发群团组织的生机活力、有效参与社会治理提供了动力。除此之外，最重要、最紧迫的是规范和发展社会组织，鼓励和支持社会组织参与社会治理。

### （三）发展社会组织

社会组织也是中国式的概念。它是对传统的非政府组织、非营利组织、第三部门、民间组织等称谓的改造。主要有两种情况，一是在民政部门管理的社会组织，包括社团、基金会、民办非企业单位三类。截至2015 年底，中国共有 60 多万家社会组织。二是实际存在但是没有在民政部门正式登记备案的社会组织。这类社会组织通常规模不大、内部结构比较简单甚至不怎么规范，例如，社区老年志愿服务组织、钓鱼协会、棋牌协会等。据估计，这类组织的数量远远超过在国家机关登记备案的社会组织数量，而且生命力很强。中国政府对于社会组织的改革发展思路，一是盘活存量，即用改革的办法规范已有社会组织的行为，激发社会组织活力。中共十八大以后社会组织改革进入新的历史阶段。对于现有社会组织改革的目标是政社分开，促使社会团体、行业协会商会真正按照社会组织的要求独立运转，建立完善的法人治理结构，提高服务能力和水平。十八届二中全会决定限期实现行业协会商会与行政机关真正脱钩。经过两年的调研论证，2015 年，中央办公厅、国务院办公厅印发了《行业协会商会与行政机关脱钩总体方案》。《总体方案》阐述了改革的总体要求和基本原则，明确了脱钩主体、范围、任务和措施，对配套政策和组织实施方式也做了详细的说明。其中，最为核心的内容是，推进行业协会商会与行政机关在机构、职能、资产财务、人员、党建外事等方面的"五分离五规范"。目前，行业协会商会与行政机关脱钩进入实质性阶段。二是做大增量。与发达国家相比，与社会治理创新的现实要求相比，中国社会组织数量远远不足，迫切需要大力发展。2013 年，中国政府明确要求改革社会组织登记管理制度，对行业协会商会类、科技类、公益慈善类、城乡社区服务类社会组织，除依据法律法规和国务院决定需要前置审批外，不再需要有主管部门，可直接向民政部门依法申请登记。这在一定程度上有利于社会组织的发展。

# 三　社会治理方式改革

社会治理方式是指运用何种方法和工具治理社会。是否能够依法治理是社会治理与社会管理最重要的区别之一。在强调法治方式的同时，社会治理积极运用社会管理中有效的方法，例如，道德约束、市民公约、村规民约、行业规范、单位管理等方法和工具。

## （一）运用法治方式

十八大以来，法治成为社会治理方式改革创新的主旋律。十八届四中全会提出推进法治社会建设的重大任务，要求把社会治理纳入法治化轨道，提高社会治理法治化水平。坚持依法治理，领导干部是重点。习近平总书记多次强调，各级领导干部要提高运用法治思维和法治方式的能力，在法治轨道上推进各项工作。要求各级领导干部自觉带头守法，善于运用法治思维和法治方式开展工作、解决问题，引导和支持人们依法理性表达诉求、依法律按程序维护权益，预防和化解矛盾，有效实施社会治理。要求在领导干部中树立法治首先是"治官"而不是"治民"的理念。十八大以来开展的严厉打击腐败和全面从严治党都是依法推进社会治理的有力保障和重要体现。

法治要求规范约束政府权力，保护公民权利。因此，严管"官"的同时要构建公民权利的保护机制。十八大以来，中国政府致力于依法建立健全群众利益表达维护和矛盾纠纷解决机制。一是着力构建群众利益表达机制和协商沟通机制。要求各级政府建立决策听证制度，凡是群众切身利益的重大决策，都要通过听证等方式广泛听取群众意见。完善人大代表联系群众机制，听取和反映群众诉求。构建程序合理、环节完整的协商民主体系，拓宽国家政权机关、政协组织、党派团体、基层组织、社会组织的协商渠道，充分发挥协商民主在群众利益表达和协商沟通中的独特作用；发展基层民主，维护基层群众利益；健全以职工代表大会为基本形式的企事业单位民主管理制度，维护和保障职工民主权利和利益。改革信访工作制度，建立涉法涉诉信访依法终结制度，启动信访立法工作，努力把信访纳入法治化轨道，引导群众依法理性表达诉求，通过法律渠道维护合法权益。二是着力构建社会矛盾预警机制。总结和推广一些地方创造的网格化管理、社会化服务经验，加大力度建设基层党组织、政法综合治理机构、人民调解组织，发挥其扎根基层、联系群众的优势，及时了解群众疾苦，倾听群众呼声，反映群众利益诉求，及早发现和掌握社会矛盾线索，为党委、政府和有关部门决策、管理提供依据。三是健全社会矛盾纠纷预防化解机制。各地开展大下访、大排查、大调处活动，坚持抓早抓小抓苗头、及时就地化解，最大限度地把矛盾解决在基层、解决在萌芽状态，防止矛盾激化升级。在社会矛盾纠纷化解方面，中国已经建立了调解、仲裁、行政裁决、行政复议、诉讼等纠纷解决制度，这些制度各具特色、各有优势，在化解矛盾纠纷中各自发挥独特作用。2014年以来，根据十八届四中全会精神，进一步完善各项纠纷解决制度，致力于建立不同纠纷解决制度运行顺畅、有机衔接、相互协调的多元纠纷解决机制。具体来说，就是要求进一步完善调诉对接、裁审协调、复议诉讼衔接的机制，不同纠纷解决制度既能在各自领域和环节中有效发挥作用，又能够顺畅衔接、相互配合、相互支撑，强化纠纷解决效果。例如，调解是中国特色的纠纷解决制度。《人民调解法》规定了人民法院对调解协议效力的确认和执行制度，有效实施这一制度，对于提高人民调解的公信力，防止经过调解的纠纷又涌入法院，从而减轻法院案件压力，具有重要作用。因此，需要坚持和完善调解制度，同时，还要坚持调处结合、调判结合，能调则调，当处则处，该判则判，依法妥善化解纠纷。

### （二）运用信息技术

中国正处于信息化、互联网乃至物联网深度发展的时代。信息化与互联网为信息互通、资源共享、社会合作提供了极大的可能性和便利性，既给社会治理带来挑战，也给社会治理方式创新带来机遇。中国政府充分意识到新一代"互联网＋"技术与社会治理服务融合在社会治理中的重要作用，把它作为提升社会治理精细化水平的有力支撑。近年来兴起的网格化管理模式就是信息化在社会治理中的运用。网格化管理模式是运用数字化、信息化手段，以社区、网格为区域范围，以事件为管理内容，以处置单位为责任人，通过管理信息平台，实现网格内单位联动、资源共享的社会治理模式。2015 年 7 月，国务院颁布《国务院关于积极推进"互联网＋"行动的指导意见》，提出了 10 个方面的任务，其中有多项涉及社会治理的内容。与"互联网＋"相关的是大数据、云计算等信息化技术手段，越来越成为社会治理的重要工具。2015 年 8 月 31 日，国务院出台《促进大数据发展行动纲要》，勾画了未来 5—10 年打造精准治理、多方协作的社会治理新模式。建设智慧城市、智慧社区、智慧警务，实行"阳光信访"[①] 正在成为热潮。

## 四 社会治理重心调整

社会治理重心涉及社会治理的范围、领域和重点任务。随着工业化、城市化、信息化、市场化和国际化的深入推进，中国社会治理的形势和任务发生了极大的变化，社会治理的重点领域和工作着力点也随之变化和调整。

### （一）重视网络社会治理

21 世纪以来，互联网技术迅猛发展，快速形成了一个庞大复杂的网络社会。由于网络社会的匿名性、平等性、参与性和互动性等特点，它的发展速度远远超出人们的想象。它既独立于现实社会，又与现实社会紧密相连，成为人类历史上新的生存交往空间和方式。2010 年中国网民数量为 4.57 亿人，到 2015 年 12 月则跃升为 6.88 亿人，5 年多时间增加 2 亿多人。网络社会的诞生既给人们的生产生活、学习购物、交流交友等带来极大方便，但是，同时，网络信息鱼龙混杂、真假难辨，往往充斥着暴力、色情、欺诈、谣言等有害信息，信息安全存在隐患，一些言论不理

---

① 阳光信访，是一种形象的比喻，这是国家信访局 2013 年以后实践和大力倡导的一种新型信访工作模式。它是指国家依托互联网建立信访信息系统。国家机关与国家信访信息系统互联互通，运用信息系统受理、办理信访事项，方便信访人查询信访事项的处理进展和办理结果，接受监督。

性、不负责甚至有政治目的，对社会秩序和政治稳定构成威胁。为此，统筹现实社会的治理和网络社会的治理成为一项紧迫的任务。

2011 年 5 月，国务院办公厅成立国家互联网信息办公室，负责落实互联网信息传播方针政策，推动互联网信息传播法制建设，指导、协调、督促有关部门加强互联网信息内容管理等。2014 年 2 月，国家互联网信息办公室升格为正部级。2014 年 8 月，国家互联网信息办公室颁布实施了《即时通信工具公众信息服务发展管理暂行规定》，对即时通信工具服务提供商、使用者的服务和使用行为进行了规范。2015 年，全国人大常委会起草了《网络安全法（草案）》，已向社会公开征求意见。2014 年以来，多次开展针对网络谣言、网络犯罪的专项治理行动。成立专门的管理机构、制定专门的政策法律，依法实施网络治理，将促进网络社会健康有序发展。

### （二）重视城市社会治理

2011 年，中国城市化率达到 51.27%，标志着城市人口超过农村人口，也意味着自此以后中国不再是一个农村和农民占主导的国家，而是城市和城市人口占主导的国家。2015 年底，中国城市化率进一步提高到56.1%，而且据预测 2020 年中国城市化率将达到 60%。中国快速城市化的秘密在于大量农村人口转移进入城市工作和生活。1978 年，中国城市化率不到 18%，30 多年间中国城市化率提高了 38 个百分点，数以亿计的农村人口离开农村进入城镇。中国快速城市化进程带来两个极化效应，一是城市特别是大城市人口急剧膨胀，造成人口"过密化"，公共资源紧张，公共服务不足，外来人口难以融入当地社会，社会治理面临诸多困境。这种情况在北京、上海、广州和深圳等特大型城市特别明显。二是农村特别是中西部经济欠发达地区农村人口"空心化"，出现大量"空心村"和"空壳村"。青壮年外出以后形成的"留守儿童""留守妇女""留守老年"有 1 亿多人，成为新的弱势群体。城市化带来的新变化、新挑战，给中国的社会治理提出了一个崭新的课题，一方面要积极探索建立适应城市特点的社会治理体制，另一方面要加强和创新农村社会治理。2015 年底，在时隔 37 年之后，中央召开了改革开放后第一次城市工作会议，要求各级党委政府高度重视城市工作，科学规划、建设和管理城市，加强城市管理机构建设，改革城市执法体制，提高社会治理水平。城市社会治理在城乡社会治理格局中的地位将进一步上升。

### （三）重视基层社会治理

基层社会治理是社会治理的根基，城乡社区则是基层社会治理的主要载体，社区治理已经成为基层社会治理的主要形式。各级党委政府越来越清醒地认识到，社会治理的重点和难点都在基层，上面千条线下面一根针。以乡镇街道和社区居委会为主体的基层直接面对和服务群众，基层社会治理水平的高低直接反映和决定着整个国家的社会治理水平。近年来，各地按照"重心下移、力量下沉、保障下倾"的要求，推进街道和社区管理体制改革。很多地方进一步把社会服务与城市职能下沉到街道，发挥街道开展公共服务、统筹辖区治理、组织综合执法、指导社区建设等职能，街道办事处在辖区社会服务与城市管理中的综合协调作用得到加强，推进街道政务服务中心建设。社区建设进一步得到加强，各地普遍开展社区减负工作，要求制定社区任务清单，社区有权拒绝任务清单之外的政府部门和有关单位提出的工作要求，社区工作进一步规范。按照费随事转的要求，政府向社区投放和转移的资源更多。同时，遵循社区治理规律，动员居民委员会、社会组织、物业公司、业主委员会、驻区单位等各方面力量，搭建社区成员交往交流的平台，鼓励和支持社区成员互帮互助，加强社区公共事务民主管理，增进社区成员的联系，增强社区成员的社区认同感和归属感。

### (四)重视公共安全与应急管理

公共安全事关人民安居乐业、社会安定有序，健全公共安全体系、加强应急管理工作，确保公共安全是社会治理的重要内容。21 世纪以来，我国自然灾害进入多发频发期，特重大事故灾难时有发生，食品药品安全事件经常发生，公共卫生事件防控难度增大，社会矛盾和群体性事件数量居高不下，反恐维稳形势严峻、任务艰巨。特别是随着工业化和城市化加速推进，城市高层建筑物、水电油气运等生命线工程，一些大型关键设备、化工园区等重大风险源在增多，一旦发生事故，可能导致重大经济社会损失和人员伤亡，造成社会混乱。2003 年抗击"非典"疫情之后，中国政府开始建设以"一案三制"① 为核心的现代应急管理体系。经过十多年的建设和发展,中国应急管理的机构、制度逐步建立和完善,预防和处置突发事件的能力大大增强。但是,2015 年,发生长江航道上"6·1""东方之星"客轮翻沉事件、天津港"8·12"火灾爆炸事故、深圳市光明新区"12·20"渣土受纳场滑坡事件,造成重大人员伤亡,暴露出我国公共安全体系和应急管理工作的不足,也说明加快公共安全体系建设任重道远。作为非常态社会治理的应急管理工作,受到了前所未有的重视。有关部门正在制定《国家突发事件应急体系"十三五"规划》,致力于织密织牢公共安全网,补好应急管理的短板,提升公共安全保障和应对突发事件的能力。

## 参考文献

[1] 丁元竹:《中国社会体制改革:战略与对策》,国家行政学院出版社 2013 年版。

[2] 《〈中共中央关于全面深化改革若干重大问题的决定〉辅导读本》,人民出版社 2013 年版。

[3] 龚维斌主编:《中国社会治理研究》,社会科学文献出版社 2014 年版。

[4] 龚维斌编:《当代中国社会治理实例分析》,云南教育出版社 2014 年版。

[5] 韩春晖:《社会管理的法治思维》,法律出版社 2013 年版。

[6] 李培林:《社会改革与社会治理》,社会科学文献出版社 2014 年版。

[7] 李汉林:《中国单位社会:议论、思考与研究》,上海人民出版社 2004 年版。

[8] 李友梅等:《中国社会生活的变迁》,中国大百科全书出版社 2008 年版。

[9] 陆学艺主编:《当代中国社会建设》,社会科学文献出版社 2013 年版。

[10] 马庆钰、廖鸿主编:《中国社会组织发展战略》,社会科学文献出版社 2015 年版。

[11] 马福云:《户籍制度研究:权益化及其变革》,中国社会出版社 2013 年版。

[12] 闪淳昌、薛澜主编:《应急管理概论——理论与实践》,高等教育出版社 2012 年版。

[13] 魏礼群:《社会建设与社会管理》,人民出版社 2011 年版。

[14] 吴群刚、孙志祥:《中国式社区治理——基层社会服务管理创新的探索与实

---

① "一案三制"中"一案"是指编制和管理应急管理预案,"三制"是指应急管理的体制、机制和法制。

践》，中国社会出版社 2011 年版。

[15] 张林江：《走向"社区 +"时代》，社会科学文献出版社 2015 年版。

[16] 张林江：《社会治理十二讲》，社会科学文献出版社 2015 年版。

（作者：龚维斌　国家行政学院社会治理研究中心主任、教授）

# 第 六 章

# 公共财政改革

　　1978 年前，与同期的经济体制与政治体制相适应，中国财政的主要模式是"生产建设型财政"，其基本特点是国家财政与企业财务合二为一。1978 年以后，中国开启了改革开放的伟大进程，财政体制随之发生了巨大的变化。截至 2015 年，中国财政改革总体上可划分为四个阶段：一是党的十一届三中全会后放权让利、建立财政"分灶吃饭"的分级包干体制；二是 20 世纪 90 年代前期构建中央与地方之间以划分税种为基础的适应社会主义市场经济体制的分级财政体制；三是 1998 年后实施以建立公共财政框架为取向的全面创新；四是 2013 年以来以建立现代财政制度为取向的系列改革。分述如下。

## 一　1978 年以前的中国财政

　　总体而言，改革开放前中国财政改革主要集中于财权在中央与地方之间的收收放放。新中国成立之初，主要实行的是高度集中、"统收统支"的财政管理体制。1951—1953 年，"高度集中"有所松动，实行了收入分类分成（即将财政收入划为中央、地方的固定收入与固定比例分成收入和中央调剂收入）、支出按隶属关系列预算、地方预算每年由中央核定的"划分收支、分级管理"体制。1958 年，随着中央对地方下放企业、下放财权，实行了"以收定支，五年不变"的财政管理体制，规定地方可在五年内，按照收入情况自行安排支出。但由于经济出现问题，这一体制只执行了一年。1961 年，以自 1959 年开始实行的"总额分成，一年一变"体制为基础，与调整时期上划企业等措施相配合，重新将财权向中央集中，扩大中央固定收入，基建支出全归中央专案拨款。这一体制在1965年之后，做过一些旨在"调动地方积极性"的小改进，除了在"文革"动乱的非常时期（1968年）暂时实行"收支两条线"（即收入全部上缴，支出由中央分配）外，一直执行到1970年。1971年，再次下放企业，下放财权，实行"收支包干"的财政管理体制，扩大地方财政的收支范围，按核定的绝对数包干，超收全部留归地方。1974年，在经济受"文革"严重破坏的情况下，"包干"体制已执行不下去，改行"收入按固定比例留成，超收另定分成比例，支出按指标包干"的体制，简称"旱涝保收"体制。1976年，为解决固定比例留成体制收支不挂钩、不能体现地方财政权责关系的问题，再次实行"收支挂钩、总额分成，一年一变"的财政管理体制。总体而言，这一时期财政体制频繁变动，财权在"放"与"收"、"集中"与"分散"之间屡经周折，也在很大程度上反映了持续、反复进行的对于"社会主义经济如何更有活力地发展"的探索。

## 二　1978—1992年的中国财政

1978年，党的十一届三中全会召开，会议确定了将全党的工作重心转移到经济建设上来，由此启动了波澜壮阔的30年改革开放。1980年2月，根据中共中央十一届三中全会的有关精神，国务院颁发了《关于实行"划分收支、分级包干"的财政管理体制的暂行规定》，拉开了改革开放过程中财政包干制的序幕。

### （一）1980年的财政"分灶吃饭"

财政包干制的主要内容是：从1980年初起，除北京、天津、上海三个直辖市继续实行"收支挂钩，总额分成，一年一定"的财政体制以外，对各省、自治区统一实行"划分收支，分级包干"的财政体制。并在此前提下，对不同地区，根据具体情况，采取不同的做法。大体上有以下几种：

1. 对四川、陕西、甘肃、河南、湖北、湖南、安徽、江西、山东、山西、河北、辽宁、吉林、浙江等大多数省份实行"划分收支、分级包干"的办法。

2. 对内蒙古、新疆、西藏、宁夏、广西、云南、青海、贵州等民族自治或按民族自治待遇的自治区和省，仍然实行民族自治地方财政体制，在保留对民族自治区特殊照顾的同时，也实行"划分收支、分级包干"的办法，确定中央补助的数额，并由一年一定改为五年一定不变。

3. 对广东、福建两省，在实行财政"包干"制度的同时，采取特殊政策和灵活措施，即实行"划分收支，定额上缴或定额补助"的办法，给予更多的财政自主权。

4. 对江苏省继续实行"比例包干，四年不变"的财政体制，但对包干范围和留交比例做了适当调整。

5. 1980 年的这一次财政体制改革力图将地方政府从中央政府的机体上剥离出去，各有其财、各有其责，并各自对自己的财政结果负责，相当于打破"财政大锅饭"，故常被简称为"分灶吃饭"。

### （二）1985 年的财政"分级包干"

到了 1985 年，鉴于五年已经到期，特别是 1982 年、1983 年两步"利改税"以后，国有企业上缴利润已改为以所得税、调节税的形式上缴，国家与企业之间的财政分配形式已经发生了很大变化，各级财政收入分割也有了新的基础，新的调整势在必行。根据中共十二届三中全会《关于经济体制改革的决定》的精神，国务院决定从 1985 年起对各省、自治区、直辖市实行"划分税种，核定收支，分级包干"的财政体制，其主要内容如下。第一，在第二步利改税的基础上，划分各级财政收入的范围。第二，中央与地方财政支出的划分，基本上按照原来的体制，即按隶属关系划分的支出范围不变，只对个别事业管理体制的改变做出相应的调整。少数不宜实行包干的专项支出，则由中央专案拨款。第三，核算分成基数，确定分成办法。较之于此前的"分灶吃饭"，1985 年改革中"包干"的成分明显增加。但这一体制也出现了一些始料未及的问题，主要是中央财政收入占全国财政收入的比重连年下降，中央财政赤字增加，运转困难，需要进一步的改革。

### （三）1988 年的"财政大包干"

1988 年 7 月，国务院发布了《关于地方实行财政包干办法决定》，规定在全国分别实行不同形式的财政包干。主要有六种。一是收入递增包干，即以 1987 年的决算收入和地方应得的支出财力为基数，参照各地近几年收入增长情况，确定收入递增率（环比）和地方留成、上解比例，在递增率以内的收入，实行中央与地方固定比例分成，超过递增率的收入，全留地方，地方收入达不到递增率影响上解中央的部分，由地方自有财力补足。实行这种包干办法的有北京等 10 省（市）。二是总额分成，即根据核定的收支基数，以地方支出占总收入的比重，确定地方留成、上解比例。实行这种包干办法的有天津等 3 省（市）。三是总额分成加增长分成，具体做法是基数以内部分，按总额分成比例分成，实际收入比上年增长的部分，另计分成比例，以使地方从增收中得到更多的利益。采用此法的有大连等 3 个计划单列市。四是上解额递增包干，以上解中央的收入为基数，每年按一定的比例递增上缴。广东、湖南实行这种办法。五是定额上解，即按固定数额向中央上解收入。上海等 3 省（市）采用这种办法。六是定额补助，即中央按固定的数额补助地方。吉林等 16 省（自治区）实行这种办法。

可以看出，1988 年的"财政包干"制是 1980 年、1985 年两次财政体制重大调整的自然延续，一方面承袭了"分灶""包干"的思维逻辑，另一方面将"财政承包"发展到新的阶段。该体制从 1988 年执行到 1993 年，与同期国有企业广泛推行的承包经营责任制结合起来，对这一时期的政治、经济和财政运行机制本身产生了重大影响。

# 三 1994 年的分税制改革

1994 年是中国财政史上具有里程碑意义的一年，中国正式采用了与市场经济相符合的分税制。所谓分税制，是指在划分事权的基础上，按税种划分中央、地方财政收入的一种分级预算管理体制。其要点有三个：首先是合理划分中央与地方政府的事权和支出责任；其次，按事权与财权匹配的原则，将全部税种分别划分为中央税、地方税和共享税三类，明确中央与地方政府各自的收入范围；最后是建立规范的转移支付制度，以调剂余缺、弥补困难地区政府的财政收支缺口。当时分税制的主要内容如下：

### （一） 明确中央与地方事权和支出范围

中央财政：主要承担国家安全、外交和中央国家机关运转所需经费，调整国民经济结构、协调地区发展、实施宏观调控所必需的支出以及由中央直接管理的事业发展支出。具体包括：国防费，武警经费，外交和援外支出，中央级行政管理费，中央统管的基本建设投资，中央直属企业的技术改造和新产品试制费，地质勘探费，由中央财政安排的支农支出，由中央负担的国内外债务的还本付息支出，以及中央本级负担的公检法支出和文化、教育、卫生、科学等各项事业费支出。

地方财政：主要承担本地区政权机关运转所需支出以及本地区经济、事业发展所需支出。具体包括：地方行政管理费，公检法支出，部分武警经费，民兵事业费，地方统筹的基本建设投资，地方企业的技术改造和新产品试制经费，支农支出，城市维护和建设经费，地方文化、教育、卫生等各项事业费，价格补贴支出以及其他支出。

### （二） 按税种划分中央与地方财政收入

当时划分税种的基本原则是：将维护国家权益、实施宏观调控所必需的税种划为中央税；将同经济发展直接相关的主要税种划为中央与地方共享税；将一些与地方经济和社会管理关系密切以及适合地方征管的税种划为地方税。具体如下：

中央税：关税，海关代征消费税和增值税，消费税，中央企业所得税，地方银行和外资银行及非银行金融企业所得税，铁道部门、各银行总行、各保险总公司等集中缴纳的收入（包括营业税、所得税、利润和城市维护建设税），中央企业上缴利润等。外贸企业出口退税，除1993年地方已经负担的20%部分列入地方上缴中央基数外，以后发生的出口退税全部由中央财政负担。

地方税：营业税（不含铁道部门、各银行总行、各保险总公司集中交纳的营业税），地方企业所得税（不含上述地方银行和外资银行及非银行金融企业所得税），地方企业上缴利润，个人所得税，城镇土地使用税，固定资产投资方向调节税，城市维护建设税（不含铁道部门、各银行总行、各保险总公司集中缴纳的部分），房产税，车船使用税，印花税，屠宰费，农牧业税，对农业特产收入征收的农业税（简称农业特产税），耕地占用税，契税，遗产或赠予税，土地增值税，国有土地有偿使用收入等。

中央与地方共享税：增值税、资源税、证券交易税。增值税中央分享75%，地方分享25%。资源税按不同的资源品种划分，大部分资源税作为地方收入，海洋石油资源税作为中央收入。证券交易税，中央与地方各分享50%。

### （三）建立中央对地方的税收返还制度

为了保持当时的地方既得利益格局，逐步推进改革，建立了中央财政对地方的税收返还制度：按照1993年地方实际收入以及税制改革和中央与地方收入划分情况，核定1993年中央从地方净上划的收入数额（即消费税+75%的增值税–中央下划收入）。1993年中央净上划收入，全额返还地方。1994年以后，税收返还额在1993年基数上逐年递增，递增率按全国增值税和消费税的平均增长率的1:0.3系数确定，即上述两税全国平均每增长1%，中央财政对地方的税收返还增长0.3%。若1994年以后中央净上划收入达不到1993年基数，则相应扣减税收返还数额。

### （四）分设中央和地方两套税务机构

为了保证各自的财政收入，设计了新的税收征管体系，即国家税务局和海关系统负责征收中央固定收入和中央与地方共享收入，地方税务局负责征收地方固定收入。

1994年分税制在中国财政改革中，具有里程碑意义，其影响一直持续到当下，具有重大的历史意义。一是确立了流转税和所得税为主体的税收制度。在这个制度下，企业不分大小、所有制和行政级别，统一依法经营，按章纳税，打破了企业"条块分割"的行政隶属关系，有利于从根本上将企业从政府的肌体上剥离，逐步塑造其独立的市场主体地位。二是在各级政府的责任与税收收入之间建立了直观联系，有利于推进政府职能转变，深化行政改革。三是有利于规范中央与地方政府的财政关系，提高财政分配的透明度。同时也要看到，1994年的分税制具有明显的过渡色彩，在此后的20多年执行过程中，由于后续改革和配套改革没有跟进，原分税制体制设计上的固有缺陷随着时间的流逝而不断放大，造成了中央与地方之间事权过于下移而财力过度上收的状况，并由此引出了一系列问题。

# 四　2013年的现代财政制度

党的十八届三中全会《关于全面深化改革若干重大问题的决定》指出，"财政是国家治理的基础和重要支柱，科学的财税体制是优化资源配置、维护市场统一、促进社会公平、实现国家长治久安的制度保障"，新一轮财政改革再次成为重点，而改革的基本取向是建立现代财政制度。

## （一）继续推进税收制度改革，建立现代税收制度

1. 实施结构性减税，全面实施"营改增"。理论研究表明，增值税属于"中性税"，对生产经营活动的扭曲效应最小，应当大力发展。目前，"营改增"试点已全面收官，2016年5月1日起，增值税已全面替代了营业税，为我国经济转型升级创造了制度条件。

2. 调整征收范围与环节，改革消费税。改革将主要集中在两个方面，一是适当扩大并调整消费税征收范围，把高耗能、高污染产品及部分高档消费品纳入征收范围。二是将消费税由目前主要在生产（进口）环节征收改为主要在零售或批发环节征收，逐渐将消费税改造成为地方主体税种之一。

3. 加快资源税改革步伐。改革的主要内容是将原油、天然气、部分金属和非金属矿的资源税由从量计征改为从价计征，从源头上理顺资源型产品的价格形成机制，以节约使用有限资源、促进环境保护与生态建设。

4. 适时开征房地产税。目前，房地产税已进入全国人大的立法程序，有望于两三年之内推出。通过五年左右的建设期，房地产税应当成为继营业税之后最大的地方主力税种，在促进地方收入体系建设、加强地方性公共产品提供方面发挥主要作用。

5. 建立健全综合与分类相结合的个人所得税制度。改革的重点是适当合并相关税目、降低边际税率、完善税前扣除、完善个人所得税征管配套措施，形成综合与分类相结合的个人所得税制度，以此提高政府调节收

入分配的能力，促进社会稳定和谐。

6. 开征环境保护税。环境税已进入全国人大立法程序，有望于尽快出台。

7. 加强和改进税收优惠政策设定。重点是加强对税收优惠特别是区域税收优惠政策的规范管理，区域发展规划应与税收优惠政策脱钩，对现有的税收优惠政策，即将执行到期的应彻底终止不再延续，对未到期限的要明确政策终止的过渡期，对带有试点性质且具有推广价值的，应尽快在全国范围内实施，严格禁止各种越权税收减免，以维护税收制度的统一性与严肃性。

### （二）推进现代预算制度改革

1. 实行全口径预算。其基本含义是将全部财政收入和支出纳入预算管理。为此，我国将实行四本预算：一般公共预算、国有资本经营预算、社会保障预算和政府性基金预算，另外还要考虑地方政府性债务，以此将全部政府性资金统一纳入预算管理，增加财政的宏观调控能力。

2. 加强重点环节的预算管理。未来一个时期，改革的重点主要是建立以权责发生制为基础的政府会计报告制度、深化绩效预算、加强财政问责等方面，以真正形成一个符合现代政府管理要义的政府收支管理制度体系。

3. 实施中期预算框架。即在3—5年的时限内，综合考虑财政收支和预算安排，形成以计划（国家大政方针）引领预算资源的配置、以预算资源对计划形成硬约束的正确关系，既提高财政资金的配置效率，也切实支持国家中长期规划与政策的顺利实施。

4. 加快推进预算公开。改革的重点是扩大公开范围、细化公开内容，不断完善预算公开工作机制，强化对预算公开的监督检查等。与此同时，加强人大对政府预算的审查监督，审核的重点由平衡状态、赤字规模向支出预算和政策拓展，以增强预算的约束力，提高政府预算的刚性。

### （三）建立事权与支出责任相匹配的政府间财政体制

1. 清楚划分中央与地方之间的事权范围。未来，我国政府间事权将划分为以下三类：一是中央事权，主要包括国防、外交、国家安全、司法等关系全国政令统一、维护统一市场、促进区域协调、确保国家各领域安全的重大事务；需要在全国范围内统一标准的基本公共服务事权；二是中央与地方共同事权，主要指具有地域管理信息优势但对其他区域影响较大的公共产品和服务，如部分社会保障、跨区域重大项目建设维护等；三是地方事权，凡地域性强、外部性弱并主要与当地居民有关的事务，如各类地方公共产品和公共服务的提供等。

2. 构建地方税体系，促进地方政府职能转型。凡税基难于移动、产权明晰、有助于提高本地公共服务质量的税种，原则上应当划为地方税，如房产税、资源税等。另外，那些在本地从事生产经营活动的公司、企业，由于消费了地方政府提供的基础设备和公共服务，因此其税收中的一部分也要交给地方政府，可结合消费税的改造，逐渐将其培养成地方税的主要来源之一。

3. 构建更加规范的转移支付体系。即增加一般性转移支付，减少专项转移支付，将各地区之间的财力差距控制在适当的范围之内，促进全国范围内的基本公共服务均等化。

此外，根据我国的实际情况，今后财政改革还要进一步深化财政投融资制度改革，推动我国科技创新与技术进步。构建地方债务管理体制，为新型城镇化建设提速寻求长期、稳妥的资金来源。同时大力推行 PPP，鼓励政府与社会资本合作。

总之，财政是国家治理的基础和重要支柱，担负着促进宏观经济稳定、调节收入分配、保证社会稳定等方面的重要职责。必须发挥财政制度对于经济发展、政府管理、社会稳定等方面的重要作用，一方面要学习、借鉴市场经济国家成熟的经验与做法，另一方面也要随着我国自己社会经济形势的需要不断进行适应性调整，建立起一套既有我国特色也符合市场经济规律的现代财政制度，以适应我国从经济大国迈向经济强国的需要，为完成"双百"目标、实现中华民族的伟大复兴做出贡献。

**参考文献**

[1] 吴敬琏：《当代中国经济改革》，上海远东出版社 2004 年版。

[2] 贾康、冯俏彬：《中国财政管理体制十年回顾》，《经济研究参考》2004 年第
　　2 期。

［3］周飞舟：《分税制十年：制度与影响》，《中国社会科学》2006 年第 6 期。

［4］胡鞍刚：《分税制：评价与建议》，《中国软科学》1996 年第 8 期。

［5］项怀诚主编：《中国财政五十年》，中国财政经济出版社 1999 年版。

［6］财政部预算司编：《中国政府间财政关系》，中国财政经济出版社 2003 年版。

［7］贾康：《"十二五"时期中国的公共财政制度改革》，《财政研究》2011 年第 7 期。

［8］楼继伟：《建立现代财政制度》，《人民日报》2013 年 11 月 6 日。

［9］楼继伟：《中国政府间财政关系再思考》，中国财政经济出版社 2013 年版。

［10］高培勇：《新一轮财税体制改革的战略定位》，《人民日报》2014 年 6 月 9 日。

［11］刘尚希：《基于国家治理的新一轮财税改革》，《当代经济管理》2013 年第 12 期。

（作者：冯俏彬　国家行政学院经济学部教授）

# 第 七 章

# 公共部门人事制度改革

20世纪70年代末期以来,中国政府积极适应国际发展趋势和国内经济社会发展需要,始终围绕政府中心工作大局,紧密契合不同阶段发展的实际,逐步深入推进公共部门人事制度改革。随着经济体制改革的逐步深入和行政管理体制改革的不断推进,稳步建立和推行公务员制度,积极稳妥地进行事业单位人事制度改革,逐步健全符合现代企业制度要求的国有企业人事制度。公共部门人事制度改革以制度化建设为根本,不仅继承优良传统,体现时代特征,而且与时俱进,不断创新。公共部门人事管理逐步实现了科学化、专业化、法治化。

中国通过公共部门人事制度改革,逐步形成了干部分类管理的基本格局。1987年,中共十三大从推进政治体制改革的高度提出人事管理分类改革,按照党政分开、政企分开、政事分开、管人与管事既紧密结合又合理制约的原则,分类管理各类人员,国家干部的分类管理工作迈出重要步伐。建立公务员制度,是创新干部工作管理体制,突破政企、政事大一统管理体制的战略选择。公务员制度的建立和推行,标志着适合机关特点的干部人事管理制度的建立,奠定了机关、事业单位、国有企业干部分类管理的基本格局,基本形成了与社会主义市场经济相适应的干部人事管理体制,逐步构建了独具中国特色的人事管理制度。

## 一 建立健全具有中国特色的公务员制度

1978年至今,中国公务员制度已经经历了近40年的发展。1993年,《国家公务员暂行条例》正式颁布,这是国家公务员管理的第一个基本行政法规。① 从 1993 年到 1997 年，是公务员制度全面实施的阶段。原人事部出台了多个与《国家公务员暂行条例》相配套的规定和实施办法，包括公务员录用、考核、晋升、工资保险福利、交流、辞职辞退、退休等内容，公务员制度在全国范围内建立。2006 年，《公务员法》开始实施，公务员管理迈向法制化阶段。到 2013 年，公务员法实施后，先后出台了多项配套法规和规章，这些法律法规和规章与《党政领导干部选拔任用工作条例》等党内法规相互配套，构成了中国特色公务员法律法规体系的基本框架，公务员队伍的进、管、出各个环节基本实现了有章可循、有规可依。

### （一）构建中国特色公务员制度体系

中国公务员管理工作立足制度建设的根本，既注重政策制度的稳定性，维护法治的权威，又为吸收干部人事制度改革新成果和下一步改革保留空间，保持一定的灵活性。各类国家机关同时将制定新政策法规与修订已有政策法规相结合。在《国家公务员暂行条例》颁布后，先后制定出台了一批配套政策规定，基本形成了以《条例》为主体的法规体系。《公务员法》在全面总结《条例》实践经验的基础上，对相关法律条文进行了进一步的概括、提炼和完善，标志着公务员管理法制化进入一个新的历史阶段。② 目前，公务员法的相关配套政策法规体系基本确立，已出台包括条例、部门规章在内的多个配套法规，内容涵盖公务员录用、考核、奖励、任职定级、调任、职务任免与升降、交流、处分、申诉、培训等各方面，使公务员管理的各个主要环节基本达到了有章可循、有法可依。

### （二）健全科学的公务员管理机制

逐步健全科学的公务员管理机制，促进了公务员管理的科学化水平不断提高。1993 年，《国家公务员暂行条例》正式颁布，到 1997 年底，在全国基本建立起了公务员制度，公务员管理法规体系初步形成，凡进必考

---

① 尹蔚民主编：《人力资源和社会保障事业改革开放 30 年文集》，中国人事出版社 2009 年版。

② 盘名德：《我国公务员制度的发展历程及其特色》，《时代人物》2015 年第 4 期。

机制基本确立，竞争择优机制普遍建立，激励保障机制普遍推行，新陈代谢机制初步形成，职业开发机制效益明显，监督制约机制逐步健全。切实发挥公务员管理综合效能，突破了机关人事管理侧重人事福利等方面的传统工作视野。① 随着公务员制度改革逐步深入，选人用人渠道进一步拓宽，选拔任用方法进一步完善，公务员聘任制逐步推行。作为全国聘任制公务员制度试点城市，深圳于 2007 年、2009 年分两批招聘了聘任制公务员，并规定从 2010 年起所有新进入行政机关的公务员，一律实行聘任制。

### （三） 推进公务员分类管理制度改革

建立公务员分类管理制度是实行公务员科学管理的基础。《公务员法》将分类管理作为公务员制度坚持的一项基本原则，贯穿于公务员管理的实践，特别是改革了过去用一种管理模式管理所有公务员的做法，在公务员中实行了综合管理类、专业技术类、行政执法类、司法管理类分类管理的新模式。《公务员法》全面总结了《公务员暂行条例》和《干部选拔任用工作暂行条例》推行的实践经验，吸收了干部人事制度改革的最新成果，积极借鉴了近年来国外公务员制度改革的有益做法。作为中国干部人事管理第一步具有总章程性质的法律②，标志着公务员分类管理走上了科学化和制度化的轨道。

### （四） 全面推进司法管理体制改革

随着改革开放的深入，中国先后颁布《中华人民共和国法官法》（修正）、《中华人民共和国检察官法》（修正） 等法律法规，全面推进司法管理体制改革。建立符合职业特点的司法人员管理制度，健全法官、检察官、人民警察统一招录、有序交流、逐级遴选机制，完善司法人员分类管理制度，健全法官、检察官、人民警察职业保障制度。中央《关于全面推进依法治国若干重大问题的决定》从推进法治专门队伍正规化、专业化、职业化，提高职业素养和专业水平的要求出发，提出建立从符合条件的律师、法学专家中招录法官、检察官制度，这是对中国现行法官、检察

---

① 仲组轩：《干部人事制度改革取得重大进展》，《中国组织人事报》2012 年 10 月 17 日。

② 穆敏：《我国干部人事制度改革的历史回顾与前瞻》，《理论学刊》2003 年第 1 期。

官遴选制度的一项重大改革。

### （五）推动公务员工资与社保制度改革

公务员工资制度改革，是收入分配制度改革的重要内容。中国公务员工资制度主要经历了 1985 年以职务工资为主的结构工资制、1993 年以职务和职级为主的职级工资制、2006 年职务与职级相结合的工资制。2013年，中共十八届三中全会明确提出要"改革机关事业单位工资和津贴补贴制度，完善艰苦边远地区津贴增长机制"。促进人力资源合理流动和优化配置，积极推进公务员养老保险制度改革。2015 年，国务院发布《关于机关事业单位工作人员养老保险制度改革的决定》，标志着公务员社会保险制度改革开始启动。除了基本养老保险制度要改变模式、改变待遇确定机制与调整机制，在多层次的养老保险体系方面做出了建立职业年金的重要改革举措。

建立健全具有中国特色的公务员管理制度，贯彻中央关于深化干部人事制度改革的方针政策和决策部署，实行公务员制度改革通盘考虑、统筹兼顾，有计划、有步骤地协调推进。加大公务员竞争性选拔力度，完善公开选拔、竞争上岗制度，积极探索多种形式竞争性选拔干部办法，坚持标准条件，突出岗位特点。

## 二　积极稳妥地进行事业单位人事制度改革

中国政府一直高度重视事业单位人事制度改革。改革开放以来，按照"脱钩、分类、放权、搞活"的路子，在合理划分政府和事业单位职责权限的基础上，进一步扩大事业单位的人事管理自主权，建立健全事业单位用人上的自我约束机制。[①] 根据社会职能、经费来源和岗位工作性质的不同，逐步建立符合不同类型事业单位特点和不同岗位特点的人事制度，实行分类管理。贯彻公开、平等、竞争、择优的原则，引入竞争激励机制，通过建立和推行聘用制度，搞活工资分配制度，建立充满生机活力的用人机制。通过制度创新和配套改革，充分调动各类人员的积极性和创造性，

---

① 　郭艳平：《和谐推进事业单位人事制度改革》，《人事人才》2006 年第 4 期。

增强事业单位活力和自我发展能力。《事业单位人事管理条例》是深化事业单位人事制度改革的重大举措，在事业单位人事制度改革进程中具有里程碑意义。

### （一）全面建立和推行合同聘用制度

随着中国社会主义市场经济体制的建立和加入世界贸易组织，迫切要求转换事业单位用人机制。国务院于 2002 年颁布《关于在事业单位试行人员聘用制度的意见》，事业单位在全国范围内试行聘用制，逐步破除干部身份终身制，引入竞争机制，全面建立和推行合同聘用制度，把聘用制度作为事业单位一项基本的用人制度。所有事业单位与职工按照国家有关法律、法规，通过签订聘用合同，确定单位与个人的人事关系，明确单位与个人的义务和权利。通过建立和推行聘用制度，实现用人上的公开、公平、公正，促进单位自主用人，保障职工自主择业，维护单位和职工双方的合法权益。通过聘用制度转换事业单位的用人机制，实现事业单位人事管理由身份管理向岗位管理转变，由单纯行政管理向法制管理转变，由行政依附关系向平等人事主体转变，由国家用人向单位用人转变。

### （二）建立符合事业单位性质和工作特点的岗位管理制度

适应社会主义市场经济体制和政治体制改革的要求，事业单位要科学合理设置岗位，明确不同岗位的职责、权利和任职条件，实行岗位管理。国务院先后颁发《事业单位登记管理暂行条例》和《关于修改〈事业单位登记管理暂行条例〉的决定》，事业单位的独立法人地位得到明确。随着事业单位登记管理制度的实施与调整，原人事部于 2006 年颁发《事业单位岗位设置管理试行办法》和《〈事业单位岗位设置管理试行办法〉实施意见》，这是事业单位首次开展岗位设置和岗位聘用。2007 年，《中华人民共和国劳动合同法》颁布，对事业单位与实行聘用制的工作人员订立、履行、变更、解除或者终止劳动合同等情形做了规定。国务院相继颁布了《关于分类推进事业单位改革的指导意见》《事业单位人事管理条例》，逐步建立起符合事业单位性质和工作特点的岗位管理制度。对专业技术岗位，按照岗位要求择优聘用，逐步实现专业技术职务的聘任与岗位聘用的统一；对责任重大、社会通用性强、事关公共利益、具备一定专业技术才能胜任的岗位，逐步建立执业资格注册管理制度，实行执业准入控制；对管理岗位，建立体现管理人员的管理水平、业务能力、工作业绩、资格经历、岗位需要的等级序列，推行职员制度；对工勤岗位，建立规范工勤人员"进、管、出"等环节的管理办法。逐步建立固定与流动相结合的用人制度，促进专业技术人才资源配置的社会化、市场化。

### （三）实行选人用人公开招聘和竞聘上岗制度

事业单位逐步实行公开招聘制度和竞聘上岗制度。2000年，中央组织部、原人事部发布《关于加快推进事业单位人事制度改革的意见》，事业单位人事制度改革力度开始加大。2010年，中央组织部、人力资源和社会保障部发布《关于进一步规范事业单位公开招聘工作的通知》，制定具体的招聘办法，从制度上规范事业单位选人用人的程序和做法。2011年，国务院出台《关于进一步深化事业单位人事制度改革的意见》，从全面规划、整体推进的高度对事业单位人事制度改革进行指导。2014年，国务院颁发《事业单位人事管理条例》，标志着中国事业单位人事制度改革取得较大进展，以聘用制度、岗位管理制度和公开招聘制度为主要内容的人事管理制度基本建立。[①] 同时，改革事业单位领导人员单一的委任制，在选拔任用中引入竞争机制，建立健全领导人员竞聘上岗制度。

### （四）推进事业单位分配和养老保险制度改革

事业单位人事制度改革与工资制度、社会保险制度等改革协调推进。事业单位贯彻按劳分配与按生产要素分配，效率优先、兼顾公平的分配原则，扩大事业单位内部分配自主权，逐步建立重实绩、重贡献，向优秀人才和关键岗位倾斜，形式多样、自主灵活的分配激励机制。发挥工资政策的导向作用，实行一流人才、一流业绩、一流报酬，对到艰苦边远地区事业单位和在关键或特殊岗位工作的人员，在工资待遇上适当给予倾斜。同时，积极推进事业单位养老保险制度改革。2008年国务院出台《关于印发事业单位工作人员养老保险制度改革试点方案的通知》，决定在山西、上海、浙江、广东和重庆5省市先期开展养老保险制度改革试点。2015

---

[①]　俞贺楠：《我国事业单位人事制度相关改革发展历程》，《实践与探索》2015年第4期。

年国务院发布《关于机关事业单位工作人员养老保险制度改革的决定》，标志着事业单位社会保险制度改革正式启动，事业单位人事制度改革取得重大进展。

在全面深化改革的背景下，深化事业单位人事制度改革是经济社会发展的必然要求。按照加快推进事业单位分类改革的总体要求，事业单位人事制度改革要以健全聘用制度和岗位管理制度为重点，创新管理体制，转换用人机制，健全以合同管理为基础的事业单位用人机制和事业单位领导人员选拔任用制度，探索不同行业、不同类型事业单位实行聘用合同制度的具体办法，完善岗位设置管理制度，形成权责清晰、分类科学、机制灵活、监管有力，符合事业单位特点的人事制度。

# 三  逐步完善符合现代企业制度<br>要求的国有企业人事制度

中共十一届三中全会以后，社会主义市场经济逐步形成与发展，必然要求国有企业积极推进人事管理制度改革，国有企业人事制度以符合现代企业制度为要求得到逐步完善。1993 年，中共十四届三中全会明确规定，建立现代企业制度是国有企业的改革方向，到 2000 年，大多数国有大中型骨干企业初步建立起现代企业制度，适应新制度要求的企业用人机制、岗位聘任制度逐步发展。国有企业逐步实现了企业人事管理形式的多样化，使企业人事制度改革与企业改革相适应、相同步，在领导制度、聘用制度、工资分配等制度上不断进行探索、创新和发展。国有企业通过系列人事制度改革，创造了一个较为公开、平等、竞争、择优的用人环境，健全了一种经营管理者能上能下、能进能出、充满活力的用人机制，完善了一套管理严格、制度完备、群众参与的监督体系，建立起了符合市场经济规律和中国国情的企业领导人员管理机制。

## （一） 建立健全国有企业岗位聘任制度

1978 年改革开放以后，中国政府的工作重心开始转移到为经济建设服务上来，对国有企业的人事管理制度改革在此背景下逐步启动。国有企业适当下放人事管理权限，实现人事管理形式的多样化，使人事制度改革与经济体制改革相适应、相同步。中共十五届四中全会《关于国有企业改革和发展若干重大问题的决定》，标志着国有企业改革和发展以崭新的局面跨入新世纪。国有企业的独立法人地位得到明确，特别是在大规模推行聘用制度、建立岗位管理制度、完善分配制度、健全人事监督制度、裁减冗员等方面进行了改革，很大程度上激发了自身活力。随着社会主义市场经济体制的发展，大多数国有大中型骨干企业逐步建立现代企业制度，适应现代新型企业制度要求的岗位聘任制度和公开招聘机制得以健全发展和持续推进。国有企业根据新形势新情况逐步完善竞聘上岗实施细则，突出岗位特点、丰富竞聘形式、加大空缺岗位竞聘力度，实现竞聘上岗的制度化、程序化、规范化。同时，拓宽选人视野，敢于打破单位限制、专业限制、地域限制、体制限制，按照企业发展战略和市场取向选人用人，为人才脱颖而出开辟通道。

### （二）改革完善企业领导人员管理制度

在领导人的任用上，大多数国有企业采取组织任命制。随着社会主义市场经济体制改革的深入和发展，国有企业人事制度逐步以改革和完善企业领导人员管理制度为重点，完善企业领导人员选拔方式，实行组织选拔与市场化选聘相结合。2009年，中央办公厅、国务院办公厅印发了《中央企业领导人员管理暂行规定》。同时，为深入贯彻落实《管理规定》，中央组织部、国务院国资委还联合下发了《中央企业领导班子和领导人员综合考核评价办法（试行）》。为规范国有企业领导人员廉洁从业行为，促进国有企业科学发展，依据国家有关法律法规和党内法规，制定了《国有企业领导人员廉洁从业若干规定》。2013年，《中共中央关于全面深化改革若干重大问题的决定》提出，国有企业要合理增加市场化选聘比例，岗位聘任形式更加灵活。

### （三）积极推进国有企业薪酬制度改革

全面推进国有企业薪酬制度改革，符合经济体制改革深化发展的要求。2009年，人力资源和社会保障部等六部门联合出台《关于进一步规范中央企业负责人薪酬管理的指导意见》，对中央企业发出高管"限薪令"。2015年，由人力资源和社会保障部等部门制定的《中央部门管理企业负责人薪酬制度改革方案》正式实施，薪酬制度改革的重点是规范组织任命的国有企业负责人薪酬分配，对不合理的偏高、过高收入进行调整。

深化国有企业人事制度改革，是适应经济体制改革深化发展的需要。健全符合现代国有企业制度要求的国有企业人事制度，重点改革和完善企业领导人员管理制度，逐步完善与公司治理结构相适应的企业领导人员管理体制。健全中央和地方党委对国有重要骨干企业领导班子和领导人员的管理体制，探索建立符合现代企业制度要求的企业领导人员管理办法，依法落实董事会和企业经营管理者的选人用人权。完善企业领导人员选拔方式，把组织选拔与市场化选聘结合起来。

# 四　公共部门人事制度改革经验总结

中国改革开放以来，政府人事工作坚持广纳英才、任人唯贤干部路线，坚持德才兼备、以德为先用人标准，坚持民主公开、竞争择优改革方针，推动人事制度改革不断向深层次推进、向宽领域拓展、向科学化迈进。公共部门人事制度改革围绕中心、服务大局更加有力，尊重实践探索、注重典型示范更加有效，加强总体规划、统筹协调更加科学，改革路径、用人导向更加鲜明。

## （一）鼓励基层创造，协调推进改革更加科学

人事制度改革的许多重大举措源于基层的实践创造。比如公开选拔、竞争上岗、任前公示等，都经过基层探索、总结提炼、规范完善而上升到制度层面。公共部门人事制度改革要尊重基层首创精神，鼓励从实际出发，坚持自下而上探索与自上而下推动相结合、重点突破与整体推进相结合，积极稳妥地把握好改革的进程，保证改革有序顺利推进。一是宏观指导、健全制度，加强改革总体规划。中央高度重视改革的顶层设计，在总结基层实践经验基础上，注重把成熟改革探索完善上升为制度规范，增强制度设计的科学性、合理性、协调性，注意改革措施的衔接配套，防止随意性、盲目性。二是重点突破、整体带动，科学把握改革路径。地方把握好改革的时机、重点、力度和节奏，加强试点、集中攻关，总结经验、推

广应用，以重点突破带动改革整体推进。三是典型示范、舆论引导，营造改革良好氛围。加大对人事制度改革新举措、新进展、新成效的宣传力度，加强舆情分析和舆论引导，形成有利于推进改革的舆论导向和社会氛围。

### （二）坚持扩大民主，用人民意基础更加坚实

扩大民主是推进公共部门人事制度改革的基本方向。中国公共部门人事制度改革把扩大民主的要求贯穿到干部选拔任用的全过程，以坚实民意基础促进选人用人公信度提高。根据干部选拔任用不同情形，对不同主体推荐提名方式、程序做出规范。坚持民主推荐、民主测评，增强推荐测评的科学性和真实性。把民主推荐、民主测评作为干部选拔任用的必经程序，按照代表性、知情度和相关性原则，合理确定民主推荐、民主测评、民主评议人员范围。着力增强考察民主，保证人选质量。普遍推行干部任用票决，实现好中择优。

### （三）服务中心大局，制度建设根本更加凸显

改革开放以来，中国公共部门人事制度改革始终服从和服务于政府的中心工作和改革发展稳定的大局，围绕中心大局选人才、用人才、聚人才，优化人才成长的环境。只有准确把握政府人事工作的科学定位，把干部人事工作放在中国政府的工作大局下来谋划，围绕中心工作任务来展开，公共部门人事制度建设才会具有前瞻性、全局性、稳定性。中国一直把干部人事工作的制度建设作为转变工作方式的重要内容，把工作落脚点放在建立起一套行之有效的制度上。干部人事制度是否有生命力，关键是看能否适应新形势，做到审时度势、大胆探索、与时俱进。人事制度改革的实践证明，在公共部门人事制度建设过程中，既要立足国情构建制度，又要积极学习、借鉴国外行政体制改革的先进成果；既注重落实已有制度，也注重不断总结公共人事管理制度推行的实践经验，吸收人事制度改革所取得的最新成果并将之上升为国家的政策制度，使公共部门人事制度植根于中国特色社会主义制度建设，充满生机和活力。

### （四）　契合发展实际，人事分类管理更加合理

干部人事制度是经济体制和政治体制的重要组成部分。公共部门人事制度改革，必须符合经济社会发展需要，并与政府职能转变的整体进程相适应。纵观人事制度改革历程，我们发现，干部人事制度改革首先是伴随着经济体制改革开始的。经济改革初期，中央提出要下放权力，为企业"松绑"，把生产经营权还给企业。在这种情况下，企业提出要有相应的用人权、分配权，中央决定改革干部管理体制，变下管二级为下管一级，把企业中层干部交给企业自己管理，把适应计划经济的人事管理体制调整到与社会主义市场经济相配套的人事管理体制上来。随着市场经济迅速发展，中共十三大明确提出人事分类管理原则，改革高度集中的管理体制和单一的管理模式，根据国家机关、企业、事业单位不同特点，逐渐分离政企、政事职能，逐步建立健全符合各自特点的人事管理制度，实行分类管理。

### （五）　完善选拔方式，择优选人机制更加有效

人事制度改革政治性、政策性和敏感性很强，必须科学设计、扎实推进、务求实效，构建有效管用、简便易行的选人用人机制，着力提高人事制度改革的科学化水平。有效管用，就是改革措施的推出要服务于选准用好干部的需要，更加注重实际效果，遵循干部人事工作规律，坚持形式服从内容、过程服从结果。简便易行，就是改革制度的设计要坚持于法周延、于事简便，既坚持标准、严格程序，又提高效率、降低成本。公开选拔、竞争上岗，是用人制度的重大创新，是最有成效的选人用人改革措施。中国公共部门全面贯彻公开、平等、竞争、择优方针，加大竞争性选拔力度，完善公开选拔、竞争上岗等竞争性选拔干部方式，着力提高竞争性选拔质量和选人用人公信度，推进竞争性选拔方式常态化、科学化、多样化。

### 参考文献

[1] 尹蔚民主编：《人力资源和社会保障事业改革开放 30 年文集》，中国人事出版社 2009 年版。

［2］盘名德：《我国公务员制度的发展历程及其特色》，《时代人物》2015 年第 4 期。

［3］仲组轩：《干部人事制度改革取得重大进展》，《中国组织人事报》2012 年 10 月 17 日。

［4］穆敏：《我国干部人事制度改革的历史回顾与前瞻》，《理论学刊》2003 年第 1 期。

［5］郭艳平：《和谐推进事业单位人事制度改革》，《人事人才》2006 年第 4 期。

［6］陆学艺：《中国事业单位制度改革研究》，社会科学文献出版社 2008 年版。

［7］俞贺楠：《我国事业单位人事制度相关改革发展历程》，《实践与探索》2015 年第 4 期。

（作者：李学明　中国人事科学研究院助理研究员）

# 第 八 章

# 政务公开与大数据治国战略

改革开放以来，伴随着经济的快速有序发展，我国的行政体制改革进程也逐步深入。作为我国政府治理工具变革的一个重要内容，我国的政务公开工作得到了全面而有效的推行，大数据战略得以多方面应用，电子政务和智慧政府的建设粗具雏形。政务公开和大数据战略的全面有效推行，有助于改变政府治理的方式和方法，优化政府治理的生态环境，是我国改革开放以来的重要成果之一。同时，深化政务公开对推进我国行政体制改革、加强对行政权力监督制约、从源头上防治腐败和提供高效便民服务具有重要意义。中国政府在推行政务公开和大数据战略方面迈出了积极的步伐，取得了各方面的积极意义，并且对下一步推进全面政务公开、全面实施大数据战略、建设智慧政府做出了周密的部署。

## 一 当代中国推行政务公开的理论创新

与我国推行政务公开、电子政府、智慧政府建设同步进行的是，我国行政学界也对政务公开及大数据战略的理论和实践进行了不懈的探索，并取得了较多的理论创新和研究成果，为当代中国推行政务公开和大数据战略提供了很大的理论支撑和智力支持。如中国行政管理学会在 2000 年 10月 24—25 日组织全国各地政府部门和理论界的有关专家、学者近 200 人就"政府政务公开理论与实践"等问题开展了研讨，专家学者们从政治学、行政学、法学、党建学等学科角度阐述了政务公开对于我国政权建设、政治发展、行政改革、民主法制建设的重要意义。① 在后续的阳光政府、法治政府、政务公开、政府信息公开等的研究中，很多学者投入其中，取得了一系列的理论创新和成果。

### （一）关于政务公开的概念诠释

针对"政务"含义的三种理解："政治之事务""行政之事务"和"公共事务"的理解，政务公开的含义也分为大中小三种概念：一是大概念，广义的政务公开是指所有享有公权力、承担公共责任、履行公共义务的组织机构信息公开，其中包括政党信息公开、立法机关信息公开、司法机关信息公开；二是中概念，即行政管理的政务公开，既包括政府工作部门，也包括部分社会团体和企业组织；三是小概念，狭义的政务公开仅限于政府机关范围内及与公共行政管理密切相关的事项。

基于以上三种政务的理解，我国的政务公开是指依照法律或道德，与公共权力相联系的各项事务要向全部或部分特定对象公开。政务公开应以行政公开为主，兼顾与公共权力相关的各种公共事务和公共信息的公开，包括村务公开、政府事务公开和法律事务公开，以及相关的公共事业和公共企业等事务的公开。②

### （二）关于政务公开的目的、形式与内容探讨

对于政务公开的目的可以从三个角度来理解。第一种是权利本位的视角，强调政务公开是一个赋权的过程，让社会及公众的知情权、表达权、参与权、监督权得到保障；第二种是效用本位的视角，强调政务公开要使政府掌握的海量信息得到充分应用，促进市场和社会的活力；第三种是管理本位的视角，强调推进政务公开的目的在于构建法治政府、创新政府、服务型政府、廉洁政府。与此相适应，我国推进政务公开的目标在于：一是要更好地落实宪法所赋予的公民知情权、参政权；二是要增强政府公信力；三是要增进施政的民意基础，形成社会的协同合作。

---

① 胡仙芝：《"全国政务公开理论与实践"研讨会综述》，《中国行政管理》2000 年第 12 期。

② 胡仙芝：《政务公开与政治发展研究》，中国经济出版社 2005 年版。

关于政务公开的形式与内容。有专家认为，在公开范围上应该是符合公众需求、应该是有选择性的；在公开形式上应该是主动公开的，侧重于网上主动公开，而不是纸质上的；在费用上应该是免费的，而且不受版权保护之限制；在公开的利用上，要强调保护商业秘密、个人隐私与国家秘密。也有专家主张明确界定政府信息公开的范围，将政务信息分为两类：一类是政府公共政策过程中依据的信息、获取的信息和制造的信息；另一类是公共服务的信息。有专家强调，一定要明确界定政府信息公开的范围，其次才涉及如何公开等技术问题。政务公开，包括政务信息公开，都要确保议程公开，信息可获得、可转发、简便易读。

### （三）推进政务公开工作的重要意义

加快推进政务公开及政务公开信息化是国家治理体系现代化的题中应有之义。党的十八届三中全会指出，"全面深化改革的总目标是完善和发展中国特色社会主义制度，推进国家治理体系和治理能力现代化"。政府治理现代化是国家治理体系的重要组成部分，而政务公开是实现政府治理现代化的首当其冲的重要内容。它是现代政府的重要制度安排，也是我国政府性质和职能的内在要求，更是顺应经济全球化和信息化时代的一个战略举措。

首先，政务公开是实现国家治理能力现代化的重要路径。大数据包括政务公开信息化对于政府而言是一场深刻的革命，是一种规则的再造、流程的再造、职能的再造，是推动政府革命或者行政体制改革的一个突破口和关键环节。具体而言，一是能进一步提高政府的透明度、公信力及政府施政的民意基础；二是能进一步消除产生腐败的黑箱环境，推进廉洁政府建设；三是能进一步规范政府行政行为，推进法治政府建设，进而推进社会主义法治国家建设；四是能进一步促进公众广泛参与的公共政策形成机制，推进服务型政府建设，让政府做出的决策更好地服务于人民。

其次，政务公开有利于增强政府与民众的互动，改善政府的治理环境。政府在推行政务公开的过程中，一方面保证了公民的知情权，加强了政府与公民之间的信息沟通，提高了民众对政府权威和政策的认同度；另一方面也使政府更加关注公民的需求，从而增强了政府与公民的互动，优化了政府的治理环境，大大增强了政府的公信力。[①]

最后，政务公开有利于提升政府形象和工作作风，实现阳光政府、透明政府的目标。政务公开是整个政治系统的防腐剂，它对于优化政治环境，规范政治行为主体的公务行为，纯化政治氛围，保证政治民主的实现和市场经济的良性运行具有不可忽视的作用。作为监督政府行政的一个重要基础条件，政务公开强化了对政府部门和工作人员的监督，尤其是一些服务比较规范、办事有标准承诺的行政服务和审批事项，在公开办事程序、办事标准、办事人员和办事时限后，政府和社会公众都加强了对政府行政审批事项的监督，有利于实现我国提出的法治政府、责任政府、高效政府、廉洁政府等建设目标。

**(四) 关于政务公开要处理的内外部关系**

政务公开是一个综合的系统过程，学者们认为，需要注意处理好几大关系：一是要处理好发展政务公开、行政服务改革与服务型政府建设、深化行政体制改革之间的关系。二是要注意处理好电子政务平台建设中的硬件建设与政务公开和行政审批的软件建设关系。三是要注意处理好行政审批窗口与派出机构、行政服务机构与各职能部门之间的协作关系。四是要处理好电子政务平台和行政服务机构的外部服务与内部管理之间的关系。五是要注意处理好当前急迫问题的解决与未来长效机制建设的关系。

## 二 当代中国推行政务公开的发展历程

新中国成立以来，政务公开在我国的实践是从村务公开开始的。经过半个多世纪以来尤其是改革开放以来的发展，政务公开经历了一个从行政层级上由低到高、从局部到全面的发展过程，即从村务公开到乡镇政务公开，并逐步扩大到县、省和中央政府部门的政府信息公开，以及后来的依托电子政务和政务服务的政务公开，到目前的全面政务公开等发展过程。主要经历的阶段和表现有：

---

① 胡仙芝：《政务公开提升政府公信力》，《瞭望》新闻周刊2012年3月6日。

### (一) 农村经济体制改革推进村务公开

20 世纪 80 年代初，随着农村家庭联产承包责任制的实行，原来公社、生产队的管理组织形式已经解体，广西壮族自治区宜山县合寨大队果作等 6 个生产队自发地成立了由村民实现自我管理、自我教育、自我服务的农村基层群众性自治组织。[1] 1987 年 11 月全国六届人大常委会第 23 次会议通过了《中华人民共和国村民委员会组织法（试行）》，1998 年 11 月 4 日全国九届人大常委会第 5 次会议通过了正式的《中华人民共和国村民委员会组织法》，农村居民的民主选举、民主决策、民主管理、民主监督的自治形式得到了法律的保证。作为村民自治基础要件的村务公开工程也在全国各地得到了推行和发展。

对于在广大农村推行村务公开的工作，中央在 1991 年就进行了有关部署。1991 年，中共中央与国务院在有关农业和农村工作的决定中提出建立村务公开制度；1998 年颁布的《中华人民共和国村民委员会组织法》明确地实现了村务公开的五项内容；1998 年中共中央办公厅、国务院办公厅联合发布了《关于在农村普遍实行村务公开与民主管理制度的通知》，要求在全国农村基层组织推行村务公开。此后，中纪委、农业部和民政部等都分别把推行村务公开当作一项重要的工作，予以重视。自此，村务公开已在全国农村政治生活中成为一项基本制度和工作。

### （二）乡镇政府推行政务公开实践

20 世纪 90 年代后期，在村务公开和村民自治取得较好效果的情况下，乡镇作为基层政权的政治载体，其政务公开的任务就被提上了日程。根据中纪委的部署和要求，该时期乡镇推行政务公开的重点是：群众最关心、反映最强烈的问题；影响本地区经济发展和社会稳定的问题；行政工作中容易滋生腐败问题。各地根据这个原则来确定要公开的重点事项、重点部门和重点岗位。从各地的实际情况看，乡镇政务公开的特点主要有：乡镇政务公开的内容比较集中，主要以财务情况、经济事项作为重点，主要是为了解决好廉政问题，改进党政机关施政方式和工作作风，密切党

---

[1]  本刊评论员：《依法而选则安  违法而行则乱》，《乡镇论坛》1999 年第 2 期。

群、干群关系，促进经济社会的稳定发展。因此，相对而言，乡镇政务公开的制度设计和运作方面就没有村务公开的那一套组织和程序架构，而是主要依靠国家行政体制框架来执行。乡镇政权政务公开的动力具有自上而下的特点和典型的行政特征。

### （三）地方政府对政务公开的探索

在改革开放的历史进程中，地方政府在不断创新的浪潮中，在市场经济竞争和地方政府治理逐步改进的背景下，一些地方政府为了配合经济发展的特定目标，为优化环境和加强治理，开始自觉地推行政务公开。该过程中，有的是以县市为单位推进的，有的是一些地级市在特定的区域开始探索的。20世纪90年代后，一些县市和地市乃至一些国家职能部门相继进行了政务公开以及相关制度的探索。主要特点有：

首先，以办事公开为主，主要是办事程序、规则和依据的公开，目的是为企业和公民办事提供方便，这也为政务公开的广泛推行提供了社会支持和动力。有的地方进行了财务公开的探索，有的还探索了收支两条线和国库统一支付制度，这些对于防治腐败和加强廉政建设起到了较好的作用。有的部门则以权力制约为主线，加强了对组织、人事和重大决策的公开力度，如人事决策的组织公示制度、岗位公布和服务承诺制度以及重大事项的公示咨询制度等，这些都为政务公开的推进积累了很好的经验。

其次，在组织机构上，这个过程体现为政务公开的载体逐渐走向了专门化的趋势——也就是以"一站式""一门式"等集中的行政许可为主要特色的行政服务机构的发展与崛起。据2005年不完全统计，全国县以上规模集中的行政审批服务机构近3300家。到2007年10月，全国地市级以下政府建立的行政许可服务中心由2005年的3300多家增至4500多家。有1002个行政服务中心的独立网站，其相关内容的网页达到了1159万多页。① 这些行政服务机构被认为是行政审批制度改革的新生事物，在《行政许可法》颁布后得以大量快速的出现。目前，行政服务机构不仅在全国范围内普遍建立，而且在政务公开的推行方面也成了一个主要的"阵地"和"战场"。

---

① 胡仙芝：《历史回顾与未来展望：中国政务公开与政府治理》，《政治学研究》2008年第6期。

### （四）《中华人民共和国政府信息公开条例》颁布后的政务公开

2007 年 4 月 5 日，温家宝签署了国务院第 492 号令，公布了《中华人民共和国政府信息公开条例》（以下简称《条例》），并规定自 2008 年 5 月 1 日起施行。《条例》从总则、公开的范围、公开的方式和程序、公开的监督和保障等各个方面对政府的信息公开做了基本规范，为全国范围内推行政府信息公开工作提供了准绳和依据。《条例》的公布，标志着我国政务公开进入了一个全国推行、全面深入，并且实现了法制化、制度化、经常化的全新阶段。该阶段的特点有：

第一，政务公开的责任主体开始实体化、全面化。根据要求，所有的行政机关都成为政府信息的主体，也就是政府信息公开的义务主体。在主要责任主体方面，《条例》把国务院办公厅及各级人民政府办公厅定为信息公开工作的主管机构，还要求设立专门机构负责这项工作。据统计，仅 2006 年一年时间，中央人民政府门户网站就发布国务院和国务院办公厅文件 500 多件、国务院公报 250 多期；整合 71 个部门约 1100 项网上服务；发布 8 个部门的 47 项行政许可项目，被誉为 "24 小时不下班的政府"。此外，国务院的 74 个部门、单位和 31 个省（区、市）政府还建立了新闻发布和发言人制度。

第二，明确了政府信息公开的内容和范围，并扩展了相关内容。《条例》确定了 "以公开为原则，以不公开为例外" 的基本原则，并规定行政机关对符合下列基本要求之一的政府信息应当主动公开：1. 涉及公民、法人或者其他组织切身利益的；2. 需要社会公众广泛知晓或者参与的；3. 反映本行政机关机构设置、职能、办事程序等情况的；4. 其他依照法律、法规和国家有关规定应当主动公开的。显然，这些规定对于原先仅以 "办事公开" 为基本内容的公开范围有了更大的扩展。此外，还增加了申请需要公开的相关事项。

第三，公开的方式和公开的程序走向制度化和规范化。《条例》规定，每年的政务公开主管机构都要编制政务信息公开指南、政府信息公开目录、公开年度报告，实际上已经将政务公开工作作为一个制度化的行政管理内容，政府信息公开成为政府向社会和公众提供的一种公共服务和公共物品，成为人们日常生活决策不可缺少的部分。《条例》对政务公开的制度和类型也作了较为明确的规定。

第四，政务公开中政府与社会公众的互动逐步强化。自《条例》明确了信息公开的义务主体，并规定了依申请公开的具体程序之后，公民的知情权得到了保障，公民、法人等根据需要而向有关部门申请可以公开的内容，政务公开由政府单方面的公开开始走向政府部门与社会互动的一种信息交换机制。

总之，自从《条例》颁布和贯彻实施之后，我国的政务公开走向了法制化、制度化的道路。

### （五）从政府信息公开到全面推进政务公开——政务公开工作进入新征程

《政府信息公开条例》颁布和实施后，我国政务公开日渐成为各级政府的工作常态，与此同时，我国的电子政务建设和信息化工作也大步提升，接下来的几年，政务公开工作逐步与电子政务、行政审批等改革走向融合，互为支持，互相推进，开创了全面推进政务公开的新局面。

2011年6月8日，中共中央办公厅、国务院办公厅联合印发《关于深化政务公开加强政务服务的意见》（以下简称"2011年《意见》"），该意见为深入贯彻落实党的十七大和十七届三中、四中、五中全会精神，促进服务政府、责任政府、法治政府、廉洁政府建设，提高依法行政和政务服务水平，明确提出深化政务公开，加强政务服务总体要求是要以邓小平理论和"三个代表"重要思想为指导，深入贯彻落实科学发展观，坚持以人为本、执政为民，坚持围绕中心、服务大局，按照深化行政体制改革的要求，转变政府职能，推进行政权力运行程序化和公开透明；按照公开为原则、不公开为例外的要求，及时、准确、全面公开群众普遍关心、涉及群众切身利益的政府信息；按照便民利民的要求，进一步改进政务服务，提高行政效能，推进政务服务体系建设，为人民群众提供优质便捷的高效服务。明确对"以改革创新精神深化政务公开工作"做出工作安排和部署，主要有创新政务公开方式方法、推行行政决策公开、推进行政权力公开透明运行、加大行政审批公开力度、深入实施政府信息公开条例、着力深化基层政务公开、加强行政机关内部事务公开以及统筹推进政务服务体系建设，强化监督保障措施等主要内容。在统筹推进政务服务体系建设方面，还专门对行政服务机构、职能、作用、运行方式等做出安排，并明确加强组织领导、制度建设和监督考核。以"2011 年《意见》"为起点，2011 年 9 月 13 日，国务院办公厅又转发全国政务公开领导小组《关于开展依托电子政务平台加强县级政府政务公开与政务服务试点工作的意见》，重点对县级政务公开工作提出指导意见。2012 年该意见在全国选取了北京东城等共 100 个县市区进行了工作试点，有效地推进了政务公开在全国范围内的深化和开展。①

　　时隔近五年之后，2016 年 2 月 17 日中共中央办公厅、国务院办公厅（以下简称"两办"）印发并最新公布了《关于全面推进政务公开工作的意见》（以下简称"新《意见》"）对政务公开工作作出专门的全面部署。"新《意见》"开篇宗义，指出："公开透明是法治政府的基本特征。全面推进政务公开，让权力在阳光下运行，对于发展社会主义民主政治，提升国家治理能力，增强政府公信力执行力，保障人民群众知情权、参与权、表达权、监督权具有重要意义。"这可谓自中国实行改革开放，推行政务公开政策，启动信息公开法治建设以来，对政务公开性质、意义及其法理基础的一次精确阐述，反映了国家党政领导机关对政务公开和政府信息公开制度建设认识的深化与理念的提升。"新《意见》"在指出"党中央、国务院高度重视政务公开，做出了一系列重大部署，各级政府认真贯彻落实，政务公开工作取得积极成效"之后，针对"与人民群众的期待相比，与建设法治政府的要求相比，仍存在公开理念不到位、制度规范不完善、工作力度不够强、公开实效不理想等问题"，而继续做出全面推进政务公开的一个总动员和总部署。为进一步做好当前和今后一个时期的政务公开工作，"新《意见》"对 2016 年至 2020 年的政务公开共做出了五个方面、二十一项重要部署。主要内容有：

　　1. 关于全面推进政务公开工作的总体要求。全面推进政务公开工作的指导思想是认真落实党的十八大和十八届三中、四中、五中全会精神，深入贯彻习近平总书记系列重要讲话精神，紧紧围绕"四个全面"战略布局，牢固树立创新、协调、绿色、开放、共享的发展理念，深入推进依法行政，全面落实党中央、国务院有关决策部署和政府信息公开条例，坚

<hr />

　　①　胡仙芝、姜秀谦、王君琦等：《我国县级政务公开改革研究》，华夏出版社 2014 年版。

持以公开为常态、不公开为例外，推进行政决策公开、执行公开、管理公开、服务公开和结果公开，推动简政放权、放管结合、优化服务改革，激发市场活力和社会创造力，打造法治政府、创新政府、廉洁政府和服务型政府。

全面推进政务公开工作要坚持如下基本原则：紧紧围绕经济社会发展和人民群众关注的问题，以公开促落实，以公开促规范，以公开促服务。依法依规明确政务公开的主体、内容、标准、方式、程序，加快推进权力清单、责任清单、负面清单公开。坚持改革创新，注重精细化、可操作性，务求公开实效，让群众看得到、听得懂、能监督。以社会需求为导向，以新闻媒体为载体，推行"互联网＋政务"，扩大公众参与，促进政府有效施政。

全面推进政务公开工作的工作目标是"到 2020 年，政务公开工作总体迈上新台阶，依法积极稳妥实行政务公开负面清单制度，公开内容覆盖权力运行全流程、政务服务全过程，公开制度化、标准化、信息化水平显著提升，公众参与度高，用政府更加公开透明赢得人民群众更多理解、信任和支持"。

2. 全面推进政务公开工作的重点内容：首先，推进政务阳光透明。这方面主要包括：一是推进决策公开；二是推进执行公开；三是推进管理公开；四是推进服务公开；五是推进结果公开；六是推进重点领域信息公开。着力推进财政预决算、公共资源配置、重大建设项目批准和实施、社会公益事业建设等领域的政府信息公开，有关部门要制定实施办法，明确具体要求。

其次，扩大政务开放参与。这方面的主要工作有：一是推进政府数据开放；二是加强政策解读；三是扩大公众参与；四是回应社会关切，建立健全政务舆情收集、研判、处置和回应机制；五是发挥媒体作用，加强舆论引导。

再次，提升政务公开能力。这方面的工作有：一是完善制度规范；二是建立政务公开负面清单；三是提高信息化水平；四是加强政府门户网站建设；五是抓好教育培训。

最后，加强组织领导，强化保障措施。整合政务公开方面的力量和资源，进一步理顺机制，加强政务公开工作经费保障，加强考核监督等。

# 三　大数据战略和智慧政府的
理论探索和实践创新

中国的政府公开的实施和战略与大数据技术相结合，电子政务和智慧政府的建设也就有了实质性的突破和推进。近年来，中国新一代的领导人紧扣技术革新和创新经济，提出了国家大数据战略。国家治理在数据开放和智慧政府建设方面也取得了很大的进展。具体而言，主要有以下几个方面：

### （一）关于"大数据时代"

大数据时代，数据正在成为一种生产资料，成为一种稀有资产和新兴产业。任何一个行业和领域都会产生有价值的数据，而对这些数据的统计、分析、挖掘和人工智能则会创造意想不到的价值和财富。人们的生产生活都离不开大数据，大数据成为一种基础的战略资源和公共设施。

### （二）关于"大数据经济"

"数据已经成为一种新的经济资产类别，就像货币或黄金一样，将形成数据材料、数据探矿、数据加工、数据服务等一系列新兴产业。"因此大数据不只是一个产业这么简单。它在社会的各个领域中都无所不在，可以与 N 个产业"相加"，形成"大数据＋"，"大数据＋"的本质是连接和数据。2014 年 3 月 5 日，李克强在十二届全国人大二次会议上做政府工作报告时说，要设立新兴产业创业创新平台，在新一代移动通信、集成电路、大数据、先进制造、新能源、新材料等方面赶超先进，引领未来产业发展。

### （三）关于大数据战略与政府治理

大数据不仅是一场技术革命，一场经济变革，也是一场国家治理的变革。大数据时代，互联网是政府施政的新平台。单纯依靠政府管理和保护数据的做法会使政府在面对大规模而复杂的数据时应接不暇、不堪重负。而通过电子政务系统，可以实现在线服务，做到权力运作有序、有效、

"留痕"，促进政府与民众的沟通互联，提高政府应对各类事件和问题的智能化水平。大数据正有力地推动着国家治理体系和治理能力走向现代化，正日益成为社会管理的驱动力、政府治理的"幕僚高参"。而有些地方政府的实践充分表明，实施大数据战略，可以把执法权力关进"数据铁笼"，让失信市场行为无处遁形，权力运行处处留痕，为政府决策提供第一手科学依据，实现"人在干、云在算"。

### (四) 关于大数据战略的政府规划及措施

对于实施大数据国家战略，"十三五"规划建议指出："运用大数据技术，提高经济运行信息及时性和准确性。"而在此之前，大数据战略在国家的行业治理以及市场经济运行方面都开始有了较为系统的应用。2014年7月23日，国务院常务会议审议通过《企业信息公示暂行条例（草案）》，推动构建公平竞争市场环境。其中要求建立部门间互联共享信息平台，运用大数据等手段提升监管水平。2014年9月17日，部署进一步扶持小微企业发展，推动大众创业，万众创新，其中包括加大服务小微企业的信息系统建设，方便企业获得政策信息，运用大数据、云计算等技术提供更有效服务。2014年10月29日，要求重点推进六大领域消费，其中强调加快健康医疗、企业监管等大数据应用。2014年11月15日，提出在疾病防治、灾害预防、社会保障、电子政务等领域开展大数据应用示范。2015年1月14日，部署加快发展服务贸易，以结构优化拓展发展空间，提出要创新模式，利用大数据、物联网等新技术打造服务贸易新型网络平台。2015年2月6日，确定运用互联网和大数据技术，加快建设投资项目在线审批监管平台，横向联通发展改革，城乡规划，国土资源，环境保护等部门，纵向贯通各级政府，推进网上受理、办理、监管"一条龙"服务，做到全透明，可核查，让信息多跑路，群众少跑腿。2015年7月，国务院办公厅印发的《关于运用大数据加强对市场主体服务和监管的若干意见》提出，要提高对市场主体服务水平；加强和改进市场监管；推进政府和社会信息资源开放共享；提高政府运用大数据的能力；积极培育和发展社会化征信服务。

### (五) 关于开放数据和政府再造

国家大数据战略的核心之一就是数据开放战略，这与政府信息公开和政务公开的工作是相辅相成的。在开放数据战略的制定和实施中，政府再造成为必须和可能。一般而言，数据开放战略中，政府扮演着如下的角色和责任：一是数据开放生态系统的架构师，为数据开放提供系统保障；二是数据开放战略的建立者，推动该战略的规划制度和行动计划的实施；三是数据开放立法体系的推动者，为数据开放的法律责任立法立规；四是数据开放进程加速的助推者；五是数据开放应用的引导者；六是数据开放模式创新的探索者。[①]

### 参考文献

［1］《乡镇论坛》评论员：《依法而选则安　违法而行则乱》，《乡镇论坛》1999 年第 2 期。

［2］胡仙芝：《历史回顾与未来展望：中国政务公开与政府治理》，《政治学研究》 2008 年第 6 期。

［3］中国行政管理学会编：《政务公开与政府建设》，知识出版社 2001 年版。

［4］胡仙芝：《政务公开提升政府公信力》，《瞭望》新闻周刊 2012 年 3 月 6 日。

［5］胡仙芝：《政务公开与政治发展研究》，中国经济出版社 2005 年版。

［6］胡仙芝、姜秀谦、王君琦等：《我国县级政务公开改革研究》，华夏出版社 2014 年版。

［7］周汉华主编：《我国政务公开的实践与探索》，中国法制出版社 2003 年版。

［8］赵永伟、唐璨：《行政服务中心理论与实践》，企业管理出版社 2006 年版。

［9］段龙飞：《我国行政服务中心建设》，武汉大学出版社 2007 年版。

［10］本书编写组：《大数据领导干部读本》，人民出版社 2015 年版。

（作者：胡仙芝　国家行政学院博士生导师、研究员，中国行政体制改革研究会研究部主任；吴文征　北京航空航天大学公共管理学院硕士研究生）

---

[①]　本书编写组：《大数据领导干部读本》，人民出版社 2015 年版，第 247—249 页。

# 第 九 章

# 政府绩效管理与行政问责

政府绩效管理是创新政府管理方式和加强政府自身建设的重要手段。20 世纪 80 年代以来，以英国新公共管理运动和美国企业家政府改革为代表的行政改革运动开始兴起，主张将分权化管理、责任机制、结果导向、顾客为本等企业管理理念引入到政府的内部管理中来。在这一过程中，企业普遍流行的绩效管理和评估工具也随之被引入到政府管理中来，成为推动政府改革和管理创新的重要工具，并在改良传统的官僚体制、减轻财政压力、回应民众诉求、提高政府服务意识和服务能力方面发挥了重要作用。

中国于 20 世纪八九十年代引入了政府绩效评估工具，经过二三十年的快速发展，政府绩效评估已经成为政府管理的常态化运行机制。2008 年，温家宝在政府工作报告中指出，要"推行政府绩效管理和行政问责制度"。党的十八大报告进一步提出："创新行政管理方式，提高政府公信力和执行力，推进政府绩效管理"，十八届三中全会通过的《关于全面深化改革若干重大问题的决定》中，又进一步要求"严格绩效管理，突出责任落实，确保权责一致"，在中国行政体制改革的进程中，政府绩效管理和行政问责制度在中国政府创新政府管理方式、提高政府效能、改进公共服务质量方面发挥了重要作用。

## 一 政府绩效管理的发展与成效

20 世纪 70 年代末开始的改革开放为中国政府官员走出国门，了解世界先进管理经验提供了机会。80 年代开始，一些地方政府和基层部门走出国门，借鉴了已经被西方发达国家证实行之有效的政府绩效管理这一工具，结合本地区、本部门的实际情况进行实践。在30多年的实践中，中国政府绩效管理从80年代在个别部门个别领域开始起步阶段，逐步发展为在90年代的多领域多部门探索，以及21世纪头十年引起中央政府的高度重视得到大力发展，并在2011年全面试点高位推进的快速推进。从推行情况来看，一些专家认为中国的政府绩效管理已经取得了很好的效果，在某些方面甚至超过了西方发达国家。

**（一）中国政府绩效管理的发展历程和主要做法**

中国政府的绩效管理实践首先是由一些地方政府和部门自发做起的，从20世纪80年代以来经过了一个长期的探索过程，从整体上看，中国政府绩效管理大致经历了四个发展阶段。

1. 四个发展阶段①

（1）20世纪80年代初到90年代初的实践起步阶段

这个时期绩效管理的理念还没有形成，实践中评估主要是对部门的粗放式考评，评估的方式主要是对部门某一方面或对整体印象的评价。80年代的大检查、大评比、专项调查等可以看作这一阶段的主要形式。虽然一些地方和部门贯彻人事部的要求，探索实施岗位责任制，但还没有形成规范性文件。80年代后期对目标管理责任制进行了探索和尝试。

（2）20世纪90年代初到90年代中后期的实践探索阶段

这一时期绩效评估作为特定管理机制的一个环节，在很多政府机关、事业单位开始普遍应用。具体包括目标考核责任制、社会服务承诺制、效能监察、行风评议等。如青岛市运用了目标考核方式，北京市、陕西省、四川省都相继发布了目标管理规定；烟台市建委率先提出了社会服务承诺制，掀起了政府的"承诺"浪潮；行风评议成为政府自我约束的重要手段，不同地区把不同行业作为评议重点，如铁路、电力、通信、旅游、司法等诸多行业都曾是关注的重点对象；纪检监察部门推动效能监察，对提高政府工作效率、转变工作作风起到

---

① 刘旭涛主编：《基于最佳实践的中国政府绩效管理案例研究》，国家行政学院出版社2015年版。

了很好的促进作用。

（3）21 世纪头十年的快速发展及全国试点推行阶段

据中央纪委监察部绩效管理监察室统计，截至 2012 年底，全国已有 27 个省（自治区、直辖市）不同程度地开展了政府绩效管理工作。[①] 这一阶段，地方政府和部分中央部委从单纯使用政府绩效评估这一工具到逐渐认识和建立政府绩效管理制度和体系，探索建立起适应各部门发展需求的评估体系，在评估内容、评估主体选择、评估程序设定和评估方法使用方面更加注重科学性和系统性。理论界大量翻译介绍西方发达国家政府绩效管理的经验和做法，并对政府绩效管理在中国内地的运用情况进行研究探讨。

此外，随着这一阶段政府绩效管理理论和实践的蓬勃发展，中央高层领导和有关部门也开始日益重视政府绩效管理和评估的重要作用并下决心在全国推行政府绩效管理。在 2005 年和 2008 年的国务院政府工作报告中分别提出"抓紧研究建立科学的政府绩效评估体系"和"推行政府绩效管理制度"；2008 年 2 月，中共十七届二中全会通过的《关于深化行政管理体制改革的意见》也明确提出了"推行政府绩效管理和行政问责制度"，从而把中国全面推进政府绩效管理工作列入了议事日程。

2010 年 4 月，中央编办批复中央纪委、监察部增设绩效管理监察室[②]，其职责包括组织开展政府绩效管理情况调查研究和监督检查工作，指导协调各地各部门绩效管理监察工作等。2010 年下半年到 2011 年全年，中纪委监察部绩效管理监察室组织进行了深入细致的调研工作。2011 年 3 月 10 日，国务院批复同意建立由监察部牵头的政府绩效管理工作部际联席会议制度。联席会议由监察部、中央组织部、中央编办、国家发展和改革委员会、财政部、人力资源和社会保障部（公务员局）、审计署、国家统计局、国务院法制办 9 个部门组成。联席会议办公室设在监察部，承担联席会议的日常工作。

3 月 14 日，十一届全国四次会议通过的《十二五规划纲要》明确提

---

① 2013 年中纪委监察部网站信息。

② 根据工作职能需要，十八届三中全会后中纪委绩效管理监察室与执法监察室被撤销，改为执法与效能监察室。

出："推行政府绩效管理和行政问责制度。建立科学合理的政府绩效评估指标体系和评估机制，实行内部考核与公众评议、专家评价相结合的方法，发挥绩效评估对推动科学发展的导向和激励作用。"根据纲要要求，政府绩效管理部级联席会议选择北京市、吉林省、福建省、广西壮族自治区、四川省、新疆维吾尔自治区、杭州市、深圳市政府、国家发展和改革委员会、财政部、国土资源部、环境保护部、农业部、国家质检总局开展政府绩效管理试点工作。2012年底中纪委监察部组织国家行政学院等部门共同对试点工作进行验收评估，试点工作成绩突出，为全面推行政府绩效管理制度探索和积累了丰富的实践经验。

（4）政府绩效管理工作的调整阶段

2013年7月，新一届政府上台后，对中纪委监察部工作职能进行调整和转变，原有的绩效管理监察室撤销，职能转交。中央机构编制委员会办公室承担起政府绩效管理牵头工作。目前中央机构编制委员会办公室已经完成了调研工作，正在研究出台全国政府绩效管理指导意见建议。各地方政府绩效管理也在前期工作的基础上进行反思和调整，政府绩效管理工作进入调整阶段。

2. 中国政府绩效管理工作的主要做法

中国政府绩效管理工作开展主要是从地方政府及其部门在实践中推动的，这与西方发达国家政府绩效管理做法有很大不同。西方国家政府绩效管理是由中央政府自上而下地推动开展，一般有专门的中央牵头机构，通过立法支持，统一的绩效评估指标体系和程序。中国政府绩效管理最初由地方政府开始探索，各地方政府内部牵头部门不同，评估指标体系各有侧重，在实际操作中政府绩效管理有些与目标考核责任制、社会服务承诺制、效能监察、行风评议、社会评议、预算管理、领导干部考核等相结合，形成了各自不同的做法。

（1）目标考核责任制模式

20世纪90年代以来，中国地方政府、公共部门和企事业单位逐步引入目标考核责任制，将其作为推动组织年度工作任务的"推手"。如北京市1991年发布了《党政机关目标管理岗位责任制试行方案》，陕西省1991年出台了《机关目标管理岗位责任制试行办法》，四川省1992年发布了《四川省人民政府目标管理工作细则》。目标考核责任制是一种典型的"任务导向"的政府绩效评估模式，它将目标管理与评估工具结合起来。目前，中国大量政府部门开展的关键绩效指标考核（KPI）和专项内容考核，如人口、安全、节能、减排都有明确的目标约束，因此可以归为目标考核责任制模式。

（2）社会评议模式

20 世纪 90 年代末以来，沈阳、南京、杭州、武汉等城市政府，陆续开展大规模的"万人评政府"活动，从而将外部评议主体正式引入政府绩效评估领域。社会评议模式引入外部公众、专家、人大代表、政协委员、服务对象等对政府部门工作，尤其是对承担公共服务职能的政府工作部门的工作进行评议，评议内容包括机关工作作风、服务质量、办事效率等，评估结果在当地主要媒体进行公布。社会评议模式是一种典型的"公民参与导向"的政府绩效评估模式。

（3）效能建设模式

效能建设，始于 20 世纪 80 年代末中国监察部门提出的"效能监察"，本意是指对各级政府和部门及其工作人员的履行职责、办事效率、工作作风等勤政情况进行行政监察。中国福建等地方政府在此基础上提出了"效能建设"，通过系统引入各种现代管理理念和做法，不断提高政府的办事效率和服务质量，提高政府能力和公务员的素质能力。效能建设模式是一种典型的"能力建设导向"的政府绩效评估模式。

（4）党政领导干部和公务员考核模式

20 世纪 80 年代以来，根据改革开放的新形势，中国不断完善领导干部和公务员考核制度，明确了"德、能、勤、绩、廉"考核内容，并且将考核结果作为干部选拔任用、交流轮岗、奖惩、培训等方面的重要依据。中央组织部 2009 年下发了《地方党政领导班子和领导干部综合考核评价办法（试行）》《党政工作部门领导班子和领导干部综合考核评价办法（试行）》《党政领导班子和领导干部年度考核办法（试行）》。从各地方政府对领导干部及班子考评情况来看，逐渐重视生态文明、社会建设、公共服务等民生问题、腐败治理等指标，考评指标体系不断调整和完善。

（5）督察督办模式

督察督办模式是各级政府为督促、检查和落实政府的重点工作和专项工作的评估模式。该模式是各级政府根据当年党政中心工作和重大决策部署，制定工作目标，确定考核指标体系，并根据各部门职责和各地区情况，进行目标分解和任务落实，督察部门根据目标计划安排，进行跟踪督查督办。中国从中央政府到地方各级政府几乎都设置了专门的督察督办部门，建立了较为完整的制度，信息化手段也广泛使用，是中国政府普遍采用的一种绩效管理模式。

（6）全面质量管理模式

提高公共服务质量和内部管理规范化是政府长期的趋势性追求。源自企业管理的全面质量管理（TQM）思想正好适应了这一需要。中国不少地方和部门曾引入国际标准化组织的全面质量管理体系 ISO 9000。一些政府机构尝试以全面质量管理为基础，做好标准化管理工作，与绩效评估相结合，建立了适合自己部门特色的绩效管理制度。如北京市出入境检验检疫局结合质量管理、能级管理和实绩管理建立了"三位一体"的绩效管理体系。

（7）第三方评估模式

第三方评估是独立于政府，由调查机构、研究机构独立开展的对政府及其相关部门绩效的评价。目前中国内地主要有委托第三方评估和独立第三方评估两种模式。2004 年年底至 2005 年年初，甘肃省政府委托兰州大学中国地方政府绩效评价中心组织非公有制企业对政府绩效的评价，对所辖 14 个市（州）政府和所属 39 个部门的绩效进行了评价，并于 2005 年 3 月向社会公布了评价结果。2013 年起，国务院委托国家行政学院、全国工商联、中国科学院和国务院发展研究中心四家单位分别对行政审批改革情况、国务院重大水利工程及农村饮水安全政策措施等重大政策开展第三方评估。此外，2007 年开始，华南理工大学公共政策评价中心，针对广东省 21 个地级以上市和 121 个县（市、区）的整体政府绩效评价开展独立第三方评估，并定期公布评估数据。

2014 年，国务院委托国务院发展研究中心、中国科学院、国家行政学院和全国工商联分别针对"取消和下放行政审批事项""加快棚户区改造""加快重大水利工程建设""向非国有资本推出一批投资项目"等事项开展第三方评估，从中央层面委托第三方开展评估开始形成常态化机制。

除上述几种模式外，中国地方政府和中央有关部门还进行了多种绩效管理方法的探索。财政部和上海浦东新区政府等开展了绩效预算，审计署和云南昆明市政府等开展了绩效审计，等等。这些实践探索为中国政府绩效管理积累了十分有益的经验，为在更广范围使用奠定了基础。

### （二）中国政府绩效管理取得的成效

截至目前，绝大部分中国地方政府和大部分中央部委已经开展了政府绩效管理工作。政府绩效管理工作的理念认识、体系建设取得了高速的实践发展和应用，中国政府绩效管理工作成效显著。

1. 中国政府绩效管理制度化法制化建设逐步完善

中共中央十八届三中全会强调"严格政府绩效管理，突出责任落实，确保权责一致"；十八届四中全会提出"深入推进依法行政，加快建设法治政府"的新要求。习近平总书记也多次强调"凡属重大改革都要于法有据"。国内地方政府绩效管理工作开展相对成熟的地区，先后加强了政府绩效管理工作制度化法制化的力度。如哈尔滨市政府2009年就制定出台了国内首部地方性法规，杭州市2015年也出台了《杭州市绩效管理条例》，其他地方政府如广西、浙江、湖南及部分市级政府也纷纷出台了相应的绩效管理办法。

2. 政府绩效管理科学化规范化程度得到很大提升

各地方政府和中央各部委在推进政府绩效管理实践工作中，逐渐注重加深绩效管理理念认识，由传统的侧重于GDP考核为主逐步扭转为重视环境建设和当地的可持续发展，如国家发改委把生态补偿工作成效纳入到对地方政府的绩效考核之中，环保部把各地方政府节能减排工作成效纳入到绩效考核工作之中。同时，在推行绩效管理的过程中，大部分地区采用了绩效任务（合同）形式，如农业部绩效办每年年初与各司局商定绩效目标，并与各司局一把手签订绩效协议，年底根据绩效协议中工作任务进行绩效评估。北京市、杭州市、青岛市、深圳市等地方重视绩效评估中发现的问题，及时反馈给各部门，要求各部门根据反馈意见建议进行绩效改进。各地方政府和中央部委绩效评估指标体系也根据地方政府和部门战略规划，每年进行调整，加大定量评估内容，减少人为操作因素。在绩效结果应用方面也进行多方面探索，把绩效评估结果与干部选拔任用、绩效奖惩等结合起来。政府绩效管理的科学化规范化程度得到比较大的提升。

3. 公众参与政府绩效评估的范围与途径扩大

在推行政府绩效管理的地方政府和部门中，只要承担公共服务职能，都会吸纳公众参与到政府绩效评估之中。有些部门采用第三方评估方式，由第三方调查公司采用入户调查、电话调查、问卷调查、网上问卷调查等多种方式，了解公众对政府和部门提供公共服务质量满意程度。有些地方采用万人评议政府方式，通过电视、网络等方式集中时间段了解公众意见建议。有些地方，如广东省佛山加大公众对政府预算绩效评估的参与力度。公众参与政府绩效评估的范围与途径得到较大拓展。

# 二　行政问责的发展与成效

行政问责，是指有权主体，依法对在行政管理过程中，由于故意或者过失不履行或者不正确履行法定职责，影响管理秩序和管理效率，贻误工作，或者损害管理相对人合法权益，造成不良影响和后果的行政人员的责任追究。[①] 中国历来重视政府责任制建设，但真正意义上的行政问责始于1978年改革开放后。随着中国深入推进依法行政，加快建设法治政府，中国不断强化对行政权力的制约和监督，通过建立科学有效的权力运行制约和监督体系，加强行政问责规范化、制度化建设，完善纠错问责机制，健全问责方式和问责程序，提高了政府的公信力和执行力。

## （一）中国行政问责的发展历程

1978年改革开放以来，中国行政问责的发展历程，可以2003年为界限，分为两个阶段。

1. 行政问责的萌芽阶段（2003年以前）

中国改革开放后，公众对政府责任的要求日益增加。这促使中国加强党政机关国家工作人员责任体系的建设，表现为干部人事制度改革和推进

---

① 参见沈岿、林良亮、蒋季雅《"行政问责制度研究"课题报告》，2011年。

公务员制度的建立。虽然这一阶段对公务员责任有了一些新的认识，但是，还没有形成行政问责这样的概念，对领导职公务员的责任承担也还没有形成明确的、成体系的认识。对领导职公务员的责任认定，没有通过制度方式加以规定，主要是以事件的方式推进。

这一阶段，中央有关党政领导干部责任体系建设的比较重要的文件有：（1）1988年《党员领导干部犯严重官僚主义失职错误党纪处分的暂行规定》。（2）1995年《党政领导干部选拔任用工作暂行条例》。（3）1993年《国家公务员暂行条例》。（4）1997年5月9日八届全国人大常委会第25次会议通过的《行政监察法》。（5）2001年国务院出台的《关于特大安全事故行政责任追究的规定》，规定了特大安全事故中的行政责任问题。

与此同时，地方公务员责任制度建设的尝试主要是两个方面：一是与当时推动的行政执法责任制相关的官员责任追究制度。很多地方都相继出台了关于执法责任制的地方性法规、规章和其他规范性文件。例如，《海南省行政执法责任制实施办法》《青海省行政执法责任制实施办法》等。二是与重大责任事故相关的责任追究制度。例如，《北京市关于重大安全事故行政责任追究的规定》《福建省人民政府关于重大安全事故行政责任追究的规定》等。①

2. 行政问责的发展阶段（2003年以后）

中国行政问责，因2003年"非典"事件掀起"问责风暴"后快速发展。行政问责成为依法行政建设法治政府的重要内容。2004年3月22日国务院颁布《全面推进依法行政实施纲要》，提出依法行政应权责统一。2008年6月国务院发布《国务院关于加强市县政府依法行政的决定》，要求加快实行以行政机关主要负责人为重点的行政问责。2010年10月10日，国务院颁布《关于加强法治政府建设的意见》，强调要严格行政问责。

这一阶段，中央有关党政领导干部责任体系建设的比较重要的文件有：（1）2003年12月，中共中央印发《中国共产党纪律处分条例》。（2）2004年2月，中共中央颁布《中国共产党党内监督条例（试行）》。

---

① 参见沈岿、林良亮、蒋季雅《"行政问责制度研究"课题报告》，2011年。

（3）2004年4月，中共中央批准实施《党政领导干部辞职暂行规定》，详细列举了9种应该引咎辞职的情形，为问责制度化提供了依据。（4）2006年1月1日《中华人民共和国公务员法》颁布实施，将"引咎辞职"与"责令辞职"引入公务员管理制度，使责任追究制度上升为法律规定。（5）2007年，国务院常务会议通过《行政机关公务员处分条例》。（6）2009年7月，中央颁布《关于实行党政领导干部问责的暂行规定》，这是第一部在中央层面对官员问责的专门法规，具体规定了党政领导需要接受问责的7种情形。（7）2010年11月，中共中央国务院颁布经过修订的《关于实行党风廉政建设责任制的规定》，具体细化了对各级党政领导班子及领导干部施行问责的情形、条件、方式、类型等内容。（8）2015年10月12日，中共中央政治局会议审议通过新修订的《中国共产党纪律处分条例》。

地方也以地方性法规、地方政府规章和其他规范性文件的形式对行政问责制进行了规定。2003年7月，国内首个政府行政问责办法——《长沙市人民政府行政问责制暂行办法》出台。2004年7月1日，国内首个省级行政首长问责办法——《重庆市政府部门行政首长问责暂行办法》正式实施。之后，其他地方政府也以地方性法规、规章或规范性文件形式，先后出台并启动了行政问责制。例如，2004年《天津市人民政府行政问责制试行办法》、2007年《安徽省人民政府行政问责暂行办法》、2008年《云南省人民政府关于省人民政府部门及州市行政负责人问责办法》等。2011年7月，北京市发布《北京市行政问责办法》，明确规定各级行政机关工作人员出现不履行、违法履行、不当履行行政职责等26类违规问题，将受到行政问责，情节严重的将责令辞去领导职务、免职。2012年2月15日，黑龙江省哈尔滨市发布行政问责规定，对于应予行政问责的情形做出多达36项的详细规定，内容涉及行政工作人员的行政决策、办事效率低下、不作为、乱作为、慢作为、假作为等各种情形。2016年2月25日《湖北省行政问责办法》颁布，其中规定对于行政机关集体违法要追责负责人。

与此同时，政府还出台了与绩效问责相关的规定。2009年6月，广东省佛山市南海区政府出台《佛山市南海区财政专项资金使用绩效问责暂行办法》①。2008 年，湖南省辰溪县出台了《辰溪县县直机关行政绩效问责考核办法》②。2011 年，北京市财政局印发《北京市预算绩效管理问责办法（试行）》③。2012 年，财政部发布《预算绩效管理工作规划》(2012—2015 年)④。2012 年，四川省政府印发《四川省人民政府绩效管理过错问责及结果运用办法（试行）》⑤。2013 年，辽宁省铁岭市出台《铁岭市机关作风和绩效问责暂行办法》⑥。

　　行政问责实践，也出现了新的变化，政府在绩效评估结果运用中越来越注重绩效问责。福建对绩效管理和评估中发现的一些机关工作人员不认真履行职责、推诿扯皮、效率低下、贻误工作，甚至"吃拿卡要"等问题，严格进行责任追究。新疆把政府绩效考评结果作为问责的依据，对分类考评排名靠后的单位部门的主要负责人进行约谈，对绩效考评结果被确定为较差等次的单位部门的主要负责人按有关规定进行诫勉谈话，对连续两年被评为较差的部门的主要负责人予以组织处理。⑦

### (二) 中国行政问责取得的成效

　　中国行政问责的实施，促进了责任政府的建设，增强了各级政府部门的责任意识和做好工作的动力，增进了官员的责任心和使命感，提升了政府执行力，保障了公民的知情权、参与权和监督权，取得了重大成效。

---

　　①　中华人民共和国财政部：《佛山市南海区建立财政专项资金绩效问责制度》，2009 年 7 月 17 日，http：//www. mof. gov. cn/pub/mof/xinwenlianbo/guangdongcaizhengxinxilianbo/200907/t20090717＿182810. html。

　　②　中共辰溪县委组织部：《辰溪县出台行政绩效问责考核办法拷问领导干部作风》，怀化党建网，2008 年 7 月 1 日，http：//www. hnredstar. gov. cn/huaihua/gbgz/t20080701＿184843. htm。

　　③　法律图书馆，北京市财政局关于印发《北京市预算绩效管理问责办法（试行）》的通知，http：//www. law-lib. com/law/law＿view. asp？id＝385230。

　　④　《预算绩效将纳入行政问责》，《新京报》2012 年 10 月 31 日，http：//www. bjnews. com. cn/news/2012/10/31/230728. html。

　　⑤　中国国情网，四川省人民政府关于印发《四川省人民政府绩效管理过错问责及结果运用办法（试行）》的通知，2012 年 8 月 2 日，http：//www. china. com. cn/guoqing/gbbg/2012-08/02/content＿26098298. htm。

　　⑥　崔博：《铁岭市机关作风和绩效问责暂行办法》出台，中国共产党铁岭市委员会网，2013 年 2 月 26 日，http：//www. zgtlsw. gov. cn/Article＿1628＿1/。

　　⑦　薛刚、薄贵利、刘小康、尹艳红：《服务型政府绩效评估结果运用研究：现状、问题与对策》，《国家行政学院学报》2013 年 5 月。

1. 初步建立了行政问责的制度框架体系

尽管目前国家层面尚无专门规范行政问责的法律法规，相关规定散见于《公务员法》《行政监察法》《行政机关公务员处分条例》《关于实行党政领导干部问责的暂行规定》等法律法规和党内法规，不过，地方以地方性法规、地方政府规章和其他规范性文件的形式对行政问责制进行了规定。目前已初步形成行政问责的制度框架体系，既涉及重大工作失误导致的政治问责、个人品行问题导致的道德问责，也涉及绩效问责。各级官员的责任意识、问责意识与公众的监督意识、社会舆论的问责意识都得到显著增强，初步形成了对公权力持有者滥用权力追究责任的政治生态氛围，开始呈现出"常态化问责"与发生重大事件掀起的"问责风暴"并存的局面。

2. 促进了责任政府的建设

责任政府意味着政府要积极地满足和实现公民的正当要求，要勇于承担道德的、政治的、行政的、法律上的、管理上的责任，要建立一整套控制约束行政行为的制度化规范。行政问责的实施，通过问责抑制政府官员对公权的需求，避免公权的无限扩大可能对私权的侵犯；增强了权力行使者的责任感，使其不断改善行政行为，树立敢于承担责任的良好的政府形象。特别是，通过政府绩效评估结果开展行政问责，使行政问责有了可靠基础，有力地增强了官员的责任心和使命感。基于政府绩效评估结果实施的问责机制，建立健全了官员问责制度，通过对领导干部失职失误行为做出硬性的制度约束，疏通了"能下"的渠道，为干部能上能下拓展了新的路径。

3. 促进了效能政府建设

加强绩效问责，推动了对质量和效率问题的关注，把官员和公众的关注点在明确责任的基础上吸引到"事情做得如何"上来。绩效问责，对公务员的"慵、懒、散"作风是高悬的利剑，有利于引导广大公务员高质量、高效率完成工作。以实实在在的业绩评定工作成绩，推动了政府工作中务实作风的形成。组织、人员、项目、财政预算等绩效管理结果与领导干部的责任挂钩，不仅扩大了绩效管理结果的使用渠道，而且拓宽了领导干部的责任追究范围，达到"治庸、治懒"目的，推动了领导干部树立"无功也是过"的施政理念。

4. 促进了服务型政府建设

服务型政府建设是中国政府改革的重要目标。人民满意的服务型政府建设，要求政府职能实现向创造良好的发展环境、提供优质高效的公共服务、维护社会公平正义的根本转变。要实现这一转变，就必须"将权力关在笼子里"，暴露在阳光下接受人民的监督和问责。行政问责制的实施，既强化了对权力的约束，又增强了政府运行的透明度。特别是，通过绩效问责制度的实施，把绩效管理结果面向社会公开，接受公众的评议、监督，大大推进了政府管理的民主化进程，同时也搭建了一个落实公众知情权、参与权、表达权和监督权的平台。这对推动公民参与政府事务，有效监督政府行为，肃清吏治，起了重要的作用。①

## 三　政府绩效管理与行政问责正在开展的工作

### （一）中国政府绩效管理正在开展的工作②

伴随着党十八大报告提出的"创新行政管理方式，提高政府公信力和执行力，推进政府绩效管理"的新要求，中国地方政府绩效管理进入了全面发展的新阶段，各地方政府绩效管理调整工作重心，重点从以下方面开展工作。

1. 统筹兼顾，突出社会管理和公共服务内容

对地方政府来说，既要关注经济增长，又要兼顾当地经济、社会、生态环境等方面的整体协调发展。多数省市地方政府绩效管理的评估内容已开始由侧重于经济发展转向兼顾经济发展、社会建设和公共服务等内容，并且关乎民生的比例逐渐扩大。

2. 科学论证，逐步完善政府绩效管理体系建设

各地政府在推进政府绩效管理工作过程中都意识到，好的绩效管理理念需要有完善的绩效管理制度和具体细致的绩效管理环节来支撑，否则仍然是空中楼阁，无法实现提升政府行政效能、提高政府执行力、改进政府绩效的最终目标。近年来，随着政府绩效管理工作的不断深入，地方政府在完善政府绩效管理体系建设和系统优化方面进行科学论证，做了很多创

---

① 参见刘旭涛、杜义国等《基于政府绩效评估的绩效问责研究报告》，2014 年。

② 尹艳红：《地方政府绩效管理发展新趋势》，《学习时报》2013 年 4 月 22 日。

新型的工作。如北京市政府确定 2011 年政府绩效管理要 "强基础、抓规范、谋发展"，为把公众评价做实，搭好政府工作与公众知情的桥梁，委托学术机构把政府各部门的职责进行全面梳理，并与百姓身边事相对接，整理出数千条百姓非常关心、涉及切身利益、易于感知、易于评价的评价题目，形成公众评价数据库，从而使公众评价指标体系更加科学和具有针对性，有利于形成倒逼机制，促进部门工作规范化发展。这些工作表明，中国地方政府绩效管理工作正在朝着逐步完善政府绩效管理体系、促使政府绩效管理工作科学化和制度化的方向有序推进。

3. 扩大参与，努力提升政府公信力和引导公民有效监督和评价政府绩效

公民参与对中国政府部门的绩效评价工作，已经开展多年。当前越来越多的地方政府绩效管理注重引入公众评价，公众满意度评价占总体评价的比例逐步提高，很多地方政府把公众参与评估的权重扩大到 30% 以上，杭州市甚至达到 50%。公众参与绩效评估的人数比例逐步增加，如广东省鹤山市常住人口 46 万，每年约有 1.2 万名社会各界人士参加镇级政府和市级部门的绩效评价，成为中国参与人口比例最大的县级城市。公众参与评估的渠道也逐步得到拓展。很多地方通过网站、电话、信函、入户调查、焦点座谈会、街头拦访等多种形式拓展公众参与评估的渠道。青岛市开展多年的 "三民活动" 2013 年有望通过电视直播全面展示公众评估过程。公众评议对政府绩效改进形成了强大的压力，拓宽了公民参与的渠道，切实提升了政府公信力。

4. 强化改进，加大绩效结果运用力度

国外经验和国内试点实践表明，政府绩效管理能否持续并取得实效，绩效评估结果运用是关键。近年来，各地方尝试通过通报批评、表扬、奖励、问责等激励措施，强化绩效评估的结果运用。如福建省最早将绩效评估结果作为行政问责依据，并逐渐在各地政府绩效管理中得到运用。一些地方将政府绩效评估与政府领导班子考核结合起来，把绩效评估结果作为干部晋升的依据。如杭州市在干部选拔任用中，将最近四年绩效评估结果作为考核领导干部的重要依据。尤其是近两年，各地政府开始强化绩效改进方面的结果运用。如北京市海淀区政府要求各部门必须根据绩效评估结果，提交三千字的绩效改进报告，详细说明绩效改进计划，并督促落实。

河北省南宫市在 2013 年的两会上，将 25 个政府组成部门 2012 年度的《绩效管理评估建议书》提交"两会"讨论。有些地方政府还准备下一步尝试把绩效结果与部门财政预算相挂钩，充分加大绩效结果的运用力度。

5. 整合资源，努力提高政府执行力

政府绩效管理是一项牵扯面广、涉及多部门和多领域的系统工程。为有效发挥政府绩效管理的作用，目前很多地方加强了政府绩效管理的相关资源整合。一是整合以往分散到各部门各系统的考核办法，实行扎口考核，既提高了绩效管理的工作效率，又减少了基层被评估对象的负担；二是建立上下级政府之间、不同部门之间的工作协调机制，互联互通、信息共享，协同解决政府工作中遇到的难题，提升行政效能，改进政府绩效；三是建立有效绩效信息系统，将政府绩效管理与网上办事大厅、行政服务中心、公共资源交易中心、电子监察平台、对外服务窗口、行政审批等系统进行有效整合和对接，推行信息资源共享共用。有效的绩效信息系统能够节省大量的信息重复采集的成本实现绩效的实时比对，有利于动态监控政府绩效，随时发现问题和改进工作，提升政府执行力。如北京市海淀区在推行政府绩效管理工作中，充分发挥绩效信息系统的作用，对推进和完善政府绩效管理工作产生了非常好的效果。

### （二）中国行政问责目前正在开展的工作①

党的十八届三中全会以来，为了落实全面深化改革重大战略举措，中国行政问责目前正在开展以下工作：

1. 大力推行权力清单、责任清单、负面清单制度

在全面梳理、清理调整、审核确认、优化流程的基础上，将政府职能、法律依据、实施主体、职责权限、管理流程、监督方式等事项以权力清单的形式向社会公开，同时逐一厘清与行政权力相对应的责任事项、责任主体、责任方式，形成责任清单。另外，实行统一的市场准入制度，在制定负面清单基础上，各类市场主体可依法平等进入清单之外领域。三个清单，旨在划定政府与市场、企业、社会的权责边界。权力清单，明确政府能做什么，"法无授权不可为"；责任清单，明确政府该怎么管市场，

---

① 《法治政府建设实施纲要》（2015—2020 年）。

"法定职责必须为";负面清单,明确对企业的约束有哪些,"法无禁止即可为"。通过建立"三个清单",依法管好"看得见的手",用好"看不见的手",挡住"寻租的黑手"。

2. 严格决策责任追究

完善重大行政决策程序制度,明确决策主体、事项范围、法定程序、法律责任,规范决策流程,强化决策法定程序的刚性约束。一是决策机关通过跟踪决策执行情况和实施效果,对重大行政决策进行后评估。二是健全并严格实施重大决策终身责任追究制度及责任倒查机制,对决策严重失误或者依法应该及时做出决策但久拖不决造成重大损失、恶劣影响的,严格追究行政首长、负有责任的其他领导人员和相关责任人员的党纪政纪和法律责任。

3. 全面落实行政执法责任制

建立健全权责统一、权威高效的行政执法体制,严格确定不同部门及机构、岗位执法人员的执法责任,建立健全常态化的责任追究机制。通过建立统一的行政执法监督网络平台,建立健全投诉举报、情况通报等制度,加强执法监督,排除对执法活动的干预,防止和克服部门利益和地方保护主义,防止和克服执法工作中的利益驱动,惩治执法腐败现象。

4. 全面推进政务公开

坚持以公开为常态、不公开为例外原则,推进决策公开、执行公开、管理公开、服务公开、结果公开。一是完善政府信息公开制度,拓宽政府信息公开渠道,进一步明确政府信息公开范围和内容。二是重点推进财政预算、公共资源配置、重大建设项目批准和实施、社会公益事业建设等领域的政府信息公开。三是完善政府新闻发言人、突发事件信息发布等制度,及时回应人民群众关切。四是创新政务公开方式,加强互联网政务信息数据服务平台和便民服务平台建设,提高政务公开信息化、集中化水平。

5. 完善纠错问责机制

加强行政问责规范化、制度化建设,增强行政问责的针对性和时效性。一是加大问责力度,坚决纠正行政不作为、乱作为,坚决克服懒政、庸政、怠政,坚决惩处失职、渎职。二是认真落实党风廉政建设责任制,坚持有错必纠、有责必问,对"四风"问题突出、发生顶风违纪问题或者出现区域性、系统性腐败案件的地方、部门和单位,既要追究主体责任、监督责任，又要严肃追究领导责任。

**参考文献**

[1] 刘旭涛主编：《基于最佳实践的中国政府绩效管理案例研究》，国家行政学院出版社 2015 年版。

[2] 尹艳红：《地方政府绩效管理发展新趋势》，《学习时报》2013 年 4 月 22 日。

[3] ［美］小威廉·T. 格姆雷、斯蒂芬·J. 巴拉：《官僚机构与民主——责任与绩效》，俞沂暄译，复旦大学出版社 2007 年版。

[4] ［美］马克·G. 波波维奇：《创建高绩效政府组织》，孔宪遂、耿洪敏译，中国人民大学出版社 2002 年版。

[5] 刘旭涛、杜义国等：《基于政府绩效评估的绩效问责研究报告》，2014 年。

[6] 中华人民共和国财政部：《佛山市南海区建立财政专项资金绩效问责制度》，2009 年 7 月 17 日，http：//www. mof. gov. cn/pub/mof/xinwenlianbo/guangdong-caizhengxinxilianbo/200907/t20090717_ 182810. html。

[7] 中共辰溪县委组织部：《辰溪县出台行政绩效问责考核办法拷问领导干部作风》，怀化党建网，2008 年 7 月 1 日，http：//www. hnredstar. gov. cn/huaihua/gbgz/t20080701_ 184843. htm。

[8] 法律图书馆，北京市财政局关于印发《北京市预算绩效管理问责办法（试行）》的通知，http：//www. law-lib. com/law/law_ view. asp？ id=385230。

[9] 《预算绩效将纳入行政问责》，《新京报》2012 年 10 月 31 日，http：//www. bjnews. com. cn/news/2012/10/31/230728. html。

[10] 中国国情网，四川省人民政府关于印发《四川省人民政府绩效管理过错问责及结果运用办法（试行）》的通知，2012 年 8 月 2 日，http：//www. china. com. cn/guoqing/gbbg/2012-08/02/content_ 26098298. htm。

[11] 崔博：《〈铁岭市机关作风和绩效问责暂行办法〉出台》，中国共产党铁岭市委员会网，2013 年 2 月 26 日，http：//www. zgtlsw. gov. cn/Article_ 1628_ 1/。

[12] 薛刚、薄贵利、刘小康、尹艳红：《服务型政府绩效评估结果运用研究：现状、问题与对策》，《国家行政学院学报》2013 年第 5 期。

[13] 沈岿、林良亮、蒋季雅：《"行政问责制度研究"课题报告》，2011 年。

[14] 《法治政府建设实施纲要》（2015—2020 年）。

（作者：刘小康　国家行政学院公共管理教研部公共政策教研室主任；尹艳红　国家行政学院公共管理教研部副教授）

# 第 十 章

# 法治政府建设

依法治国作为中国基本治国方略，强调科学立法、严格执法、公正司法和全民守法，其中执法是关键。政府的决策与执法活动是否合法、是否适当，不仅关系到人民福祉和社会稳定，也关系到依法治国这一基本方略能否落实。因此，依法行政、建设法治政府，是全面落实依法治国基本方略的重要内容，成为中国政府施政的基本准则。法治政府建设是依法治国的关键，也是当代中国行政改革的重要内容与目标，没有进入法治化的政府就不可能是现代政府。多年来，中国政府采取一系列措施切实推进建设法治政府，法治政府建设的指导思想和具体目标、基本原则和要求、主要任务和措施，日益明确与完善。目前，中国各级人民政府的行政权力已逐步纳入法治化轨道，规范政府权力取得和运行的法律制度基本形成，依法行政取得了重要进展。

## 一 走向法治政府的路径选择

### （一）法治政府建设目标的确立

1978 年十一届三中全会提出"有法可依、有法必依、执法必严、违法必究"十六字方针，表明法治意向，显示出党和国家进行法制建设的坚定决心；1984 年中央进一步明确应"从依政策办事，逐步转变为既要依政策办事，又要依法律办事"，其中蕴含了法治政府的基本含义和要求；1993 年国务院工作办法中规定"依法办事，依法行政"，"依法行政"四字第一次出现在政府文件中。

1997 年党的十五大首次将"依法治国"确立为党领导人民的治国理

政方针；1999 年九届全国人大二次会议修订宪法时，将"依法行政，建设法治国家"写入宪法，作为治理国家的基本方略；同年 11 月，国务院关于《全面推进依法行政的决定》中提出了推进法治政府建设的具体要求；为了落实"依法治国"的战略任务，2002 年党的十六大确立了"推进依法行政"的法治任务；2004 年，国务院为落实党的十五大、十六大关于"依法治国"和"推进依法行政"的要求，制定公布了《全面推进依法行政实施纲要》，首次将"全面推进依法行政，经过十年左右坚持不懈的努力，基本实现建设法治政府"确立为全面推进依法行政的目标。

2012 年 11 月党的十八大首次将"法治政府基本建成"确立为"全面建成小康社会"的重要目标之一，并同时确定了完成这一重任的时间表：到 2020 年"法治政府基本建成"。2013 年 2 月十八届二中全会审议通过了《国务院机构改革和职能转变方案》，要求深入推进政企分开、政资分开、政事分开、政社分开，健全部门职责体系，建设职能科学、结构优化、廉洁高效、人民满意的服务型政府，丰富了法治政府的内涵。2013年 11 月十八届三中全会通过了《关于全面深化改革若干重大问题的决定》，将"完善和发展中国特色社会主义制度，推进国家治理体系和治理能力现代化"确定为全面深化改革的总目标，提出了"建设法治政府和服务型政府"的任务。2014 年 10 月十八届四中全会通过了《关于全面推进依法治国若干重大问题的决定》，对"深入推进依法行政，加快建设法治政府"作了全面部署，明确提出了"加快建设职能科学、权责法定、执法严明、公开公正、廉洁高效、守法诚信的法治政府"的任务。2015年 10 月十八届五中全会审议通过了《关于制定国民经济和社会发展第十三个五年规划的建议》，进一步提出了经济法治建设要求。

2015 年 12 月，党中央国务院发布了《法治政府建设实施纲要（2015—2020 年）》。《法治政府建设实施纲要》共分三个部分，确立了法治政府建设的指导思想、总体目标、基本原则、衡量标准和 44 项工作措施。这是我国"十三五"期间的一个法治建设纲要。它既是对党的十八大及二中、三中、四中、五中全会所确立的法治政府建设目标任务的具体落实，又是对未来五年法治政府建设工作的系统布置。

**（二）走向法治政府建设的客观动因**

制度是社会发展的内在选择结果，中国走向法治政府建设之路符合社会发展自身的规律。

首先，改革开放所启动的市场化进程催生了对法治的需求。随着市场化进程的深入，传统熟人社会关系模式逐渐松动，人们摆脱了血缘、地域等的限制，人口流动加速，交流和交往的范围越来越大，对规制的需求和依赖增强；同时随着社会分工的发展和个人收入水平的提高，个人的独立性越来越强，对产权保护、契约制度和安全制度的需求就越来越强烈，直接刺激了"法治"需求的增加。

其次，利益的分化和利益群体的形成提供了法治建设的参与主体。[①]随着市场经济的逐步建立，利益分化加剧，逐渐形成了各种利益群体。有利益分化就意味着需要利益整合，在利益整合的相互作用过程中不可避免涉及各种法律问题，从而使各类利益主体都在不同程度上参与法治建设。而且随着各利益群体的利益诉求渠道的逐步畅通、组织形式逐步合法，他们参与法治建设的成本越来越低，法治就越容易形成。

最后，执政能力的提高为法治建设提供了契机。推进法治建设已经成为党内共识和国家建设的重要目标，应成为国家重要政策，实际上也成为了法制建设的主要推动者，在法治建设过程中发挥着积极作用，从而大大加速法制建设的进程，提高法治建设成功的可能性。

**（三）法治政府建设的总体目标和衡量标准**

《法治政府建设实施纲要》确立了法治政府建设的总体目标，即经过坚持不懈的努力，到 2020 年基本建成职能科学、权责法定、执法严明、公开公正、廉洁高效、守法诚信的法治政府。

那么，如何来衡量法治政府如何建成呢？法治政府的实质在于依法治理政府，政府是法治的客体，公民和社会是法治政府的主体。法治政府的基本内涵就是政府受到法的支配，判断法治政府的唯一标准是国家有一个良好的法律法规规章体系和这个体系在阳光下运行的机制，对行政活动进

---

① 刘靖华等：《中国法治政府》，中国社会科学出版社 2006 年版，第 149—150 页。

行规范、制约、监督和问责；这个体系和机制能够在行政活动中被政府、政府工作部门、各种公共服务机构严格执行和有效运作。① 基于此，《法治政府建设实施纲要》第一次确立了法治政府是否建成的七项具体衡量标准，即政府职能依法全面履行、依法行政制度体系完备、行政决策科学民主合法、宪法法律严格公正实施、行政权力规范透明运行、人民权益切实有效保障、依法行政能力普遍提高。这七项做到了，法治政府也是基本建成了。

## 二　法治政府建设的主要举措及成就

### （一）建立健全行政法律规范体系，夯实政府活动的法治基础

十一届三中全会以来中国法制建设取得巨大成就的重要标志，就是基本改变了新中国成立以来长期无法可依的局面，立法工作取得了重大进展，初步形成了社会主义法律体系，有关政府管理的法律制定及政府立法工作也成就斐然。

截至 2015 年 12 月 31 日，全国人民代表大会及其常务委员会制定的、现行有效的法律共计 273 件，其中行政管理方面的立法占 89%。② 尤其是《国务院组织法》《地方各级人民代表大会和地方各级人民政府地方组织法》《公务员法》《行政处罚法》《行政许可法》《行政强制法》《行政诉讼法》《行政复议法》《国家赔偿法》等主干法律的出台，构建了较为完整的、贯穿行政过程"主体—行为—救济"的体系性规范，为法治政府建设奠定了坚实的基础。

与此同时，国务院还制定了《行政法规制定程序条例》《规章制定程序条例》，直辖市和国务院各部门也相继制定各自的立法程序和规则，使政府立法工作有章可循、稳步推进。截至 2016 年 2 月，国务院制定的现行有效的行政法规共计 683 件，地方性法规 12747 件，部委规章 4926 件，

---

① 王宝明：《法治政府——中国政府法治化建设的战略选择》，研究出版社 2009 年版，第 5 页。

② 该数据根据北大法宝提供的信息分类统计得出。

地方政府规章 12455 件。① 这些法规规章涵盖了政府行政领域的各个主要方面，对政府行政管理做出更加全面、细致的规范。此外，为避免法规规章以及各级政府的规范性文件，违反效力更高的上位法规定或相互之间发生冲突，2001 年 12 月国务院公布了《法规规章备案条例》，旨在加强对地方性法规地方政府规章和国务院部门规章备案审查制度的执行力度，维护法制统一、保证法律法规的正确施行。2007 年 3 月国务院办公下发《关于开展行政法规规章清理工作的通知》，要求对各现行行政法规规章进行全面清理，对行政法规规章清理活动正在向制度化方向迈进。

建立健全科学完备的行政法律法规，长效的法律法规清理、法规跟踪评估、备案审查机制，确保行政立法数量与质量的提升，有助于夯实政府活动的法治基础。

**（二）明确政府活动的权责依据，提高行政机构组织设置的法治化程度**

中国目前有两部行政机关组织法律，即 1979 年的《地方各级人民代表大会和地方各级人民政府地方组织法》与 1982 年的《国务院组织法》。这两部法律的制定为实现行政机构职能的法定化起到了积极的作用，但从条款内容上看，两部立法均较为简单，不能适应法治政府建设的现实需要。实践中，政府职权职责的划分多通过"三定方案"来实现，这在一定程度上影响了政府行为依据的规范性与权威性。

2013 年 11 月，党的十八届三中全会上首次提出"推行地方各级政府及其工作部门权力清单制度，依法公开权力运行流程"；2014 年 10 月，党的十八届四中全会通过的《关于全面推进依法治国若干重大问题的决定》再次强调，"推行政府权力清单制度，坚决消除权力设租寻租空间"是实现全面履行政府职能的重要措施，也是加快建设法治政府的重要内容；2015 年 3 月，中共中央办公厅、国务院办公厅印发《关于推行地方各级政府工作部门权力清单制度的指导意见》，要求"将地方各级政府工作部门行使的各项行政职权及其依据、行使主体、运行流程、对应的责任等，以清单形式明确列示出来，向社会公布，接受社会监督"，据此，各

---

① 上述数据出自北大法宝数据库。

级政府及政府部门大力推进权力清单的公布工作。通过建立权力清单和相应责任清单制度，进一步明确地方各级政府工作部门职责权限，大力推动简政放权，加快形成边界清晰、分工合理、权责一致、运转高效、依法保障的政府职能体系和科学有效的权力监督、制约、协调机制，全面推进依法行政。

此外，中国公务员制度的法治化建设也取得一定成效。1993 年国务院正式颁布了《国家公务员暂行条例》，之后又先后出台了一系列与之相配套的暂行规定，如职位分类、录用、考核、奖惩、职务升降、职务任免、培训交流、工资、福利、保险、退休规定，涵盖公务员管理各个环节；2005 年十届全国人大常委会十五次会议审议通过了《中华人民共和国公务员法》，它的制定和颁布标志着公务员管理法治化建设有了重大突破。公务员法治化管理，凸显了竞争激励机制，激发了公务员队伍的活力，同时也强调监督制约机制，规范公务行为。

**（三）健全行政决策机制，推进政府决策的科学化、民主化和法治化**

行政决策是政府所有行政活动的起点。起点错误，必然导致所有行为错误。推进行政决策的科学化、民主化和法治化，历来是建设法治政府的基本要求，也是衡量法治政府建设的标准。2004 年国务院《全面推进依法行政实施纲要》将"科学化、民主化、规范化的行政决策机制和制度基本形成"确立为法治政府建设的具体目标之一。2015 年党中央国务院《法治政府建设实施纲要》又将"行政决策科学民主合法"确定为法治政府的衡量标准之一，并明确要求达到"行政决策制度科学、程序正当、过程公开、责任明确，决策法定程序严格落实，决策质量显著提高，决策效率切实保证，违法决策、不当决策、拖延决策明显减少并得到及时纠正，行政决策公信力和执行力大幅提升"这一具体目标。

为保证决策的科学性，政府一方面加强中国特色新型智库建设，建立行政决策咨询论证专家库，借助外脑提高决策质量；另一方面落实重大决策社会稳定风险评估机制，提高风险评估质量。

为推进行政决策民主化，政府既注重增强公众参与实效，又坚持集体讨论决定。一方面，各级政府建立和加强公众参与平台建设，事关经济社会发展全局和涉及群众切身利益的重大行政决策事项，广泛听取意见，与利害关系人进行充分沟通，及时反馈意见采纳情况和理由。对于文化教育、医疗卫生、资源开发、环境保护、公用事业等方面事关重大民生的决策事项，建立和推行民意调查制度。另一方面，重大行政决策经政府常务会议或者全体会议、部门领导班子会议讨论，由行政首长在集体讨论基础做出决定。

为推进行政决策民主化，政府一方面着重完善重大行政决策程序制度，制定行政程序规定，将决策纳入法定程序和正当程序之中；另一方面加强合法性审查，普遍建立政府法律顾问制度，保证法律顾问在制定重大行政决策、推进依法行政中发挥积极作用。此外，还严格决策责任追究，建立和完善重大行政决策后评估制度和有关人员的责任追究制度。

### （四）大力推进行政审批制度改革，促进政府职能转变

受传统高度集中计划经济体制的影响，行政审批一度被广泛地运用于中国许多行政管理领域。随着中国社会主义市场经济的建立和完善，行政审批中存在的问题就越来越突出，有些已成为生产力发展的体制性障碍。因此，改革行政审批制度，规范行政审批行为，建立结构合理、配置科学、程序有效的权力运行机制，保证权力沿着制度化和法治化的轨道行进，便成为建设法治政府的内在要求。

中国行政审批制度改革，随着经济体制改革的深化而逐渐发展，迄今已走过 30 年的历程。1978 年党的十一届三中全会把全党工作重点转移到以经济建设为中心之后，针对计划经济体制下政府权力过分集中，管得过多、过死的弊端，1982 年中央明确提出"放权让利"；1993 年为建立社会主义市场经济体制的要求，政府开始增加企业的自主性，减少政府对企业的具体审批事务；1998 年国务院各部门划转出 280 多项职能，将属于企业和社会中介组织的职能，交给企业和社会中介组织，将该由地方办的事情交给地方；2001 年国务院办公厅下发《关于成立国务院行政审批制度改革工作领导小组的通知》，成立国务院行政审批制度改革工作领导小组，积极、稳妥地推进行政审批制度改革，改革工作全面启动；2004 年中国在加入世贸组织之后，行政许可制度步伐明显加快，以削减审批事项为主要内容的行政改革被提上议事日程；2005 年《行政许可法》的颁布

施行，压缩了审批范围，明确了权力边界，加强了对行政许可行为的监督实施以及问责机制，还权于社会和公民，对政府职能正确定位产生深远影响。

行政审批制度改革启动后，国务院先后于 2002 年、2003 年、2004 年、2007 年、2010 年、2012 年分六批，决定取消和调整行政审批项目共计 2374 项；党的十八大以来，国务院继续简政放权，深入推进行政审批制度改革，截至 2016 年 2 月，先后十四次发文，（部分）取消、调整和下放管理层级的行政审批项目 844 项，取消职业资格许可和认定事项 268 项，取消评比、达标、表彰项目 118 项，取消的行政事业性收费项目目录 3 项，决定改为后置审批的工商登记前置审批事项目录 134 项。通过对行政审批的全面清理，最大限度减少对生产经营活动的许可，最大限度缩小投资项目审批、核准的范围，最大幅度减少对各类机构及其活动的认定。

扎实深入推进行政审批制度改革，有力推动了政府职能转变和管理创新，促进了法治政府建设，也从源头上预防和治理腐败创造条件。

### （五）改革行政执法体制，提高执法效率，提升执法品质

行政执法体制是政府行政体制的重要组成部分，深化行政执法体制改革是全面深化改革的具体内容和任务。

改革行政执法体制，重点要改革行政执法机构，合理配置执法力量。为解决城市管理中长期存在的多头执法、职权交叉问题，提高行政执法水平和效率，降低行政执法成本，政府在食品药品安全、工商质检、公共卫生、安全生产、文化旅游、资源环境、农林水利、交通运输、城乡建设、海洋渔业、商务等领域内推行综合执法。综合执法的制度基础源于相对集中处罚权制度，该制度最早规定于 1996 年《行政处罚法》；1996 年 4 月国务院发布《关于贯彻〈行政处罚法〉通知》，特别强调要求各省自治区直辖市做好相对集中行政处罚权试点工作；2000 年 9 月国务院办公厅发布《关于继续做好相对集中行政处罚权试点工作的通知》，进一步加快推行相对集中行政处罚权工作的步伐。随着《行政许可法》《行政强制法》的出台，相对集中许可权制度、相对集中强制权制度也相应出现，综合执法体制日渐完善。通过推行综合行政执

法，执法队伍得到整合，执法水平进一步提高。综合执法行政机关与原有的行政执法队伍相比，在执法人数大幅度精简的情况下，执法专业化更为增强、执法效率显著提高。

行政执法体制改革的另一项重要内容为落实行政执法责任制。行政执法责任制是规范和监督行政机关行政执法活动的一项重要措施。2005年国务院办公厅颁发了《关于推行行政执法责任制的若干意见》，各级政府依法界定执法职责工作取得初步成效。实践中，各地方各部门还积极探索各种类型的责任制度，如创新行政执法评议考核机制、实施行政首长问责制、建立完善行政执法人员资格管理制度，以及听证、重大处罚备案等行政执法程序制度等。实行执法责任制，通过确定不同部门和不同岗位人员执法责任，建立健全常态化的责任追究机制，行政机关内部层级管理职能和岗位工作权限，得到重新整合并进一步理顺，规范执法从机制上得到了保证，大大提升了行政效能的提升。

### （六）全面推行政务公开，落实法治政府建设的内在要求

政务公开是社会主义民主法制建设的一项基础性工作和政府施政的一项基本制度，也是转换政府职能、建设法治政府的内在需要。

随着中国法治进程的加快，行政公开制度已逐步在全国范围内全面推行。就目前来看，中国已经初步建立了较为全面的国家法律法规公告制度；听证制度作为行政公开的重要方式，在《行政处罚法》《行政许可法》《立法法》中均有明确规定。政务公开的主要途径是政企的信息公开。2008年5月开始施行的《中华人民共和国政府信息公开条例》，将信息公开作为整个行政过程的一个重要原则在行政实践中落实，极大地推动法治政府建设。各部门各地方在实践中采用"两公开一监督"、政府采购制、窗口式服务等更为灵活多样的政务公开形式，取得良好效果。

同时，电子政务建设进一步推动政务公开。1999年1月由中国电信和国家经济贸易委员会经济信息中心牵头，联合40余家部、委、局、办信息主管部门，倡议发起"政府上网工程"。政府上网工程的全面启动，直接推动了中央和地方政府信息化进程。2005年10月1日中央政府门户网站试运行，并于2007年1月1日正式开通。政府上网工程实

施以来，各政府部门通过互联网向社会发布政务信息，绝大多数地级市政府在网上设立了办事窗口，制定了电子政务规划，从技术上推动了政府信息公开。

政务公开，尤其是电子政务建设，推动各级政府由管理型向管理服务型的角色转换，大大提高办公效率，有力促进廉政建设。

### （七）建立高效的行政纠纷处理机制，及时依法化解社会矛盾

妥善迅速解决社会矛盾和纠纷是保护公民权益、建设法治政府的重要环节。以行政复议、行政诉讼、国家赔偿作为解决社会矛盾的主要途径，凸显了解决社会矛盾方式的制度化和法治化含量。

行政复议是政府系统内部提供的纠纷解决渠道，有利于快捷地解决行政争议，化解人民内部矛盾，密切政府与人民群众的关系。各政府部门通过依法办理行政复议案件，纠正违法的或不当的行政行为，切实维护了公民、法人和其他组织的合法权益；行政诉讼和国家赔偿制度则是在政府系统外解决行政争议。中国自 1982 年开始施行行政诉讼制度，到 1990 年制定实施《行政诉讼法》之后，行政诉讼制度得到了进一步的发展和完善，对于进一步保护公民、法人和其他组织的合法权益、监督行政行为起着重要作用。尤其是 2014 年 11 月十二届全国人大常委会第十一次会议表决通过了《关于修改〈行政诉讼法〉的决定》，修改后的《行政诉讼法》通过扩大行政诉讼受案范围，规定立案登记、行政诉讼案件跨区域管辖等制度，强调行政首长出庭应诉义务、加重复议机关当被告的责任等，进一步保障了公民、法人和其他组织的合法权益，也对政府法治建设提出了更高的要求。

## 三 法治政府建设的基本经验

经过多年来的政府法治建设，中国各级政府在推进依法行政、建设法治政府等方面做了大量工作，取得了显著成绩，积累了不少宝贵经验，这些经验主要表现为以下几个方面。

**（一）党的领导、人民当家作主和依法治国三者有机统一是法治政府建设的首要前提**

党的领导是中国特色社会主义的本质特征，是社会主义法治的根本保证。党的领导和社会主义法治是一致的：社会主义法治坚持党的领导，党的领导依靠社会主义法治。在党的领导下依法治国、厉行法治，人民当家作主充分实现，国家和社会生活法治化得以有序推进。党是社会主义法治的倡导者、主导者和引领者，依法治国以加强和改善党的领导为指向；同时，作为现代国家治理基本方式的法治，是党领导人民实现中华民族伟大复兴的选择，党的领导也必须依靠社会主义法治。依法治国是党领导人民治理国家的基本方略，依法执政是党治国理政的基本方式，建设法治政府以实现党的领导、人民当家作主和依法治国三者的有机统一为基本前提。

**（二）坚持宪法原则是法治政府建设的根本保证**

宪法所确立的基本原则国家根本制度和公民基本权利义务的规定，体现了全国各族人民的共同意志和根本利益，是一切国家机关和武装力量、各政党和社会团体的根本活动准则，也是法治政府建设的基础和依据，建设法治政府的各项措施都必须符合宪法的规定。

**（三）以经济建设为中心是法治政府建设的主导方向**

法治政府建设作为经济社会发展的促进力量和保障力量，其全面推进无法脱离经济发展水平和社会条件。过于超前，法治政府建设目标和各项措施就会落空，从而根本无法实现推动经济和社会发展的作用；过于滞后，则可能成为经济和社会发展的阻碍，影响经济和社会的发展。[1] 所以，建设法治政府，需要围绕经济建设这个中心，把改革发展和稳定的重点当作法治政府建设的重点，坚持与经济和社会发展相适应，凸显法治政府建设在依法治国方略中的重要地位，是为建设法治政府不断增添动力的源泉。

---

[1]　袁曙宏、宋功德：《依法行政干部读本》，人民出版社 2004 年版，第 54 页。

**（四）政府职能转变和深化行政体制改革是法治政府建设的核心内容**

建设法治政府，是对旧的行政管理模式的深刻革命，必然要求建立与之相适应的新的行政管理体制。法治政府建设既是政府职能转变和行政管理体制改革的重要内容，也是政府职能转变和行政管理体制改革的必要手段。[①] 在我国社会转型过程中，建设法治政府既要在现有行政管理体制下逐步推进，与行政管理体制改革和政府职能转变相衔接，通过法治政府的建设促进政府职能向经济调节、市场监管、社会管理和公共服务方向转变，又要为行政管理体制改革和政府职能转变，提供足够的创新空间，保障行政管理体制改革和政府职能转变的逐步到位。

**（五）及时转变观念为法治政府建设提供发展动力**

加快法治政府建设应当在现有成绩的基础上，进一步通过转变观念。观念上的转变，重点是解决几个过渡：一是从无限政府到有限政府的过渡。事实证明，政府不是万能的，也不该是万能的。政府若将社会所有事务包揽起来既不应该也做不到。在观念上不能实现从无限政府到有限政府的过渡，政府职能就无法得到转变。二是从管理政府到服务政府的过渡。管理政府的手段侧重于命令、强制和处罚，而服务政府的手段侧重于指导、给付和帮助。要有效地转变政府职能，观念上从管理政府到服务政府的过渡是必要的。三是从传统政府到现代政府的过渡。传统政府是习惯于传统方式管理社会的政府，大多靠"运动之治""会议之治""口号之治""领导之治"，现代政府是指在国家治理现代化的要求背景下，能够做到管理科学化、民主化、文明化、法治化，能够实现"规则之治"的政府。

**（六）依法治官治权、保护公民权利是法治政府建设的重点任务**

法治政府的实质在于依法治理政府，政府是法治的客体，公民和社会才是法治的主体。法治政府的基本内涵，就是政府受到法的支配，政府必须依照法律的内容、目的、原则和精神行政，依法对社会进行管理。政府要维护宪法和法律的权威，依法提供公共服务，依法接受监

---

[①]　袁曙宏、宋功德：《依法行政干部读本》，人民出版社 2004 年版，第 54 页。

督。建设法治政府的重点是依法治官，而非治民；依法治权，而非治事，核心是保护公民权利。我国建设法治政府的实践充分表明，只有紧紧抓住这个重点和核心，不会使政府行政偏离正确方向，才能真正把行政区纳入法治轨道。

### （七）立法、执法、监督互相协调整体推进是法治政府建设的有效方式

立法是建设法治政府的前提，担负着为行政机关提供公正有效的行为规则的功能；执法是建设法治政府的关键，是人民群众的权益最直接相关的行政行为；对行政权力的监督，则是建设法治政府的保障，承担着防止和纠正行政机关违法行政的重任。推进法治政府的建设，应坚持立法、执法、监督，三位一体，互相协调，整体推进。

**参考文献**

[1] 袁曙宏、宋功德：《依法行政干部读本》，人民出版社 2004 年版。

[2] 王宝明：《法治政府——中国政府法治化建设的战略选择》，研究出版社 2009 年版。

[3] 刘靖华等：《中国法治政府》，中国社会科学出版社 2006 年版。

[4] 曹康泰：《政府法制建设三十年的回顾与展望》，中国法制出版社 2008 年版。

[5] 国务院法制办公室、国家行政学院：《加强法治政府建设文献汇编》，国家行政学院 2011 年版。

[6] 《〈中共中央关于全面推进法治国若干重大问题的决定〉辅导读本》，人民出版社 2014 年版。

[7] 中国政法大学法治政府研究院：《中国法治政府发展报告（2015）》，社会科学文献出版社 2015 年版。

[8] 王万华：《法治政府建设的程序主义进路》，《法学研究》2013 年第 4 期。

[9] 周汉华：《构筑多元动力机制　加快建设法治政府》，《法学研究》2014 年第 6 期。

[10] 马怀德：《我国法治政府建设现状观察：成就与挑战》，《中国行政管理》2014 年第 6 期。

[11] "中国法治政府评估"课题组：《中国法治政府评估报告（2013）》，《行政法学研究》2014 年第 1 期。

［12］马凯：《关于建设中国特色社会主义法治政府的几个问题》，《国家行政学院学报》2011 年第 5 期。

［13］关保英：《论法治政府的新内涵》，《南京社会科学》2015 年第 1 期。

［14］姜明安：《关于法治政府建设的两个问题》，《法制与社会发展》2015 年第 5 期。

（作者：胡建淼　国家行政学院法学部主任、教授；华燕　国家行政学院博士后、福州大学法学院副教授）

# 第十一章

# 当代中国的行政学研究

1978 年以来，伴随着中国改革开放和现代化建设进程，政府行政体制改革和提高行政效率成为一个迫切需要重视的问题。在思考和解决这一问题中，中国的行政学经历了倡导与恢复、研究与教学、应用与检验的过程，在学科建设、人才培养、社会服务等方面都取得了长足的进步，为中国的政府改革做出了自己的贡献。

## 一 中国行政学的发展历程与特征

### （一）发展历程

中国是一个有着极为丰富的行政管理思想传统的国度。古代中国曾经在行政管理实践领域创造过许多优秀文明成果，如体系完善、特点突出的政府体制、区划体制、监察制度等，特别是形成了体系完备、历史久远、运行发达的文官制度，在考选、铨叙、品阶、薪俸、考绩、监察、迁转、赏罚、致仕，品官与吏胥的划分、限任制与常任制的区分等诸多方面，都有突出的建树。① 中国传统的政治智慧实现了几千年来帝国的延续，维系了治理的周期性效率和稳定。19 世纪末 20 世纪初，在西方国家行政学体系逐渐形成和完善的同时，康有为、梁启超等思想家提出中国也应当研究行政之学问②，此后中国的一些学者开始翻译和引进当时较有影响的论

① 白钢：《中国政治制度通史 01 卷总论》，人民出版社 1996 年版，第 35—76 页。
② 余兴安：《梁启超真的讲过"我国公卿要学习行政学"吗?》，《中国行政管理》2011 年 2 月；毛桂荣：《关于"行政"、"行政学"概念的形成——兼答余兴安先生》，《中国行政管理》 2011 年第 10 期。

著。到 20 世纪 30 年代，国内学者陆续出版、发表了一些专著，如《行政学的理论与实际》《行政学原理》《欧美员吏制度》。当时国内很多大学也逐渐开设行政学课程，设立研究机构，并开始在实践领域影响实际行政过程。

1949 年到 1978 年这段时间，中国政府从国情和历史任务出发，对改善国家行政管理状况做出了积极的探索与努力。但是，由于 1952 年高校院系调整导致了行政学学科的撤销，在相当大程度上影响了我国行政管理实践经验的总结和科学化的进程，影响了公共行政学科的历史积累和发展。20 世纪 80 年代初，中国老一辈的行政学家（夏书章、周世述、黄达强、刘怡昌等）极力呼吁行政学学科的发展和建立。1984 年，国务院办公厅和劳动人事部召开"行政科学研讨会"，论证行政科学研究和教育的重要性，建议筹建中国行政管理学会。1985 年《中国行政管理》（月刊）正式公开出版发行，为行政管理科学研究和行政管理体制改革研究提供了重要的学术阵地。1988 年由国务院办公厅作为主管机关的中国行政管理学会在北京正式成立，标志着改革开放以来中国的行政学恢复建立的倡导和准备工作已经完成，行政学作为一门独立学科在中国得到公认。

在确立学科地位的背景下，专业教育的发展成为行政学发展的"主力"。中国行政学形成了相对独立的教学与科研体系。20 世纪 80 年代中期，中国人民大学、武汉大学、兰州大学、郑州大学、山西大学等开办行政管理专业和院系。1997 年教育部设立公共管理一级学科，以适应市场经济和现代化建设对复合型、应用型的公共管理人才的需求。1998 年之后，部分高校开始培养行政学博士，2001 年开始举办公共管理专业硕士学位（MPA）教育。行政学教育实现了从间接地提供知识到直接向实践工作者培训，从而进入决策和管理的深刻转变，大大缩短了科学研究与实践应用的距离。

与此同时，行政学学科的分化整合与国际化趋势也不断加速。行政学是综合性学科，科际整合特征比较明显。当代公共问题的复杂性，使得任何一个单一学科的知识与理论实不足以解决公共问题，多元科学的研究途径符合复杂世界的本质。行政学作为社会科学的一部分，它的发展本身就与社会发展密切相关，在实践中不断分化和发展。与此同时，中国行政学科的发展始终都是伴随着国际化的步伐并在此过程中得到发展的，中国行政学界十分重视吸收和借鉴外国的经验教训。通过引入跨越国界的对比研究，在更广阔的视野下思考中国的行政实践与改革。因此，行政实践和行政改革的比较研究也得到迅速发展。总之，中国行政学的发展，走势十分清晰，既是中国改革开放的实践需要引发大规模的行政学研究，又有国际行政学发展对我国的积极影响。

## （二）发展特征

政府改革与创新成为行政学发展的"主线"。[①] 中国行政学的发展一方面遵循学科规律，相对独立地构建自身的体系；另一方面则围绕着政府职能改革与管理方式创新进行行政管理理论和实践研究。中国传统上一直是政治权力和行政权力占主导地位的行政国家，要建立市场经济体制，前提就是要取消和减少政府对微观经济活动的干预，面对经济、社会和政治不断发展的新形势，政府体制出现了许多不适应的方面，如政府职能转变不到位、政府直接干预微观经济活动的现象仍然很多、市场监管体制不完善、社会管理体制不健全、公共服务体系薄弱等。政府管理自身也出现了许多问题，如公共服务赤字（公共服务不能满足公民的需要）、财政赤字（主要在地方政府，特别是县以下政府财政赤字）、制度赤字（政府管理的许多方面缺乏制度的保障）、能力赤字（政府能力不能适应社会快速变化的需要）、绩效赤字（官僚主义和效率不彰）、信任赤字（腐败、滥用权力导致的公民对政府信任的降低）。改革政府需要科学的理论作为指导，政府改革与创新直接成为中国行政学发展的推动力，亦成为中国行政学研究的核心主题。从一定意义上说，后者决定了前者的方向和构成，是中国行政学发展的一条"红线""主线"。如何建立与经济社会发展需要相适应的行政管理体制，成为时代对行政学发展的要求。行政学研究者针对涉及政府管理改革和创新的热点、难点问题进行了系列研究和探索，对改革开放条件下政府机构的设置原则、组织架构、运行流程、层级关系、事权划分等重大问题进行深入的研究。

公共行政的职业化是行政学发展的重要推动。公职人员是推动国家建

---

① 高小平：《中国改革开放以来行政管理学研究的进程和成就》，公共管理高层论坛，2010年。

设的基石和发展动力，其素质和能力乃一国施政的成败所在。为适应建立现代化公共行政的需要，中国政府急需一支掌握公共行政专门知识和技能、具有职业精神和伦理的公职人员队伍。20 世纪 80 年代至今，中国公职人员的教育和培训逐步走向经常化、制度化和正规化。特别是中国实施国家公务员制度以后，中国公职人员的发展逐步走向职业化的发展方向。公共行政的职业化，最根本的在于确保公职人员的专业能力与能力胜任。公职人员的大规模、经常化、制度化的教育培训，他们研究和学习公共行政，为公务职务做好准备，同时结合技术与管理训练，提升公职人员的管理能力，都为公共行政学科的发展提供了良好的土壤。

公共领域的问题与危机是行政学发展的内在动力。行政学在本质上是一门如何透过有效的集体行动解决公共问题的科学。改革开放以来，中国社会发生了巨大的变化，取得了举世公认的成就，但在社会经济领域，也出现了诸多问题，面临许多的危机和挑战，最突出的是经济的稳定和可持续发展问题、环境污染和生态危机问题、能源与能源安全问题、社会矛盾和社会稳定问题、粮食和粮食安全问题、公共卫生问题、反贫困与分配不公问题等。当代社会在公共事务领域所遭遇的问题高度复杂，而公共行政与公共政策的知识可以帮助我们解决实际的社会问题，行政学的价值完全系于其解决公共问题的能力。在当今社会，公民对政府解决诸多社会问题寄予更大的期望，并要求其承担更大的责任，这便大大改变了公共行政的本质和角色。正是当代中国社会出现的问题，对行政学的研究取向构成了影响，促使行政学研究者寻找新的解决问题的方式。[1]

## 二  中国行政学的发展成就

### （一）学科建设

在 30 年的发展历程中，公共行政研究社群的自我意识逐步觉醒并不断得到强化。随着改革开放对公共行政的时代需要，公共行政作为一门科学研究的领域，其地位得到了社会科学界的认同和政府的认同。这种自我

---

[1]  张成福：《变革时代的中国公共行政学：发展与前景》，《中国行政管理》2008 年第 9 期。

意识觉醒产生的一个结果便是学科发展趋于自主性，趋于专门化，公共行政逐渐从政治学科和其他学科中分离出来，拥有了合法的身份。一是教育主管行政部门对学科地位的认同和确认；二是公共行政现代化对公共行政专业人才的需要以及公共管理专业学位的推动；三是高等院校扩展和发展新专业的冲动。学院化和专业迅速发展，公共行政的社会地位不断提高，影响不断扩大，行政理论和知识得到广泛传播，培养了一大批公共行政管理的专门人才，促进了学科的研究和发展。

目前，中国行政学形成了比较完整的学科框架。公共管理、行政领导、行政生态分析、公共部门人力资源管理、公共经济研究以及制度分析等次级分支研究纷纷发展起来；同时，专门的行政研究领域如市政学、教育行政、卫生行政、交通行政、工商行政等也逐步拓展。公共行政研究领域不断拓展和深化，专业性研究逐步强化。中国公共行政研究在宏观、中观以及微观层面都有更大的拓展。从宏观研究方面，公共行政的研究逐步拓展到研究政府与市场、政府与社会、政府与企业、政府间关系等领域。在中观层面上，更加关注公共政策的制定、执行与评估问题以及具体公共事务领域的政策与管理问题（如公共卫生政策与管理、环境政策与管理、土地资源政策与管理、教育政策与管理、能源政策与管理等）。在微观层面上，研究的核心更加关注政府内部体系的科学管理问题（如公共组织的管理、公共部门的人力资源管理、公共财政与预算的管理、公共部门绩效的管理、公共部门的战略管理等）。研究领域的不断拓展，使得中国的公共行政研究更趋于符合中国的行政现实，更趋于以解决公共问题为导向，更趋于运用多学科的知识研究行政问题。行政学与相关学科的交叉融合增多，开始更多地与经济学、管理学、法学等相关学科的研究结合起来，互相借鉴与渗透。政治学、心理学、法律学、经济学、管理科学、统计学、历史学等相关的知识，为公共行政学的研究提供了诸多专门领域的知识来源。

### （二）人才培养

中国行政学注重应用多样灵活的人才培养方式。1994 年 9 月，国家行政学院正式成立，成为国务院直接领导的培养公务员的高级学府，全国各地、各级政府都成立了行政学院。截至目前，全国已有近千所高校设有行政管理、公共事业管理、公共管理本科专业，200 多所高校开设 MPA 硕士点，超过 50 所高校可以培养行政学专业的博士。① 这些行政学团体和教学、研究机构的建立，形成了一支强大的行政学研究、教学和实践三者相结合的队伍，为社会培养了大批行政学人才。

行政学教学强调理论素养与实践经验的结合。为了能面向政府、面向社会培养行政管理应用型专门人才，高等学校行政学科在建立教学队伍时坚持引进来和走出去相结合的策略，积极促进从事行政学理论研究和教学的队伍与实际行政管理人员之间的交流互动。聘请实际行政部门中既有丰富实践经验又有理论素养的行政人员到高校授课；与此同时，让高等学校中的科研人员和教师走出去，到政府部门挂职或兼职，取得实际的锻炼和工作经验。课程建设方面，强调基础知识与实用技能并重。行政学课程以适应转型时期的现代化管理需求为出发点，综合设置了政治学、管理学、公共政策分析、法学、基本技能训练等方面的基础课程。为了提高学生的实践综合能力，使行政学专业的学生更能适应社会发展，课程的设置还增加了行政绩效评估技术、公共政策分析技术、公共预算和部门预算编制技术、政府部门会计技术、政府部门审计技术以及政府公关形象设计新技术等技术性课程。在教材建设方面，强调学术性与应用性相结合。根据新的形势和社会发展需要，组织编写了行政学重点课程教材，教材更新及时，知识内容根据实际社会发展不断完善。教材在注重行政学理论的同时融入实际操作的技术，实用且可读性强，实现了理论与实践紧密结合，学术性与现实应用性有机统一，能够有效地服务于行政学的教育教学以及人们的自学。

行政学教育采用课堂教育和社会教育相结合的方式，培养兼具理论知识和实务经验的行政管理人才。通过教学、科研机构与实际部门合作共同培养的方式，提升学生的专业理论知识与实际操作技能。此外，高校还与政府合作给学生创造深入基层单位进行挂职实践和顶岗学习的机会。使学生走出校门，广泛地接触社会生活，将所学的理论知识应用于解决实际问题上，积累实务经验，加深学生对中国特色的政治和行政实际的认识。通

---

① 娄成武：《我国当前公共管理学科发展的若干问题探讨》，《中国大学教学》2010 年第 5 期。

过科学的人才培养体系，每年都向政府和社会的各个领域输出了大批专业人才。

### （三）国际交流

随着全球化的发展，中国的行政学也在不断走向国际化，与国际的交流不断发展和加深。

第一，组织翻译国外的行政学经典著作。在中国行政学学科创建和理论研究的初期，国际交流更多地集中在引进、学习国外行政学的先进理论和实践知识上。中国人民大学、北京大学、清华大学、中山大学等学术研究机构组织翻译了公共行政领域众多国外经典与教材，如中国人民大学出版社出版的《公共行政与公共管理经典译丛》、国家行政学院出版社出版的《西方行政改革系列丛书》、商务印书馆出版的《中外政治制度比较丛书》等。这些翻译著作的出版将国外行政学理论与实践发展最新动态展现给国内，推动了国内行政学科的发展。

第二，举办国际性的学术研讨会。从 1984 年开始，我国政府和学界承办了多次大型国际公共行政研讨会（如 1984 年联合国文官制度改革研讨会、1991 年东部地区行政组织第 14 次大会、1995 年世界反贪大会、1996 年国际行政学会第三届国际大会等）。进入 21 世纪之后，随着中国行政学的日益发展，国际交流日益增加，中国行政管理学会、中国人民大学和美国行政管理学会、美国罗格斯大学以及电子科技大学联合举办了 8 届中美公共管理研讨会和 11 届公共管理国际研讨会，在国际行政学界产生了广泛的影响。中国的著名高校如复旦大学、中山大学也纷纷举办各种专题的国际会议，这些研讨会的主题涉及当代公共行政面临的许多重大问题，推动了中国行政学的国际学术交流。

第三，学者之间的交流和国际合作研究。中国行政学界每年均向国外派遣交流学者、留学生以学习国外最新的行政学理论与实践经验。与此同时，国外许多著名的公共行政学者到国内进行定期或不定期的学术交流活动，交流最新行政学研究成果和探讨学科发展。国内的大学、研究机构、学者经常与国际机构（如联合国计划开发署、世界银行、亚洲开发银行）在共同关心的许多议题领域（如政府改革、环境管理、治理与发展、公共服务等）开展共同研究。

### （四）中国行政学的贡献

中国行政学经过几十年的研究和探索，取得了长足的进步，为我国的社会科学发展、学术研究、人才培养和推进行政改革做出了重要贡献。

第一，行政学为政府改革提供了强大智力支持。中国从中央政府（国务院）到地方政府将行政学的理论研究和应用放到推进行政管理体制改革以及提高政府效能、执行力和公信力的重要位置，政府积极实施科学行政、民主行政、依法行政，将公务员的行政管理实践与理论学习、学术研究结合起来，并在政府机关或事业单位中设立行政管理研究机构，加强行政管理研究。政府从加强指导、安排任务、沟通信息、物质支持等方面给行政学研究创造条件，支持研究机构和社会团体的研究工作，把这种研究机构和社团组织当作政府改进行政管理的"参谋"，在制订改革方案、实施改革进程中主动听取他们的意见和建议，作为决策的重要力量，联系社会、团结专家学者的"桥梁"，充分发挥作用。行政学界对行政管理体制改革中热点、重点和难点问题，特别是涉及全局性、战略性、前瞻性的重大课题进行研究，大批的行政学专家开展了科学化的政策研究和管理咨询。几十年来，围绕着政府管理和改革中的许多重大理论和现实问题，如政府职能转变、机构改革、人事制度改革、公共财政改革、公共服务体制与机制改革、政策制定的民主化与科学化、公共危机管理、环境保护体制改革、公共医疗体制改革、反腐败等，公共行政学者皆提供了诸多有价值的政策建议。这些研究成果，使行政管理研究机构成为政府的重要"智库"。[①]

第二，中国行政学促进了中国行政人员素质和能力的提升。在中国行政学发展的历程中，行政学者展现了一种强烈的公共责任感，这主要表现在：一是公民教育。在大学向大学生们传授了中国政府管理的理念、体制、机制和公共政策方面的知识，使他们了解中国的行政现实，理解自己作为一名公民的权利、义务和责任；二是为公共机构和官员提供教育和培训。无论是大学的公共行政院系，还是专门的行政官员的教育培训机构

---

① 高小平：《中国改革开放以来行政管理学研究的进程和成就》，公共管理高层论坛，2010年。

（如国家和地方行政学院、党校），公共行政知识的传授均占有相当重要的地位。公共行政知识的传授使官员了解如何更加明智地做出选择，如何更有效率地工作，如何以更负责任的精神为公众服务。这种专业培训随着MPA教育的发展而尤为突出。1999年年底全国541万公务员中，大专以上文化程度的只有52%左右，即使受过高等教育的多是单一的专业教育，现代行政管理知识以及财税、金融、法律知识及宏观决策能力普遍薄弱。中国行政学界在政府支持下，2001年开始进行公共管理硕士专业学位教育。MPA教育以公务员为主要培养对象，招生时必须保障80%以上的学生是公务员。截至2015年，MPA培养院校从24所发展到223所，招生规模从3506人扩大到128363人①，MPA教育迅速发展，有效地促进了公共管理队伍结构的良性调整，提高了公共管理队伍尤其是公务员队伍的学历层次和基本素养。MPA研究生将公共管理的最新研究成果引入中国公共治理的实践，对提升中国公共管理的质量起了非常重要的作用。不仅如此，MPA教育提倡的公共精神、公共关怀等理念，以及学术讨论、社会实践等活动，对公共管理变革也起到重要的推动作用。

第三，行政学成为中国社会科学和世界行政学体系中一个具有自身特色的学科。中国的行政学专业性研究逐步强化，分化出了如公共管理、公共政策、行政领导、决策科学、公共部门人力资源管理、行政心理学、公共经济研究以及制度分析等次级分支研究，同时，专门的行政研究领域如市政学、教育行政、卫生行政、交通行政、工商行政等也逐步成长起来。中国行政学结合中国现实，提出了符合中国国情的行政学理论，建立起了适用中国行政实践与改革的知识体系，为中国的行政实践与改革赢得了一定的国际话语权。社会对公共行政学的研究寄予很高的期望，公共行政领域的学者也有信心能够帮助解决这些问题，他们怀有强烈的使命感去分析和研究走向现代化政府过程中遇到的种种障碍，梳理中国公共行政的历史和现实，力图正确地阐述与解释它，从而提出建设性的对策与建议。②

---

① 周建国、陈谦：《中国MPA教育中长期发展的困境与出路》，《中国行政管理》2015年第11期。

② 张成福：《变革时代的中国公共行政学：发展与前景》，《中国行政管理》2008年第9期。

第四，中国行政学的国际贡献。随着中国行政学与国际行政学之间的交流沟通日益增加，中国行政学的影响力也越来越大。中国行政学界牵头成立了亚洲地区公共行政网络（AGPA），其宗旨是通过举办学术交流活动吸引和集聚亚洲地区在公共行政领域的机构和组织共同推动亚洲行政科学的发展。通过在亚洲范围内开展比较研究，发展公共行政理论，从而为亚洲的实践者、学者和公务员搭建了交流平台。2009 年，国际行政科学评论中文版开始在中国出版，国际行政科学评论是国际行政学会的官方刊物，是反映国际公共行政实践与理论发展的重要载体，在国际公共行政科学领域具有权威地位和影响。中国的行政改革实践也吸引着世界各地的行政学者，他们越来越关注中国。比如 2016 年中国行政管理学会、中国人民大学等合作举办的第八届中美公共管理国际研讨会，就有来自数十个国家的几百位学者参加。中国学者也越来越多走上国际行政学界，介绍中国的实践和经验。国际行政科学学会、美国行政管理学会每年的年会上，都能听到很多中国学者的声音。与此同时，国家行政学院、北京大学、清华大学等机构还为来自亚洲、非洲、拉美、中东欧等地区的各级公务人员开展了各类培训，为他们介绍中国的改革经验和发展成就。

# 三　中国行政学的研究内容

随着中国全方位改革的启动，中国行政学努力把中国行政改革现实问题作为研究和关注的重点，着重研究中国行政的规律和特点，有力地推动和促进了行政改革的步伐。同时，学者们结合中国实际做出了许多独立思考和探索，取得了大量独创性的成果。总体来看，中国行政学研究领域较为广泛，主要的研究内容如下。

## （一）行政学基础理论研究

一是行政哲学研究。中国的行政哲学研究有丰富的思想渊源，可以从中国历代的治国理政实践与思想体系中吸收精华。中国行政学界对行政管理方法创新、行政文化、行政伦理、公共性、行政战略、行政发展等问题进行了深入的探讨，研究的内容既具有很强的外张力，又具有一定的内聚力。行政哲学研究主题阶梯推进，构筑了行政哲学的理论基础和核心范畴。理论求索与现实追问相互结合、相互观照，为研究行政管理体制改革和创新中的深层次问题提供了哲学支撑。

二是服务型政府的研究。服务型政府是中国行政学界重要的理论成果，并对中国政府实践产生了深刻的影响。中国学者梳理了政府行政模式的历史演变，即从近代以前的"统治行政"向近代的"管理行政"再向现代的"服务行政"转变，这是统治和管理、管理和服务此消彼长的动态变化过程。从服务行政的角度，政府职能在于提供公共服务，纠正市场失灵，提供公共产品，创造安全、民主、平等的制度环境，处理社会面临的公共问题，促进社会健康发展。政府购买公共服务是服务型政府建设的重点，政府购买公共服务需要解决法规制度、服务标准、工作机制、社会组织、督察评估等方面问题。树立科学合理的公共服务质量评价标准，则是其中的基础性环节。

三是现代治理研究。中国政府提出要"推进国家治理体系和治理能力现代化"，这也是中国行政学界重要的研究课题，行政学研究者们围绕这一主题展开了大量的研究工作。国家治理体系是国家实施国家治理目标的基本制度体系。国家治理制度和治理能力的现代化，即治理制度和治理能力作为现代政治要素，不断地、连续地发生由低级到高级的突破性变革的过程。在此过程中，国家治理体系更加完备、更加成熟、更加定型，包括一整套政治的、经济的、社会的、文化的、生态环境的治理体系；同时在这一治理体系下，治理能力的运用能够更加有效、更加透明、更加公平，这包括各种政治的、经济的、社会的、文化的、生态环境的、科技的、信息的现代化手段。

### （二）行政改革研究

一是行政体制改革。行政体制改革是行政改革的重要内容。改革开放以来，中国政府相继进行的七轮大规模体制改革引起中国行政学界的广泛讨论。我国行政体制改革的制度基础在于社会主义市场经济体制的建立以及中国与世界在一系列制度平台上所建立起来的开放与合作关系。改革的核心是适应经济和社会发展的需要，按照经济与社会发展的规律来调整政府机构的结构与运行，重点调整政府与社会、政府与市场、中央与地方的关系。行政学关于政府机构改革的研究主要关注的议题是：如何通过由全能政府向有限政府、管制政府向服务政府的转型来调整政府与社会的关系；如何通过政府体制改革来调整政府与市场、政府与企业的关系；如何通过政府的向下分权来调整中央与地方的关系，以解决集权与分权的问题。

二是政府职能转变。行政改革另一个重要内容是政府职能转变。行政学的学者们就推进政府职能根本转型亟须解决的若干深层问题进行研究，这些研究主要着眼于政府、市场、社会，诸如三者之间究竟是什么关系、政府究竟应当推进怎样权力清单制度体系、地方政府应该保持哪种改革动力、如何避免行政审批陷入外延式数字游戏、如何保证改革不再沉入碎片化的低效循环中、如何使各类非政府组织和社会主体以及基层具备承接能力等。针对这些问题学者们在研究中认为要对政府与市场、社会之间，央地政府之间的关系做出明确系统的理论界说；建立健全标准统一的政府权力清单体系；增强各级地方政府主导改革的内在动力；深化行政审批制度改革必须注重内涵式推进；正确确定政府转移给市场和社会的职能的管理属性，明确市场监管维度、强化事中事后监管；在全国一盘棋中协同推进各地各级政府改革；培育基层政府、市场和社会主体的接收能力；切实加强政府事中管理事后监管；为改革提供合法性保障；同时，聚焦于组织结构、政府流程优化，尝试梳理政府内部不同层级和不同部门之间的关系，实现政府体系内部的有机整合与协同，进而改进政府职能履行方式。当前，特别要注重简政放权、放管结合、优化服务。

三是依法行政和廉洁政府建设。建设法治政府和廉洁政府是中国政府行政改革的战略目标，也是行政学界研究的重点。建立法治政府的核心是推进依法行政，行政学界对依法行政的关注主要在确保各类行政主体依法从事行政管理行为，严格履行法定职责；提供高效的行政管理活动和优质的公共服务，确保行政人员的积极性与主动性，以较低的成本获取较好的服务效益，各级行政主体及其工作人员享有的行政职权和行政职责、行政责任承担呈现出完整、均衡的状态。行政学界提出了廉洁政府的衡量标准：政府官员廉洁奉公；政府机关和公共部门等法人单位奉公守法；公共权力和公共资源的获取和运用无私且合法；司法、执法公正无私；法律、政策无私为民。建设廉洁政府需要建立分权制衡的权力运行机制，促进政府管理现代化，建立完备、周密的反腐败法律体系和坚强有力的反腐败执法机构，建设一个强大而活跃的公民社会。

### （三）政府管理创新研究

政府管理方式创新是行政学关注的一个重要领域，政府管理创新是政府发展永恒的主题，也是行政学研究永恒的主题。当代行政学在这一领域研究的主要问题有以下几个：

一是提高政府公开性和透明度。在行政学界和其他学科专家推动下，中国的政府信息公开立法取得重要进展，公开机制日趋健全，范围不断扩大，保障了人民群众的知情权、参与权、监督权。提高公开性可以促进政府的科学民主决策机制建设，如建立公众参与、专家论证和政府决策相结合的决策机制。当前，还特别关注大数据时代的政府改革与创新，大数据科技的运用不仅使得行政管理精准化程度得到提升，而且数据的开放性将分析和使用数据的权利给予民众，使得"数据民主"成为可能。同时，"移动政府"也为提高政府工作提供了一个高效、全方位的公共服务新平台。①

二是如何构建政府应急管理体系。当代中国正处于深刻的社会转型之中，呈现出了风险社会的许多特征，日益频发的公共危机事件严重威胁着社会的安宁与稳定。近年来，公共危机治理问题研究一直是学者们关注的热点，行政学界及时关注和回应社会风险，推动政府初步建立了分级响应、属地管理、信息共享、分工协作的应急体系。提出了完善公共危机管理机制，提高公共安全危机应对能力的很多建议，比如公共危机的舆情管理等。

三是提高政府的执行力和公信力。中国的行政学研究讨论了提高政府执行力和公信力的主要工具。1. 绩效管理方法，政府的整体绩效问题开始受到越来越多的关注。一些地方政府及部门开始对政府绩效评估进行积极的探索，在强化责任、改进服务、提高效能、深化公开、完善奖惩、推动落实等方面起到了积极作用。2. 通过督察进行反馈控制。政府督察部门要通过开展督促检查，获取信息，发现政府执行中的问题并及时修正，达到管理控制的目的。强有力的督促检查工作，对促进政府执行事项的落

---

① 许开轶：《2015 年中国行政学研究综述》，《云南行政学院学报》2016 年第 1 期。

实有较大作用。3. 组织文化建设。倡导政府执行力文化，形成"立即反应、立即行动"的政府执行文化，把提高执行力作为考核政府机关、政府官员和公务员最基本的标准，培育以"马上就办"理念为核心的政府执行文化。4. 流程再造。不少地方政府推进以政府公共需求为导向的政府流程再造，优化审批流程，理顺工作关系，解决职能交叉，改进技术手段，从而压缩政府层级，简化行政程序，实现流程的跨部门化和集约化管理，提高行政效率和政府执行力。5. 推进政府质量管理。将质量管理的基本理念、工作原则、运筹方式运用于行政管理之中，以全员参与为基础，强调政府内部个人与个人、部门与部门、个人与部门之间的相互协调与合作，将其他个人或部门作为自己服务的顾客，建立充满活力的政府组织，从而为公众提供高质量的公共产品和公共服务。

## 参考文献

[1] 白钢：《中国政治制度通史》第 1 卷总论，人民出版社 1996 年版。

[2] 余兴安：《梁启超真的讲过"我国公卿要学习行政学"吗?》，《中国行政管理》2011 年第 2 期。

[3] 毛桂荣：《关于"行政"、"行政学"概念的形成——兼答余兴安先生》，《中国行政管理》2011 年第 10 期。

[4] 高小平：《中国改革开放以来行政管理学研究的进程和成就》，公共管理高层论坛，2010 年。

[5] 张成福：《变革时代的中国公共行政学：发展与前景》，《中国行政管理》2008 年第 9 期。

[6] 娄成武：《我国当前公共管理学科发展的若干问题探讨》，《中国大学教学》2010 年第 5 期。

[7] 周志忍：《迈向国际化和本土化的有机统一：中国行政学发展 30 年的回顾与前瞻》，《公共行政评论》2012 年第 1 期。

[8] 刘鹏：《中国公共行政学：反思背景下的本土化路径研究》，《中国人民大学学报》2013 年第 3 期。

[9] 何艳玲：《我们在做什么样的研究：中国行政学研究评述》，《公共管理研究》2007 年。

[10] 刘熙瑞：《服务型政府——经济全球化背景下中国政府改革的目标选择》，《中国行政管理》2002 年第 7 期。

［11］迟福林：《全面理解"公共服务型政府"的基本涵义》，《人民论坛》2006 年第
　　　5 期。

［12］中国行政管理学会课题组：《服务型政府的定义和内涵》，《理论参考》2006 年
　　　第 6 期。

［13］杰伊・D. 怀特：《使多样性有意义：公共行政研究、理论和知识发展的背景》，
　　　《公共行政研究：对理论与实践的反思》，清华大学出版社 2005 年版。

［14］何颖：《公共行政研究方法及其走向评价》，《中国行政管理》2005 年第 10 期。

（作者：刘杰　中国行政管理学会联络部副主任、副研究员）

# Administrative Reform in Contemporary China

Organized and Edited by Chinese Academy of Personnel Science

# Preface

The 2016IIAS-IASIA Joint Congress ( hereinafter referred to as Joint Congress) was held in Chengdu from September 19 to 23, 2016. The Congress was co-hosted by the Ministry of Human Resources and Social Security of People's Republic of China and Chinese Academy of Governance, and organized by Chinese Academy of Personnel Science, Sichuan University and Chengdu Municipal Government, with Chinese Public Administration Society, China Society of Administrative Reform and China Society for Public Sector Reform as supporting organizations.

The Joint Congress is one of the highest-level and most influential international academic conferences in the field of administrative science, attracting more than 500 experts, scholars and government officials from over 50 countries and regions. The attendees exchanged views and discussed broadly on the theme of "Building Capacity for Sustainable Development" . During the Congress, dozens of special panels were held, including Intercontinental Administrative Forum, Host Country Panel, BRICS Panel, UN Panel and OECD Panel. All of these produced excellent academic outcomes.

As the main organizer of the Congress and the Vice-President member of IIAS, Chinese Academy of Personnel Science invited a number of Chinese scholars to consult during the preparation. It was agreed that on the one hand, we needed to encourage Chinese scholars to participate in the Congress and have their own voice heard on the issues with common concerns in the area of international administrative science; on the other hand, we also needed to show the achievements of administrative reform in China and introduce our experiences to international counterparts. Hence comes the idea of compiling this book, *Administrative Reform in Contemporary China* and the following writing and editing works.

The book aims at comprehensively expounding on the development course, main measures, practical results and basic experience of administrative reform in China since the Reform and Opening-up, especially in recent years. Topics covered in this book include reform of governmental agencies, transformation of government functions, reform of administrative review and approval system, innovation of social governance, government affairs disclosure, e-governance, reform of public service units, reform of public fiscal system, reform of the human resources system, government performance management, administrative accountability and advancing law-based administration. Progresses in administrative science research during the last three decades are also reviewed and summarized in the book. After the Chinese version of the book was completed, we had professionals to translate it into English. We also had both Chinese and English versions issued for distribution during the Joint Congress.

Experts from Chinese Academy of Governance, Chinese Public Administration Society, China Society of Administrative Reform, China Society for Public Sector Reform and Chinese Academy of Personnel Science contributed to the writing of the book. Among them are distinguished professors, such as Liqun Wei, President of China Society of Administrative Reform, senior experts in this field, as well as young scholars. The authors of this book are Liqun Wei, Liping Li, Feng Chen, Lili Yi, Weibin Gong, Qiaobin Feng, Xueming Li, Xianzhi Hu, Wenzheng Wu, Xiaokang Liu, Yanhong Yin, Jianmiao Hu, Yan Hua, Jie Liu, in the order of chapters. (The authors' organizations, positions and professional titles are stated at the end of each chapter, hence not include here.)

Xing'an Yu, President of Chinese Academy of Personnel Science and Secretary-general of the Organizing Committee of the Joint Congress, presided over the writing and editing of the book, including the outline and style of the book and review of the manuscript. Senior experts in the field of administrative science, such as Xiaoping Gao, Jingjun Shao and Jie Gu also participated in the discussion of manuscript revising. Jiang Wu, member of the National Committee of CPPCC and former President of Chinese Academy of Personnel Science provided advice for the writing and editing works. Xuezhi Liu, Ying Xiong, Lina Qiao, Yi Wang, Tianchun He and Yuejun Guo from Chinese Academy of Personnel Science assisted the editor-in-chief in organizing, liaison and proofreading work.

Undoubtedly, administrative reform in China in the last three decades can be seen as one of the most magnificent pictures in the development of contemporary administrative science in the world. This book provides a panoramic view of such picture. We did further revision after it was submitted as conference materials for the Joint Congress in last September. Now the book is officially published to provide a reference for readers, as well as for broader criticism and advice.

Xing'an Yu

President, Chinese Academy of Personnel Science

April, 2076

# Contents

# Chapter Ⅰ

# Basic Course and Essential Experiences of Administrative Reform in China

Administrative reform is an important component of political reform and and development in China, which includes evolution of administrative power structure, adjustment of administrative organization, improvement of administrative management system, innovation of administrative instruments, and so on. Over the past four decades since China adopted the policy of reform and opening up, administrative reform has made significant progress. Reviewing the great course and valuable experiences of administrative reform in China and discussing the key issues to be addressed in the next-step reform will have great significance for understanding the great achievements of the reform and opening up, keeping on deepening administrative reform, and promoting the Four-Pronged Comprehensive Strategy. ①

## 1.1 Background of Administrative Reform in China

Administrative system is an important part of national political superstructure. It is determined by the social and economic system and the development level of a country. Therefore, the development of administrative

---

① In 2014, the Chinese Communist Party and the Chinese government developed the Four-Pronged Comprehensive Strategy, which includes finishing building a moderately prosperous society; deepening reform; advancing the law-based governance of China; and strengthening Party self-discipline.

reform in China cannot be separated from the specific administrative traditions of China, the deepening of economic and social reform, and the development of international theory and practice on public administration.

### 1.1.1 Tradition of Chinese public administration and changes in administrative system before the reform

On October 1, 1949, the People's Republic of China was founded. The establishment of a socialist system in China has created the conditions for exploring the establishment of a new administrative management system. In 1951, the Central People's Government Administration Council issued *Decision on the Adjustment of Organizations and Reducing Staff (Draft)*, and conducted streamlining administration work for the first time after the founding of new China. In 1954, the First National People's Congress promulgated the first *Constitution*, selected the President and established the State Council, forming the basic administrative framework of the new China. From the end of 1954, it took more than one year to carry out a larger-scale simplification on the central and local authorities at all levels. In 1956, the relation between the central and local authorities was adjusted again. The national system conference held that year proposed that: the first step in the improvement of national administrative system was to firstly divide the administrative functions and powers of the central government and provinces, autonomous regions and municipalities directly under the central government and expand the administrative rights of the local authority appropriately, and then gradually divide the administrative functions and powers of province and county, county and township. This reform continued until 1960. In the early 1960s, in order to meet the needs of the national economic adjustment, the "simplifying and concentrating" administrative system reform was carried out. In general, after the founding of new China, the construction of China's administrative system has made significant progress: firstly, an administrative mode conforming to the requirements of socialist country nature was initially constructed; secondly, an administrative system adapted to the planned economic system was created; and thirdly, the experience in both positive and negative aspects of Chinese administrative system construction was accumulated. It can be said that although there were many twists and turns in the development course of administrative system in this historical period, the relation between the central and local authorities was explored, streamlined administration was implemented, government institutions were adjusted, the basic framework of a socialist administrative system was established and economic and social development was promoted. The construction of administrative system in this historical period provided a basic premise and important reference for the reform of administrative system after the reform and opening up, of which the most fundamental lesson was not to go beyond the economic and social development level and the corresponding objective conditions but to focus on adapting to the needs of productivity development and to steadily adjust and change, based on national conditions and actual situations.

## 1.1.2  Sustained and rapid economic and social development and deepening of reform and opening up

Since 1978, China has opened the prelude to the great reform and opening up. From countryside to city and from economic field to other fields, the process of a comprehensive reform was carried out. From opening up domestically to opening to the outside world, from coast to the areas along rivers and borders, and from East China to the central and western parts, the process of opening up surged forward with great momentum. Such an unprecedented reform and opening up greatly stimulated the enthusiasm of hundreds of millions of people, immensely liberated and developed the social productivity and promoted the overall progress of the society. As a result, China successfully achieved its great historic turn from a highly centralized planned economy to a vitalized socialist market economy, and from a closed and semi-closed state to an overall opening state. The image of Chinese people, the image of socialist China and the image of the Communist Party of China have undergone historic changes. China's comprehensive national strength has been greatly improved and its international status and influence been significantly promoted. Even more significant was the sustained and rapid economic development, which remained at a rate rarely seen in the world. Chinese economy has grown from the brink of collapse to rank No. 2 in the world and people's standard of living developed from the lack of food and clothing to a comprehensive well-off level, all of which have made great contributions to the development of the world economy and the progress of human civilization. Sustained and rapid economic and social development and deepening of reform and opening up have provided impetus and fundamental support for the administrative reform in China.

### 1. 1. 3  Theory and practice of international administrative reform

Since the 1970s, with the changes of international situation, the theory and practice of international administrative reform has made positive progresses, with government administrative reform theories represented by new public management movement, public choice theory and governance theory emerging successively, and achieving great success in practices in the United States, Britain, France, Australia, New Zealand and other countries. The main contents and measures of the theory and practice of international administrative reform include the following four aspects. First is the optimization of government functions. Redefining government functions is one of the key points of government reform in contemporary western developed market economies. In view of new public management movement, government is free from a large number of social matters and delegates or returns such functions to the society (borne by social and economic organizations or intermediary organizations), while only responsible for formulating, supervising and executing the laws and regulations. Second is the marketization and socialization of public service. Government takes full advantage of the power of market and society to promote the marketization and socialization of public service. Third is decentralization. One of the goals of administrative reform in contemporary western countries is to decentralize government management functions and to narrow government administration scope. Therefore, it is necessary to implement decentralization and devolution of administrative power to lower levels. Fourth is the introduction of modern management technology. Modern management technologies, especially the management technology of private sectors, are introduced for "Reinventing government" so as to realize the modernization of government management and to establish a "Marketization" and "Entrepreneurial" government. The theory and practice of administrative reform in China are made on the basis of the theory and practice of the latest international administrative reform. Due to political, historical, cultural and other reasons, the reform paths of administrative system between countries may be different and we cannot indiscriminately imitate international administrative reform modes, however, the theory and practice of international administrative reform has positive enlightenment significance for China to broaden horizons and open ideas. In fact, the administrative reform in China is exploring and deepening constantly based on beneficial theories and practices of international administrative reform, and has developed a road of administrative reform with Chinese characteristics.

## 1.2  Course of Administrative Reform in China

The Third Plenary Session of the 11th Central Committee of the Communist Party of China (CPC) was convened at the end of 1978, opening a new era of China's reform and opening up and socialist modernization construction. The great reform and opening up of the past 40 years had successfully realized historical turnings from highly centralized planned economic system to vitalized socialist market economic system and from a closed and semi-closed state to an all-round opening state, which led to world well-known achievements in economic and social development. In this process, in accordance with the overall goal of building socialism with Chinese characteristics and the fundamental requirements of establishing a superstructure adapting to economic basis and of liberating and developing productivity, unremittingly advancing administrative reform and the new breakthroughs and significant progresses had been reforming and improving the socialist administrative system with Chinese characteristics. In general, the administrative system reform in this period had experienced three stages:

### 1.2.1 Breaking the shackles of highly centralized planned economic system (1978 – 1992)

From the Third Plenary Session of the 11th Central Committee of the Communist Party of China (CPC) to the Fourteenth National Congress of the Chinese Communist Party, the main mission was to break through the highly centralized planned economic system and administrative mode, and to explore a socialist administrative system with Chinese characteristics. In this stage, from 1982 to 1988, two centralized administrative system reforms were implemented. In 1982, the key-points of institutional reform by the State Council were to adapt to the shift of work focuses, improve the efficiency of government work, and streamline and adjust organizations. After the completion of the reform at central level, the local institutional reform was carried out and the focuses were to streamline the bloated body, overcome the bureaucracy and improve work efficiency. In 1988, a new round of administrative system reform was implemented. The task of this reform was to further transform the functions, straighten out the relationship, streamline the institutions and personnel, and improve the administrative efficiency. This reform put forward for the first time that the focuses were to grasp functional transformation and closely merge with economic system reform; and merge and reduce specialized management departments and professional institutions within the comprehensive departments in accordance with the requirements of economic system reform and the separation of government and enterprises; to appropriately strengthen the decision-making consultation and the regulation, supervision, audit, information departments, change the working mode of comprehensive departments and improve the government capability of controlling macro economy in accordance with the scientificity and integrality of organizational establishment; to implement the principle of simplification, unification and effectiveness, clear up and rectify the administrative companies, revoke the organizations established for individual affairs, and cut the bloated departments and personnel; to suggest using legal means to control the organization establishment and the size of personnel force in order to consolidate the results of institutional reform and make the administration up to a legalized road; and to implement the work of "Three Determinations" for the first time, namely, the determination of functions, determination of institutions and determination of establishment. As a whole, through this stage of reform, china had initially gotten rid of the fetter of administrative mode adapting to highly centralized planned economic system, stimulated its economic and social vitality and promoted the liberation and development of productivity.

### 1.2.2  Adapting to the socialist market economic system ( 1993 – 2012 )

From the Fourteenth National Congress of the Chinese Communist Party to the Eighteenth National Congress of the Chinese Communist Party, the main task was to promote the reform comprehensively in accordance with the requirements of developing a socialist market economy, and the reform of socialist administrative system with Chinese characteristics had made significant progress. From 1993 to 1998 in this stage, two centralized administrative system reforms were implemented.

In 1993, the main contents of institutional reform by the State Council were as follows: the first was to transform the functions and adhere to the separation of government and enterprises, which required to decentralize the power to enterprises, let enterprises deal with their own issues, and reduce the concrete approval items and the direct management to enterprises. The second was to straighten out the relationship. One was to straighten out the relations between the State Council departments, especially between the integrated economic sectors and between integrated economic sector and professional economic sector, reasonably divide the duty and authority to avoid the crosscutting and overlapping. The other was to straighten out the relation between the central and the local, and reasonably divide the administration authorities to make the local governments develop local economy and various social undertakings according to local conditions under the guidance of the central guidelines and polices. The third was to streamline the institutional establishment. Since 1993, the local institutional reform was carried out all over China. Taking the transformation of government functions as the key, the reform had greatly streamlined the institutions and personnel, especially the specialized economic management departments.

In 1998, a most profound administrative reform was carried out. The main contents of the reform included: one was to adjust the functions of departments. According to the principle of *integration of power and responsibility*, more than 100 functions were transferred between departments and the same or similar functions were transmitted to and undertaken by one department as far as possible, which greatly improved the problems that had existed for a long time but not been solved, such as functional crosscutting, multi-body management, inconsistent policies, and unclear powers and responsibilities. The other was to streamline the organizational establishment. The main task was to greatly streamline the central industrial and economic departments and then take the corresponding reform in provincial, municipal, county and township institutions.

Since the Sixteenth National Congress of the Chinese Communist Party in 2002, the main task of administrative reform was to promote the construction of a service-oriented and law-based government, and deepen the reform of socialist administrative system with Chinese characteristics in all-round way. The key was to build the architecture and mechanisms conducive to the promotion of scientific development and social harmony, and to focus on the innovations of institutional mechanisms and management instruments. It mainly included: to pay more attention to people-oriented development and to promote an overall, coordinated and sustainable economic and social development and a people's all-round development; to pay more attention to the development of socialist democratic politics, the vigorous promotion of scientific and democratic decision-making, the improvement of decision-making information and intellectual support system, and the enhancement of decision-making transparency and public participation; to pay more attention to the transformation and full implementation of government functions, the strengthening of social management and public service functions, the acceleration of social construction focusing on the improvement of people's livelihood and public services, and the enhancement of social creation vigor; to pay more attention to regulating government behaviors, comprehensively promoting administration according to law, and accelerating the construction of a law-based government; to pay more attention to the improvement of management methods, the vigorous promotion of openness in government affairs and e-government, and the implementation of administrative performance management system.

The 2nd Plenary Session of the 17th CPC Central Committee put forward the goal of establishing a socialist administrative system with Chinese characteristics by 2020. Since 2008, the administrative reform in China has made a new breakthrough. The positive progress in functional transformation, the important breakthrough in departmental relations and the new steps explored in the implementation of giant department system had intensively solved 70 more problems of crosscutting responsibilities and relationships in macroeconomic control, resources and environment, market supervision, culture and health and so on.

### 1.2.3 Promoting the modernization of government governance (since 2013)

The task of administrative reform at this stage was mainly to promote the streamline administration and decentralization, the combination of delegating power and strengthening regulation, and the optimization of public services. It was the stage of promoting administration system reform further into the depth. After the 18th National Congress of the Communist Party of China, China entered the decisive stage of building a comprehensive well-off society. The Third Plenary Session of the 18th Central Committee of the CPC put forward that the general goal of comprehensively-deepening reform was to develop and perfect the socialist system and promote the modernization of national governance system and governance capacity. Concentrating on this general goal, administrative system reform accelerated the establishment of socialist administrative system with Chinese characteristics. The Third Plenary Session of the 18th Central Committee of the CPC proposed that, "we have to effectively change the government functions, deepen the administrative system reform, innovate the administrative management mode, enhance the credibility and executive ability of government, and build a law-based and service-oriented government". The main line was to further promote the separation of government and enterprise, the separation of government and capital, the separation of government and public service units and the separation of government and community, to continuously promote the reforms of streamlining administration and decentralization, the combination of delegating power and strengthening regulation, and optimization of public services, to build a service-oriented government with scientific functions, optimized structure, honesty and high efficiency, and people-satisfaction, and to provide supports for boosting China's economy adapting to and leading the new normal, realizing the medium and high speed growth and stepping into the middle and high-end level.

## 1. 3  Main Contents of Administrative Reform in China

Chinese administrative reform after the policy of reform and opening-up is an exploration process of continuously deepening the understanding and gradually promoting the nature, characteristic, law, relationship, goal and task of administrative system in the context of economic system reform, social system reform, cultural system reform and political system reform, and it is also a significant law exploration process for building socialism with Chinese characteristics. The practice has shown that the reform and exploration at this stage had made great successes, which fundamentally abandoned the highly centralized planned economic system and administrative management mode and basically built an administrative system in conformity with the development of a socialist market economy. The main contents were as follows:

### 1.3.1  Transformation of government functions

The transformation of government functions is inevitably necessary to the transformation from traditional planned economy to socialist market economy. Transformation of government functions is not only the red line that runs through China's administrative reform process for nearly 40 years since the reform and opening-up, but also the core of China's administrative reform. The 14th National Congress of the Communist Party of China put forward that the fundamental way of functional transformation was to separate the government from enterprises. The 16th National Congress of the Communist Party of China clearly put forward that the main government functions were economic adjustment, market supervision, social management and public service. Since the 18th National Congress of the Communist Party of China, Chinese administrative reform has grasped more tightly "the nose of an ox" — transformation of government functions, and accelerated in transforming government functions by taking streamline administration and decentralization as a breakthrough, which made the market play a decisive role in resource allocation and gave a better play to government functions, effectively promoted government functions to the creation of good development environment, the delivery of high quality public services and the safeguarding of social fairness and justice. Through nearly 40 – year administrative reform, government intervention in micro-economic operation has been significantly reduced, the enterprise status as a competitive subject in the market has been determined, the decisive role of market allocating resources has been obviously enhanced, the new type of macroeconomic regulation and control system has been gradually improved and the social management and public service functions has been continuously strengthened.

### 1. 3. 2  Adjustment of administrative division

The adjustment and optimization of administrative division is an important content of China's administrative reform. Since the reform and opening up, China's administrative reform has been adapting to the needs of economic and social development, urbanization development and productivity revolution. A series of administrative division reform attempts such as establishing special zones, creating new provinces (municipalities directly under the central government), transforming prefecture into city, changing county into city, city governing county and changing county into district, have greatly enriched the practical connotation of China's administrative division. Affected by urbanization process, spatial expansion of central city, agglomeration and growth of population, improvement of traffic and communication conditions and policy factors, the adjustment of China's administrative division mainly includes five main modes: change of organizational system, division of administrative region, merging of administrative region, upgrade of organizational system and newly-established administrative region. Among them, transforming county into city (county level) was the most important administrative division adjustment mode since China's reform and opening up, which had been carried out for about 19 years from 1979 to 1997. Since the city establishment standards were adjusted by the central government for twice in this period, the whole process and cycle for the change of administrative division were greatly influenced.

### 1. 3. 3  Reform of government organizational structure

Organization is the carrier of functions, while the allocation of functions needs a scientific organization establishment to perform. One of the important contents of China's administrative reform is to reform the government organizational structure. Since the reform and opening up, China has successively carried out seven-time great reforms of government organizational structure, whose general trend and requirements were to scientifically divide and reasonably define the functions of various departments of government, further straighten out the relationships between vertical and horizontal administrative organizations and between government departments, and perfect the inter-departmental collaboration mechanism in accordance with the change of economic and social development and the requirements of full performance of government functions. The reasonable adjustment of organization establishment and optimization of personnel structure can not only solve the overstaffing problems in some departments and organizations, but also overcome the problems of insufficient establishment and personnel in some departments due to strengthening of functions, thus making the functions match with the organization and the task match with personnel and establishment. One important characteristic of institutional reform in 2008 was to actively promote the reform of giant department. This reform aimed to merge the institutions with similar functions but decentralized management, merge and adjust the institutions with crosscutting and overlapping responsibilities, disputed functions and difficult coordination for a long term, and meanwhile, appropriately set up new institutions with too wide function range and excessively centralized power to change the imbalance of department structure and the phenomena of catching one and losing another in operation. The reform in 2013 further optimized the department setup, coordinated the relationship between departments, continuously improved the administrative operation mechanism that the decision-making power, execution power and supervision power were unified and coordinated with each other, and built a government institutional framework focusing on macro-control department, market supervision department and social management and public service department, thus made the institutional setup and responsibility system tend to be reasonable. It could be said that each institutional reform was driven by economic system reform, aiming to adapt to the demands of development and improvement of socialist market economy and carry out fundamental transformation and reinventing for government management system.

### 1. 3. 4  Transformation of government management mode

Since the reform and opening up, Chinese government has taken an initiative to adapt to the requirements of domestic and international environmental changes and economic and social development. While improving and perfecting existing administrative management modes, Chinese government adhered to the principle of people-centered, made use of market mechanism, adopted modern scientific and technological achievements, simplified administrative procedures, adjusted management process, and combined various kinds of management methods and instruments such as government regulation, planning and plan, public opinion guidance, economic incentive, information service, so as to make administrative management modes more scientific, humanized and simplified. First was to innovate the way of macro-control. Facing the bigger economic downward pressure, we need to actively innovate the way of macro-control, clearly maintain the lower limit of steady growth and employment guarantee and the upper limit of inflation prevention, and safeguard the reasonable range for economic operation; to concentrate on transforming the way and adjusting the structure, duly and appropriately pre-adjust and finely adjust to improve the pertinence and coordination of macroeconomic regulation and control. The second was to transform government management more from prior approval to mid and post supervision, plug up supervision gaps and loopholes, increase the intensity of punishment on law breakers and violators, strive to achieve "easy entering but strict managing" and make efforts to create a market environment with fair competitions. The third was to promote the government purchase of services and innovate the government functional ways. The fourth was to strengthen the construction of e-government, strive to promote "Internet + government service" and make use of e-government platform to implement management and service, which enhanced the responsiveness of public demands, improved the administrative efficiency, reduced management costs and provided convenience for the public.

### 1. 3. 5  Promotion of law-based government construction

The construction of a law-based government was a great achievement for China's administrative reform since the policy of reform and opening up, of which one prominent sign was that the government had gradually realized the transformation from an all-round government to a limited government and from a regulation government to a service government, the goals and requirements of a law-based government had been further clarified, the citizens' right consciousness and the concepts of rule by law were continuously enhanced and the construction of a law-based government had made significant progress. The core of a law-based government was the administration according to law. *The Administrative Procedural Law* promulgated in 1989 was considered as a milestone in the course of legalization in China. In March 2004, Chinese government issued *Enforcement Outline of Completely Advancing Administration according to Law* and clearly put forward to use about ten years to basically achieve the goal of building a law-based government. After that, the construction pace of a law-based government had been accelerating. With a series of laws and regulations including *Administrative License Law, Administrative Procedural Law and Implementing Regulations of the Administrative Review Law*, the framework of legal system of a law-based government in China was basically established, the laws and regulations system of administration according to law was constantly improved, the work of administrative legislation, law enforcement and supervision was further strengthened, the legalization and institutionalization of government construction and administrative work was accelerated and the government could effectively use the system to govern the rights, affairs and people. Through years of efforts, a law-based government was built in 2015, administrative laws and regulations were continuously improved, the reform of administrative law enforcement system was further deepened, the administrative law enforcement organizational system was much perfected, the routinization and standardization level of administrative law enforcement was significantly increased, the construction of administrative supervision system was strengthened, and the legislation, standardization and openness of administrative power operation and administrative actions implementation was greatly improved.

### 1. 3. 6 Strengthening the construction of civil servants rank

Civil servants rank is the subject of government management, whose quality and ability will directly affect government execution and credibility. Since the reform and opening up, China had established a modern national civil servant system. In April 1993, the State Council approved and issued *The Temporary Regulation of Civil Servants* and implemented it in October that year, which marked the initial formation of civil servants system in China. After that, all regions throughout the country began to gradually build and implement the national civil servants system from top to bottom and strengthen the construction of civil servants rank. The laws and regulations system of civil servants management gradually improved, including the basic mechanisms of recruitment, incentive and wjthdrawal, which basically established a national civil servants system with Chinese characteristics. At the same time, the construction of government work style and clean government was promoted continuously and the overall quality and ability of civil servants was obviously improved so as to form a rank of civil servants who could cherish posts and wholeheartedly devote to work, be loyal to their duties, have good quality and excellent working style and be honest and diligent, thus laying a solid foundation for further building and perfecting a socialist administrative system with Chinese characteristics.

### 1. 3. 7    Promotion    of    anti-corruption    and    establishment    of clean government

Honesty is the bottom line of official morality and also the footstone of government credibility. Since three decades of reform and opening-up, especially entering the 21st century, Chinese government has unremittingly promoted the construction of clean government and made important progress in investigating key and major cases, punishing corrupt officials, strengthening system construction, enhancing the supervision of leading cadres, governing commercial bribery, and remedying the unhealthy tendency that caused damages to the interests of the masses. The State Council held the working conference of clean government every year and made the deployment for the construction of anti-corruption and clean government in the whole government system. All regions and departments in China had included the construction of anti-corruption and clean government into the overall planning of economic and social development and implied it into various reforms and important policy measures. The second was to formulate a series of legal systems for building a clean government such as *The Law of Government Procurement of PRC*, *Anti Monopoly Law of the People's Republic of China* and *Tendering and Biding Law of the People's Republic of China*, to standardize the discretion in administration, play the basic role of market in resources allocation and effectively prevent the occurrence of corruption behaviors. The third was to build a clean government through the innovation of system and mechanism. We need to promote the reforms of the administrative approval system, the cadre and personnel system, the judicial system and working mechanism, and the finance, investment, resource and other systems, investigate and punish corruption cases according to laws, make great efforts to build a clean and honest culture and actively carry out international exchanges and cooperation in anti-corruption construction. It is a common aspiration for all the people in the world to fight against corruption and build a clean and honest politics, and also a common theme that all governments and political parties around the world needed to face. China will play a positive role in international and regional anti-corruption exchange and cooperation and make arduous efforts to build a fair, honest and beautiful world.

# 1. 4  Basic Experience of Administrative Reform in China

Since the reform and opening up, the administrative reform in China has not only made remarkable progress, but also accumulated valuable experience in practice. It mainly includes the following six aspects:

### 1. 4. 1  Adhering to top-level design and overall planning

This is not only the valuable experience of administrative system reform in China, but also the basic conformance for deepening the reform of administrative system in the next period. Deepening the reform of administrative system needs to be overall planned in the whole development situation of the party and the country, and under the unified leadership of central government, it needs to be integrally planned and deployed together with other reforms and conducted in a holistic way. In his *Party and State Leadership System Reform*, Deng Xiaoping pointed out "Reforming the system of party and state leadership and other systems aims to take full advantage of the superiority of socialism and speed up China's modernization ⋯⋯ We shall regularly sum up historical experience, carry out intensive surveys and studies and synthesize correct views so as to continue the reform vigorously and systematically, step by step and from the central down to the local. " The administrative system reform in China is conducted through overall plan and coordination under the leadership of the Communist Party of China. Report of the Eighteenth National Congress of the CPC suggested "We improve the mechanism for coordinating structural reforms and conduct major reforms in a holistic way. " This is of great significance for administrative system reform in strengthening top-level design and overall planning, and collaboratively progressing all kinds of reforms. Chinese Government always takes the administrative reform as a key part of comprehensively deepening reforms, studies in depth about the relationships between the administrative reform and the economic reform, the political reform, the cultural reform and the social reform, seizes the regularity of inter-adaptation and inter-supporting and the complexity of inter-constraint and interaction of reforms of all aspects, correctly handles the relationships among reform, development and stability, improves the scientificity and authority of decision-making for system reforms, strengthens the coordination, matching and effectiveness of reform measures of all aspects, and ensures the correct direction and smooth progress of socialist reform.

### 1. 4. 2  Adhering to the strategy of progressive reform

The four decades of reform and opening-up in China has pursued a successful path of progressive reform. The administrative system reform is an important part in deepening the entire reform and an inevitable requirement for establishing and improving a socialist market economic system and developing the socialist democratic politics. Therefore, the administrative reform in China adheres to the path of progressive reform. The basic characteristics of reform path is an orderly, exploratory and innovative self-improvement and development revolution of a socialist administrative system under the premise of adhering to the political leadership of the Communist Party of China and adhering to the basic institutional framework of socialism with Chinese characteristics. Orderliness means the administrative reform in China correctly handles the relationship among reform, development and stability, overall coordinates the intensity of reform, the speed of development and the national tolerance, and it is a reform for the administrative system on the basis of maintaining China's basic political system and regime. Exploration means the administrative reform in China correctly handles the relationship between socialism and market economy. It is an unprecedented career without reference, which shall be carried out all by "Crossing the River by Touching the Stones" and all by adapting to the needs of socialist market economy. Each step of the reform shall be done correctly, accurately and firmly. Innovation means the administrative reform in China is not only a significant adjustment for the original structure of administrative power and interest pattern, but also a profound change of concept and ideological revolution. We must run the spirit of innovation through the whole process and each link of the reform. The practice has proved that each progress of Chinese administrative reform in theory and practice is the result of adhering to emancipating the mind, seeking truth from facts, and advancing with time. To promote the administrative reform, we shall not only have long-term objectives, overall planning and clear path and direction, but also determine the key tasks of each period. It is impossible to accomplish the whole task at one stroke. We shall not only make full use of the favorable conditions of all aspects, seize the favorable opportunity, firmly and decisively push forward the reform measures and take large steps in some important areas, but also comprehensively analyze the contradictions and risks that we face, fully consider the tolerance of all aspects and actively and steadily carry out the reform.

### 1. 4. 3  Adhering to public participation in reform process

The public is the subject of reforms in China, so as the administrative reform. Serving the people wholeheartedly is the fundamental purpose of the Party and the Government. For the people and by the people are the fundamental starting points and driving forces to promote the various reforms. From the view of value goal, since the opening-up, the administrative reform in China has always adhered to by the people, for the people and serving the people, focused on adapting to the promotion of economic and social development, constantly improved the people's material and cultural life and promoted people's all-round development; adhered to respecting the dominant status of the masses and safeguarding their rights and interests; fully reflected the interests and appeals of the broad masses and enabled all the people to share the fruits of reforms and development. From the view of dynamic mechanism, the administrative reform in China attaches great importance to the enthusiasm, initiative and participation of the public, which enhance social economic vitality and creativity. The practice has proved that only the administrative reform in China is in line with the interests of the people, reflects the voice of the people, firmly relies on the people and builds the government satisfying the people, can it get the wholehearted advocacy and strong support from the general public.

### 1.4.4  Adhering to the focus on development as a central task

China is a large developing country. Achieving sustained, rapid and sound development of China's economy is not only the first priority of contemporary China, but also a great contribution of Chinese people to the world development. Therefore, focusing on economic development, serving economic development and adapting to the development are always the internal driving forces of the administrative reform in China. As a basic component of national system the administrative system is an important part of Chinese political superstructure, and also a binding point of economic system, political system, social system and other systems, all of which have close relationships with each other. The administrative reform in China, especially the government institution setting and function adjustment, involves national economy, politics, culture and other aspects in social life. It also involves a series of important relationships between the central and local government, the government and society, the government and enterprises, and the whole and partial interests. Therefore, the administrative system reform must be overall planned in the situation of China's economic and social development, submit to and serve the demand of promoting economic and social development, adapt to the process of improving socialist market economic system and be coordinated with the construction of socialist democratic politics and the improvement of national governance system.

### 1.4.5  Encouraging innovation and practicing with courage

Many of the major policies and practices of the Party and Government come from the innovations of the people and the practices at basic levels. In the process of deepening the administrative reform, we should always encourage and support local governments and departments to proceed from the reality, adapt to local conditions, explore bravely, promote innovation and accumulate experience for deepening the reform. For example, in recent years, many local governments and departments have explored actively around the organization structure, hierarchy, management system, operation mechanism, service mode and other aspects of the government, including promoting the reform of super ministry system, exploring the reform of province directly managing counties ( cities ), innovating the modes of administrative management, building the government service standardization, and reforming the comprehensive law enforcement system. The relevant departments and local governments have investigated, studied and objectively evaluated the effect of those reform measures, carefully studied and solved the problems appeared in the process of reform, improved and promoted the effective reform measures that have been proved in practice, and reflected them in the top-level overall planning and decision-making deployment.

### 1. 4. 6 Adhering to the combination of learning from international experience and conforming to China's reality

Opening-up is a basic state policy of China. Since the Reform and Opening-up, China has vigorously carried out administrative cultural exchanges between China and foreign countries in a more open mind, better mentality and broader perspective, and make due efforts for promoting the progress of human civilization in learning and drawing lessons from each other. The administrative reform involves the relationship adjustment of administrative powers and the structure change of government organizations, but without copying foreign modes blindly, it is good at studying and drawing lessons from the beneficial results of international public governance and conforming to the trend of development and changes of the times. Moreover, based on the vast territory of China, quite different situations between different regions, very uneven development, profound influence of traditional administrative concept and other realities, the administrative reform in China not only proceeds from overall situation and uniformly deploys, but also fully considers the characteristics of different regions, guides by categories and achieves the combination of learning from international experience and conforming to China's reality.

## References

1. Xi, J. P.  (2014) . *The Governance of China* (1st ed. ) . Beijing, China.

2. Wei, L. Q.  (2013) . *On the Reform of Administrative System.* Beijing, China: People's Publishing House.

3. Wei, L. Q.  (2009) . The Review and Prospect of 30 Years' Reform on Administrative System. *Qiushi*, 2, 33 – 36.

3. Wei, L. Q.  ( Ed. ) .  ( 2015 ) . *Innovating Government Governance and Deepening Administrative Reform.* Beijing, China: Chinese Academy of Governance Press.

(Written by: Liqun Wei, President of China Society of Administrative Reform, Former Director of Research Office of the State Council, Former Secretary of Party Committee and Executive Vice-President of Chinese Academy of Governance)

# Chapter Ⅱ

# Government Organization Reform

Over the past 30 years, China has undertaken its administrative reform in a comprehensive and progressive way. The reform incorporates diverse content as functional and institutional adjustment, as well as operational and managerial innovation; in addition, it also covers a wide range of fields as both internal and external supportive reforms. To be specific, the government institutional reform has been an important part of the overall administrative reform. The government is the main body to perform duties; in other words, the government solve the issue of who carry out actions and who shoulder responsibilities. Therefore, the adjustment of government organizational structures and changes in government institutional systems are both the manifestation and inherent content of administrative system reform. Since 1982, the Chinese government has undertaken 7 government organizational reforms in a row. The background and features of these reforms have embodied the general trend of Administrative Reform in China.

## 2.1 Background and Features of Government Organization Reform

Since the reform and opening up, China has undertaken 7 central Organization Reforms respectively in 1982, 1988, 1993, 1998, 2003, 2008 and 2013. Each reform carried out in particular time and with specified mission, is to respond to objective needs of economic and social development at that time. And each reform is introduced hierarchically and implemented accordingly by the State Council, provincial governments and municipal departments to the county level.

### 2. 1. 1  1982 Reform: Toward lean leadership and staff

The reform was put forward against the background of opening up new prospects in Chinese modernization construction. To meet the demand of shifting focus of national work to economic development, the reform, by cutting and merging party and government institutions, by diminishing cadres and leaders, centralized leadership innovation, in a way to transform the situation of overstaffing and sluggishness.

First, to re-shape leadership. According to the guideline of Four Modernizations, the reform was undertaken to select elite as leaders while reducing deputy leaders at all levels and in all departments.

Second, to abolish life tenure for leading officials and establish a cadre retirement system.

Third, to streamline institutions and cut personnel force size. The number of ministries and institutions under the state council was cut from 100 to 61. The personnel size was reduced by 25% , and personnel size of departments under the state council especially diminished from 51,000 to 30,000.

The reform in 1982 was implemented under specified historical situations and did not touch upon the issue of government functional transformation.

### 2. 1. 2  1988 Reform : put forward transforming government functions the first time

This time, the reform centralized on transforming government functions, adjusting relations, reducing government interference on business operation, enhancing macro-control, increasing administrative efficiency and rationalizing institutional setting.

First, function transformation was regarded as the key issue while handling the relations between governments, enterprises and public institutions. The overall functional configuration of departments under the State Council was adjusted considerably to shift government functions from micro-management to macro-control, from direct supervision to indirect control, and from divisional management to industrial administration. Certain specialized departments were dismantled, cut or merged, while around 30 departments' functions were enhanced. The content of functional transformation was specified in the scheme of "determining the function, post and size".

Second, the reform solved the function intersection issue among departments. Statistics show that almost 50 intersection issues were settled through consultation, which laid sound foundation for clarifying responsibilities, reducing disputes and establishing scientific administrative system.

Third, a few professional economic departments as well as a majority of bureaus were cut while several comprehensive industrial management departments formed; in the meanwhile, departments that perform supervision and economic regulation were enhanced. Corresponding to the changes of functions, the personnel adjustment among sectors was carried out accordingly.

Forth, approaches to institutional reforms and functional transformation were explored, laying foundation for implementing civil servant system. Local governments recruited according to fixed personnel size, gradually assigned concrete functions for each position and formulated post description. These altogether promoted the application of civil servant system.

Mindset of this reform is brand new and for the first time, the core issue of transforming government functions is put forward. From then on, government organization reforms are closely related to China's macro development and economic system reform.

### 2. 1. 3 1993 Reform: deepen government function transformation to meet the need of building socialist market economy

In 1992, the 14th National Congress of the Communist Party of China put forward the goal of establishing a socialist market economy, denoting that under the national macro-control, the market played a fundamental role in resource allocation. The government organization reform in 1993 was thus conducted against this backdrop. To fulfill the need of building socialist market economy, national administrative management system was adjusted accordingly so as to step up functional shift and to restructure institutions.

First, further shift government functions to satisfy the demand of socialist market economy. During this reform, priority was given to reform management systems of planning, investment and finance. Also some professional economic departments and function intersected institutes are merged or removed. Comprehensive economic sectors shift their work pattern to macro-control and regulation.

Second, to clarify relations among sectors. Upon transforming government functions, more focuses were given to clarify relations among professional sectors and relations between comprehensive sectors and professional ones. The responsibilities and authorities among sectors were clearly defined.

Third, to cut institutes and personnel. After the reform, the composition departments under the State Council were reduced from 42 to 41 and non-standing organizations under the State Council were substantially deducted from 85 to 26. More than 2 million staff quotas were cut nationwide.

Main features of this reform: one, against the background of establishing socialist market economy, government function transformation was treated as the key issue. The reform gave full play to government's macro management role while diminished its control in micro economic sectors. Efforts were also made to separate government administration and enterprise management, encourage corporation autonomy, and upgrade company managerial mechanisms. Two, substantially reduced professional economic management departments. Most of such departments were transferred into economic or service entity. Some that shoulder heavy management responsibilities and could hardly shift into economic entities largely reduced their personnel and internal institutes. Governments narrowed their direct management on enterprises' production-supply-marketing activities and on enterprises' property of personnel-finance-belonging. Three, drastically downsize personnel and institutes. Four, initiate the civil servant system.

## 2. 1. 4    1998    Reform: separate government functions from enterprise management

The reform plan of the State Council was approved at the first session of the ninth National People's Congress on March 10, 1998. The plan specified the target of the reform, i. e. , establish an administrative management system characterized by efficient services, coordinate mechanisms and standardized behaviors, build high-caliber and professional cadres, and gradually construct an administrative management system with Chinese characteristics that adapts to the socialist market economy.

This time, efforts were made to separate the relationship between party and government departments with their associated economic entities and companies. Tangible improvement was shown regarding function transformation. Specifically, the reform strove to cut government departments sharply, dismantle almost all professional economic management departments in the industrial sector, such as ministry of electric power, ministry of coal, ministry of metallurgical industry, ministry of machine building, ministry of electronics, ministry of chemical industry, ministry of geology and mineral resources, ministry of forestry, light industry association and textile association. By this way, the organizational foundation for intersection of governments with enterprises was eliminated. After the reform, organs of the State Council were cut from 40 to 29. The comprehensive economic departments were adjusted as macro control sectors, and a great many professional economic departments were dismissed and over 100 functions were handed over to enterprises, social intermediary agencies and local organs. Each and every professional economic department strictly clarified their liabilities with enterprises and was free from company management thereafter. In the meantime, size of the personnel force was reduced at a great margin. The State Council emphasized a decrease of 50% personnel force, the largest one ever among all the Administrative Reform. After the reform, the number of personnel among departments of the State Council diminished from around 32,300 to 16,700 . Altogether, the reform downsized almost 1.15 million persons.

The 1998 reform showed the following features: one, the government organization reform was combined with the establishment of modern enterprise system. The reform highlighted functional transformation and realized the separation of government and enterprises functions. Also, a standardized relationship between governments and the state-own enterprises was specified. Professional economic departments were unhooked with company management. Government economic management sectors were basically formed and a modern governing system adapted to the socialist market economy was initially developed. Two, combine the government organization reform with the civil servant system. The reform explicitly defined the improvement of civil servant system and establishment of high-caliber professional managerial cadres as significant part of the reform target. The reform also integrated personnel adjustment with cadre structure optimization and public service improvement. Three, incorporate the reform with the enhancement of legal construction among administrative organs.

### 2.1.5 2003 Reform: function integration and structure adjustment after joining the WTO

To satisfy the requirement after joining the WTO, the 2003 Reform aimed at prominent contradictions and issues occurred in economic and social development. Simultaneously promote and improve democratic decision-making mechanism and enhance administrative supervision and other institutional construction.

The reform generally maintained the original government institutional pattern, i.e., 28 composition departments under the State Council apart from the General Office. Priority was given to solve prominent issues and contradictions within the management institutions that impeded the overall reform and development, so as to promote the shift of government functions. First, to deepen state property supervision and management structure reform. Set up State-owned Assets Supervision and Administration Commission, which helped segregate the government role of social and economic administrator from property owner, and the role of public administrator from enterprise operator. In a word, separate government functions from enterprise management. Second, to improve macro control and regulation system and establish State Development and Reform Commission. Third, to strengthen financial supervision system and establish China Banking Regulatory Commission ( CBRC ) . In the meantime, a separated and compatible financial supervision system characterized by a clear responsibility division among CBRC, CSRC ( China Securities and Regulatory Commission) and CIRC ( China Insurance and Regulatory Commission ) is formed. Forth, to set up a circulation management system including both internal and external trade and establish Ministry of Commerce. Fifth, to reform the supervision management system of food security and production safety.

The reform was conducted with distinct historic features. One, the reform adapted to the development of market economy and met the demand of entry into the WTO. Function transformation was emphasized; the government's functions of macro control and regulation as well as supervision were also enhanced. Two, the reform generally maintained the original government institutional pattern, and emphasized on identifying functions and deepening existing transition. Three, the reform paid attention to functional integration and internal structure adjustment. Four, it was underlined that the reform would be a progressive one. In general, no major adjustment was made on government institutions this time and main focus was given to solve prominent issues.

### 2.1.6 2008 Reform: active exploration on super ministry establishment

The second plenary session of the 17th CPC central committee examined and adopted the Opinions on Deepening Administrative Management System Reform ( The Opinions ), which comprehensively stipulated the guiding ideology, basic principle, overall target and main tasks of further reforms. The Opinions formed the top-level design for administrative management reform in China.

According to the Opinions, the Reform made tangible trials on some key issues, to name a few, accelerating government function transformation, improving social management and public service, exploring the establishment of super-ministry system that integrates functions organically, clarifying responsibilities and liabilities among sectors and enhancing department duties. First, to reasonably allocate functions among macro control and regulation departments. The National Development and Reform Commission shrank their duties on micro affairs and concrete approval items, in a way to concentrate on macro-control. The Ministry of Finance improved budget and tax management, strengthened systems in which central and local rights on handling matters are compatible with their financial powers. Public fiscal system was reinforced. The People's Bank of China further developed the monetary policy scheme, enhanced overall consistency with financial regulators to safeguard national financial security. Second, to establish related resource management institutes. Set up high-level consultancy and coordination agency—National Energy Commission and initiate National Energy Administration. Third, to establish Ministry of Industry and Information. Former duties of industries that were incorporated in NDRC, former responsibilities that other than nuclear power supervision performed by the National Defense Commission of Science, Technology and Industry and former obligations of Ministry of Information Industry and Informationization Office under the State Council, are all re-scheduled as part of the newly established Ministry of Industry and Information (MII). Set up State Administration of Science, Technology and Industry for National Defense. MII became the new supervisor of the State Tobacco Monopoly Bureau. Forth, to establish Ministry of Transport. Found Civil Aviation Administration. Integrate the responsibilities of former Ministry of Transportation, of the General Administration of Civil Aviation and of the Ministry of Construction in terms of urban passengers transport guidance, into Ministry of Transport. Also, the newly established Aviation Administration was in the charge of the Ministry of Transport. Besides, the State Postal Bureau was affiliated to the Ministry of Transport. The Ministry of Railways is maintained, to be further reformed. Fifth, to build Ministry of Human Resources and Social Security ( MOHRSS ) . Duties that formally belonged to the Ministry of Personnel and the Ministry of Labor and Social Security are integrated into MOHRSS. Set up National Public Servant Bureau. Sixth, Organize Ministry of Environmental Protection. Seven, establish Ministry of Housing and Urban-Rural Development. Eighth, China Food and Drug Administration became part of the Ministry of Public Health. Clearly define that the Ministry of Public Health should shoulder the responsibilities of comprehensive coordination on food safety and of investigating grave food safety accidents. After the Reform, apart from the General Office, there are in total 27 organizing departments within the State Council.

Features of the 2008 Reform are: one, some government functions were abolished, delegated or transferred, according to the principles of separating government from enterprises, from capital resources, from public service institutions, and from market intermediaries. Meanwhile, social management and public service responsibilities that are closely related to people's immediate interests and to national welfare and people's livelihood were enhanced, such as macro-control and regulation, energy management, environmental protection and housing and social security, safety production. Two, initial explorations on establishing super-ministry system was conducted in areas of industry and information, transportation, human resources and social security. This is the first trial that China adopted ever to probe a new route for government organizational structure. Three, rationalize responsibilities among sectors. In line with the principle that one single duty is performed within one sector, department responsibilities were further defined to solve the issue of function intersection among areas like environment and resources, foreign economy and trade, market supervision, culture and sanitation. Four, emphasized department responsibilities. While endowing departments with authorities, duties were underlined to ensure that authority comes along with responsibilities.

### 2.1.7   2013 Reform: government function transformation as a major task

In the spirit of the CPC eighteenth National Congress and the second plenary session of the Eighteenth Central Committee, the Reform complied with the requirement of building socialist administrative system with Chinese characteristics, carried forward institutional reforms with functional transformation as the core, in a mind to improve mechanisms and efficacy.

To transform functions and streamline responsibilities, the State Council promoted the "super-ministry" reform, further separated government functions from enterprise management within the railway system, and integrated institutes of health care and family planning, food and drug, press and publications, radio, film and television, energy and ocean management. After the Reform, apart from the General Office, composing departments at the ministerial level of the State Council totaled 25, and the other 4 were cut.

Features of the 2013 Reform: one, to highlight government functional transformation. Functional transformation was regarded as soul and main stream of the Reform. Together with the institutional reform, functional transformation was another key word inscribed within the title of reform plan. Two, to integrate decentralization, macro-management and postmortem supervision. Specifically, while empowering the market, enterprises, society and individuals, governments enhanced necessary duties, emphasized macro-management and intensified postmortem supervision. Three, to make tangible steps on government organization reforms among some key areas. Further separate government functions from enterprise management within the railway system, and integrate institutes of health care and family planning, food and drug, press and publications, radio, film and television, energy and ocean management. These targeted steps solved enduring problems of high attention. Four, to make major breakthroughs in enhancing the construction of fundamental, long-range and far-sighted systems. For example, the real estate registration system was established, and a united social credit code system in which citizens are recognized by identity numbers and institutes by organizing bar code was designed and applied. All these fundamental systems, by guiding citizens' behaviors and exerting corresponding constraints, are of great significance in pushing forward the entire administrative reform and ensuring effective management.

## 2.2  Achievements of Government Organization Reform in China

After over 30 years' efforts, the government organization reform has made tremendous achievements and a system .that is adapted to socialist market economic mechanism was initially formed. From the perspective of government construction, the achievements are as follows:

### 2.2.1  Government management concepts evolved

Compared with situations before the reform and opening-up, the government has formed a modernized character positioning and basic concept, in line with contemporary development and national realities. One, to introduce the concept of responsible government. Governments and departments at all levels gradually identified and reinforced their responsibilities. Two, to introduce the concept of service-oriented government. Governments' functions of public service and social management are enhanced, and even become a significant part in their function structure. Whether a department provides more public service of higher quality becomes an important standard for performance measurement. Three, to introduce the concept of a law-based government. The government and its staff shall respect and safeguard the authority of law, and the consciousness of acting within the constitution and laws is gradually formed. Four, to introduce the concept of clean government. A government department should be diligent, frugal, clean and efficient. Government power should be operated in the sun, and acceptance of public supervision becomes important criterion.

**2. 2. 2  Government functional transformation gained tangible improvements**

After continuous reforms, government functions gradually adapted to the requirements of socialist market economic development, and to the increasing public needs. One, the relationship among the government, market and enterprises has been streamlined. Separation of government functions from enterprises management is basically realized. The market exerts a decisive effect on resource allocation. The system in which the government plays an indirect role in macro-control and regulation is improving. Especially since the New Government, administration simplification and decentralization are promoted vigorously that are unseen before. A large number of items requiring administrative review and approval are cancelled; proceedings that could be resolved by market adjustment and enterprise independent decisions are left to the market and enterprises at the most; these combined releasing the market vitality. In the meantime, decentralization is not neglecting responsibilities, but concentrating on service optimization, and on supervision during or after the course. Two, functions of social management and public services are valued increasingly. Safeguard social stability and promote harmony are of great importance; mechanisms of social interest coordination, conflicts resolution and emergency coping are established step by step. Develop social undertakings and improve people's livelihood are also on the agenda; compulsory education, public health and social security system construction have made great strides. Three, the impact of social organizations are intensifying in economic and social affairs. All types of organizations are flourishing and the governing scheme is transforming from sole management by governments to a coordinated governance between governments and society.

**2. 2. 3  Government organizational structure optimized**

After the Reforms, the institutional framework formerly adapted to the planned economy was thoroughly changed, and replaced by one that is consistent with socialist market economy. Before, planning is the driving force, comprehensive departments supervise specialized sectors and specialized ones directly control enterprises. Nowadays, an institutional framework in which departments of macro-regulation, the industry management, the market supervision, social administration and public services play major roles is basically established.

### 2. 2. 4 Governments and departments at all levels gradually defined their responsibilities

Reasonable delimitation of responsibilities among local and central governments are basically realized. Rights and liabilities of managing economic and social affairs among governments at all levels are gradually and rationally defined. The situation of functional parallelism at all levels is altered. In the last two years, the Chinese government vigorously promoted "the list of government rights and liabilities system". Governments could only exercise its power rigidly by items. The system also laid foundation for legal delimitation of governments' rights and liabilities. Government responsibilities are further clarified and intersected items among departments of major fields are gradually defined. Coordination and cooperation mechanisms among sectors are also formed.

### 2. 2. 5 Government systematic construction and capacity building strengthener

Government operation mechanism and managerial mode are reinvented constantly, thus raising administrative efficacy as a whole. One, significant steps forward are witnessed in terms of scientific and democratic policy-making mechanism. The mechanism involves public participation, expert judgment and government decision-making as a whole. Two, the mechanism of keeping the public informed of government affairs is propelled. The improved and expanded mechanism guarantees people's rights to know, to participate and supervise. Three, an emergency response system is initiated, featuring grading responses, localized management, information sharing and labor division and coordination. Four, administrative supervision and accountability are intensified. An administrative supervision system that involves external control, hierarchical overseeing, monitoring and auditing takes its initial shape. Accountability system plays a vital role in handling major incidents. Five, substantial progress has been seen in terms of fundamental system construction concerning people's immediate interests.

## 2. 3  Understanding of Government Organization Reform in China

The governmentorganization reform in China has gained tremendous experiences through over 30 years' exploration. A proper summary would be of significance to deepen the recognition on some fundamental rules of government organization reform.

### 2. 3. 1  Reform shall adhere to the leadership of the Communist Party of China

Ever since thereform and opening up, the reforms are conducted under the leadership of Communist Party of China and pursue a correct political direction. The reforms deem the safeguard of people's fundamental interests as the starting point and standing point. Reform shall account for and serve the people. The only yardstick for reform success is people's satisfaction, pleasure and recognition.

### 2. 3. 2  Reform shall be based on the general situation of economic and social development

Development is the absolute principle. The reforms are introduced to constantly emancipate and develop the productive forces, and promote economic and social development in an all round way. The government organization reforms aim to build a comprehensively well-off society, adapt to improving socialist market economy and coordinate with building socialist democracy and running the State according to the law.

### 2. 3. 3 Reform shall intensify top level design and overall planning

The governmentorganization reform is a long-term systematic project. Reform priorities and emphasis need to be identified. Long-standing and periodical targets shall be balanced. Equal attention shall be paid to coordinate the relationship between the reform and economic, political, social and cultural development, between the overall reform and corresponding reforms within institutions, so as to promote the reform in a harmonized way. Give full play to local and central governments' initiatives, and to initiatives of the general public, in a way to push forward the reform as a whole. Besides, to properly handle the relationship among the reform, development and stability and take into account of the requirements and limitations are essential. In sum, the reform dynamics, the development speed and the general affordability should be balanced.

### 2. 3. 4 Reform shall emphasize the improvement of social security and people's livelihood

Guarantee the improvement of people's livelihood is a major task for social and economic development in China. The governmentorganization reform shall prioritize the guarantee and improvement of people's livelihoods, propel the function transformation, and also lay emphasis on social management and public service. Provide better systematic arrangement to guarantee and improve people's livelihood. Give full play to the government's leading role in offering public services.

### References

1. Li, J. P. (2005) . *Review and Reflection: Experiences and Lessons Learned from Chinese Government Institutional Reform. Chinese Public Administration*, 2, 19 – 20.

2. Wang, Y. C. (2006) . *Progress and Challenge within Chinese Institutional Reform. CASS Journal of Political Science*, 3, 1 – 7.

3. The General Office of State Commission for Public Sector Reform. ( 2008, December 18) . Further Boost in Overall Layout—Reflection of the Institutional Reform in China. *People's Daily*, p. 7.

4. Wang, Y. K. ( 2008) . Reflection and Outlook: Chinese Government Institutional Reform over 30 Years. *Journal of Cadres of Party and Government*, *1*, 23 – 26.

5. He, Y. Review on the Chinese Government Institutional Reforms over the Past 30 Years. *Chinese Public Administration*, *12*, 21 – 27.

6. Wang, Y. K. ( 2008) . *Reflection and Outlook: Chinese Government Institutional Reform over 30 Years*. Beijing, China: People's Publishing House.

7. Zhu, G. L. , & Li, L. P. ( 2009 ) . Retrospect and Suggestion: Thirty years ' of Government Institutional Reform. *Journal of Beijing Administrative College*, *1*, 18 – 22.

8. Wei, L. Q. ( 2009) . Establish and Improve the Institutional Management System with Chinese Characteristics—Reflection and Outlook of Institutional Reform. *Qiushi*, *2*, 33 – 36.

9. Wang, L. M. ( 2009) . Review and Reflection on Six Concentrated Institutional Reforms since the Reform and Opening up. *Chinese Public Administration*, *10*, 7 – 16.

10. The General Office of State Commission for Public Sector Reform. ( 2011, July 25) . The Glories Past of Chinese Institutional Management Reform since the the Reform and Opening up. *People's Daily*, p. 10.

11. Zhang, Z. J. ( 2012 ) . *Witness to the Institutional Reform and Personnel System Reform*. Beijing, China: National School of Administration Press.

12. Zhou, Z. R. , & Xu, Y. Q. ( 2014 ) . An Examination of Government Institutional Reform during the Last Thirty years from the perspective of the Change of Management. *Social Science in China*, *7*, 66 – 86.

( Written by: Liping Li, Deputy Director, Editorial Office of *China Institutional Reform and Management* )

# Chapter III

# Transformation of Government Functions and Reform on Administrative Review and Approval System

The government functions reflect the basic direction and main functions of the government activities. It shall necessarily continuously adjust and change with the development of economy and society. The transformation of government functions is the core of the reform on administrative system in China, which runs through the entire process of reform, opening-up and modernization construction. As a part of the government's management, the administrative review and approval system is important content of improving the socialist market economic system. The reform on the administrative review and approval system is not only the breakthrough point of the transformation of government functions, but also an important means of releasing market dynamics and endogenous power of social development.

## 3.1 Historical Process and Characteristics of Transformation of Government Functions

In 1978, a decision was made at the Third Plenary Session of the 11th Central Committee of the Communist Party of China to shift the focus of work to socialist modernization construction. This is the strategic requirement proposed for the transformation of government functions in the new historical period. In

1982, at the 12th National Congress of the Communist Party, it was proposed that the institutional reform and the economic system reform must be completed systematically. Since 1982, China has carried on 7 centralized reforms on the system and organization of administrative management. The transformation of government functions has always been the important task of administrative management system reform. The Third Plenary Session of the 12th Central Committee of the Communist Party of China requires the government organs to "implement separation of the responsibilities between government and enterprises, and correctly play the functions of the government in managing the economy". The Fourth Plenary Session of the 12th Central Committee of the Communist Party of China put forward the requirement of transformation of government functions for the first time. At the 13th National Congress of the Communist Party of China, the important judgment of "the transformation of government functions is the key of successful institutional reform" was proposed. At the 14th National Congress of the Communist Party of China, the objective of establishing socialist market economy system and the requirement of accelerating the transformation of government functions were proposed. At the congress, it was also proposed that the fundamental approach of transformation is to separate government functions from enterprise management. The transformation of government functions and establishment and improvement of the macroscopic-control system was proposed at the Third Plenary Session of the 14th Central Committee of the Communist Party of China. The economic managing function of the government is mainly to establish and execute macro-control policy, do well in infrastructure construction and create a good environment for economic development. At the 15th National Congress of the Communist Party of China, it was proposed to transform the government functions in accordance with the requirement of the socialist market economy and realize the separation of government and enterprises. The institutional reform of 1998 revoked most of the professional economic departments. It marks the function transformation with the main content of transforming government functions and promoting separation of government and enterprise. At the 16th

National Congress of the Communist Party of China, it was proposed to deepen the reform on the system of administrative management and further transform government functions. At the Third Plenary Session of the 16th Central Committee of the Communist Party of China, it was proposed to accelerate the transformation of government functions, deepen the reform on the system of administrative review and approval and faithfully transform the economic managing function of the government to serving the market subjects and creating a good environment for development. At the 17th National Congress of the Communist Party of China, it was proposed to accelerate the reform on the system of administrative management, build a service-oriented government and require to "focus on transformation of functions, accelerate separating the government from enterprises, separating the government from investment, separating the government from public service units and separating the government from the market intermediary organizations, so as to reduce the government intervention in micro-economic operations". At the Second Plenary Session of the 17th Central Committee of the Communist Party of China, it was proposed to "achieve fundamental transformation of government functions to creating good environment for development, providing high-quality public services, and safeguarding social fairness and justice". Especially the Central Committee of the Communist Party of China put forward a series of major strategic thoughts, including the scientific development concept, building a harmonious socialist society, strengthening and innovating social management and so on and put forward higher requirements for promoting the transformation of government functions under the new situation. At the 18th National Congress of the Communist Party of China, it was proposed to further promote the work of separating the government from enterprises, separating the government from investment, separating the government from public service units and separating the government administration from commune management and build a service-oriented government with scientific functions, optimized structures, honesty, high efficiency and the people's satisfaction; deepen the reform on the system of administrative review and approval, continuously streamline administration and delegate power to the lower levels and promote the transformation of government functions to creating good environment for development, providing high-quality public services and safeguarding social fairness and justice in accordance with the objective of establishing the socialist administrative system with Chinese characteristics. At the Third Plenary Session of the 18th Central Committee of the Communist Party of China, the government was required to strengthen the formulation and implementation of the development strategies, planning, policies, standards and so on, strengthen the supervision of market activities and strengthen delivery of various public service; strengthen the macro-control responsibilities and ability of the central government, strengthen the responsibilities in public service, market supervision, social management, environmental protection and other aspects of the local government.

Through the continuous reform of more than 30 years, the transformation of government functions in China has made significant progress. The historical process of the transformation of government functions has shown an increasingly deepened clear track.

### 3. 1. 1  From adaption to needs of economic construction and economic system reform to needs of implementation of concept of scientific development and economic & social harmonious development

The administrative reform in China closely hinges on the core work of the party and country in different periods and stages. The transformation of government functions transfers from adaption to needs of the economic system reform to needs of economic & social development situation and administrative system reform; the transformation of government functions shall pay more attention to people orientation so as to spare no effort to solve problems of unbalanced and incongruous development of economy and society according to requirements on scientific outlook on development, construction of socialism harmonious society and building of moderately prosperous society. From adaption to needs of economic construction as the part to needs of economic, political, social, cultural and ecological construction, the government shall fully and properly perform its functions so as to enhance economic regulation and market supervision as well as pay more attention to social management and public service.

### 3.1.2 Enrichment and development of connotation of government functions and clearer target of transformation of government functions

Sixteenth National Congress of the Communist Party of China explicitly put forward four basic government functions under conditions of socialist market, namely "economic regulation, market supervision, social management and public service". Opinions on Deepening the Reform of the Administrative System, which is passed at the Second Plenary Session of 17th central committee of CPC, puts forward firstly and clearly targets of transformation of government functions, namely "to realize fundamental changing of government functions to creation of good development environment, provision of high-quality public service and safeguarding of social fairness and justice". It proposes "to better play the basic role of market in resource allocation and citizens and social organizations in public affairs management as well as more effectively provide public products". It also clearly defines key points in performance of functions by central government and local governments. The Third Plenary Session of 18th central committee of CPC firstly puts forward to " deal with the relationship between government and market so as to guarantee decisive effect of market in resource allocation and better government functions". Therefore, targets of transformation of government functions are clear gradually.

### 3.1.3 Close integration of transformation of government functions and institutional restructuring leads to new requirements on transformation of government functions

The relationship between scientific definition of functions and rational institutional setting is interrelated and interdependent; government functions shall be performed via certain institutions while institutions survive via function performance. For 7 administrative system and institutional reforms in the part, it is the process for structural change and adjustment based on the development requirement of core work and economy & society, which represents requirements on function transformation; the task of institutional restructuring shall be implemented via change and adjustment of functions. The 17th CPC National Congress of CPC puts forward to explore and implement super-ministries system with integrated functions. The Fifth Plenary Session of 17th central committee of CPC proposed to firmly push super-ministries system reform; the Third Plenary Session of 18th central committee of CPC proposed that "deepening reform of institutional restructuring is a must for transformation of government functions" and "proactively and steadily implement super-ministries system". This further clears the direction and key points of transformation of government functions in near future.

## 3. 2  Reform of Administrative Review and Approval System

Since the reform and opening-up, local governments and departments of all levels have performed reform of administrative review and approval system to different degrees; however, there are still many problems existing, making it inconsistent with requirements of economic & social development and construction of government under law. Government functions shall be further transformed and administrative review and approval system shall be further reformed. Since the establishment of new government, deepening reform of administrative approval system becomes the breakthrough to transform government functions. With constantly innovated ideas, the transformation of government function enters a new phase.

### 3. 2. 1  Reform of administrative review and approval system from 2001 to 2012

In September of 2001, the State Council established the leading group for administrative approval system reform with office headquartered in Ministry of

Supervision. In October of 2011, the State Council issued *Circular of the State Council for Approving and Transmitting Opinions on Implementation of Reform of Administrative Approval System* and proposed general requirements on reform of administrative approval system, namely administrative approval inconsistent with principles of separation of government from enterprise and public services and hinders market opening and fair competition with little effect shall be canceled; market mechanism shall replace the administrative approval for operation; for administrative approval that must be kept, establish sound supervision and restriction mechanism so as to realize strict approval process with less procedures and higher approval efficiency. In this way, system of accountability for administrative approval is strictly implemented. Since the Sixteenth National Congress of the Communist Party of China, the State Council further substantiates and strengthens the leading team and office. Since the Seventeenth National Congress of the Communist Party of China, in order to meet the needs of restructure of the State Council, the original leading team for reform of the administrative review and approval system of the state council is canceled and inter-ministerial meeting of the State Council, led by Ministry of Supervision and consisted of 12 departments such as State Commission Office of Public Sectors Reform and State Development and Reform Commission for reform of the administrative review and approval system, is established so as to further promote reform of administrative approval system. Meanwhile, all local governments established leading organizations for reform, forming the work pattern of unified leadership by party committees and governments, coordination organized by administrative body and charging by relevant departments to promote the reform of administrative approval system with wisdom and power from all aspects.

From 2002 to 2012, the State Council conducted reform of administrative approval system for 6 times successively; the first reform was conducted in October of 2002, in which 789 items requiring administrative approval were canceled; the second one was in February of 2003, in which 406 items requiring administrative approval were canceled and management of 82 items were regulated; the third reform was conducted in May of 2004, in which 475 items requiring administrative approval were canceled or regulated, among which 409 items were canceled while 39 items were regulated; the forth reform was conducted in October of 2007, in which 186 items requiring administrative approval were canceled or regulated, among which 128 items were canceled, 29 items were delegated to lower levels, 8 items were regulated while 21 items were integrated; the fifth reform was conducted in July of 2010, in which 184 items requiring administrative approval were canceled or issued, among which 113 items were canceled while 71 items were delegated to lower levels; the sixth reform was conducted in August of 2012, in which 314 items requiring administrative approval were canceled or regulated, among which 184 items were canceled; 117 items were regulated and 13 items were integrated; in these six reforms, the State Council totally canceled and regulated 2497 items requiring administrative approval, accounting for 69.3% of original quantity.

In order to regulate reform of administrative approval system, policies and documents, such as Opinions on Reform of Administrative Approval System, Some Problems on Principles for Implementation of Reform of Administrative Approval System and Opinions on Deepening the Reform of the Administrative System, were issued to clear guiding principles, basic ideas, work target and methods & procedures the reform shall abide by.

Through the efforts of more than ten years, the reform of administrative approval system has wide and positive influence on politics, economy and society. The first one is the acceleration of transformation of government functions. Through transformation of government functions, the government transfers what is not its business to the enterprise, society and market so as to gradually tease out its relation with market and society. The phenomenon of excessive centralization of power is changed to a certain degree. Besides strengthening and improvement of macroeconomic regulation and control as well as enhancement of market supervision, governments at all levels are paying more attention to fulfill the social management and public service functions so as to promote the harmonious development of economy and society. The second one is promotion of administration according to law. Administrative License Law of The People's Republic of China was officially implemented in July of 2004, representing the reform of administrative approval system and work have marched on the legalized and standardized track. According to unified arrangement by the State Council, local governments and departments comprehensively clean up, abolish and revise administrative rules, regulations and normative documents that are inconsistent with laws. Meanwhile, new laws, regulations and systems related to administrative approval were formulated to regulate government permission and procedures for function performance according to laws; the third one is enhancement of governmental administration innovation. Take promotion of governmental administration innovation as the main content of deepening reform of administrative system; all links of administrative approval, unless national and commercial secrets and personal privacy are involved, shall be public to all people so as to perform open approval. Local governments also proactively explore and establish government affair center to realize one window to public and one stop services; development of electronic government affair as well as online declaration and approval; these reforms plays a significant role in deduction of government work procedures, optimization of government structure and improvement of administrative efficiency. The forth one is promotion of construction of a clean government; administrative responsibility system and the accountability system are further perfected via deepening reform of administrative system as well as to further curb the spreading of disciplinary violations and corruption phenomena of power abuse and abuse of power for personal gain; it also promotes the construction of clean government.

### 3.2.2 Reform of administrative review and approval system since 2013

After the formation of new State Council, acceleration of government function transformation and streamline administration & institute decentralization are the priorities for the government. Take the deepening reform of administrative approval system as the hand and breakthrough to promote streamline administration & institute decentralization, combination of issuance and control as well as optimized services to promote the reform. In June of 2013, the State Council confirmed that the department in charge of reform of administrative approval system is State Commission Office of Public Sectors Reform, replacing previous Ministry of Supervision. The Office for reform of administrative approval system under the State Council is located in State Commission Office of Public Sectors Reform. In April of 2015, the State Council decided to change the name of coordination team for function transformation under the State Council to coordination team for function transformation promoted by the State Council; as the deliberation and coordination agency of the State Council, it also has reform team for administrative approval, who is responsible for organization and promotion of reform of administrative approval system of the State Council; meanwhile, there are also specific teams for reform of investment approval and reform of commercial system as well as function teams such as comprehensive team and legal team.

At beginning of the new government, there are more than 1700 items requiring approvals by departments under the State Council; there are lots of obstacles for investment and public issues; the procedures of approval are complicated and time consuming and of higher cost and lower efficiency. It not only severely inhibits the market activity and restricts economic and social progress but also leads to power rent-seeking and rise of corruption. Enterprises and masses have strong opinions against this. Therefore, the new government proposes to delegate powers to the market and society with courage like a solder cuts his wrists and solemnly commits to canceling more than one third of items requiring administrative approval. In the part three years from 2013 to 2015, departments under the State Council canceled and issued 618 items requiring administrative approval, accounting for 36% of total original ones. The target committed by the new government is completed in advance with excessive amount. The approval of non-administrative licensing is finally and thoroughly terminated. The investment project directory approved by the government is modified for twice consecutively. The project quantity approved from central party level is decreased by 76% in accumulation; 95% of foreign investment projects and 98% overseas investment project are approved and registered on the internet. Promote the reform of commercial system: the industrial and commercial registration is changed from previous "first approval certificate then business license" to "first business license then approval certificate", in which the pre-approval is simplified by 85%; the registered capital is changed from paid-in capital to subscription; full implementation of "integrate the business license , the organization code certificate and the certificate of taxation registration into one document" and "one license with one code"; the items requiring approval for personal and enterprise qualification were decreased by 44%; in order to realize more tax reduction and general deduction, a series of preferential tax policies are issued successively such as constant expansion of pilot project of "replacement of business tax with VAT" and cut off most intermediary service items during administrative approval as well as cancellation, halt and derate large amount of administrative fees and government-managed funds. The pricing items by central government were canceled by 80%; half of special transfer payments from the central government to local government are deducted. Along with power delegation, supervision in and after course shall be innovated and enhanced. Establish the system of list of power and obligations for government department; when handover or accepting delegated power, all local governments shall proactively promote reform of "delegation, control and service" responding to expectation for optimization of public services by the mass; items requiring administrative approval by most provinces are decreased by 50%, even 70% in some provinces.

The reform effectively stimulates the market vitality and social creativity, particularly the promotion of rapid development of new driving force. The enthusiasm for mass entrepreneurship and innovation is high while the new market entities are developing rapidly and constantly. Since 2015, the increase of new enterprises reached 40, 000 daily across the country, among which 12,000 are newly registered enterprises. The enterprise vitality remains at 70%; the business environment in China is improved significantly; the cost for market access and operational system is decreased dramatically and total factor productivity was improved steadily.

There are mainly five features in reform of administrative review and approval system in recent three years: one is that we not only vigorously cancel and delegate items of administrative approval but also pay attention to innovation of supporting systems. When we cancel and delegate administrative approval items in batches, we also promote innovation of relevant systems, such as reform of industrial and commercial registration system, transforming "first approval certificate then business license" to "first business license then approval certificate"; promote convenient industrial and commercial registration system and change the paid-in system to subscription system; change the annual inspection system to annual report system so as to make it easier to establish a business; explore to establish system of negative list in free trade zone and implement the principle of "Absence of Legal Prohibition Means Freedom" for the market entity. The Second is to pay attention to promote reform with idea and method of rule of law. The essence of administrative approval system reform is the transformation of government functions; regulate and restrict government behaviors to realize law-based administration of government; legal idea and method shall be applied from the arrangement and implementation of deepening reform of administrative approval system; strictly abide by requirements on power & rights by law, legal procedure and openness & transparency; in order to promote reform of administrative approval system and transformation of government functions according to laws, the State Council submitted relevant laws to Standing Committee of the National People's Congress for revision according to legal procedures so as to abolish some administrative laws & regulations as well as modify some administrative regulations & provisions. The third, implement reform measures via open mechanism and mechanism of reversed transmission of the pressure. For detailed measures involved in streamline administration & institute decentralization and transformation of government functions, the new government specified responsible unit, participating unit and time table of reform completion; the government also committed to reducing more than one third of administrative approval items, demonstrating the determination and target of comprehensively deepening reform ; publish administrative approval items of the State Council on websites of all departments and SCOPSR as well as publish power list system so as to accept supervision by the mass and the society. Meanwhile, bring in evaluation mechanism by a third party for canceled or delegated approval items so as to form reverse pressure against the reform to promote substantial process of reform as well as implementation of all measures. The fourth, empty the stock and strictly control the increment simultaneously. During the cancellation and delegation of administrative approval items, we shall consider not only the stock reform but also control of increment. The State Council successively issued *Notice of the State Council on Strictly Controlling the Establishment of New Administrative Licensing Items* and *Notice of the State Council on Cleaning Up Non-Administrative License Examinations and Approvals by Departments under the State Council*, in which the State Council explicitly request to strictly control new approval items with strict requirements on standard settings and procedures for new administrative approval items; approval in other form is prohibited beyond the list even for necessary administrative approval so as to avoid corruption and to realize clear standards, strict procedures, effective restriction and clear rights & responsibilities. Meanwhile, existing non-administrative license examinations and approvals by departments under the State Council are cleaned up and canceled. The fifth, innovation of government supervision mode. Innovate the supervision mode via perfection of supervision measures as well as realize full utilization of market mechanism and social power to realize transformation of government attention from prior approval to supervision in the course and afterwards.

## 3.3  Main Achievements and Basic Understanding of Transformation of Government Functions

The  Chinese  government  made  great  progress  and  achievements  in transformation of government functions. Government function of economic regulation and market supervision is enhanced; social management and public service receive more attention; problems of insufficient transformation of government, such as absence, offside and mal-position have been improved. All these lay solid foundation for further comprehensively deepening reform.

Firstly, to enhance and improvemacroeconomic regulation and control. To meet needs of accelerated transformation of economic development pattern and promote development of science and technology, we shall constantly enhance and improve macroeconomic regulation and control; comply with laws in socialist market economy and further perfect macroeconomic regulation and control system to regulate economic activities with more economic and legal means; enhance the force on regulation of economic structure and lay the emphasis on promotion of transformation of economic development pattern and promotion of supply-side structural reform so as to further enhance the foreseeability, pertinence and effectiveness of macroeconomic regulation and control.

Secondly, to enhance and improve market regulation level. Regarding market supervision, spare no effort to solve division of management responsibilities and insufficient supervision so as to establish and perfect unified, open and competitive modern market system. Strengthen reform of market supervision system and rationally define market supervision scope to gradually form market supervision integrated with administrative enforcement of law, industry self-regulation, supervision by public opinions and mass participation; regulate market supervision behaviors and improve market supervision pattern; supervise and manage market entities and behaviors according to laws so as to maintain market order with fairness and competition; strive to cultivate and regulate intermediary organizations and professional services organizations in all markets to promote and guide the social power to participate in market supervision.

Thirdly, to pay attention to social management and public service. More resources shall be allocated to field of social management and public services; reform the financial system, adjust the revenue and expenditure structure, increase gross supply of public products and expand coverage of public services; promote classified reform of public institution, scientifically and rationally define relation between government and public institutions, enhance responsibilities by public institutions for provision of public services and improve level of public services; innovate the supply pattern of public services and solve shortcomings in provision of public service by the government via procurement of services; promote reform of industry system according to plans and regulate & develop social organizations; delegate responsibilities of coordination, service and technical assistance to the social organization to guarantee the key role of social organization.

Fourthly, to further promote the cleanness of authority-responsibility relationship between different levels and departments so as to constantly improve administration efficiency. Further clarify the authorization clarification between central and local governments and segregation of duties between different departments; key point of government service and social management shall be highlighted; the situation of same status of responsibilities at different levels is improved; the ability for macroeconomic regulation and control by central government is further improved while the service level by local government for grass-roots level and the masses is improved as well; define intersected responsibilities between different key departments and gradually establish mechanism of coordination and cooperation between departments so as to clarify and strengthen department responsibilities; administrative law enforcement system shall be further teased out to gradually solve highlighted problems of law enforcement with interference to citizens by different departments at different levels; proactively promote the reform of provincial governing county system and reform pilot in economically developed towns; expand the administration authority for county government and economically developed towns and increase decision-making power for development.

Generally speaking, the transformation of functions of Chinese government basically meets the development of economy and society, promoting the continuous deepening of administrative system reform and accelerating the construction and development of service-oriented government. We now have the following basic understandings. First, to promote administrative reform with transformation of government functions as the core and government functions will constantly be regulated and changed with the development of economy and society. Second, to general requirements on separation of government from enterprises, capital, business and market intermediary organizations as well as transform government functions to main standards to test results of the administrative system. Third, to take clarification of department responsibilities, sorting of authority-responsibility relationship and regulations on relation between central and local governments as the key content during transformation of government functions. Fourth, to organically combine transformation of government functions with setting of regulation organs, innovation of government administration pattern and administration operation mechanism. Fifth, adhere to the principle of gradual and constant promotion of transformation of government functions.

## References

1. The General Office of State Commission for Public Sector Reform. ( 2008, December 18) . Further Boost in Overall Layout—Reflection of the Institutional Reform in China. *People's Daily*, p. 7.

2. Zhu G. Y. ( 2008 ) . Construction of Service-Oriented Government, a New Phase for Transformation of Government Functions—Review on and Expectation of Process of Function Transformation of Chinese Government. *CASS Journal of Political Science*, 6, 67 – 72.

3. Center Group of Theory Studying of State Commission Office of Public Sectors Reform. (2011, July 25) . Glorious History of Administrative Restructuring in China since Reform and Opening-up Policy. *People's Daily*, p. 10.

4. Ying S. N. (2012) . Reform of Chinese Administrative Approving System: Retrospection and Innovation. *Academic Frontier*, 3, 48 – 53.

5. Wang L. M. ( 2014 ) . Deduction, Delegation, Reformation and Administration shall be

done together for Deepening Reform of Chinese Administrative Approval System - Opinions and Suggestions to Deepen the Reform of Administrative Approval System by Departments under the State Council. *Chinese Public Administration*, *1*.

6. Tang Y. L. ; Zhu C. （2004）. Basic Experience and Optimization Path for reform of Chinese Administrative Approving System by Central Government Since 2001. *Theoretical Discussion*, *5*, 148 – 153.

7. Wang P. Q. （2015）. Discussion on Several Theoretical Issue Concerning Government Functions. *Academic Journal of National School of Administration*, *1*, 31 – 39.

8. Ran H. （2015）. The Process, Issue and Trend of China's Streamlining and Power Delegation and The Reform of Administrative Approval System. *New Vision*, *5*, 26 – 32.

（Written by: Feng Chen, Deputy Secretary General, China Society for Public Sector Reform）

# Chapter IV

# Reform of Public Service Units in China

In China, one of the major Administrative Reform is the reform of public service units. Since the 1980s, reform of public service units has been an important reform parallel to that of the rural areas, SOEs and administrative system along with China's reform and opening-up progress. Public service unit is an organization form of the public sector unique to China. Today, public service units have become the main providers of public services as they can be found in major sectors related to people's livelihood, such as education, science and technology, culture, and health care in the forms of schools, research institutes, cultural organizations, medical institutions, etc. It now refers to "public service units or public service institutions subordinated to government agencies that are established for the purposes of public services, funded by state owned property and engaged in education, scientific, cultural and health care undertakings"[1]. Although the concept of *public service unit* or *public service institutions* is unique to China, institutions of similar functions can also be found worldwide, such as independent agencies, executive agencies, non-departmental public bodies, bodies of public law, semi-autonomous bodies, according to OECD[2].

Further promoting reform of public service units is important because such

---

① State Council: "Provisional Regulations on the Registration and Administration of Public Service Units", Decree No. 411 of the State Council, 2004.

② OECD: Distributed Public Governance: Agencies, authorities and government bodies, CITIC, 2002.

reform is about improving people's livelihood and scientific, educational, cultural and health care undertakings that are closely related to people's welfare. Only by deepening reform can the government meet the society's increasing need for public services. Moreover, such reform is crucial for transforming government function and building a public service-oriented government. In addition, such reform is critical to sustainable economic growth, as public service is an indispensable part of the tertiary industry and a potential area to boost consumption. It is also vital for structural improvement of economic engines, economic transformation and upgrading. In a word, pushing forward reform of public service units is critical to the overall layout of reform and opening-up.

## 4. 1  A Review of Reform of Public Service Units in China

According to General Principles of the Civil Law of the People's Republic Of China, there are mainly four types of legal persons: corporate legal person, government agency legal person, public service units legal person, and social organization legal person. Public service units is independent legal person. Currently, there are 1. 11 million public service units in China, with a total of over 31 million employees. Classified by industries, public service units can be divided into 25 major categories and over 100 minor categories. In 10 industries, there are public service units with more than over 400, 000 officially budgeted posts. Over half of the public service units belong to the education sector, with a total of 14. 83 million employees. The health care sector and the cultural sector has the second and third largest number of public service units. Public service units first appeared during the period of planned economy. In the 1950s, following the pattern of the Soviet Union, China adopted a series of actions to transfer private ownership to public ownership, thus forming a mechanism with the government as the arranger, and public service units as the sole providers of public services. In 1955, the word "public service units" was first used in an official document, referring to "government agencies or departments whose budget are listed by state finance as expenses for public undertaking. "

The reform on public service units can be divided into the following phases:

### 4.1.1 Power Delegation and Profit Sharing to Invigorate Public Service Units

Taking economic development as the central task was identified at the Third Plenary Session of the 11th Central Committee held in December, 1978. However, due to the influences of the Cultural Revolution, financial support forscientific, education, cultural and health care undertakings had been highly insufficient. Meanwhile, the planned economy mentality and strict policy restrictions resulted in public service units' lacking of vigor. Under such circumstances, initial reform on public service units centered on delegating administrative power to public service units at all levels. It started within the scientific sector first, as it is closely related to economic development, followed by exploration of further reform in health care, education and cultural sectors. In 1985, reform of the fund appropriation for research institutes was proposed in a document of the central government, which involved classification management of funds according to features of different research activities. In this way, research institutes were granted more decision-making power. A system whereby the director of a research institute takes responsibility was adopted, and it was made clear that trial implementation of the system of employment under contract could be carried out in research and design institutes and higher education institutions. In the cultural sector, trial reform of the art performance troupes was put forward by the Ministry of Culture through the introduction of the contract responsibility system. Paid services and commercial activities enjoyed policy encouragement, and contributed to the thrive of the cultural sector in turn. In the health care and education sectors, power delegation invigorated local public service units and institutions. For instance, in the health care sector, state subsidies to hospitals all followed the rule of fixed subsidy, and decision making by individual hospital except for major maintenance and purchase of large scale medical equipment. In the education sector, the state implemented the principle of local government taking the responsibility for basic education and carrying out classification management in 1985. Later, reform of the enrollment plan and graduation assignment system of higher education institutions were also implemented, which showed that higher education institutions were granted more decision-making power.

Through policy incentives of delegating power and sharing profits during 1985-1992, public service units were invigorated. However, due to insufficient fund and other difficulties, reform of the public service units was still comparatively passive. The main focus of the reform would thus be on expanding resources for funds. It should also be noted that during this period of time, the line between public service units and enterprises was blurred as public service units were starting to "make profits", which showed early signs of unclear functions of public service units.

### 4.1.2 Separating the Government and the Public Service Units, and Conducting Special Reform

After the goal of pushing forward reform towards socialist market economy was proposed in 1992, establishing a government administration system compatible to socialist market economy became a priority. Reform of the public service units thus entered a new phase of establishing a system for the operation of public service units and human resource management compatible to socialist market economy. In 1993, reform of the wage system in public service units was carried out. As a result, classification management for three different public service units, namely full allocation, balance allocation, and self control of revenue and expenditure was adopted. The reform was mainly about the transition from full allocation to balance allocation, and from the latter to self control of revenue and expenditure, which enabled market-oriented public service units access to the market. Since 1996, exploration on targeted reform of public service units began. Intermediary agencies in the field of finance and securities underwent ownership transformation. Meanwhile, application based research institutions and geotechnic investigation and design units were reformed as enterprises.

In 1998, the reform of government institutions, personnel downsizing and the transfer of government function took place. Public service units thus undertook part of the personnel as well as part of the government functions. "As a result of the 1998 reform, the number of government agencies was cut by half, leaving a huge amount of administrative tasks unattended. Therefore, the number of public service units soared at that time. " On the other hand, along with economic and social development, government function also expanded, requiring new public service units that had administrative and law enforcement functions for supervising the environment, labor security, cultural market management and other conditions for administrative functions. Such public service units include China Securities Regulatory Commission, China Banking Regulatory Commission, China Insurance Regulatory Commission, State Electricity Regulatory Commission, etc. However, this only made the line between public service units and government agencies more blurred.

In 1996, the first administrative document on public service units, *Opinions of the State Commission Office of Public Sectors Reform on the Reform of Public Service Units* was launched, which marked the shift from reform according to sectors to overall reform. The underlying guideline was "design an overall reform plan in a scientific way, unswervingly follow the trend of social development, encourage diversified ways of classification management, and institutionalize total amount control"[1] . In this way, progress had been made in the reform of public service units in terms of human resource system, distribution system, social security, etc. In 1999, with the launching of *Provisional Regulations on the Registration and Administration of Public Service Units*, public service units were under unified registration and administration

---

① Fan, H. S. (2010) . Exploration on the Reform of Public Service Units in China. Beijing: People's Publishing House.

nationwide.

In 2000, classification reform on non-profit research institutes subordinated to State Council and departments directly under the State Council was carried out. Those non-profit research institutes that engaged in fundamental and applied research or public services were subsidized by state finance, and operated and managed as non-profit organizations. During this time, reform on the human resource system in public service units was intensified.

In this period, the reform direction became clearer. The public service units legal person registration system enabled public service units to become independent legal persons, which separated public service units from administrative departments in a legal sense. Meanwhile, the reform followed the principle of socializing public service units, which coincided with the introduction of market mechanism in the new global public administration movement. At the same time, the concept of "non-profit" appeared in official documents, which marked its presence in policy design of the reform. Also, the principle of separating public service units from the government stipulated during this period granted public service units with the status of independent social entities, which was also the main theme for ensuing reform of public service units and the administration structure. The trend of marketization emerged as well during the reform in sectors such as science and technology, education, cultural and sports. In public services sectors such as medical care and education, the trend of profit orientation rather than non-profit appeared. On the one hand, new systems were being established as public service units were gradually separated from the government. On the other hand, the incomplete reform of government bodies or new functions required of public service units again blurred the boundary between the government and public service units. Problems of "unclear distinction between the government and public service units, unclear distinction between the government and enterprises, and unclear distinction between government and social organizations" became eminent, which showed that public service units still had blurred functions, and were inadequate regarding their non-profit nature.

**4. 1. 3 Breakthroughs of Personnel Reform and Deepening Reform by Sectors (2002 – 2011)**

During this period, the reform focus of personnel system in public service units was on promoting the system of employment under contract and post manage system in all industries, in order to gradually develop a personnel management system for public service units that was different from that of administrative organs and SOEs. In 2002, the State Council forwarded a document by the Ministry of Human Resource and Social Security, which stipulated that the system of employment under contract shall be adopted in public service units, and all employees should sign contracts. In 2006, with the launch of Post Management Methods in Public Service Units (Trial, Ministry of Human Resource and Social Security ([2006], No. 70), which marked the transformation from personnel management to post management. The same year, reform of income distribution was carried out with the introduction of wage based on performance. In 2008, pilot programs of endowment insurance in public service units were carried out in provinces and municipalities such as Shanxi, Shanghai, Zhejiang, Guangdong, and Chongqing.

Public service units can be found in various sectors. Reform of public service units by sectors has always been on the way. In 2003, public service units in the cultural sector underwent major reforms. Pilot programs of the reform were carried out in 35 public service units in 9 regions nationwide. As a result, public service units in the cultural sector were divided into two categories: non-profit and profit. The reform focus on the non-profit public service units in the cultural sector included more input, system transformation, vitality enhancement, and service improvement. In 2009, structural reform of public service units in the medical and health care sector was initiated, bringing forth the separation of government and public service units, supervision and operation, hospital and medicine business, profit and non-profit. Pilot programs of the reform of public funded hospitals were also implemented. In an effort to combat the defect of blurred line between management and operation, in areas such as radio, film and television, cultural undertakings, news and press, business groups were formed, which enabled the separation of management and operation.

During this period, public service units were significantly invigorated due to reform of personnel system, together with deepening reform of the finance system, and pilot programs of reform of the endowment insurance system. Classified reform of public service units were first proposed in the 2005 Government Work Report. And pilot programs of classified reform started in certain provinces and municipalities. From personnel system reform to the reform of public service units, from pilot programs to full implementation, from unified reform to targeted reform, from single item reform to comprehensive reform, all these progresses have laid a solid foundation for ensuing reform of public service units.

### 4.1.4 Back to Its Non-profit Nature —the period of comprehensive reforms (2011 – now)

On March, 2011, Opinions of the CPC Central Committee and the State Council to Promote the Reform of Public Service Units ( [2011] No. 5) was launched, marking a new round of reforms of public service units. This is also the first top-level design that targeted at reform of public service units as a whole. One distinct feature of the new round of reform is that based on scientific classification, public service units were divided into three categories, namely public service units that undertake administrative functions, public service units that provide public services, and public service units that undertake business operations. On such basis, targeted policies were designed for public service units of different kinds to further promote the reform. As non-profit public service units are the main body of public service units, they were thus the core of the new round of reform. After the official document was released, 11 supporting documents were also launched, aiming at solving issues such as the classification of public service units, management of officially budgeted posts, finance related policies, legal person management structure, income distribution and other basic issues public service units had in common during the transition process.

Since 2011, based on the criterion of social functions, the first step of the reform was to clarify the functions of public service units. During the process, the administrative functions undertaken by public service units were given back to administrative organs, where as technical, supportive and service-oriented functions were given to public service units, and work that can be undertaken by social organizations, such as assessment, appraisal, inspection and standard making were returned to social organizations and the market. Scientific classification was mainly based on such clarification. During this period, Regulations on Personnel Management in Public Service Units was launched, which marked another step of law based reform of public service units. The endowment insurance system followed a dual system, where employers in public service units enjoyed the same basic endowment insurance system as enterprise employers. By 2015, classification of public service units that undertake administrative functions and public service units that engage in business operation was basically completed. With the launch of Opinions on the Purchase of Services by the Government to the Private Sector, such practice formed a trend, and the institutional environment for the private sector to engage in the development of public undertakings has been further optimized.

## 4.2  Main Achievements of Reform of Public Service Units

### 4.2.1  Contribution to Social Development

Along with the reform of public service units, a batch of public service units in the fields of sales and production, technology and application, intermediary and services were all restructured and became enterprises. They no longer enjoyed preferential policies for public service units, and had to follow market competition rules, carry out autonomous operation and assume sole responsibility for profits or losses. Such a move gave public service units back its non-profit nature.

Meanwhile, public service units engaged in education, scientific, cultural and health care undertakings, which take up the largest proportion of public service units have been playing a significant role in promoting social development in the past three decades through constant reform.

In the education sector, the popularization of education is significant. As a result, more people are having access to education. Furthermore, efforts towards education equality have seen important progress, with the gap between urban and rural areas, different regions, schools and groups narrowing. The retention rate of Nine Year Compulsory Education reached 92.6%, and the total number of students in higher education institutes reached 35.59 million, ranking the 1 st in the world. [1]

In the health care sector, universal health care system has been established. The proportion of individual expenditure on health care in total medical expense dropped to 30%. Over 1.3 million people have been covered by three major basic medical security and insurances, namely employee basic medical insurance, the new rural cooperative medical insurance, and urban residents basic medical insurance, contributing to a participation rate of over 95%. With further improvement of the medical service system, the number of medical institutions exceeded 980,000, and the total amount of medical workers exceeded 10 million. Basic medical service system that covers both urban and rural areas has been established, which resulted in significantly improved medical service conditions: each village has clinics, each township has health care centers, and each county has eligible county-level hospitals. The proportion of residents that can arrive at a medical treatment places within 15 minutes has

---

[1]    Yuan, G. R.. Reform and Development of Employment and Social Security since the "12th Five Year Plan", Especially after the 18th CPC National Congress. Retrieved on June 10, 2016 from http: // news. 12371. cn/2015/10/21/ARTI1445365460334897. shtml.

reached 84% and 80.2% in urban and rural areas respectively[1].

In the science and technology sector, for scientific research public service units, all the projects are no longer subject to the administrative approval of the supervising unit or financial department. Instead, the undertaking unit will be in charge of the transformation of research outcomes and the income generated[2]. Meanwhile, in response to requirements of classification reform of public service units in terms of the use of research outcomes and profit management, pilot reforms have been carried out in several public service units subordinated to the central government in National Innovation Demonstration Zone, or provincial level pilot zones such as the Hefei-Wuhu-Bengbu Pilot Zone, etc[3].

In the cultural sector, with constant improvement of modern public cultural services system, a public cultural services network at the national, provincial, municipal, county-level, township, village, and community levels has been established. Moreover, in rural areas, 40,000 township level cultural service centers have been established, over 600,000 Rural Libraries have been set up, and farmers can enjoy free movie once a month[4].

Besides, reform of public service units propelled equalized public services and contributed to the building of a service oriented government that is dedicated to maintaining social security and improving people's livelihood. A considerably improved public service system has been established, which is a major driving

---

① Wang. G.. Reform and Development of Health Care since the "12th Five Year Plan", Especially after the 18th CPC National Congress. Retrieved on June 10, 2016 from http: // news. 12371. cn/2015/10/20/ARTI1445278350425253. shtml.

② Wan. G. (2005). China's Scientific Innovation Since the "12th Five Year Plan" (Particularly after the 18th CPC National Congress). Party members' website, http: //news. 12371. cn/2015/10/22/ARTI1445451095310860. shtml.

③ *Notice on Further Implementing Pilot Programs of the Use, Distribution and Profit Making of Scientific Research Results in Public Service Units Directly Subordinated to the Central Government.*

④ Yin, W. M. (2015). Reform and Development of Employment and Social Security since the "12th Five Year Plan", Especially after the 18th CPC National Congress. Retrieved on June 10, 2016, from http: //news. 12371. cn/2015/10/21/ARTI1445365460334897. shtml.

force to equalized public services, more public service-oriented government function, optimized government structure and administrative mechanisms. With more investment in public finance, significant progress has been made.

### 4. 2. 2 Separation from the Government-Clarification of the functions of public service units

Long after the Reform and Opening-up, public service units were still affiliated to governments without being independent legal persons, and their functions were mainly based on government functions. Many public service units that were administrative and entrepreneurial in nature took up much administrative and profit-making functions. Before the Reform and Opening-up, "some public service units did not have clear functions, and could not separate from government and enterprise functions", as a result, " social service development in China was relatively backward, with inadequate social welfare services, single way of service provision, irrational resource distribution, and low quality and efficiency" .

With the new round of reform of public service units in 2011, a series of reform measures were launched and implemented. Public service units were qualified as independent legal persons. While the government delegated micro management to public service units, public service units continued to provide the society with public service as independent legal persons.

In the process of realizing the separation of the government and public service units and further straightening the relationship between the the two, it was proposed that government departments should reduce micro-management and direct management on public service units. On the other hand, their role in stipulating policies, laws and regulations, planning the development for different sector, improving standardization, supervision and instruction, in order to ensure the independent legal persons status of public service units as independent legal persons. For public service units that are providers of public service, " we actively explore effective ways to separate management and operation, and will work on gradually eliminate administrative ranks. " In a sense, reform of public service units further strengthened the public service function of the government by further clarifying the role of public service units as the main provider of public services, and the main force in basic public service area. Clearer functions also ensured that public service units could play a more important role in improving public services.

### 4. 2. 3  Reform of internal management system-bringing invigoration

Reform of public service units resulted in the development of an internal management system that is compatible to public service units, one that is different from that of the government and enterprises, with innovation in cadre management, personnel system, performance management, etc.

First and foremost, executive accountability system was widely adopted. Meanwhile, construction of legal person governance structure was promoted. Since 2012, State Commission Office of Public Sectors Reform led the launching of pilot programs of legal person governance structure in public service units. Over the past few years, the pilot program has achieved initial results, with the governance structure built in over 600 public service units, and considerably complete legal governance structure and systems developed by pilot units.

Second, personnel management system that is compatible to the features of different public service units and demand of different posts has been built. Furthermore, public service units are endowed with more authority in terms of personnel management, represented by the introduction of competition mechanism and the wide adoption of employment by contract system. By the end of 2014, the implementation rate of employment by contract system reached 93%, and the implementation rate of employment by job posting reached 91%.

Third, the previously adopted unitary income distribution system was changed to adapt to different features of public service units of different kinds, which effectively invigorated the motivation of professionals. Since 2009, salary based on performance system was fully implemented in compulsory education institutes and public service units in the public health system and grassroots medical institutes. Pilot programs of the reform were also carried out in other public service units, which further motivated employers and formed effective incentives to strengthen the vitality of public service units.

### 4. 2. 4  Breaking up Monopoly-diversified options for public services

Through reform, providers of public service gradually shifted from the government as the sole provider to the combination of government, social organizations and enterprises. Meanwhile, the private sector also has access to participate in the area of profitable public services by means of bidding, contracting, franchise, and sole proprietorship.

In the education sector, joint education programs such as "state run and private funded", "private run and government funded", and "joint program by the public and private sector" appeared. Private invested elementary schools, middle school and, universities, and other education institutes are becoming an important part of China's education. In the science and technology sector, private invested research institutes, such as R&D institutions, intermediary organizations, and high-tech technology entities supplement to state run research oriented public service units in a positive way. In the cultural sector, private funded cultural undertakings and cultural industries have seen rapid development. Freelancer writers, private booksellers, free lance performers, rural individuals engaged in the cultural industry, private invested book stores, libraries, recreation centers and community recreation groups all emerged, which resulted in the boom of urban and rural cultural markets and development of the cultural undertaking and cultural industries. In the health care sector, policies to encourage private invested medical services have been stipulated, which changed the situation of the state as the sole provider of medical services. Medical institutions funded by public donation, private clinics and private funded hospitals are allowed, forming a new picture where the state, public entities and individuals all join hands in providing medical services.

Although public service units are still the major provider of public services, with the reform of financial investment method, the procurement system has separated the government's role of service procurer from service provider and arranger. The government no longer provide all public services, but instead, procure public services from entities other than public service units. In this sense, the previous monopoly with government as the sole public service provider had been broken up. As a result, public service market has been on the rise, bringing forth diversified providers and channels of public services.

## 4.3  Features of Reform of Public Service Units in China

Reform of public service units over the past three decades has generated some valuable experiences. To summarize, these experiences include classified reform, pilot reform, progressive reform, and systematic reform.

### 4.3.1  Classified reform-attending to the differences of public service units

Classified reform has been stressed since the beginning of reform of public service units, due to the variety and complexity of public service units. In different phases of the reform, different classification criteria were adopted. Since 1985, the reform was mainly based on different features of different industries, along with systematic reform in education, cultural, health care, science and technology sectors in order to fully unleash the motivation of administrative departments. For a while, reform of public service units followed such a pattern, where administrative departments were given more space to avoid one-size-fits-all kind of deal, which was also an internationally prevalent practice. In the 1990s, reform on public service units was based on different budget channels of public service units. Based on budget channels, public service units were divided into three categories: full allocation, balance allocation, and self control of revenue and expenditure. In this way, the government could realize more effective management of the finance of public service units. For the past decade, however, classified reform was mainly based on the social functions of public service units and more focus was put on scientific classification. Such classified reform is one valuable experience of reform of public service units in China, as it would make the reform more targeted with concerns of the differences of public service units.

### 4. 3. 2  Pilot reform-wide application based on successful experiences

"Looking before you leap is a reform approach that has Chinese characteristics and applies to the realities of China. Looking before you leap also means to learn from practice. "[1] Just as reforms in other areas, the reform of public service units also started with pilot programs, which is a way to learn from practice. For instance, pilot programs structural reform of art performance groups started in the latter half of 1988, in some large and medium-sized cities that undertook comprehensive reform of economic systems appointed by the State Council. The 1992 deepening reform of scientific research system also started with pilot programs. "Pilot programs shall be adopted in 3 – 5 research institutes in their respective fields for structural adjustment, and in 5 – 10 research institutes in trying out structural optimization and operation system reform as an effort to explore ways for major research institutes to operate towards a commercialized direction. " Pilot program of reform of public service units is also a way to accumulate experiences, identify problems, and lay foundation for wide adoption. During the personnel system reform of public service units in the health care sector in 2000, pilot programs of new types of management systems, such as board decision making system and the establishment of board of supervisors were introduced under approval in institutions where reform on proprietorship was under trial. In 2008, pilot programs of classified reform of public service units were carried out in five provinces and municipalities such as Shanxi, Shanghai, Zhejiang, Guangdong and Chongqing. Important reforms such as this usually start with pilot programs. In the process, based on local

---

① Xu, S. S. (2003, November 19). "Reforms Must Start with Pilot Programs, and Knowledge Lies in Practices". People's Daily.

realities, these provinces and municipalities can propose detailed implementation plans, and issue the plan to local party committee, government and commission of sector reform for approval, and the plans can then be implemented after they are put in files by State Commission Office of Public Sectors Reform. In the implementation process, local authorities will coordinate with finance, human resource and social security departments and summarize important experiences. Another example is that in 2010, Opinions on Pilot Programs of Reform of Public Funded Hospitals were released, requiring 1 – 2 cities (districts) in each province, autonomous region and municipality to be the pilot city for reform of public funded hospitals. The state then chose 16 cities to carry out pilot programs under state direct instruction. In this way, we can research on problems arising from the pilot program and solve the problems in a timely manner. By constantly summarizing experiences, we can further improve the general idea and main policy measures of the reform.

Pilot programs are important for the reform for they are based on realities and conform to specific conditions of the areas and organizations where these programs are carried out. Moreover, they ensure power delegation, which better motivates local authorities and encourages explorations of different kinds, and results in an accumulation of experiences. When problems arise, relevant departments and organizations can communicate and coordinate, which ensures proper management of the relationship between reform and development.

### 4.3.3 Progressive reform-ensuring smooth transition

Public service units cover a lot of sectors and industries, with a large number of organizations and personnel. Under such circumstances, progressive reform that starts from easy to difficult is necessary. First, a one-size-fits-all kind of deal should be avoided, and targeted measures should be adopted for personnel of different age, for instance. In another sense, reform is the re-distribution of interests, which concerns every individual. No matter it is the reform of endowment insurance or system transformation of public service units, targeted measures for certain issues were adopted to reduce obstacles from the employers' side. Second, policy making during the transition period of the reform ensured smooth transition. The official document on the reform of public service units in 1996 embodied the idea of progressive reform. " Promote eligible full allocation public service units to offer paid services according to certain regulations; balance allocation public service units shall further create conditions to transit to self control of revenue and expenditure or enterprise management. " During the reform, all regions and department were required to propose the range, standard, proportion and time line for the transition of public service units. For instance, if a public service unit is transformed to an enterprise, it was clearly stipulated that " during the transition period, government budget will still be granted to solve the social security issue of people who retired before the system transformation. " For classified reform, " public service units that fully conform to certain categories should be identified; those that almost fit in certain categories shall be put in an assumed category before they are identified according to all conditions. " Progressive reform was a way to reduce the resistance of reform, and to minimize the impact of reform on stability, while protecting the rights of employers. Thirdly, state finance as the support. During the transition period of system transformation, for instance, if the enterprise's pension calculated according to the enterprise standard is lower than the that calculated according to the former public service units' standard, the government would subsidize the difference by using the basic endowment insurance fund. The fund was undertaken by the Ministry of Finance, and under the joint management of the human resources and social security departments and finance departments. The latter would fill in the gap once the fund is inadequate. In a word, progressive reform effectively mitigates possible conflicts and ensures stability during the reform.

### 4.3.4　Systematic reform-joint efforts of targeted reform and comprehensive reform

Reform of public service units is a complex and systematic undertaking which is never isolated from other social progress. First, it always goes along with the reform of administrative system and is compatible with socialist market economy, aiming at power delegation and invigoration. It can be seen as part of, or an extension of administrative reform. Second, it is related to reform of cadre personnel system, which stresses classified reform of government agencies, public service units and SOEs. Third, it concerns the commercialized operation and non-profit nature of public service units. The new round of reform of public service units in 2011 highlighted the systematicness of the reform. Official documents of the highest level since the founding of new China in 1949 were released that same year, which provided answers for the generality, transition and basic issues concerning public service units. Meanwhile, 11 documents included instructions for reform details, such as classification, sector reform, legal person management, and state asset management. The 1 + 11 documents proposed joint measures to systematically push forward the reform, and manage the relationship between the reform of public service units and that of the economic structure, administrative reform and relevant sector reform. It also provides references for how to coordinate measures of internal reform, in order to ensure the consistency and compatibility of reform measures.

Although China's reform of public service units has been effective, there are still remaining problems that need special attention: China's social development is still relatively backward; some public service units still have blurred functions, which can be hardly separated from government and enterprises, resulting in its inflexibility; the overall supply of public services is still inadequate, and supply channel is relatively unitary, resource distribution needs to be more rational, and quality as well as efficiency of the supply should be improved; policy measures supporting public services are far from enough, and supervision still needs to be strengthened. All these issues are affecting the healthy development of public services in China. By 2015, classification of public service units had been completed, and reform on public service units that undertook administrative functions or engaged in businesses had been basically accomplished. Non-profit public service units still belonged to public service units. By 2020, it is scheduled that a management and operation system featuring clear functions, improved governance, efficient operation, and strong supervision should be built, and a public service system that "prioritizes basic services, adequate supply, rational service structure and trustworthy services", one that has Chinese characteristics be established. Such a goal is consistent with the goal of building a moderately prosperous society in an all-round manner by 2020. For reform in the next step, the focus would be on non-profit public service units. And the reform shall be further carried out in education, health care, cultural, science and technology sectors, covering issues including the separation of government and public service units, and the separation of supervision and operation, legal person management structure, personnel system, income distribution, finance and taxation, social security and reform, supervision and management, etc.

## References

1. Fan, H. S. (2010). Exploration on the Reform of Public Service Units in China. Beijing: People's Publishing House.

2. Policy Research Office of the State Education Commission (1985). Selected Articles on the Reform of the Education System. Beijing: Education Sciences Publishing House.

3. State Council (2004). Provisional Regulations on the Registration and Administration of Public Service Units. Decree of the State Council, No. 411.

4. State Council (2014). Regulations on Personnel Management in Public Service Units. Decree of the State Council, No. 652.

5. OECD (2002). Distributed Public Governance: Agencies, authorities and other government bodies. Beijing: China CITIC Press.

6. Wan. G. (2005). China's Scientific Innovation Since the "12th Five Year Plan" (Particularly after the 18th CPC National Congress). Party members' website, Retrieved on June 17, 2016, from http://news.12371.cn/2015/10/22/ARTI1445451095310860.shtml.

7. Xu, S. S. (2003, November 19). "Reforms Must Start with Pilot Programs, and Knowledge Lies in Practices". People's Daily.

8. Yin, W. M. (2015). Reform and Development of Employment and Social Security since the "12th Five Year Plan", Especially after the 18th CPC National Congress. Retrieved on June 10, 2016, from http://news.12371.cn/2015/10/21/ARTI1445365460334897.shtml.

9. Yi, L. L. （2012）. Exploration on Reform of Administrative Public Service Unites-
thinking based on investigation in three pilot provinces（municipalities）. China Public
Administration（9）.

10. Yuan, G. R.. Reform and Development of Employment and Social Security since the "12th
Five Year Plan", Especially after the 18th CPC National Congress. Retrieved on June 10,
2016 from http: //news. 12371. cn/2015/10/21/ARTI1445365460334897. shtml.

11. State Council, Opinions of the State Council to Promote the Reform of Public Institutions,
［2011］ No. 5.


（Written by: Lili Yi, Associate Professor, Department of Public
Administration and Policy, Chinese Academy of Governance）

# Chapter V

# Reform and Innovation of the Social Governance System in China

Since 1978 when reform and opening up were introduced, China has witnessed tremendous economic, social, political and cultural changes. As such, the social organizational method and order establishment model experienced their due adjustment and reform from traditional social management to social governance in modern sense. The reform and innovation of social governance system are mainly reflected in the concept, subjects, methods and priorities of social governance.

## 5. 1 Innovation of Social Governance Concept

In 2012, the significant idea of "national governance system and modernization of governance capacity" was proposed during the 18th CPC National Congress. And as an integral part of the national governance system and the modernization drive of governance capacity, "social governance" was officially written into party and state theory and policy after years of popularity in academia. In essence, social governance centers on safeguarding and realizing the legal rights and benefits of the general public on the basis of fairness and justice, in an attempt to realize social harmony, settle social problems, dissolve social conflicts, guard against social risks, enhance social recognition, protect public security and safeguard social stability. It is a rather localized concept, sharing both similarities and differences with the concept of "governance" internationally accepted. At some point, we can view it as a branch or component of "governance", rendering the concept, principle, method and means of "governance" adaptive to "social governance". Social governance is consisted of two words, "social" and "governance". As to "social", it can be interpreted as a subject, namely the governing power by social forces, or as an object, referring to the social affairs being governed. Either way, social governance is only one part of governance and not all. Therefore, it differs from "governance" in that the latter is a much broader concept with its scope larger, objects more complicated and tasks heavier, while the former is relatively simpler. Social governance is a theory with Chinese characteristics and a result of both Chinese historical tradition and reality. It is one of a kind.

### 5.1.1 Transition from social management to social governance

Social governance evolves from social management. The Chinese have long grown accustomed to the concept of social management, yet are unfamiliar with the closely related social governance. The concept of social management is deeply rooted in China. It is only natural that as long as human society exists, there is a need for social management. In the 21st century, with the high-speed economic development and advancing urbanization, the economic and social structures as well as the demand structure and social classes in China have been profoundly transformed, leaving frequent outbreaks of social problems and conflicts, old and new and the need of enhanced and innovated social management even more urgent. In 2004 during the 4th Plenary Session of the 16th Central Committee of CPC, the central government emphasized that we need to strengthen social development and management and push forward the innovation of social management system. Since then, social management has been taken as another important task of the party and the government in addition to economic development and management. It also gained attention from the academia to become a key research field with a set of valuable research results. But social management used to inherit traditional thinking pattern and instruments and take safeguarding social stability as the sole objective. Then inspired by the theory of governance and ·drawing upon the social management practices, the open-minded CPC and the Chinese government took out their boldness of theoretical innovation to introduce the new concept of social governance. The newborn concept is a further development of social management theory. It is a more reasonable and cultural version of social management that suits the requirements of the times.

### 5.1.2 Building on fairness and justice

Social governance requires the basis of fairness and justice which are both the important principles and measurements of social governance. More importantly, they are the criteria of the effects and quality of social governance. As the Chinese saying goes, when injustice happens, people feel wronged and upset, making harmony difficult to achieve. Injustice and unfairness are the root causes of many a social problem and conflict. In recent years, the Chinese government are committed to promoting fairness in people's rights, opportunities and rules by reforming the household registration system to narrow urban-rural gap; reforming employment, education and social security policies to reduce unfairness; deepening reform of the judicial system to regulate the judicial behaviors and establish a fair and efficient judicial system, thus ensuring fairness and justice throughout the entire society.

### 5.1.3 Sticking to people-orientedness

To protect civilians' legal rights and benefits, social governance requires people-orientedness. By sticking to the people-oriented principle, the government safeguard people's dignity and rights and meet their demands. It is the most significant principle of social governance. To that end, the government first need to set sight on protecting the vulnerable, because only when the vulnerable group have their rights protected, can the society truly progresses forward and the level of civilization be elevated. In contrast to the party and government cadres, experts and scholars, the farmers, migrant workers, poor people and people who find it hard to find a job in the urban areas belong to the vulnerable group enjoying less income, lower social status and weaker social influence, but facing more difficulties in their work and life and poorer ability to deal with them. In recent years, the protection of the above-mentioned groups' rights remains the priority of the CPC and government works. The series of public policies in China aim not only at universal coverage, but also at filling the gap of social development through preferential policies and priority support. The vision of upholding shared development so that all people will reap more sense of gaining benefits during reform raised during the 5th Plenary Session of the 18th Central Committee of CPC entails the aggressive development of social undertakings and the improvement of people's wellbeing so that the jobseekers get jobs, workers get paid, students have teachers, the elderly are taken care of, the sick have medical services and residents have houses to live. Only when people have their difficulties in their work and life solved, can the social conflicts and problems be muted greatly.

### 5.1.4 Pursuit of unity between dynamism and order

Social governance pursues the unity between order and dynamism and stresses the goals of stability and order as well as releasing social dynamism. Such a pursuit is a crucial step forward from social management to social governance. We should not one-sidedly highlight the importance of social order while neglecting social dynamism, so as to avoid the dead-end situation once management steps in and the chaotic situation when unfettered. Since the new administration came to power, it has taken streamlining and delegation of power, combination of management and delegation, and upgrading government services as the central tasks of the effort to deepen the administrative approval system and even the reform of administrative system. To be more specific, for the matters that the government should not and could not manage, they are handed to the market and the society; the authority of dealing with matters that fall into the realm of local and grassroots governments is decentralized. In this way, we will properly handle the relationships between the government and the market, the government and the society, society and market and the central government and local governments, inject more vitality to the market and society, encourage and support mass entrepreneurship and innovation in a way that all sources of wealth creation will be fully vitalized, all talents will have their potential tapped, all things will have their best usage and everyone feels happy.

### 5. 1. 5  Start from the source

Social governance needs to start from the source rather than the final consequence. the government should not sit still and start contemplating solutions until the problems occur. Instead, we should have some precautions and preliminary intervention, which differ from sheer control and suppression. Such a methodology needs to guarantee the rights of citizens and improve people's livelihood by conducting risk assessment and eliminating the conflicts, problems, threats and risks in their buds.

## 5. 2  Expansion of Subjects Of Social Governance

In general, social governance has diversified subjects. By governing through multiple forces, it realizes collective governance. Before 1978, China introduced the highly centralized planned economic system where the government extended its hands to all economic, political and cultural fields. To some degree, the government (including public power organs within the CPC) was the byword of state (state power). That's why some scholars believe that before reform and opening up, China had only a state without market and society. In the framework of state-market-society, the all-powerful state swallowed the market and society, leaving no room for the survival and development of the market and society. The state (or the party and the government) was almost the sole provider of all public affairs, products, services and social order. With social forces and social space out of the equation, the social management (governance) before reform and opening up was more of political management (governance) . In the first 20 years after reform and opening up, China struggled to break the planned economic system to build a socialist market economy with Chinese characteristics, cultivate entrepreneurs and market forces and allow the market to play a decisive role in resource distribution. As a result, the direct intervention in the economic life by the state was increasingly shrinking and the relationship between the government and market gradually moved towards a scientific and reasonable direction. However, in comparison, the relationship between the government and society is still far from reasonable, which is manifested in the over-intervention of the government in social affairs and the fact that the government gets involved in many things that are beyond its capability. On the other hand, for the social members' life difficulties in urgent need of resolution, the government usually is not there to help, making the social problems and conflicts hard to be timely solved and the pursuits of the general public unable to be effectively voiced. This not only pressurizes the government, but also prevent the social forces to develop themselves. For the reform and innovation of China's social governance system, it is therefore a necessity to put in place a new arrangement featuring diversity and collective governance under the leadership of the party and the government.

### 5. 2. 1 Dominated by the CPC and the government

The social governance system with Chinese characteristics requires the party committee to play a leading role and the government a dominant role. It encourages and supports the participation of people from all walks of lives. As an innovation that both advocates something and abandons something else, it carries forward and develops the social management system. The participation by diverse players is led by the CPC and dominated by the government. Hence, to innovate social governance, the government first need to enhance party leadership, give full play to the dominant role of the government, instead of giving them up. But the way in which the party and government play their roles in social governance must not simply copy the traditional one. Rather, the government must keep up with the times and continuously reform and improve the system. The CPC leadership is conducive to ensuring that social governance will not deviate from its direction and stay on track. Social governance in China cannot imitate the experience and practices of other countries, which means we must explore to establish a social governance model that aligns with China's historical and cultural tradition and socialist market economy with Chinese characteristics. CPC leadership will help unit, organize and mobilize all forces to take part collectively, because CPC has strong cohesion and integrating power, enabling it to coordinate sorts of forces. Under new historical conditions, the CPC leadership in social governance lies in its judging the status quo, formulating major policies and principles, shaping social thinking, values, public opinions and social mentality, and selecting, utilizing and nurturing talents in this regard. The dominant role of the government is embodied in regularly studying and predicting social development trend, compiling special schemes of social governance, enacting social policies and regulations, coordinating institutional designs related to social governance, managing the general situation, gathering and properly distributing resources. In recent years, the party committees and governments at all levels stepped up their research of the macro policies of social governance, improved the top-level design, unremittingly intensifying the accountability system of social governance, strengthening the performance evaluation of governance and setting up a more detailed and strict evaluation system of indicators.

### 5.2.2 Multilateral participation

The modern society is a complicated one, with diverse and varied social needs, complex and delicate social affairs and tons of social problems and conflicts. Accordingly, the governing party and government could not take all things in their hands, thus turning to mobilize and take advantage of the market organizations and social organizations to engage in social governance. For China to foster a landscape of multiple forces and collective governance, firstly, the government will further improve urban and rural self-governing organizations and advance self-governance by the public. In this respect, the Chinese government and CPC has unveiled a series of policies and measures; secondly, we will reform people's groups represented by the Communist Youth League, the Women's Federation and Labour Union, to increase their vitality and enhance their connection with specific groups of people, thus playing their roles in social governance. In July, 2015, the central government convened a conference on the work of mass organizations where it was stated that all work related to mass organizations should center on the masses and that it need to strengthen the organizations, especially at the grassroots level, speed up the establishment of organizations in new areas and of new groups, and actively engage with and guide related social organizations. Also in July, the central government unveiled the Opinions on Strengthening and Improving the Party's Work of Mass Organizations, in which the reform direction of the Labor Union, Women's Federation and Communist Youth League was specified, releasing vitality of mass organizations and encouraging them to take part in social governance. Besides, the most important and urgent is to standardize and develop social organizations and support their participation in social governance.

### 5. 2. 3  Develop social organizations

Social organization, as an upgraded version of traditional NGOs, non-profit organizations, civil organizations and the third sector, is also a Chinese concept. It refers to two categories; first, the social organizations managed by the civil affairs departments, including mass organizations, foundations and private entities other than enterprises. By the end of 2015, the number of this type of social organizations stood at over 600000 in China; second, it refers to those that actually exist yet have not registered in the civil affairs departments. This type of organizations usually features small scale, simple or even irregular internal structure, such as the elderly volunteering organizations within communities, fishing association and chess and cards association. It is estimated that the number of this type of organizations far exceeds that registered in national agencies and they have stronger vitality. For the reform of social organizations, the Chinese government decides to firstly vitalize the existing ones by standardizing the behaviors of existing social organizations through reform and unleashing their vitality. Ever since the 18th CPC National Congress, the reform of social organizations entered a new historical stage. The objective is to separate the government and social organizations so that social organizations and industrial associations could operate independently in line with their due obligations, establish a full-fledged legal person governance structure and enhance their service capability and level. During the 2nd Plenary Session of the 18th Central Committee, it was determined that industrial associations, chamber of commerce would decouple from administrative agencies within required time. After two years of investigation and demonstration, in 2015, the General Office of the Central Committee and the General Office of State Council publicized the Overall Plan of Decoupling Industrial Associations and Chamber of Commerce from Administrative Agencies, which explained the overall requirements and fundamental principles of the reforms, identified the subjects, scope, tasks and measures of the decoupling, and elaborated on the supporting policies and ways of implementation. Among those, the most essential content is the " five separation and five standardization" in terms of organization, functions, financial assets, personnel, party building and foreign affairs. For now, the campaign is at the substantial stage. Secondly, increase the number and reinforce the organizations. Compared to developed countries, the number of social organizations in China lags far behind and falls short of the realistic requirement of social governance innovation. In 2013, the Chinese government explicated that we need to reform the registration and management systems of social organizations and that except in need of pre-approval in accordance with the laws, regulations and the decisions of the State Council, the industrial associations, chambers of commerce, scientific, non-profit organizations, urban and rural community service organizations can directly apply for registration in the civil affairs departments without the approval of authorities in charge. This will be conducive to the development of social organizations to some degree.

## 5. 3   Reform of Social Governance Method

Social governance method means the method and instruments adopted for social governance. One of the most prominent differences between social governance and social management is whether they abide by the law. While emphasizing the rule of law, social governance actively utilizes the effective methods of social management, such as moral restraint, citizen convention, village by-laws, industrial regulations and rules of entities.

### 5. 3. 1   Applying the rule of law

Since the 18th CPC National Congress, the rule of law became the mainstream reform and innovation of social governance method. According to the major task of promoting the law-based society proposed during the 4th Plenary Session of the 18th Central Committee of CPC, social governance should be incorporated into the rule of law and the level of rule of law in social governance should be elevated. To stick to the rule of law, the key is in the leaders and cadres. General Secretary Xi Jinping has mentioned on many occasions that leaders of all levels need to enhance their capability of fostering a law-based mindset and wielding the rule of law in order to press ahead with all types of work. He instructed leaders of all levels to take the initiative to abide by the law, engage in their work and problem-solving through the idea and method of rule of law, guide and support people to reasonably and legally voice their pursuits and safeguard their rights and benefits in line with the legal procedure, with a view to fending off and resolving conflicts and effectively practicing social governance. This is the "governance of officials" rather than the "governance of people" . And the cracking down on corruption and the comprehensive strengthening of party self-discipline since the 18th National Congress serve as the powerful guarantee and manifestation of such social governance on the basis of the rule of law. The rule of law calls for keeping the government power within bounds and protecting the rights of citizens. Therefore, while keeping the officials strictly accountable, the government need to set up a mechanism to protect the citizens' rights. Since the 18th CPC National Congress, the Chinese government have been dedicated to establishing and improve a mechanism for the masses to express and safeguard their interests and resolve disputes and conflicts. Firstly, it makes efforts to put in place the mechanism for the general public to express their concerns and the consultation and communication mechanism. Specifically, governments of all levels will be bound by the system of witness hearing, indicating that all the major decisions concerning the vital interests of the people need to heed the opinions of the general public on a broad scale through witness hearing. Besides, it will improve the mechanism of NPC members in contact with the masses through listening and responding to the masses' pursuits. By establishing a democratic consultative system characterized by reasonable procedures and complete links, the government will extend the consultation channels for state authorities, political consultative organizations, party groups, grassroots organizations and social organizations, thus allowing consultative democracy to play a unique role in the expression, consultation and communication of the masses when they seek their interests; Develop grassroots-level democracy to safeguard the interests of grassroots people; Improve the democratic management system in enterprises and public institutions represented by the workers' congress system to secure the legitimate rights and interests of the employees. Reform the petition system by forming a legal conclusion system for the appeals and launching the petition legislation work so as to incorporate petition into the rule of law and lead the public to express themselves legally and reasonably and safeguard their lawful rights and interests through legal channels. Secondly, the Chinese government attempt to construct a social conflict early warning mechanism by organizing and promoting grid management and social service experience of some localities, intensifying the development of grassroots party organizations, political and legal governance organs and people's mediation organizations to take advantage of their deep roots in the grassroots level and connection with the masses in order to timely grasp the concerns and worries of the public, listen to their voices, respond to their pursuits and discover any clue of social conflict for the reference of the party committee, governments and related departments for their decisions and management. Thirdly, the Chinese government will improve the social disputes prevention and resolution mechanism. Localities carry out massive visits, investigation and mediation campaigns by upholding the principles of early actions, small details, sign detection and resolution instantly on the spot, thus stiffening the conflicts in the cradle to the largest degree and circumventing any escalation of the conflicts. In terms of dissolving social disputes and disagreements, China has already established a system of mediation, arbitration, administrative adjudication, administrative review and litigation, all of which have their own characteristics and strengths and play their unique roles in the resolution of conflicts. Since 2014, in line with the spirits of the 4th Plenary Session of the 18th Central Committee of CPC, the government have further improved the series of disputes resolution systems and strove to establish a multiple disputes resolution mechanism guarantee the smooth operation, seamless alignment and mutual coordination between different systems. In details, the government aim to further improve the mechanisms of aligning arbitration and litigation, coordinating arbitration and trials, and combining reconsideration with litigation, enable all mechanisms to effectively play their roles in various fields and links and reinforce each other as they work together to resolve disputes. For example, mediation is one of the systems with Chinese characteristics. The People's Mediation Law lays down the confirmation and implementation of the efficacy of the mediation agreement by the people's courts. Effectively exercising this system will improve the credibility of mediation and prohibit the disputes already reconciled from flooding to the court, thus reducing the burden of handling cases on the courts. As a result, the government need to continue improving the mediation system. At the same time, we need to combine mediation and arbitration, and mediation and trials and see to it that while mediation comes first, those that should be arbitrated and judged should accordingly be duly arbitrated and judged.

### 5. 3. 2 Applying information technologies

China is in the era of informatization, internet and the net of things. Informatization and internet provide great possibilities and convenience for information transmission, resource sharing and social cooperation. They bring not only challenges, but also opportunities to social governance. The Chinese government are fully aware that the new generation internet + technology, once integrated with social governance service, will play a significant role in social governance and therefore takes it as an effective support of the fine social governance. The rising grid management model in recent years is one digital and information representation. It takes communities and grids as the regional scope, events as the management content, the entities as the responsible players, and it realizes connection between entities within the grid and resource sharing through managing the information platform. In July, 2015, the State Council promulgated the Directives on Actively Promoting Internet + Campaign, including 10 tasks, including items covering social governance. Other information technologies related to internet + are big data and cloud computing which are increasingly becoming important tools of social governance. On August 31st, 2015, the State Council publicized the Outline of Promoting Big Data Development in which it depicted the new social governance model in the next 5 to 10 years featuring precision governance and cooperation between multiple players. Moreover, smart city, smart communities, smart police and "sunshine petition" are becoming popular.

## 5. 4 Adjustment of Social Governance Priorities

The priorities of social governance cover the scope, areas and key tasks of social governance. With the development of industrialization, urbanization, informatization, marketization and internationalization, the situation and tasks of China's social governance go through tremendous changes, together with the adjustment of its crucial areas and focus.

### 5. 4. 1  Value the role of internet in social governance

Since the 21st century, the internet technology has enjoyed rapid development, bringing about a grand and complex internet society. Because of the anonymity, equality, wide participation and interaction of the internet society, the speed of its development is beyond imagination. It is both independent from the real society, but also closely connected with the later, becoming the new space and means of human existence and exchanges unprecedented in human history. In 2010, the number of the Chinese netizens registered 457 million, which jumped to 688 million, an increase of more than 200 million within 5 years. The birth of the internet society makes convenient people's work and daily life, learning and shopping, communication and making new friends. On the other hand, the internet is awash with mixed information, such as information of violence, porn, fraud and rumors, endangering information security. Some arguments online are unreasonable, irresponsible or even politically intended, threatening social order and political stability. To that end, it is urgent for the government to coordinate the governance of the real world with that of the internet society. In May, 2011, the General Office of the State Council set up an internet information office at national level responsible for executing the policies and principles concerning internet information transmission in an attempt to facilitate the legal transmission of internet information, guide, coordinate and urge related agencies to reinforce their management of internet information and contents. In February, 2014, the internet information office was promoted to the ministerial level. In August, 2014, the office implemented the Interim Rules on the Development and Management of Public Information Services through Instant Messaging Instruments, regulating the services of the instant messaging service providers and the usage behaviors of users. In 2015, the Standing Committee of NPC drafted the Cyber-Safety Act and solicited opinions from the public. Since 2014, the government have launched special campaigns targeting online rumors and cyber crimes for many times. Chinese Communist Party also introduced special authorities and policies and laws to govern the internet according to law and boost the healthy and orderly development of the internet society.

### 5. 4. 2  Value social governance in the urban areas

In 2011, the urbanization rate in China was 51. 27% , signifying that the urban population exceeded the rural population for the first time and that China will not be a country dominated by rural areas and farmers ever since but by cities and urban population. In the end of 2015, that rate rose to 56. 1% and is now forecast to be about 60% by 2020. The reason behind the rapid urbanization in China is the large number of rural residents migrating to the cities. In 1978, China's urbanization ratio was less than 18% . So that ratio increased by 38 percentage points within about three decades, implying that hundreds of millions of rural residents left their hometown for the urban areas. Consequently, the swift urbanization ended up with two extreme effects. First, the urban population exploded rapidly, especially in the metropolises, resulting in the high density of population which further causes the shortage of public resources and services. The migrant workers find it hard to integrate into the local lives and social governance confronts multiple difficulties. Such phenomena are quite prevalent in the mega cities, such as Beijing, Shanghai, Guangzhou and Shenzhen. Second, the population in the rural areas, especially in the less-developed central and western China, hollows out, leaving behind many hollowed out villages and ghost villages. With the young people flooding out for jobs, the left-behind children, women and elderly people stand at the number of over 100 million and become the new vulnerable group. The new changes and challenges brought by urbanization pose new problems for social governance in China. For one thing, the government need to explore the formulation of a social governance system suitable to the new features of the cities. For another, we need to strengthen and innovate social governance in the rural areas. In the end of 2015, after 37 years, the central government convened the first urban work conference since reform and opening up and asked the party committees and governments of all levels to pay high attention to the work related to the urban areas through scientific planning, construction and management, the development of urban management authorities and reform of urban law enforcement system, thus elevating our social governance level. The status of social governance in urban areas leaps upward in the general social governance landscape.

### 5. 4. 3  Value social governance at grassroots level

Grassroots-level social governance is the basis of social governance while the urban and rural communities are the carriers of grassroots social governance and community governance has become the major form of grassroots social governance. Party committees and governments at all levels are increasingly aware that the focus and difficulty of social governance lie in the grassroots. Thousands of threads have their roots in one needle—the grassroots. The primary components of grassroots are village and township subdistricts and community neighborhood committee which are directly oriented to the public and serve the public. Therefore, the level of grassroots social governance can directly reflect the general social governance level in China. In recent years, localities push forward the reform of the subdistrict and community management system according to the decentralization requirement of shifting the cores, strength and subsidies from top-down. Many places assign the social services and urban functions down to the subdistricts to give play to their roles in public services, coordinating governance within jurisdictions, organizing comprehensive law enforcement and guiding community development. In this process, the subdistrict offices have enhanced their coordinating function in the social service and urban management and the construction of a subdistrict government affairs service center is advanced. As the communities are being enhanced, the activities to reduce burden on communities are being carried out in many places. Theses activities demand the preparation of a list of communities' tasks. Communities have the right to refuse any other work allocated by government agencies and related entities that are not in the list. In line with the system of costs linked with duties, the government distributes more resources to the communities. Meanwhile, following the rules for community governance, varied forces have been mobilized, such as the neighborhood communities, social organizations, logistics companies, committee of owners and organizations in the communities. By establishing such a platform for community members to communicate, the government encourage and support them to help each other, strengthen the democratic management of public affairs, boost the connection between members and enhance their sense of belonging and recognition.

### 5.4.4 Emphasize public safety and emergency control

Public safety is a matter that concerns people's contented work and life and the social stability and order. Improving the public safety system and strengthening emergency management are the inherent contents of social governance. In the 21st century, natural disasters break out frequently; severe accidents happen from time to time; food and drug safety incidents are exposed often; the difficulty of preventing and controlling the public health problems is rising; the number of social conflicts and mass disturbances stays stubbornly high; anti-terrorism is an arduous task. In particular, with the accelerating industrialization and urbanization, the number of risk sources from high buildings, lifeline projects of water, electricity, oil, gas and transportation, large equipment, and chemical and industrial parks is mounting. Once an accident happens, there might be significant economic and social losses and injuries to men as well as social chaos. After the fight against SARS in 2003, the Chinese government started the introduction of a modern emergency management system centered on "one plan and three systems". After ten years of development, China has gradually developed and improved the emergency management agencies and systems and bolstered its capability of preventing and dealing with emergencies. But in 2015, the capsized Oriental Star along the Yangtze River, August 12th explosion in Tianjin Harbor, the December 20th landslide of residue soil in Guangming New District of Shenzhen caused severe casualties. They revealed the loopholes in our public safety system and emergency management and illustrated that we still had a long way to go to speed up the improvement of the public safety system. As the non-normal branch of social governance, emergency management has drawn unprecedented attention. Related departments are now enacting the 13th Five Year Plan of National Emergency Response System which is designed to strengthen the public safety net, fill in the loopholes of emergency management and cement the capability of guaranteeing public safety and responding to emergencies.

## References

1. Ding Y. Z. ( 2013 ) . *The Social System Reform: Strategies and Solutions*, Chinese Academy of Governance Publishing House.

2. *Supportive Readings of the Decision of the CCCPC on Some Major Issues Concerning Comprehensively Deepening the Reform* ( 2013 ) . Beijing: People's Publishing House.

3. Gong W. B. ( Ed ) ( 2014 ) . *Social Governance in China.* Beijing: China Social Sciences Press.

4. Gong W. B. ( Ed ) ( 2014 ) . *Analysis of Social Governance Examples in Contemporary China*, Yunnan Education Publishing House.

5. Han C. H. ( 2013 ) . *The Rule of Law Mindset of Social Management*, Law Press China.

6. Li P. L. ( 2013 ) . *Social Reform and Social Governance*, Social Sciences Academic Press.

7. Li H. L. ( 2004 ) . *China's Unit Society: Arguments, Thinking and Research*, Shanghai People's Publishing House.

8. Li Y. M. ( 2008 ) . *The Evolution of Social Life in China*, Encyclopedia of China Publishing House.

9. Lu X. Y. ( 2013 ) . *Social Construction in Modern China*, Social Sciences Academic Press.

10. MA Q. Y. , Liao H. ( Ed ) ( 2005 ) . *The Development Strategy of Social Organizations in China*, Social Sciences Academic Press.

11. Ma F. Y. ( 2013 ) . *Study on the Household Registration System: its legal rights and transformation*, China Society Press. 12. Shan C. C. ; Xue L. ( Ed ) ( 2012 ) . *Overview of Emergency Response—Theories and Practices*, China Higher Education Press.

13. Wei L. Q. ( 2011 ) . *Social Construction and Social Management*, People's Publishing House.

14. Wu Q. G. , Sun Z. X. （2011） . *Chinese Model of Community Governance—Exploration and Practice of Grassroots Social Management Innovation*, China Society Press.

15. Zhang L. J. （2015） . *Moving into the "Community +" Era*, Social Sciences Academic Press, 2015.

16. Zhang L. J. （2015） . *Twelve Lectures on Social Governance*, Social Sciences Academic Press.

（Written by: Weibin Gong, Director of Social Governance Research Center, Chinese Academy of Governance）

# Chapter VI

# Overhaul of Public Fiscal System

Before 1978, in compliance with the economic and political system of that era, the fiscal system in china took the form of production and construction guided fiscal, the nature of which was a combination of national finance and enterprise finance. After 1978, China initiated the great reform and opening-up scenario and its fiscal system underwent huge changes as a result. Till 2015, the overhaul of public fiscal system in China can be divided into four stages: 1. Decentralization and empowering the local governments and the establishment of a graded fiscal responsibility system that separated the local fiscal systems from the central one after the Third Plenary Session of the 11th Central Committee; 2. A tax categorization based graded fiscal system between the central and local governments that responded to the socialist market economic system in the first half the 1990s; 3. A new round of innovation for establishing new public fiscal framework after 1998; 4. A series of reforms to establish a modern fiscal system after 2013. Details are described in the ensuing passages.

## 6.1 Fiscal System in China before 1978

To put briefly, fiscal system reform in China before reform and opening-up policy was focused on the granting and withdrawal of power between the central government and local governments. At the beginning of New China, fiscal system was a highly centralized system with unified revenue and expenditure. From 1951 to 1953, the highly centralized system began to loosen up. A fiscal system featuring classified revenue sharing (fiscal revenue classified as fixed income and fixed rate distributed income of the central government and local governments and the central allocated income), expenditure budgeting according to affiliation relations and annual local budget determined by central allocation of revenue and expenditure and graded management was created. In 1958, as central government assigned management power of enterprises and fiscal power to local governments, a five-year fiscal policy of expenditure based on revenue was introduced. According to the policy, local governments were allowed to determine autonomously the fiscal expenditure considering revenue in five years time. However, the policy was only in place for one year due to economic problems. In 1961, based on the policy of totaling sharing and revision per year and the handing over of enterprises to upper management organization, fiscal power was recentralized to the central government to expand central fixed revenue. Expenditure on infrastructure construction was under central government's special provision. After 1965, the policy was slightly modified to motivate local governments. Except from the upheavals during the Cultural Revolution (1968) when separate management of revenue and expenditure were temporarily employed (revenue were totally collected by the central government and expenditure were allocated all by the central government), the policy had been implemented until 1970. In 1971, ownership of enterprises and fiscal power were again granted to local governments and a fiscal responsibility system was established. Under this system, the range of local government budget was broadened. Local government took their fiscal responsibility according to a verified absolute and extra revenue was all reserved by local governments. In 1974, under the background of economy being destroyed by the Cultural Revolution, the fiscal responsibility system was not able to survive. In its place was the system featuring fixed rate revenue reserve, additional sharing rate for extra revenue and expenditure responsibility allocated by targets, which was in short addressed as a yield guaranteed fiscal system regardless of any challenges. In 1976, to solve the disconnection between revenue and expenditure and the lack of linkage between right and responsibility in local fiscal system caused by fixed rate reserve system, the system of unified management of revenue and expenditure, totaling division and revision per year was again adopted. In summary, fiscal system of this period changed frequently. The determination of fiscal power went through twists and turns of granting and withdrawal, centralization and decentralization, which reflected to a great degree the repeated exploration of how to develop socialist economy with the greatest momentum.

## 6. 2  Fiscal System in China between 1978 and 1992

The year of 1978 witnessed the convening of the Third Plenary Session of the 11th Central Committee during which the focus of the Party's work was shifted to economic construction. A splendid thirty-year of reform and opening up was initiated since then. In February of 1980, according to the spirits of Third Plenary Session of the 11th Central Committee, the state council published the "Interim Provisions on the Implementation of Separated Revenue and Expenditure between Central and Local Governments and Graded Fiscal Responsibility System", marking the beginning of fiscal responsibility system during the process of reform and opening up.

### 6. 2. 1  Differentiation of central and local fiscal systems in 1980

The main content of fiscal responsibility system was: except from three municipal cities namely Beijing, Tianjin and Shanghai continuing with the fiscal policy of unified revenue and expenditure, totaling sharing and revision per year, the other provinces and autonomous regions all adopted the fiscal system of differentiated revenue and expenditure between central and local governments and graded fiscal responsibility system. Under this background, different implementations were carried out by different regions according to specific conditions. The followings are some major methods:

(1) A majority of provinces such as Sichuan, Shaanxi, Gansu, Henan, Hubei, Hunan, Anhui, Jiangxi, Shandong, Shanxi, Hebei, Liaoning,

Jilin and Zhejiang adopted the fiscal system of differentiated revenue and expenditure between central and local governments and graded fiscal responsibility system.

(2) Autonomous regions of minor nationalities or autonomous regions and provinces receiving the same treatment such as Inner Mongolia, Xinjiang, Tibet, Ningxia, Guangxi, Qinghai and Guizhou still maintained self managed local fiscal system. While keeping special protection to these regions, the fiscal system of differentiated revenue and expenditure between central and local governments and graded fiscal responsibility system was also implemented with specific central subsidy. Besides, the term of revision was changed from one year to five years.

(3) While implementing the fiscal responsibility system, Guangdong and Fujian province were granted a special policy and flexible arrangements, which was separated revenue and expenditure between central and local governments and fixed rate revenue turning over or fixed rate subsidy. As a result more fiscal autonomy was secured to these provinces.

(4) Jiangsu province continued with the fiscal responsibility system according to a specific ratio and the term of revision was four years. But adjustments were made to the range and reserve ratio of the fiscal responsibility system.

(5) The fiscal reform of 1980 aimed to separate local fiscal system from the central system. Governments at different levels shall control their own fiscal systems and fulfill their responsibilities for the fiscal results. The reform broke down the original fiscal situation of "everyone eating from the same big pot", and the new fiscal situation was a differentiation of local systems from the central one.

### 6.2.2 Graded fiscal responsibility system in 1985

Since the five-year period came to an end in 1985 and especially owing to the two phases of revenue turning over replaced by tax reform in 1982 and 1983, the part of revenue that should be turning over by state owned enterprises were replaced by income tax and adjustment tax. Fiscal distribution between the government and enterprises were altered greatly. Fiscal income distribution at different levels acquired new foundations and a new round of adjustment was necessary. According to the spirit of the "Decisions on Economic System Reform" of the Third Plenary Session of the 12th Central Committee, the State Council decided to implement the fiscal system featuring categorization of taxes, budget approval and graded fiscal responsibility system. The main content of the fiscal policy is as follows: 1. Define the range of fiscal revenue at different levels based on the second phase of revenue turning over replaced by tax. 2. The distribution of fiscal expenditure between central and local governments basically followed the previous system, which was scope of expenditure based on affiliation relations. Only slight adjustment was made to meet the particular changes in institutional management system. Special expenditures that were not suitable for fiscal responsibility system received special appropriation from the central government. 3. Calculation of distribution base number and determination of distribution methods. Compared to the differentiation of local fiscal system from the central one, the reform in 1985 stressed more on fiscal responsibility. But the system brought some unprecedented problems, in particular a consecutive decrease of the ratio of central fiscal income in national fiscal income. Central fiscal system was confronted with growing deficit and hardship in its operation, which all called for further reform.

### 6.2.3  Overall fiscal responsibility system in 1988

In July of 1988, the State Council issued "Decisions on Local Fiscal Responsibility Systems", stipulating fiscal responsibility system should be implemented throughout the country in different forms. There were altogether six forms: 1. Revenue increasing fiscal responsibility system. Determine revenue increase rate (compared to the previous period), local reserve and turning over ratio based on the final accounted revenue and the expenditure quota of local governments in 1987 and following the local revenue increase in recently years. Fixed rate distribution between the central and local government was applied for revenue within the increase rate threshold. Revenue extra of the increase rate threshold was all reserved ,by local government. And local fiscal system should make up for any lacking in the turning over part to the central government when local revenue did not meet the turning over amount determined by the increase rate. This type of fiscal responsibility system was implemented in 10 provinces ( cities ) , such as Beijing. 2. Total amount distribution. Determine local reserve and turning over ratio by the proportion of expenditure in total revenue based on verified budget base number. This type of contract system was implemented in 3 provinces ( cities ) such as Tianjin. 3. A combination of total amount distribution and revenue increasing distribution. Total amount distribution was employed for revenue within the base number. Additional distribution rate was adopted for the increased part of actual revenue compared to last year. In doing so, local government could receive more benefit from revenue increase. This type of contract system was implemented in three cities that were specially designated in the state plan such as Dalian. 4. Fiscal responsibility system featuring increasing turning over amount, which meant the base number of revenue turning over to the central government increased by a certain percentage every year. This type of contact system was implemented in Guangdong and Hunan provinces. 5. Fixed turning over rate, which meant the amount of revenue turning over to the central government followed a fixed rate. Shanghai and other two provinces ( cities ) adopted this method. 6. Fixed subsidy which meant the central government granted fixed subsidy to the local government. Jilin and other 15 provinces ( cities ) adopted this method.

The fiscal responsibility system in 1988 was a natural continuation of the two major adjustments of fiscal systems in 1980 and 1985. It on one hand inherited the logics of differentiation of central and local fiscal systems and fiscal responsibility system and on the other hand extended the concept of fiscal responsibility to a new level. The system was in place from 1988 to 1993. Integrated with the contractual management responsibility system of state owned enterprises in the same period, the system exerted great influence on the political, economic and fiscal system of that era.

# 6.3  Separate Tax Collection System reform in 1994

The year of 1994 is a milestone in China's fiscal history. China adopted a taxation system that was in conformity with market economy—the separate tax collection system. Based on the determination of administrative rights, the separate tax collection system was a graded budget management system that distributed revenue between central and local budgets according to tax categories. The system had three major features: firstly, it appropriately clarified responsibilities and right over expenditure between the central and local governments; secondly, all taxes were divided into three categories namely central tax, local tax and shared tax according to the matching principle of responsibilities and financial right, and the range of revenues for central and local governments were determined; lastly, a standardized transfer payment system was established for regulating supply and demand and making up for fiscal budget deficit of the governments of less developed areas. The main features of the separate tax collection system are as follows:

## 6.3.1  Clarification of responsibilities and the scope of expenditure between central and local governments

Central fiscal system was mainly responsible for expenditure on national security, diplomacy and operation of central governmental organizations, and on adjusting national economic structure, balancing regional development, implementing macroeconomic control, as well as on undertakings that were directly controlled by the central government. The scope of central fiscal expenditure included expenditure on national defense, armed police, diplomacy and foreign aid, central level administrative affairs, infrastructure that was collectively controlled by the central government, technological reform and new product R&D of directly central controlled enterprises, geological prospecting, agriculture aid arranged by central fiscal system, repayment of capital and interest of foreign debt that was assumed by the central government and on the public security organs that were directly controlled by the central government as well as on the undertakings such as culture, education, healthcare and science.

Local fiscal system was mainly responsible for expenditure of political organizations of the local area and of the local economic and institutional development. The scope of local fiscal expenditure included expenditure on local administration, public security organs, part of armed police, militia service, infrastructure that was collectively controlled by local government, technological reform and new product R&D of local controlled enterprises, agriculture aid, city maintenance and construction, as well as on local undertakings such as culture, education, healthcare and on price subsidy and other affairs.

### 6. 3. 2  Distribution of central and local fiscal revenue according to tax categorization

The fundamental principle of tax categorization at that time was that taxes requisite for protecting national interests and implementing macroeconomic control were categorized as central tax; taxes directly linked with economic development were categorized as shared tax between the central and local governments; taxes closely related to local economic and social development and suitable for local collection and management were categorized as local tax. Detailed information is as follow:

Central tax: customs, excise tax and VAT collected by the customs, excise tax, income tax of state owned enterprises, income tax of local banks, foreign banks and non-bank financial institutions, collectively collected revenue (including business tax, income tax, profit and urban preservation and construction tax) from the ministry of railways, head offices of banks and from head offices of insurance companies, and profit that should be handing over to the central government by state owned enterprises. Regarding export tax rebate of export enterprises, except for the 20% already bore by local government in 1993, which was included in the base number for handing over to the central government, any tax rebate happened after should be borne by the central government.

Local tax: business tax ( excluding collective payment of business tax by the ministry of railways, head offices of banks and head offices of insurances companies), income tax of local enterprises ( excluding income tax of the aforementioned local banks, foreign banks and non-bank financial institutions), profit handing over by local enterprises, personal income tax, tax on urban land use, tax on fixed asset investment regulation, urban preservation and construction tax ( excluding collective paid amount by the ministry of railways, head offices of banks and head offices of insurances companies), property tax, vehicle and vessel use tax, stamp duty, slaughter expense, agricultural and livestock tax, tax levied on income from agricultural products ( agricultural product tax), farmland occupation tax, contract tax, inheritance or gift tax, land appreciation tax, charges on using of state owned land, and etc.

Shared tax by central and local governments: VAT, resources tax, and securities transactions tax. VAT was shared by the central and local government by 75% and 25%. Resources tax was shared according to type of resources. The majority went to local fiscal revenue while ocean and oil resources tax went to central government revenue. Securities transactions tax was equally divided between central and local governments.

## 6.3.3 Establishing tax refund mechanism from central to local governments

To ensure social interest structure in local areas and implement reform step by step, a tax refund policy from central to local government was established: the net revenue collected by the central government from local governments in 1993 was calculated based on actual local revenue in 1993, the tax system reform and the distribution of fiscal income between central and local governments ( excise tax + 75% VAT – fiscal income allocated by the central government). Net fiscal revenue collected by the central government in 1993 was fully returned to local governments. After 1994, tax refund ratio grew year on year according to the base number of 1993. The increasing rate of tax refund was determined by a ratio of 1 : 0. 3 compared with the average growing rate of national VAT and excise tax, which meant that every 1% growth of the above two taxes, tax refund from central to local government would grew 0. 3%. In the event that the net fiscal revenue collected by the central government did not reach the base number of 1993, tax refund would be deducted accordingly.

### 6. 3. 4  Establishing separate tax authorities for central and local tax collection

To ensure fiscal revenue for both central and local governments, a new tax collection system was created. State Administration of Taxation and the Customs were responsible for collecting fixed central fiscal revenue and shared revenue between the central and local governments; local tax authorities were responsible for collecting fixed local fiscal revenue.

The separated tax collection system of 1994 was a milestone in China's fiscal reform. Its influence lasted till today and boasted of great historical importance: 1. A tax system based on commodity turnover tax and income tax were established. Under this system, enterprises, no matter of their size, ownership and administrative level, should operate and pay taxes according to regulations. The fragmented administrative subordinated relations of enterprises were broken, laying down foundation for fundamentally separating enterprises from governmental organizations and build them into independent subjects of market. 2. A direct link was created between the responsibilities and tax revenue of governments at all levels, which was conducive to promote the transformation of government functions and deepen administrative reform. 3. It was helpful to standardize the fiscal relation between central and local government and enhance the transparency of fiscal allocation. In the meantime, it was worth noticing that the separated tax collection system of 1994 in nature was a transitional tax system. During its application in the next 20 years, owning to the lack of ensued and supporting reforms, the intrinsic loopholes of the design of the original tax separation system became severer and severer as time went by. As a result, responsibilities were overly concentrated in the local governments and fiscal power was dominated by the central government and this situation had caused a series of problems.

# 6.4  The Modern Fiscal system of 2013

Decisions on Major Issues Concerning the Overall Deepening of Reform of the Third Plenary Session of the 18th Central Committee of the Communist Party of China pointed out that fiscal system was the foundation and an important pillar of state governance. Good fiscal and tax systems are the institutional guarantee for optimizing resources allocation, maintaining market unity, promoting social equity and realizing enduring peace and stability. A new round of fiscal reform has become the focus of the government and the fundamental target of the reform is to create a modern fiscal system.

## 6.4.1  Continue with tax system reform and establish a modern tax system

(1) Implement structural tax deduction and replace business tax with VAT in an all rounded way. According to scholarly studies, VAT is a neutral tax that has the smallest distortive effect to manufacturing and business activities which should widely adopted. Till now, pilot implementation of business tax replaced by VAT has been finished. From May 1 2016, business tax has been replaced by VAT nationally, laying down a structural foundation for the nation's economic transformation and upgrade.

(2) Adjust the range and procedure of excise tax collection—reform of excise tax. The reform was mainly in two aspects: one was to properly expand and adjust the range of excise tax collection by including high energy consuming and highly polluting products and part of high-end consumption goods. The other was to change the collection of excise tax from the current production (importation) process to retail or wholesale process, gradually shaping excise tax to a major type of local tax.

(3) Step up the reform of resources tax. The main content of the reform

was to change the collection of tax on crude oil, natural gas, specific metals and non-metal mining resources from quantity targeted to price targeted. Straighten out the price formation mechanism of resource products from the very beginning to economically use limited resources, promote environmental protection and ecological construction.

(4) Begin collecting real estate tax when the time has come. Currently, collection of real estate tax is in the legislative process of the National People's Congress, and may be introduced to public in two to three years' time. After around five years of construction period, real estate tax shall become another major local tax after excise tax, exerting great influence in promoting local fiscal revenue system construction and enhancing local public product supply, etc.

(5) Establish and consolidate an income tax system that combines integration and categorization. The key of the reform was to properly combine related tax items, reduce margin tax rate, improve tax deductibles and enhance supportive methods of income tax collection, and form a modern income tax system that combines integration and separation so that the government's control over income distribution will be enhanced and the stability and harmony of the society can be secured.

(6) Begin collecting environmental protection tax. Currently, collection of environmental protection tax is in the legislative process of the National People's Congress, and may be introduced to public soon.

(7) Enhance and improve preferential tax policy. The key is to strengthen standardized management of preferential tax in particular regional preference tax policy. Regional development plan shall be unhooked from preferential tax policy. Existing preferential tax policies that are going to expire shall be terminated completely. For existing preferential tax policies that are still valid, a transitional period before its termination shall be specified. For pilot preferential policies that are worth promoting, they shall be implemented throughout the country immediately. All kinds of ultra vires tax rebate shall be strictly forbidden to maintain the integrity and seriousness of tax policies.

### 6. 4. 2 Promote the reform of modern budget system

( 1 ) Implementation of inclusive budget, the key of which is to include all fiscal revenue and expenditure into budget management system. To meet this target, China has adopted a budget system of four elements: general public budget, budget for operation of state owned assets, budget for social security and budget for government managed funds. Besides, local government debts are also included so that all kinds of government managed funds are uniformly managed by the budget system and as a result the macro regulation ability of fiscal system is enhanced.

( 2 ) Strengthen budget management of key aspects. In the future, the focus of the reform will be establishing governmental accounting report system based on the accrual basis, deepening performance budgeting and enhancing fiscal responsibility, so as to form a governmental budget management system that is accustomed to the spirits of modern government management.

( 3 ) Implement mid-term budget framework. Within 3 – 5 years time, after comprehensively considering fiscal budget and fiscal arrangements, a positive relation will be established where budget resources allocation is guided by plans ( major national policies ) while budget resources in turn function as a rigid constraint for the formation of plans. The relation will not only enhance the efficiency of fiscal allocation but also support the smooth implementation of national mid and long term strategies and policies.

( 4 ) Step up transparent budget. The key of the reform is to expand the scale of transparency, specify the details that will be exposed to the public, improve the mechanism of budget transparency and enhance supervision and review of budget transparency. In the meantime, review and supervision of governmental budget by the National People's Congress shall be strengthened. Starting from the state of equilibrium and the scale of deficit, the focus of the review shall move towards expenditure budget and policies, so as to enhance the binding effect of budget and the rigidity of governmental budget system.

### 6. 4. 3 Establish an inter governmental fiscal system that matching responsibilities with expenditure rights

(1) Define the scale of responsibilities between the central and local governments. In the future, responsibilities of governments at different levels will be divided into three groups: 1. Central responsibilities, mainly including national defense, diplomatic affairs, administration of justice and other major affairs that will affect unified policy making of the state, maintain harmonization of the market, promote regional integration and ensure national security from different angles; basic public service responsibility that shall apply a unified standard nationwide. 2. Shared responsibilities between the central and local governments, mainly including public products and services that possess informational advantage in regional management but have relatively strong influence to other regions, such as some specific social security and the construction and maintenance of major cross regional project; 3. Local responsibilities, referring to affairs that bear strong regional characteristics, little externality and are mainly related to local residents, such as all kinds of local public products and services.

(2) Establish local tax system and assist the functional transformation of local governments. Any taxes as long as the tax base cannot be moved, property right is clearly defined, and they are conducive to improve the quality of local public service shall be categorized as local taxes, such as property tax and resources tax, etc. Besides, companies and enterprises that perform businesses in the region shall contribute part of their tax submission to the local government as they have utilized equipment and public services provided by the local government. With the reform of excise tax, this part of tax can be made into one of the main sources of local tax.

(3) Establish a more regulated transfer payment system. Promote unified basic public service provision nationwide by enhancing general transfer payment, reducing transfer payment of special purposes and limiting the financial power gap of different regions within an appropriate range.

In the meantime, based on the practical situation of the country, fiscal reform in the future will continue to deepen the reform of fiscal investment and financing system, promoting scientific innovation and technological advancement of the nation. A local debt management system will be constructed to promote long term and stable funding support for the accelerated construction of new type urbanization. And PPP model will be advocated to encourage collaboration between governmental and social capital.

In summary, fiscal system is the foundation and pillar of state governance. It has the important responsibilities of maintaining the stability of macro economy, regulating revenue allocation and securing social stability. To tap into its influence on economic development, governmental management and social stability, China need to the on one hand draw upon the experiences and mature methods from market economies and on the other hand make adaptive adjustment according to the social economic situation of our country. The country shall establish a modern fiscal system of Chinese characteristics that also conforms to rules of market economy, so as to meet the demands of transformation from an economic giant to an economic super power and contribute to the fulfillment of two hundred years target and the great rejuvenation of the Chinese nation.

## References

1. WuJ. L. (2004) . Chine Economic Reform (2 nd ed. ) . Shanghai: Yuandong Book.

2. JiaK. , Feng Q. B. (2004) . Review of China's Fiscal Management System in the Past Ten Years. *Review of Economic Research*, 2F - 2.

3. Zhou F. Z. ( 2006 ) . Ten Years of Separate tax collection System: System and Influence. *China Social Science*, 6.

4. Hu A. G. (1996) . Separate tax collection System: Review and Suggestions. *China Soft Science*, 8.

5. Xiang H. C. (Ed) (1999) . *Fifty Years of Fiscal System in China* (1 st ed) . Beijing: China Financial and Economic Publishing.

6. BudgetDepartment of the Ministry of Finance ( ed ) ( 2003, November 6 ) . *Inter Governmental Fiscal Relation in China.* Beijing: China Financial and Economic

Publishing.

7. Jia K. (2011) . Public Fiscal System Reform in the 12th Five Year Period of China. *Fiscal Study*, 7.

8. Lou J. W. (2013, November 6) . Establishing Modern Fiscal System. *People's Daily*.

9. LouJ. W. (2013) . *Reconsidering Inter Governmental Fiscal Relation in China* (1 st ed. ) . Beijing: China Financial and Economic Publishing House.

10. Gao P. Y. (2014, June 9) . Strategic Positioning of the New Round of Fiscal and Taxation System Reform. *People's Daily*.

11. Liu S. X. (2013) . A New Round of Fiscal and Taxation System Reform Based on State Governance. *Contemporary Economic Management*, 12.

(Written by: Qiaobin Feng, Professor, Department of Economics, Chinese Academy of Governance)

# Chapter VII

# Human Resources Reforms
# in the Public Sector

Since late 1970s, the Chinese government has been gradually deepening its human resources system reform in the public sector, with an attempt to keep up with international development trend and to meet domestic needs in economic and social development. During the reform, the government concentrated on its core tasks while giving consideration to the development needs arising in different stages of the reform. With reform in economic and administrative systems advances, the government is steadily building and implementing a civil servant regime, proactively promoting human resources system reform in the public sector, and gradually improving a human resources system for state – own enterprises SOE that satisfies a modern corporate structure. Human resources system reform in the public sector bases itself on the construction of a system, integrating refined traditions and innovations which embody the modern time. Human resources management in the public sector has by and large become more scientific, professional and legal – based.

Through reform, China facilitated the emergence of categorized management of cadres. In the 13th National People's Congress of the CPC in 1987, the idea of categorized human resources management was proposed in the context of political system reform. Following the functional separation between the Party and the government, separation of the government from SOE corporate management, separation of public service units from the government, and checks and balances between human resources management and administration, categorized human resources management laid a solid foundation for the categorized management of cadres. Establishing a civil service system is a strategic decision for innovations in the management system for cadres' work and for breakthroughs in the unified management system of the government, SOEs and public service units. The establishment and implementation of the civil servant system signifies the establishment of a cadre management system suitable for government organs, sketches the outline for categorized management of government organs, public institutions, and cadres from SOEs, forms a cadre management system compatible with the socialist market economy, and gradually constructs a human resources management system with unique Chinese characteristics.

# 7.1 Development of A Civil Servant Regime with Chinese Characteristics

Since 1978, Chinese civil servant regime has been here for 30 years. The Interim Regulations on State Civil Servant promulgated in 1993 is the first general administrative instrument on state civil servant. [1]The period from 1993 to 1997 marked efforts to fully implement a civil servant regime. The former Ministry of Personnel introduced regulations and implementation rules in support of the Interim Regulations on State Civil Servant, covering civil servant recruitment, performance appraisal, promotion, salary, insurances, benefits, exchange scheme, resignation, dismissal and retirement. By then, a civil servant regime had been established nationwide. Civil servant management has come under legal supervision since 2006, when the Civil Servant Law was promulgated. Towards 2013, after the Civil Servant Law has become effective, various support laws and regulations had been introduced. These instruments,

---

① Yin Weimin (Chief editor). Human Resources and Social Security Reforms: 30 Years Review [M]. Beijing: China Human Resources Press, 2009

aligned with the relevant Communist Party rules, such as the Regulations on the Selection of Party and State Leaders, have formed a legal framework of a civil servant management regime with Chinese characteristics, governing every stage from entry, management to termination of a civil servant.

### 7. 1. 1  A framework of support structures for the civil servant regime with Chinese characteristics has been developed

Chinese civil servant management is reform – oriented. It emphasizes both policy consistency and maintains legal authority on one hand, and reserves room for new outcomes emerged from reform programmes and next stages of reform on the other. Various state authorities have a combined task of policy development and revision of existing rules at the same time. After promulgation of the Interim Regulations on Civil Servant, a great number of support measures have been introduced, contributing to a legal framework based on the Interim Regulations. The Civil Servant Law, having drawn the implementation lessons of the Interim Regulations and also summarised, distilled and developed relevant legal instrument, signified that legal supervision of civil servant management had entered a new stage. [1] At present, a set of policies and rules have been basically established, including released rules and ministerial regulations, and covering recruitment, performance appraisal, bonus, determination of professional grade, reassignment, appointment, dismissal, promotion, exchange, disciplinary measures and grievance mechanism and training, hence the legal supervision covers every aspect of civil servant management.

### 7. 1. 2  An evidence-based management mechanism has been developed

An evident-based civil servant management mechanism has contributed to a higher capacity. The civil servant regime had been basically established by the end of 1997, several years after enactment of Interim Regulations on State Civil

---

① Pan Mingde. Evolution of the Chinese Civil Servant Regime and its Characteristics [J] . Shidai Renwu, Issue 4, 2015: pp 49 – 51

Servant in 1993. A legal framework on civil servant management had taken shape. Compulsory evaluation before recruitment had been basically established. Competitive selection of the merit had been widely applied. Staff motivation and security mechanism had been widely promoted. A human resources metabolism in which new employees replace veterans nearing retirement had taken shape. A career development mechanism had been applied with remarkable outcomes, while an oversight and checks and balances mechanism had gradually evolved. These measures facilitated overarching effects of civil servant management, had surpassing the traditional benefit-oriented human resources approach. [1]As a result of deepened reforms in which scope of staff selection had further expanded and the appointment process had been more developed, a civil servants on employment contract stream program had been gradually started. As a pilot city of the program, Shenzhen recruited a great number of staff on employment stream in 2007 and 2009, in two separate groups, and announced that, starting in 2010, all entrants to administrative authorities would have employment contracts.

### 7. 1. 3  A structured staff management system has been introduced

The structured staff management system is the foundation of an evidence-based management. The Civil Servant Law interprets structured management as a principle of the civil servant regime that should be implemented throughout management practices. Structured management is a departure from the "one for all" management model, and categorizes civil servants into general administration, professional services, administrative enforcement and judicial service. The Civil Servant Law best summarised the implementation lessons of Interim Regulations on State Civil Servant and Interim Regulations on the Selection of Cadres, incorporated the latest outcomes of human resources reforms in public sector as well as best practices from overseas models in recent

---

① Zhong Zuxuan. Great Progress Emerges From Government Human Resources Reform [N] . China Human Resources Bulletin (Zhongguo Zuzhi Renshi Bao), 17 October 2012.

years. As the first law that offers comprehensive guidance on management of government officials, [①] the Law marks that structured management has been on the course of improvement and institutionalization.

### 7. 1. 4  Great advancement in the management of legal officials

As the Reform and Opening up initiative go deep, China has made great efforts to push forward reforms to its legal management structures by adopting a series of laws, including the revised Law on Judges of the People's Republic of China and the revised Public Procurators Law of the People's Republic of China. A management structure that suits the characteristics of legal officials have been established. Recruitment of judges, prosecutors and police officers have been centralised; exchange programmes have been regulated; selection from lower courts and procuratorates have been established, and the career security measures for judges, prosecutors and police officers have been in place. The Decision on Major Issues Pertaining to Comprehensively Promoting the Rule of Law released by the Communist Party proposed, in the context of regularization, specialization and professionalization of enforcement forces and enhancement of their professionalism and expertise, to select judges and prosecutors among eligible lawyers and jurists. This is a great step forward for the current selection regime.

### 7. 1. 5  Major progress in reform of civil servants remuneration structure and social security system

The reform to the remuneration structure of civil servants is an important component of the income distribution reform. The remuneration structure of civil servants have experienced three stages: the first was the post-based regime in 1985, which was replaced by the post-or grade-based regime in 1993 and in 2006 by the one that considers both post and grade. In 2013, the 3rd plenum of

---

① Mu Min. Human Resources Management of Chinese Government Workers: History and Future [J] . Lilun Xuekan, Issue 1, 2003: pp . 69 – 72.

the 18th CPC Central Committee called for "reforms to the remuneration and allowance structure of government authorities and public service units and further steps to develop the allowance increase mechanism in harsh and remote areas" to facilitate reasonable flow of human resources and optimised allocation. Central authorities also called for efforts to reform the pension regime for civil servants. In 2015, the State Council launched the reform to the pension regime of civil servants by releasing the Decision on the Reform to the Pension Regime of Government Authorities and public service units. In addition to the need to change the delivery model, eligibility criteria and adjustment mechanism, the Decision included a major step by calling for the introduction of an annuity scheme to complement the existing pension regime.

To establish a sound civil servant management regime, it is required to implement the Central authorities' policies and decisions on advancing the human resources reforms in the public sector, to adopt a comprehensive, balanced, planned and structured approach coupled with coordinated efforts, in order to expand the competitive selection of civil servants and to promote its transparent and competitive nature through rulemaking, while explore competitive selection alternatives for particular posts on the basis of set criteria and post attributes.

## 7.2  Active yet Steady Reforms of the Human Resources Regime in Public Service Units

The Chinese government attaches great importance to human resources reforms in the public service units. Since the reform and opening up initiative, reforms had been undertaken on the basis of "unpeg, classify, decentralise and liberalise" and with a view to readjust the responsibilities of government authorities and public service units, hence the human resources authority of public service units have been expanded while a self-restraint mechanism have been in place. [1]A structured management approach, with which staff are managed based on organisational arrangement and post attributes, has been gradually introduced to public service units of different social functions, funding sources and work nature. An active human resources regime had been formed following introduction of a competitive selection process conducted on basis of transparency, equality and selection based on merit, an employment on contract regime and a remuneration diversity programme. Thanks to institutional innovation and support reforms, staff enthusiasm and creativity have been fully mobilised, contributing to dynamic and sustainable public service units. The Regulations on Human Resources Management of public service units marked a great step in advancing human resources reforms; and it is a milestone in the overall reform process.

### 7.2.1 The contract employment practice have been widely adopted

The establishment of socialist market economy system and China's accession into WTO have both created a strong urge for public service units to shift from the traditional human resources practices. The State Council, in its 2002 Comments to Pilot Contract Employment in public service units, proposed to start a nationwide pilot of contract employment, cease lifetime cadre status on a gradual basis, introduce competitive selection process, and fully adopt a contract employment regime as a basic human resources approach. All public service units and their staff are required to establish an employment relationship through contract with defined rights and obligations. The contract-based regime has contributed to a transparent, equal and fair human resources practice, while increased autonomy in staff selection and guaranteed staff freedom of employment, thereby having guaranteed bilateral legal interests. Reforms have also changed the nature of the status-based human resources management to a post-based management model, from pure administrative management to

---

[1]  Guo Yanping. A Social Harmony-conscious Approach to Develop Human Resources Practices Reform in public service units [J]. Renshi Rencai, Issue 4 of 2006: pp 9 – 10

statutory management, from the administrative hierarchical relationships to equal human resources actors in an enterprise, and from employment by the country to employment by enterprise.

## 7.2.2 A post management approach based on organisational arrangements and post attributes has been established

In order to meet needs under the socialist market economy and political reforms, public service units are required to classify their posts in a reasonable manner, and that is to define the duties, powers and requirements for each post. Public service units as independent legal persons have been clarified after the State Council, in separate occasions, released the Interim Regulations on the Incorporation of public service units and Decision to Revise the Interim Regulations on the Incorporation of public service units. In alignment with the implementation of the incorporation regime and its amendments, the former Ministry of Personnel released in 2006 Measures on the Pilot Scheme of Post Classification of public service units and Guidelines on Implementation of Pilot Scheme of Post Classification of public service units, which marked the first ever post classification and employment through contract on the part of public service units. With the promulgation of the Employment Contract Law of the People's Republic of China in 2007, public service units are required to conclude, fulfil, revise, rescind or terminate an employment contract with staff members on the employment contract stream. Following this, the State Council released Guidelines on Categorised Development of Public Enterprise Reforms and Regulations Human Resources Management for Public Enterprise, a post management approach that suits the organisational arrangements and post attributes has been gradually adopted. [1]For technical posts, it is required to be filled based on job requirements and on a competitive basis, and the alignment between recruitment for technical posts and their job requirements has been

---

① Lu Xueyi. Research on Chinese Public Enterprise Reform [ M ] . Beijing: Social Science Literature Press, 2008

gradually realised. For technical posts whose duties are significant and with high universal application and concerns public interests, it is required to place entry threshold through a certification regime. For executive posts, it is required to create a grade system that reflects the managerial expertise, work capacity, performance, qualifications and experiences of individuals who fill them as well as job requirements. For general services posts, measures should be formulated to regulate the entry, management and exit of such staff. It is required to adopt a human resources approach that offers fixed and non-fixed appointments to facilitate recruitment of technical staff through a process open to the whole society.

### 7.2.3 A transparent and competitive staff selection process has been in place

A transparent and competitive selection process has been implemented in public service units on a gradual basis. In 2000, the CPC Organizational Department and the former Ministry of Personnel jointly released Comments to Accelerate Human Resources Reforms in public service units, representing added impetus to the human resources reform. In 2010, the Organizational Department and Ministry of Human Resources and Social Security released the Announcement on Further Regulation of Public Recruitment Practices in public service units, making specific rules governing how to conduct recruitment process and recruitment practices had been institutionalised. In 2011, the State Council made comprehensive guidelines to human resources reforms in public service units by releasing its Comments on Further Advanced Human Resources Reforms of public service units. By 2014, the State Council released Regulations on Human Resources Management of public service units, which marked significant progress in the human resources reform process and a human resources regime with contract-based employment, post management and public recruitment as its chief components have been created. [1]At the same time, the single appointment for the executive leaders of public service units has been complemented by a developed and competitive recruitment process.

### 7. 2. 4 Remuneration and pension reforms has been advanced

In the context of fully advancing reforms initiatives, deepening the human resources reforms in public service units is an inevitable requirement by socioeconomic development. According to the general requirement to accelerate structured reforms in public service units, public service units need to focus their efforts to innovate management approach and shift human resources practices to develop a recruitment-based regime, a post management approach, a contract-based human resources management practice and a competitive selection process for executive leadership. Enterprises of different sectors and types need to explore unique approaches suited to their own organisations and develop post classification regimes, contributing to a well-defined, reasonably classified and flexible structure with strong supervision.

In addition to the human resources reforms, there has also been reform progress in remuneration and social security schemes. The distribution autonomy within enterprises has been expanded without prejudice to the principles of distribution according to workload and production factors, cost-efficiency while taking consideration of equality. This approach has facilitated a diversified and flexible remuneration and motivation mechanism that emphasize actual performance and contribution, coupled with focus on outstanding employees and key posts. Remuneration package have been used as an instrument to retain first-class workers with excellent performance, while workers working in harsh and remote areas or workers in key or special posts have been appropriately compensated. Meanwhile, pension reforms have been advanced with increased efforts. In 2008, the State Council released Announcement to Print and

---

① Yu Henan. Human Resources Reforms and Development in Chinese SOEs [J], Shijian Yu Tansuo, Issue 4, 2015: pp 19 – 23

Circulate the Proposal Concerning Trial of Pension Scheme Reform for Staff in public service units, in which it decided at first to start pilot programmes in Shanxi, Shanghai, Zhejiang, Guangdong and Chongqing. By 2015, with release of Decision on the Pension Reforms of Government Authorities and public service units, China has formally launched the pension reforms for public service units. By now, there has been great progress in the reform.

## 7. 3  A Human Resources Regime Aligned With Modern Corporate Management In SOEs

The development of socialist market economy following the 3rd plenum of the 11th CPC Central Committee necessitated human resources reforms in SOEs, and reforms had gradually started to modernise corporate management. In 1993, the 3rd plenum of the 14th CPC Central Committee clearly stated that a set of modernised corporate systems is where the reforms should lead. By 2000, most of the key SOEs of large and medium sizes have such systems in place, coupled with developing human resources mechanisms and a recruitment approach required under new systems. Human resources management practice has been gradually diversified, thus making its human resources reform aligned with the management reform. Efforts had been ongoing to explore, innovate and develop approaches to executives management, recruitment regime and remuneration scheme. [1]A series of reform measures has contributed to a more transparent, equal, competitive and merit-based human resources environment. A manager is now possible to be relegated as well as promoted, and replaced by a new one as well as retained. A rigorous accountability mechanism has been fully developed, open to public report, and, finally, a management approach to the executive team has been adopted that both meets market economy requirements and takes account of national circumstances.

---

① Pan Qili. Human Resources Approach to the Executive Team of SOEs [D] Thesis of a Master's program graduate, University of Electronic Science and Technology of China, 2006

### 7. 3. 1  Contract-based recruitment has been introduced to SOEs

Reforms to the human resources regimes in SOEs had been gradually launched after Reforms and Opening up in 1978, when the Chinese government shifted its focus to economic development. Human resources powers had been appropriately deregulated to the enterprise level, enabling diversification of human resources management. By then, human resources reforms had been aligned with the overall reforms to the economy. The Decisions on Questions Concerning State-owned Enterprise Reforms and Development, released from the 4th plenum of the 15th CPC Central Committee, marked that SOEs reforms and development had entered a new century. The SOEs as legal persons have been confirmed. Great potentials of SOEs have been unleashed thanks to, particularly, an extensive contract-based approach, a post management mechanism, a developed remuneration policy and a sound supervision regime as well as announced redundancies. With the continued development of socialist market economy, most of the major SOEs have developed modernised corporate systems, a contract-based employment regime and a public recruitment mechanism. SOEs have been revising rules concerning competitive selection based on new circumstances, and, for vacant posts, they have increased recruitment efforts by bringing out job features and diversifying recruitment approaches, thus making the competition process more developed as a regime. Meanwhile, according to the corporate strategy and market positioning, SOEs have expanded their scope of staff selection by transcending corporate, professional, geographical and institutional boundaries to open up new channels for talents.

### 7. 3. 2  Approach to manage executive team has been improved

Most of the executives in the SOEs are appointed by the Central authorities. As a result of the advanced socialist market economy reforms, the focus of stated-owned enterprises reforms had been shifted to reforming the management of executives and developing executives recruitment procedures, hence Central appointment had been combined with market recruitment. In 2009, the General Office of the CPC and the General Office of the State Council printed and circulated the Interim Regulations on Management of SOEs Executives. At the same time, to implement the Interim Regulations, the Organization Department of the CPC, in cooperation with the State-owned Assets Supervision and Administration Commission of the State Council, circulated the Measures on Integrated Evaluation and Appraisal of the Executive Teams and Individual Executives of Centrally Owned Companies (Trial). To ensure the integrity of state-owned enterprise executives and the sound development of such enterprises, the Regulations on the Integrity of the Executives of SOEs have been developed, taking account of relevant laws and Party regulations. Approach to recruitment has become more flexible by 2013, when SOEs were required to reasonably increase the market recruitment proportion.

### 7.3.3 Measures have been implemented to regulate the compensation structure of state-owned enterprise executives

Pushing forward regulation of the compensation structure of state-owned enterprise is in line with the advanced economic reforms. In 2009, six ministries, including Ministry of Human Resources and Social Security, released Guidelines on Further Regulating the Management of Centrally-owned Enterprise Executives Compensation to introduce a "salary cap" for these enterprises. By 2015, the Reform Package for the Compensation Structure of Centrally-owned Enterprises Executives, developed by ministries including Ministry of Human Resources and Social Security, became effective. The compensation structure reform is designed to regulate compensation of those Government-appointed executives of SOEs by adjusting higher or overpaid compensation.

Deepening human resources reforms in SOEs is to adjust to the advanced economic reforms. The efforts to establish a human resources regime required by a modern state-owned enterprise need to be focused on a sound management of its executives aligned with the governance structure, strengthen management of the executive teams and individual leaders of key SOEs by the central and local Party authorities, explore executives management practices consistent with modern corporate management, implement the statutory human resources powers granted on the board of directors and the administrators, and develop the selection approach of corporate executives by combining government appointment with market recruitment.

## 7.4  Lessons Of Human Resources Reforms In The Public Sector

Over the 30 years of reform and opening up, the Government has been conducting human resources policies on the basis of extensive acceptance of talents, merit-based appointment, and possession of moral and work capacities with moral qualities going first, while the reform scope and enhancing its evidentiary base has been expanded and enhanced with democracy, disclosure and competitive selection as its guiding principles. The human resources reforms in the public sector have grown stronger thanks to a "serve to the whole situation" approach, more effective to a respect for exploration with a focus on best practices, more coherent to an integrated and balanced approach, with its recruitment orientation more clarified to a reformed approach.

### 7.4.1  Encouraged grassroots creation and coordinated efforts enhanced outcomes

Most of the significant measures in the human resources reforms come from the grassroots. Measures such as public selection, competitive recruitment and publication of proposed candidates are all products of grassroots exploration and development before institutionalisation. It is important for human resources reforms to respect grassroots initiative, encourage action based on circumstances, adhere to the principles of bottom-up exploration and top-down facilitation as well as critical focus and coordinated efforts, and have a good control of reform process, thereby contributing to an active, secured, orderly and successful process. This means 1 ) using strategic deliberations as an opportunity to enhance reform measures. The Central authorities attach great importance to top-level design. It will draw lessons from grassroots experiences before institutionalising mature practices, thus their evidence base, reasonableness and coherence are enhanced, and compatibility is ensured to avoid arbitrary or random decision-making. 2 ) It is to adopt an integrated approach to reforms, with focus on critical points and coordinated efforts. Local authorities had a good command of the reforms in terms of timing, key points, exertion and rhythm. Critical issues have been resolved through enhanced pilot programmes, and lessons drawn and good practices have been promoted. In other words, efforts critical issues facilitated overall progress. 3 ) Good practice demonstration and influenced reactions fostered a good reform environment. Communication of the latest measures, developments and outcome have been increased, public reactions about reforms have been analyzed and directed, which had created a favourable environment for reforms.

### 7.4.2 Human resources decisions has been more broadly based thanks to expanded democracy

Expanded democracy is a basic direction of human resources reforms in the public sector. This principle has been implemented throughout cadre selection in such reform programmes to enhance public trust in human resources decisions. Under this principle, rule has been developed for appointment procedures for different actors based on recruitment situations. Adherence to popular recommendation ( *minzhu tuijian* ) and democracy questionnaire ( *minzhu ceping* ) has been ensured, and actions have taken to improve the reasonableness and credibility of such measures. Popular recommendation and democratic questionnaire have become a compulsory element of cadre selection and appointment, and deliberations were taken place after audience had been identified based on representativeness, knowledge about a concerned candidate and relevance. Enhanced inspection democracy ( *kaocha minzhu* ) measures had been taken place to ensure candidate quality. A voting system has been widely applied, contributing to a merit-based recruitment among select candidates.

### 7.4.3    A " serve to the whole situation " approach has facilitated institutionalisation

The human resources reforms in the public sector since economic reforms have been subject and serving to the central work of the Government and to the whole situation of reforms, development and social stability, and it was based on such principle that the Government's stance on recruitment of cadres had been developed, and a good worker development environment had been created. Human resources reforms in the public sector can only be forward-looking, comprehensive and sustainable when the Government stance on human resources management is accurately comprehended, that is to put the reforms in the context of Government work agenda. As always, China considers human resources development as an important agent to change how it works, and aims to establish an effective human resources institution in the end. For a human resources management approach to cadres to last, the key point is to see whether it is compatible with new situations, therefore it is necessary to gauge situations and have some pioneering spirit and keep up with changes. According to situations on the ground, it is necessary to take account of national realities in mind, while learn from best practices of overseas Administrative Reform; to emphasize implementation of existing institutions, while draw lessons from ongoing reforms from time to time and draw latest reform outcomes and institutionalise them as national policies, thus making human resources reforms in the public sector sustainable by being incorporated in the socialism with Chinese characteristics.

### 7.4.4    An accurate structured management brought more reasonable outcomes

The cadre management regime is an important element in the economic and political systems. Human resources reforms in the public sector are required to meet socioeconomic development and be aligned with the general process of government functions shift. A fact can be discovered through research on the overall human resources reform process that human resources reforms took place with economic reforms. In the preliminary phase of economic reforms, the Central leadership proposed deregulations, which means returning production and management powers to enterprises. In this context, enterprises asked for human resources and distribution powers. This prompted the Central leadership to embark on reforms the way it managed cadres, and two-tier management had been replaced by a one-tier model. By then, management of middle level cadres had been handled to enterprises themselves, while the human resources management regime aligned with a planned economy had been adjusted to one aligned with a socialist market economy. With the rapid development of market economy, during its 13th National Congress, the Communist Party of China put forward human resources structured management approach and to change the highly unified management mechanism and the single management approach by striking a clear boundary between state authorities, enterprises and public entities in terms of functions according to their different attributes, and gradually develop human resources regimes fit for each of their purposes.

### 7.4.5 Enhanced staff selection brought recruitment efficiency

Human resources reform is a highly political and sensitive policy issue, therefore must be subject to rigorous design, focused efforts to implement and a pragmatic approach, in order to create a fit for purpose and easy-to-execute mechanism, while contributing to its evidentiary base. The fit-for-purpose requirement calls for reform measures to contribute to a good staff selection and management, emphasizing actual outcomes and observe patterns in the human resource practices in public sector; in other words, form is decided by subject-matter and process by result. The easy-to-execute requirement emphasizes institutional coherence and easy to use; in other words, it is necessary to both maintain high standards through a rigorous process and be cost effective. A public and competitive selection process is a major human resources innovation, and it proved to be the most effective approach to staff selection. The principles of transparency, equality, competition and merit-based selection had been fully implemented in the Chinese public sector. The public sector organisations had contributed to a more transparent and competitive with expanded coverage by developing approaches to selection. This has enhanced the quality of the competitive process, improved credibility of selection and appointment decisions, and made the competitive selection a regular, reasonable process with diversified approaches.

## References

1. Yin W. M. ( Ed. )    ( 2009 ) . *Human Resources and Social Security Reforms*: 30 *Years Review*. Beijing: China Human Resources Press.

2. Pan M. D. ( 2015 ) . Evolution of the Chinese Civil Servant Regime and its Characteristics. *Shidai Renwu*, *4*, 49 – 51.

3. Zhong Z. X. ( 2012, October 17 ) . Great Progress Emerges From Government Human Resources Reform. China Human Resources Bulletin ( Zhongguo Zuzhi Renshi Bao ) .

4. Mu M. ( 2003 ) . Human Resources Management of Chinese Government Workers: History and Future. *Lilun Xuekan*, *1*, 69 – 72.

5. Guo Y. P. ( 2006 ) . A Social Harmony-conscious Approach to Develop Human Resources Practices Reform in public service units. *Renshi Rencai*, *4*, 9 – 10.

6. Lu X. Y. ( 2008 ) . *Research on Chinese Public Enterprise Reform*. Beijing: Social Science Literature Press.

7. Yu H. N. ( 2015 ) . Human Resources Reforms and Development in Chinese SOEs, *Shijian Yu Tansuo*, *4*, 19 – 23.

( Written by: Xueming Li, Assistant Researcher, Chinese Academy of Personnel Science)

# Chapter VIII

# Government Affairs Disclosure and Strategy of Governance by Big Data

Since the reform and opening-up policy was implemented more than three decades ago, China has achieved rapid economic growth in an orderly manner. Meantime, the reform of China's administrative system has grown deeper. Disclosure of government affairs, as an essential part of reforming the tools for governance, has also achieved comprehensive and considerable progress. The strategy of Big Data has been applied in multiple areas, and the development of E-government and "Smart Government" is also fledging. The comprehensive implementation of government affairs disclosure and the Big Data strategy are two of the most important achievements made over the last three decades of reform and opening-up because they are conducive to changing how governance is executed and improving the ecological environment of governance. Furthermore, government affairs disclosure is also highly relevant for promoting the reform of China's administrative system, enhancing supervision and restriction of administrative power, preventing corruption from the source, as well as providing efficient and convenient service to the people. The Chinese government has taken some active steps in enhancing government affairs disclosure and implementing the Big Data strategy. Moreover, elaborate plans for the next phase have already been developed to comprehensively boost government affairs disclosure, implement the Big Data strategy and build the "Smart Government".

# 8. 1   Theoretical Innovations of Government Affairs Disclosure in Contemporary China

As China is pressing ahead with government affairs disclosure, E-government and Smart Government, the ·administration academia in China is preoccupied with exploring the theories and practices of government affairs disclosure and the Big Data strategy. A good number of theoretical innovations and research findings have already been made. Such innovations and findings have proved to be strong theoretical and intellectual support for the implementation of government affairs disclosure and the Big Data strategy. For example, the China Public Administration Society held a symposium during Oct. 24th to 25th in 2000 to discuss topics such as "the theories and practices of government affairs disclosure". The symposium attracted a line-up of over 200 experts and scholars from government agencies all over China and from the academic circles. From disciplines such as political science, public administration, law and the development of the Communist Party of China, they shared their views on the importance of government affairs disclosure for China's governance, political development, public administration reform, democracy and legal system. [1]Many of these scholars became actively engaged in the subsequent research of " Sunshine Government ", rule-of-law government, government affairs disclosure, and government information disclosure, and made abundant theoretical innovations and findings.

### 8. 1. 1  Definition of Government Affairs Disclosure

There are three layers of meaning to "government affairs":  "political affairs", "administrative affairs" and "public affairs". Likewise, there are three layers of meaning to "government affairs disclosure": firstly, in the

---

[1]   Hu Xianzhi, Seminar summary of "The theory and practice of government affairs disclosure", *Administrative management in China*, 2000.

broadest sense, it means information disclosure of organizations possessing public power, shouldering public responsibilities, and fulfilling public obligations, including political parties, legislative bodies and judicial organizations; secondly, it means disclosure of administrative affairs, including those of government organizations as well as some social and corporate organizations; lastly, in the narrow sense, it exclusively means information disclosure of government affiliated agencies and affairs closely related to public administration.

Based on such an understanding, "government affairs disclosure" in China is defined as the disclosure of affairs involving public power to the general public or selected audience in accordance with law or morality. Government affairs disclosure should focus on the disclosure of administrative affairs and at the same time pay high attention to the disclosure of public affairs and information related to public power, for example, village committee affairs, government affairs, legal affairs, information about public utilities and companies. ①

## 8.1.2   Purposes, Methods and Contents of Government Affairs Disclosure

The purposes of government affairs disclosure can be examined from three perspectives. First, from the perspective of power, to improve government affairs transparency is to empower the public with the right of information, expression, participation and supervision. Second, from the perspective of efficiency, to improve government affairs transparency is to ensure that the tremendous amount of information at the hand of the government can be put to best use and the vigor of market and society can be injected. Third, from the perspective of governance, to improve government affairs transparency is to build a rule-of-law government that is innovative, service-oriented and

---

① Hu Xianzhi, *On Government Affairs Disclosure and Political Development*, *China Economy Publishing House*, 2005.

clean. Therefore, promoting government affairs disclosure has three objectives: first, to better secure right of information and right of political participation for the public as is stipulated in the Constitution; second, to enhance the credibility of the government; third, to cultivate stronger support from the people for governance and create synergies in society.

Experts have come up with many ideas about the methods and contents of government affairs disclosure. They believe that the scope of disclosure should meet the demand of the public and be selective; the government should take the initiative to make the disclosure, and the information should be disclosed online instead of on paper; the disclosure should be free of charge and copyright should not be applicable; though for public use, proprietary secrets, personal privacy and state secrets should still be protected with due attention. Some experts also suggest that the scope of disclosure should be clearly defined. Government information can be divided into two categories: one is information the government refers to, collects and creates when making public decisions, and the other is information about public services. They stress that the scope of disclosure must be clearly defined before discussing technical problems such as methods for disclosure. Disclosure of government affairs and related information should ensure that agendas are disclosed and that information is accessible, transferrable, and easy to read.

### 8. 1. 3  The Significance of Enhancing Government Affairs Disclosure

To speed up government affairs disclosure and its informatization stands at the core of modernize China's governance system. The 3 rd Plenary Session of the 18th CPC Central Committee pointed out that " the overall goal of comprehensively deepening reform is to improve and develop socialism with Chinese characteristics, and to modernize the national governance system and its capability " . Modernization of governance is essential to the national governance system, and government affairs disclosure is the top priority for the modernization of governance. For the modern Chinese government, government affairs disclosure is a crucial institutional arrangement, an inherent task set by its nature and functionality, and a strategic move adapting to economic globalization and informatization.

To begin with, government affairs disclosure is a critical method to improve governance capacity. Big Data, including the informatization of government affairs disclosure, means a revolution for the government because it reshapes rules, processes and functions. Therefore, government affairs disclosure is a key link for promoting reform of the government and its administrative system. To be specific, first, it can improve government transparency, credibility and the popular support for governance. Second, it can further eliminate the "black-box" environment that breeds corruption and thus promotes cleaning government. Third, it can improve compliance of government practices and enhance rule of law, paving the way for building a socialist country based on rule of law. Fourth, it can help build the mechanisms that engage a wider participation of the masses for the making of public decisions, which is conducive to building a service-oriented government that can better serve its people with its decisions.

In addition, government affairs disclosure will strengthen interaction between the government and the people, thus improving the environment for governance. For one thing, it protects the right to information of the citizens, intensifies information communication between the government and the people, and cultivates a stronger level of support for the government's authority and policies. For another, the make the government pay more attention to the need of citizen, thus improving government-people interaction, the governance environment and the government's credibility. ①

Lastly, government affairs disclosure will polish the image of the government and improve its style of work, helping to achieve the objectives of "Sunshine Government" and "Transparent Government". Government affairs disclosure can be compared to the preservatives for the whole political system

---

① Hu Xianzhi, *Disclosure of Government Affairs Enhances Government Credibility*, *Outlook Weekly*, 2012.

due to its indispensable role in improving the political environment, regulating political conducts, purifying the political atmosphere, achieving political democracy and ensuring the proper functioning of market economy. As a critical basis for supervising the government and its administrative services, the disclosure intensifies oversight of government departments and its public servants. And this is especially true for administrative services and approvals already with relatively clear standards. This is because, after the processes, standards, staff and timelines of such services and approvals are disclosed, both the government and the people will be further enabled to supervise. In this way, government affairs disclosure paves the way for building a government that is law-based, accountable, efficient and clean.

### 8. 1. 4  To Properly Handle the Internal and External Relationships Involved in Government Affairs Disclosure

Government affairs disclosure is a comprehensive and systematic process, in which scholars believe that the following relationships should be handled properly: first, the relationship among promoting government affairs disclosure, reforming administrative services and building a service-oriented government, as well as deepening the reform of the administrative system; second, the relationship between the infrastructure development involved in building an E-government platform and the "soft power" development of promoting government affairs transparency and streamlining approval processes; third, the coordinative relationship between administrative approval agencies, administrative service agencies and various functional departments; fourth, the relationship between external service function and internal management of the E-government platform and administrative service organizations; fifth, the relationship between solving immediate problems and establishing long-term mechanisms.

## 8.2  Evolution of Government Affairs Disclosure in Modern China

After the founding of People's Republic of China, government affairs disclosure made its first step in the field of village affairs and over half a century has passed since then. The last 30 – odd years in particular, with reform and opening-up achieving remarkable progress, have witnessed the evolution of government affairs disclosure, from lower administrative levels to higher ones, and from pilot areas to a full rollout. That is to say, government affairs disclosure has escalated from village committee level, to township level, county level, provincial level and all the way up to central government level. Now it is achieving disclosure based on E-government and e-service, and will eventually realize a full disclosure of government affairs. The stages and manifestations of government affairs disclosure are summarized as follows.

### 8.2.1  The Institutional Reform of Rural Economy Drove Disclosure of Village Affairs

As the household responsibility system (linking remuneration to output) was adopted in the early 1980s, the former practices of "communes" and "production teams" were phased out. In Hezhai Production Brigade of Yishan County at Guangxi Zhuang Autonomous Region, six production teams voluntarily established grassroots self-governing bodies that conducted self-management, self-education and self-service. [1]The 23rd Session of the 6th Standing Committee of the National People's Congress adopted *The Organizational Law of Village Committees of People's Republic of China* (*Trial*) in November, 1987. The 5th Session of the 9th Standing Committee of the National People's Congress adopted *The Organizational Law of Village*

---

[1]  Observer, *Following the Law Creates Stability and Breaking the Law Incurs* Disorder [ J ], *Village and Township Forum*, 1999 (2) .

*Committees of People's Republic of China*, which safeguards the rights of villagers to self-governance, including democratic election, decision-making, management and supervision. As a basic element of self-governance, the practice of village affairs disclosure was phased in and rolled out nationwide.

The Central Government made special instructions and arrangements for the rollout of village affairs disclosure in 1991. In 1991, the CPC Central Committee and State Council vowed to build a system for village affairs disclosure when making decisions on work related to agriculture and the rural area. In 1998, *The Organizational Law of Village Committees of People's Republic of China* was promulgated, which laid out the five core contents of village affairs disclosure. In 1998, the General Office of the CPC Central Committee and the General Office of the State Council co-issued *The Notice on the Implementation of Village Affairs Disclosure and the Democratic Management System*, which requires the village committees nationwide to disclose village affairs. Later on, the Commission for Discipline Inspection of the CPC Central Committee, Ministry of Agriculture and Ministry of Civil Affairs have all put the implementation of village affairs disclosure high on their work agenda. In this way, village affairs disclosure has become a basic system and commonplace practice in the political life of rural China.

### 8. 2. 2 Implementing Government Affairs Disclosure at Township Level

In the late 1990s, as village affairs disclosure and the self-governance of the rural people achieved fairly good effects, the topic of township government affairs disclosure was mentioned more and more frequently. In accordance with the instructions of the Commission for Discipline Inspection, the priorities of township government affairs disclosure back then were: issues that the local people were most concerned with and complained the most about; issues had a direct bearing on local economic development and social stability; administrative affairs that were vulnerable to corruption. Following the instructions, township governments determined their key items of affairs, departments and positions to disclose information about. In practice, township government affairs disclosure was characterized by a high convergence of disclosed contents, mainly about financial and economic affairs, which aimed to prevent corruption, improve governance style and culture, tighten relations of the CPC and its officials with the people, and promote stable social and economic progress. In summary, the practices of township government affairs disclosure are less systematic in terms of organizational structure, institutional design and procedures, compared with those of village affairs disclosure. The implementation of township government affairs disclosure relied on the organizational structure of national administrative system, featuring a top-down pattern and a strong administrative trait.

### 8.2.3   Exploration of Government Affairs Disclosure by Local Governments

As the reform and opening-up policy deepens, local governments have also kept making renovations. With competition from market economy increasing, local governments have made gradual progress in improving their governance. Some local governments started to promote government affairs transparency voluntarily with the aim of paving the way for hitting certain economic targets and improving governance. Some of the cases were on a county government basis, some prefecture-level cities. After the 1990s, some county governments, prefecture-level city governments and even some state functional departments set out to explore government affairs disclosure and the supportive institutional arrangements. Such experiments had the following characteristics.

First, the disclosure efforts focused on administrative services, their procedures, rules and legal bases, aiming to make it more convenient for companies and citizens to obtain such services. In this way, popular support and motivation were cultivated in the rollout of government affairs disclosure. Some governments explored the disclosure of financial affairs. Some explored the practices of separating revenue from expenditure, and centralized payment from the national treasury, which proved to be beneficial for preventing corruption and promoting clean government. Some local government departments focused their disclosure efforts on the check of balance, paying special attention to the disclosure of promotions, internal transfer and major decisions. For example, establishing the mechanism of disclosing internal transfers, new positions, service promises and major decisions. Such practices have all contributed to the experience accumulation for government affairs disclosure.

In addition, as for change of organizational structure, the medium of government affairs disclosure gradually embarked on a "specialized" route, i. e. "administrative service centers" featuring "one-stop" or "one-center" service emerged and popularized. A rough survey in 2005 revealed that nearly 3300 service centers of concentrated administrative approval functions at county level and prefecture city level had been established. By October 2007, the number rose from 3300 in 2005 to 4500. Among these administrative service centers, there were 1002 websites established and run independently with over 11. 59 million pages of contents. ①Such administrative service centers were regarded as an innovation of the administrative approval system and further popularized after the promulgation of *Law of the People's Republic of China on Administrative Approval*. At the moment, administrative service centers not only have been widely established, but also represent the "frontline" and major "battlefield" for the implementation of government affairs disclosure.

### 8. 2. 4 Government Affairs Disclosure After the Promulgation of Regulation of the People's Republic of China on Government Information Disclosure

On April 5th, 2007, the then Premier Wen Jiabao signed the Decree No. 492 of State Council, unveiling the *Regulation of the People's Republic of China on Government Information Disclosure* (the "Regulation") and announcing it would come into force after May Ist, 2008. The *Regulation* provided a fundamental framework for the disclosure of government information,

---

① Hu Xianzhi, *The Past and the Future: China's Government Affairs Disclosure and Governance* [J], *Journal of Political Science*, 2008 (6) .

including general principles, the scope, methods and procedures of the disclosure, as well as the supervision and supportive policies for the disclosure. Thus, the *Regulation* provides a legal basis and reference for implementing government information disclosure nationwide. The unveiling of the *Regulation* marked that China's government affairs disclosure entered the new stage of nationwide rollout, featuring being legalized, institutionalized and standardized. This new stage has the following characteristics. :

First, the responsible subjects for government affairs disclosure were further specified and expanded. According to the *Regulation*, all administrative departments became subjects of government information, i. e. subjects with the duty to disclose government affairs. The *Regulation* defined the General Office of the State Council and the general offices of people's governments at all levels as the subjects for the disclosure, and required them to set up special teams to manage the disclosure. It was estimated that in the year 2006 alone, the Central People's Government's official website disclosed as many as over 500 documents approved by the State Council and its General Office, and over 250 issues of State Council Gazette; roughly 1100 items of online administrative services involving 71 departments were integrated; 47 items of administrative approval involving 8 departments have been disclosed, hailed " the 24/7 government" . [3] In addition, the mechanism of releasing news and installing spokespersons has been established in the 74 departments and agencies of the State Council as well as among 31 provinces ( regions and municipalities) .

Second, the content and scope of government affairs disclosure were further specified and expanded. Putting in place the general principle of " make disclosure the norms and make withholding the exception" , the *Regulation* stipulates that administrative bodies must disclose government information that fits one of the following: first, concerning the interests of citizens, legal persons or organizations; second, requiring the general public to be widely informed or engaged; third, relating to the organizational structure, functions and procedures of administrative bodies; fourth, legally bound to be disclosed in accordance with law, regulations and rules. Notably, such requirements expanded the former content and scope of disclosure, which used to be just an abstract description as " transparent practices ". Moreover, that relevant applications shall be disclosed was added to the content for disclosure.

Third, the methods and procedures became institutionalized and standardized. The *Regulation* prescribes that the responsible government departments shall compile annual disclosure guides, annual disclosure directories and annual disclosure reports, institutionalizing government affairs disclosure as part of administrative management. The disclosure of government information evolved into a public-service product provided by the government to the masses, which became dispensable in the day-to-day decision-making of the general public. The *Regulation* also explicitly set out the mechanisms and systems involved in government affairs disclosure.

Fourth, the interaction between the government and the public in government affairs disclosure gradually intensified. Since the *Regulation* clarified the responsible subjects of the disclosure and the detailed procedures about disclosure upon application, people's right to information has been safeguarded. Citizens and legal persons can apply to relevant government departments for disclosure of particular information, shifting the disclosure from a top-down approach to an interactive approach between the public and the government.

In a word, the promulgation and enforcement of the *Regulation* embarked China's government affairs disclosure onto a more legalized and institutionalized route.

### 8.2.5 A New Journey—From Partial Disclosure of Government Information to Comprehensive Disclosure of Government Affairs

Since the promulgation and enforcement of the *Regulation*, government affairs disclosure became the norms for governments at all levels. Meantime, the efforts to build E-government and drive informatization have also been greatly boosted. In the following years, efforts of government affairs disclosure became increasingly integrated with the efforts of E-government development and the reform of administrative approval. These fields of work became mutually complementary and reinforcing, ushering in a new era of comprehensive disclosure of government affairs.

On June 8th, 2011, the General Office of CPC Central Committee and the General Office of the State Council ( the " Two Offices " ) co-issued *The Opinions on Deepening Government Affairs Disclosure and Improving Government Service* ( *"The Opinions* of 2011" ) . *The Opinions* of 2011 aims to implement the instructions of the 17th CPC Congress, and the 3rd, 4th and 5th Plenary Session of the 17th CPC Central Committee to build a government that is service-oriented, accountable, law-based and clean, and to enhance administration based on law and government service. *The Opinions* of 2011 explicitly provides: deepening government affairs disclosure and improving government service should adhere to the " Deng Xiaoping Theory" and the important thought of "Three Represents", conform to the "Science-based Development Concept", and abide by the essential principles such as people-orientation, rule for the people, change of government functions aligned with the institutional change of China's political system, and standardized and transparent use of administrative power; under the general principle of "make disclosure the norms and make withholding the exception", government information of general concern to the public and involving the interests of the public shall be disclosed timely, precisely and fully; to provide better and more convenient service to the people, government service, its efficiency and system shall be further improved. *The Opinions* of 2011 also explicitly set out that the efforts of government affairs disclosure should be made in the spirit of reform and innovation, including to innovate on new disclosure methods, promote disclosure of administrative decisions, advance transparent use of administrative power, expand disclosure of administrative approval, deepen implementation of the *Regulation*, highlight disclosure at grassroots levels, step up disclosure internally at the administrative agencies, build the government service system, and reinforce supervision. Moreover, as for building the government service system, *the Opinions* of 2011 lays out the administrative service agencies, their functions and missions as well as how they operate, giving special priority to leadership, institutional development, supervision and evaluation.

Based on *the Opinions* of 2011, on September 13th, 2011, the General Office of the State Council re-issued *The Opinions on the Pilot Programs of Improving Government Affairs Disclosure and Government Service at County-level Governments Based on the E-Government Platform* ( No. 99 of Year 2011 ) drafted by the National Steering Team of Government Affairs Disclosure, which comprises of instructions specially made to county-level governments on government affairs disclosure. In 2012, 100 county-level governments nationwide were selected as pilots for the Program, which contributed significantly to the national rollout of government affairs disclosure. [1]

Five years later, on Feb 17th, 2016, the "Two Offices" co-issued *The Opinion of Comprehensively Promoting Government Affairs Disclosure* ( *the New Opinions*) to provide special and comprehensive instructions for government affairs disclosure. *The New Opinions* points out in its very beginning that "Transparency is a fundamental feature of government based on rule of law. To comprehensively promote government affairs disclosure and let power be exercised under the sunshine is critical to advance socialist democracy, boost the country's governance capacity, enhance the government's credibility and efficiency, and safeguard the citizens' rights of information, expression, participation and supervision. " Such an exposition of the nature, significance and legal basis of government affairs disclosure is so detailed and precise that it represents a major step forward since the beginning of China's efforts to promote government affairs disclosure and develop a legal framework for it. It reflects the elevated understanding of the CPC and the Central Government of government affairs disclosure and its supportive systems and mechanisms. *The New Opinions* points out that "the CPC Central Committee and the State Council have attached great importance to government affairs disclosure and issued a serious of major

---

[1]　Hu Xianzhi, Jiang Xiuqian, Wang Junqi et al. , *On the Reform of Government Affairs Disclosure of County-level Governments*, *Huaxia Publishing House*, Edition of Feb. 2014.

orders, and that governments at all levels have conscientiously followed the orders and made great achievements in this area". Despite the remarkable progress, there remain problems, such as "compared with the public's expectation and the requirement of building a rule-of-law government, relevant governments should continue to change their mindset about the disclosure, perfect its systems, intensify the efforts and improve its timeliness". Therefore, new efforts should be made to mobilize and instruct relevant governments to comprehensively promote government affairs disclosure in a deeper manner. To achieve better transparency for now and for the next phase, *the New Opinions* issued orders about government affairs disclosure for the time period of 2016-2020 on five dimensions with 21 specific pieces of instructions. The main contents are as follows.

(1) The General Principles of Government Affairs Disclosure

Government affairs disclosure will continue to be guided by the decisions made by 18th CPC Congress, and the 3rd, 4th and 5th Plenary Session of the 18th CPC Central Committee. It will follow the instructions made by President Xi in his serious of important speeches and adhere to the national strategic goal of "Four Comprehensives (comprehensively build a moderately prosperous society, comprehensively deepen reform, comprehensively implement the rule of law, comprehensively strengthen Party discipline)". Based on the development philosophy of being innovative, coordinated, green, open and inclusive, the disclosure will practice administrative power by rule of law and earnestly implement *the Regulation* and other decisions adopted by the CPC Central Committee and the State Council. The principle to "make disclosure the norms and make withholding the exception" will be upheld, and the disclosure will cover decisions, execution, management, services and outcomes. Efforts will be made to promote simplified approval process, strike a better balance between control and relaxation of power, advance service reform, and fuel market vitality and social creativity. Special attention will be given to building an innovative government that is law-based, clean and service-oriented.

Comprehensive disclosure of government affairs should adhere to the following general principles: the disclosure should focus on matters of major concern to economic and social progress and the people; the disclosure should contribute to improving implementation, standardization and service; in accordance with relevant laws and regulations, the responsible subjects, contents, standards, methods and processes of the disclosure should be specified, and the disclosure of the list of government rights and liabilities and negative list should be sped up; the disclosure should stay innovative, meticulous about details, easy to implement and timely, so that the people can see, understand and supervise the disclosure; the disclosure should align itself with social requirements, utilize the press as a medium and activate the mode of "Internet + government affairs" so as to expand social engagement and enhance effectiveness of governance.

Comprehensive government affairs disclosure has the following goals for 2020: government affair disclosure is generally brought to a higher level; the negative listing mechanism is actively installed in accordance with law; the disclosure covers the whole process of using power and government service; institutionalization, standardization and informatization of the disclosure is significantly improved with an increased level of public engagement; a higher level of government transparency fosters stronger understanding, trust and support from the people.

(2) Key Contents of Government Affairs Disclosure

First, improving government transparency, which mainly includes, enhancing disclosure of a) decisions, b) execution, c) management, d) services, e) outcomes and f) information in key areas. It is imperative to disclose government information in such areas as fiscal budget, allocation of public resources, approval and implementation of major construction projects and social welfare programs. Responsible departments must formulate implementation guidelines and specify detailed requirements.

Second, expanding social engagement, which mainly includes strengthening a) openness of government data, b) interpretation of policies, c) social engagement, d) responses to social concerns and f) the role of media in guiding public opinion. It is imperative to establish sound mechanisms to gather, analyze, handle and respond to public opinions on government affairs.

Third, building disclosure capacities, which mainly includes a) improving standards, mechanisms and systems, b) establishing the negative lists of government affairs disclosure, c) building up IT capacities, d) enhancing the functionality of the official portal of the government and f) intensifying relevant training.

Last but not least, strengthening leadership and supportive institutional arrangements for the disclosure. Resourcesrelated to government affairs disclosure should be pooled together and relevant institutions should be straightened out. The financial support for the disclosure should be secured and evaluation of the disclosure should be enhanced.

## 8. 3 Exploring the Theories and Practices of the Big Data Strategy and "Smart Government"

When government affairs disclosure are combined with Big Data technologies, the efforts to build E-government and Smart Government will consequently intensify and be able to make breakthroughs. In recent years, the new leadership of China has given priorities to technological and economic innovations, and hence put forward the national strategy of Big Data. China has made remarkable progress as follows in the disclosure of governance data and in the development of Smart Government.

### 8. 3. 1  About the Era of Big Data

In the era of Big Data, data has become a means of production and a rare asset as well as an emerging industry. Every trade and area will produce valuable data. Gathering, analysis and digging of such data as well as artificial intelligence will bring about value and wealth beyond imagination. Our life and work are already inseparable from Big Data, which has increasingly become a fundamental type of strategic resources and public assets.

### 8.3.2 About Big Data Economy

"Data has already become a new type of economic asset, just like money and gold, and data will give rise to a series of spin-off emerging industries such as data material, data mining, data processing and data service. " Therefore, Big Data is by no means just one single industry. Instead, it has ubiquitous presence in modern society and can be connected with multiple other industries to form "Big Data +". "Internet +" in essence is all about connection and data. On March 5th, 2014, Premier Li Keqiang mentioned during his *Government Work Report* at the 2 nd Session of the 12th National People's Congress that incubation platforms for innovations and start-ups of the emerging industries will be established so that China will overtake and lead other countries in such areas as mobile communications, integrated circuits, Bid Data, advanced manufacturing, new energies and new materials.

### 8.3.3 About the Big Data Strategy and Governance

Big Data is not just a technological revolution, but also an economic evolution and governance evolution. In the era of Big Data, the Internet becomes a new platform for governance to be carried out. It will be too burdensome and overwhelming for the government alone to be counted on to manage and protect the data, especially when the data is of large scale and great complexity. By building an E-government system, online service is made possible so that power can be practiced orderly, effectively and leave a "trail". In this way, the communication and interaction between the government and the people will be enhanced, and the government will become smarter in dealing with all kinds of issues and incidents. Big Data is vigorously modernizing China's governance system and capacity. It is increasingly becoming a driving force for governance to move forward and an excellent "think tank". Practical experience at some local governments have fully illustrated that by utilizing the Big Data Strategy, the government can put the "power of law enforcement" into the "cage of data".

In this way, behaviors failing to follow the market rules will have no place to hide since power execution will always leave a "trail" . Big Data provides the government with first-hand and science-based evidence for decision-making, whereby decisions made by the government will be supported behind the scenes by analysis of big data.

### 8. 3. 4  About the Government's Plans and Measures on Big Data

The 13th Five Year Plan made suggestions on the implementation of the Big Data Strategy, stressing " utilizing Big Data technologies to improve the timeliness and accuracy of economic data" . Prior to that instruction, the Big Data Strategy has already been systematically applied in the management of industries and market economy. On July 23 rd, 2014, the executive meeting of State Council deliberated and adopted " *Interim Regulation on Enterprise Information Disclosure ( Draft )* ", aiming to build a market economy environment that is fair and competitive. It requires regulatory departments to build information-sharing platforms and utilize methods such as Big Data to improve supervision. On September 17th, 2014, the government instructed to further support the development of small and micro businesses, encourage start-ups and foster an innovative culture in society. The government vows to build a better information system that serves small and micro businesses, helps them obtain administrative information, and to provide more efficient government services by utilizing Big Data and Cloud Computing technologies. On October 29th, 2014, the government instructed to give priorities to promoting consumption in 6 areas, and to speed up the use of Big Data technology in health care and enterprise supervision. On November 15th, 2014, the government instructed to kick off Big Data pilot programs in such areas as disease prevention, disaster prevention, social security and E-government. On January 14th, 2015, the government instructed to speed up the development of the service sector and to optimize its structure for a larger growth potential, which includes building a new online platform for the service sector by utilizing technologies such as Big Data and Internet of Things. On February 6th, 2015, the government confirmed to utilize IT and Big Data technologies to build an online platform for the approval and supervision of investment projects. Horizontally, the platform will connect government agencies in charge of development reform, planning of urban and rural areas, land and resources, and environmental protection. Vertically, it will link up governments at all levels so as to put in place a "one-stop" service featuring online reception, online handling and online supervision. In this way, the government will achieve full transparency and trackability, and information will be so widely disclosed that the people no long need to run from department to department for a single approval. In July 2015, the General Office of the State Council issued *Several Opinions on Strengthening the Services and Supervision of Market Entities by Means of Big Data*, which provides that services for market entities should be improved; market supervision should be enhanced and bettered; information sharing between the government and the society should be strengthened; the government's capability of using Big Data should be elevated; efforts will be made to foster and develop social services for credit investigation.

### 8.3.5 About Open Data and Government Reengineering

A key component of China's Big Data Strategy is the open data strategy, which is complementary with disclosure of government information and affairs. In the planning and implementation of open data strategy, the government reengineering should be consistently ensured. Generally speaking, in the practice of open data, the government plays the following roles. First, it is the architect of the eco system for open data, providing system support. Second, it is the initiator of the open data strategy, making plans, building institutions and implementing action plans. Thirdly, it is the champion of building the legal framework for open data, adopting laws and rules. Fourth, it is the propeller to speed up the efforts of open data. Fifth, it is the guide of open data applications. Sixth, it is the explorer to innovate on how data is made open. ①

## References

1. Observer, （1999）. Following the Law Creates Stability and Breaking the Law Incurs Disorder, *Village and Township Forum*, 2.

2. Hu X. Z. （1999）. The Past and the Future: China's Government Affairs Disclosure and Governance, *Journal of Political Science*, 6.

3. China Public Administration Society （2001）. *Government Affairs Disclosure and Government Development*, Knowledge Publishing House.

4. Hu X. Z. （2012）. Disclosure of Government Affairs Enhances Government Credibility, *Outlook Weekly*.

5. Hu X. Z. （2005）. *On Government Affairs Disclosure and Political Development*, China Economy Publishing House.

6. Hu X. Q. , Jiang X. Q. , Wang J. Q. et al. （2014）. *On the Reform of Government Affairs Disclosure of County-level Governments*, Huaxia Publishing House.

7. Zhou H. H. （2003）. *Practices and Explorations of China's Government Affairs Disclosure*, China Legal Publishing House.

8. Zhao Y. W. , Tang C. （2006）. *Theories and Practices of Administrative Service Centers*, Enterprise Management Publishing House.

9. Duan L. F. （2007）. *Development of China Administrative Service Centers*, Wuhan University Publishing House.

10. The Editor Team （2015）. *Journal on Big Data for Party Leaders*, People's Publishing House.

（Written by: Xianzhi Hu, Ph. D. Supervisor and Researcher, Chinese Academy of Governance; Director, Research Department, China Society of Administrative Reform; Wenzheng Wu, Graduate Student, School of Public Administration, Beihang University）

---

① The Editor Team, *Journal on Big Data for Party Leaders*, *People's Publishing House*, ［M］, 2015.

# Chapter IX

# Government Performance Management and Administrative Accountability

Performance management ( PM ) serves as a major measure to innovate government's management and enhance its capacity. Since the 1980s, the administrative reform movement highlighted by the new public administration in Britain and the entrepreneurial government reform in the U. S. has prospered. Corporate management concepts, such as decentralized management, accountability mechanism, drive by the outcome, customer-centered orientation were advocated to be incorporated into government's management, so were PM and its evaluation tools that were commonly used in enterprises. PM and the tools have become essential catalyst for government reform and management innovation and exerted an important effect on optimizing the traditional bureaucracy, reducing fiscal pressure, responding to public concerns and enhancing government's awareness and capacity of service.

Chinese government introduced the PM evaluation tools between the 1980s to 1990s. After two to three decades of rapid development, the PM appraisal has become a routine mechanism of government management. In 2008, then Premier Wen Jiabao stated in the Report on the Work of the Government that "we will adhere to the administrative accountability system and government performance management system". The report to the 18th CPC National Congress put forward that "we will innovate the measures of administrative management, enhance the credibility and executive capability of the government, and promote the government PM " . The Third Plenary Session of the 18th CPC Central Committee stressed in the *Decisions of the CPC Central Committee on Several Major Questions of Comprehensive Deepening of Reforms* that the government PM should be strengthened, and responsibilities consolidated and corresponded with power. In short, during the administration institutional reform in China, government's PM and administrative accountability ( administrative accountability system ) system have played an important role in innovating government management, promoting the efficiency and capacity of the government and improving public service.

## 9.1 The Development and Outcome of Government Performance Management

Since the 1970s when the reform and opening-up policy was adopted, Chinese officials began to pay visits to foreign countries and learn of the advanced management experience in the world. Since the 1980s, some local governments and departments learned of government PM which had been proven to be effective in western countries and started the practice in accordance with local situations. The PM of Chinese government started at local governments and departments in the 1980s, was explored in various sectors by different departments in the 1990s, prospered under the great attention from the Central Government ( CG ) in the first decade of the 20th Century and entered the stage of rapid development in 2011 when pilot projects were promoted nation-wide. From the perspective of execution, some experts are convinced that the PM of Chinese government has yielded satisfactory outcome and even outperformed that in western countries in certain aspects.

### 9.1.1 Development and Major Models of Government's PM

The practice of PM in Chinese Government was initiated by some local governments and departments in the 1980s and went through a long process of exploration. Generally speaking, the development can be divided into four phases.

### 9. 1. 1. 1  Four Phases of Development[①]

(1) Starting up from the early 1980s to the early 1990s

In this phase, the concept of PM had not taken shape yet. Assessments were targeted at the general impression of a certain aspect. Major forms of assessments included general check-ups, competitions or targeted investigations. Although some local governments and departments followed the requirement of the then National Department of Human Resources to explore the post-based accountability system, no regulatory documents were formed. In the late 1980s, the target-based accountability system was also explored.

(2) Exploration from the early 1990s to the mid and late 1990s

In this phase, PM was regarded as one part of the management mechanism and was generally implemented in government departments and affiliated institutions in forms of accountability system of target fulfillment, promised public service system, efficiency inspection and work style appraisal. For example, the authority of Qingdao adopted the assessment of target fulfillment; the authority of Beijing Municipal, Shaanxi Province and Sichuan Province respectively promulgated regulations on goal management; former Yantai Municipal Commission of Urban and Rural Construction initiated the first promised public service system which was widely spread nation-wide. Also, to appraise government's style of work became an important means to maintain self-discipline. Different localities emphasized different sectors. Railway, electricity, communication, tourism, administration of justice and other sectors have all once become the emphasis. In addition, discipline inspection committees and supervision departments supervised the efficiency and performance, which increased the efficiency and change the work style.

(3) Rapid development and pilot projects in the first decade in the 21 st century

According to the statistics of PM Supervision Office of the SD of the DIC,

---

① Liu Xutao (eds.). 2015. Case Study of the PM of Chinese Government Based on the Best Practice [M]. Beijing: Press of the Chinese Academy of Governance.

Central Committee, Communist Party of China (CPC), 27 provincial governments (or governments of the autonomous regions and municipalities directly under the CG) had conducted PM work to different extents. ① In this phase, local governments and some departments/commissions of the CG no longer utilized PM simply as a tool; they recognized and established PM systems and institutions, and explored to set up the assessment mechanism that met the differentiated needs of development. The content, subject, procedure and method of assessment are more scientific and systematic. The academia translated and introduced large quantity of experience and practice of government's PM from western countries and researched on and discussed about the domestic practice of government's PM.

Moreover, with the prosperous PM development in both theories and practice, the leadership of the CG and relative departments attached growing attention to the important PM and assessment of the government; they were determined to launch PM in governments nationwide. The *Report on the Work of the Government* by the State Council (SC) in 2005 and 2008 respectively mentioned " to establish a scientific system for evaluating government performance" and "adhere to ... government performance management system" . In February 2008, *Opinions on Deepening the Reform of the Administrative System* by the Second Plenary Session of the 17th CPC Central Committee also mentioned to " adhere to the government performance management system and administrative accountability system" . In this way, to comprehensively promote government's PM was listed into the agenda.

In April 2010, the State Commission Office of Public Sectors Reform ratified the establishment of the PM Supervision Office (PMSO) under the Central Disciplinary Inspection Committee and Ministry of Supervision (the

---

① Information of 2013 from the website of the Discipline Inspection Committee, CPC Central Committee and Ministry of Supervision of China.

Committee and Ministry) . ① The PMSO's main functions are to carry out investigations, researches, supervisions and check-ups of government PM and to coordinate the PM work among different localities and government organs. From the first half of 2010 to the whole year of 2011, the PMSO had conducted in-depth and detailed researches. On 10th March 2011, the SC approved to establish the Inter-ministerial Joint Meeting System on Government's PM Work (the Joint Meeting) headed by the Ministry of Supervision. The Joint Meeting is comprised of nine central organs, namely the Ministry of Supervision, the Central Organization Committee, the State Commission Office of Public Sectors Reform, the National Development and Reform Commission, the Ministry of Finance, the Ministry of Human Resources and Social Security (the State Administration of Civil Service), the National Audit Office, the National Bureau of Statistics and the Legislative Affairs Office of the SC. The general office of the Joint Meeting was set up in the Ministry of Supervision and was responsible for the routine work.

On March 14th 2011, the *Outline of the Twelfth Five-Year Plan for the Development of National Economy and Society approved at the Fourth Session of the 11th National People's* Congress set forth the aim of "strengthen (ing) the system of government performance appraisal and administrative accountability" through "establishing a set of scientific and rational performance appraisal (PA) indicators and a mechanism that incorporates internal evaluation, public appraisal and experts' remarks, so that the performance appraisal can lead and encourage scientific development" . According to the Outline, the Joint Meeting identified Beijing Municipal, Jilin Province, Fujian Province, Guangxi Zhuang Autonomous Region, Sichuan Province, Xinjiang Uygur Autonomous Region, Hangzhou City, Shenzhen Municipal Government, the National Development and Reform Commission, the Ministries of Finance, Land and Resources,

---

① Based on the need of function performing, the PM Supervision Office and the Law Enforcement Supervision Office was combined into the Office of Law Enforcement and Performance Supervision after the Third Plenary Session of the 18th CPC Central Committee.

Environmental Protection and Agriculture, the General Administration of Quality Supervision, Inspection and Quarantine to carry out the pilot programs. At the end of 2012, the Committee and Ministry organized an assessment by the the Chinese Academy of Governance and other institutions on the programs and recorded extraordinary results. These programs gained rich practical experience for the nationwide launch of the government's PM system.

(4) Adjustment of government PM management

In July 2013 when the new session of Central Government was in office, the function of the Committee and Ministry was adjusted and the PMSO was abolished with its function transferred. The State Commission Office of Public Sectors Reform now plays the leading role in government's PM work. Until now, the Office has completed the investigation and research and is studying the issue of a national government PM guidance. Local governments are also reflecting on previous PM work and making adjustment. The government PM has entered the adjustment phase.

9. 1. 1. 2 Major PM Models

Government's PM in China was initiated by local governments and departments during their practice, which is different from the way government's PM was promoted in western countries. In western countries, government's PM was carried out from top to bottom usually with leading organizations at the central level, support from legislation and a universal assessment criterion and procedure. In China, different local governments designated different departments to take the lead; assessment criteria prioritize different aspects; and the practice varies due to the association with target-based accountability system, promised public service system, efficiency inspection, work style appraisal, public discussion, budget management and official evaluation.

(1) Target-based accountability system

Since 1990s, local governments, public service departments and affiliated institutions have gradually introduced the target-based accountability system and regarded it as the incentive to fulfilling annual targets. For example, Beijing municipal authority promulgated the *Trial Plan of Post-based Accountability*

*System of Target Fulfillment in CPC Committees and Governmental Organs* in 1991; in the same year, Shaanxi provincial authority promulgated the *Trial Measures of Post-based Accountability System of Target Fulfillment in Public Service Departments*; and Sichuan provincial authority promulgated the *Detailed Plan for Target Fulfillment of the People's Government of Sichuan Province*. The target-based accountability system is a typical target-oriented PM model for the government; it incorporates target management and assessment tool. Currently, the KPI appraisal and targeted evaluation in demography, safety, energy conservation, emission reduction and other aspects conducted by large quantity of Chinese government departments have concrete targets as the constrain. Therefore, such practice can be classified into this model.

(2) Public appraisal model

Since the 1990s, the governments of Shenyang, Nanjing, Hangzhou, Wuhan and other cities respectively carried out large-scale public appraisal campaign, introducing external appraisal into the government's PA system. The public appraisal model invites the general public, experts, representatives of local people's congresses and CPPCC committees, service receivers to appraise the performance of governmental organs, especially public service providers in terms of the style of work, service quality, efficiency, etc. The results will be published via major local media. Such a model is a typical one led by public participation.

(3) Efficiency and Capacity Building Model

The efficiency and capacity building began with the " efficiency and capacity supervision" put forward by Chinese supervision departments in the 1980s. The supervision was an administrative one targeted at responsibility fulfillment, efficiency, style of work and other aspects of the government's performance. On this basis, local governments of Fujian Province raised the concept of " efficiency and capacity building", i. e. continually improving the efficiency and service quality and enhancing the capability of the government and its civil servants by introducing various modern management concepts and practices in a systematic manner. Such a model is a typical capacity-building-oriented one.

(4) Model of Evaluation on Leaders and General Officials

Since 1980s, Chinese government has optimized the evaluation system of leaders and general officials according to the new situation after adopting the Reform and Opening-up Policy, and has identified " virtue, capability, diligence, output and incorruptibility" as the major contents. The evaluation results will be taken into account when it comes to promotion, appointment, rotation, awarding or punishment, and candidate selection of training sessions. In 2009, the Organization Department of CPC Central Committee issued the *Comprehensive Evaluation and Appraisal Measures for Leadership and Leaders of CPC Committees and Governments at Sub-national Level ( Trial) , the Comprehensive Evaluation and Appraisal Measures for Leadership and Leaders of Departments in CPC Committees and Governments ( Trial) , and the Annual Evaluation Measures for Leadership and Leaders of CPC Committees and Governments ( Trial )* . As for the evaluations of leadership and leaders conducted by local governments, ecological civilization, social development, people's livelihood and anti-corruption movement are gaining greater importance; the evaluation system has been continuously optimized.

(5) Inspection and Supervision Model

This model is mainly applied to push forward, check up and consolidate major tasks or targeted tasks. To apply this model, governments at different levels firstly identify the targets and evaluation system according the major tasks, decisions and plans of the year, and then break the target down and assign to different departments or regions according to their own situation. The inspection departments will carry out inspection and supervision in the light of the schedule to meet the targets. From top down to the grass-root level, almost every government in China has established its inspection and supervision department with universal application of IT, which forms a completed system. Such a model is a popular one among governments at different levels in China.

(6) Total Quality Management ( TQM) Model

To raise the quality of public service and standardize internal management is the long-term pursuit of government. TQM that stems from corporate management helps this pursuit along. Several local governments and departments once introduced ISO9000, a TQM system of International Organization for Standardization. On the basis of TQM, some government departments established their unique PM systems by conducting standardized management and incorporating PA. For example, Beijing Municipal Bureau of Exit-Entry Inspection and Quarantine established a trinity PM system of quality management, tier management and output management.

(7) Third-Party Evaluation Model

The third-party evaluation is conducted by independent investigation or research institutions to assess the performance of the government or its departments. Currently in mainland China, third-party evaluations are divided into designated ones and independent ones. From the end of 2004 to the beginning of 2005, Gansu Provincial Government designated the Center of PA of China's Local Governments, Lanzhou University to organize the private sector to evaluate the performance of 14 municipal governments and 39 comprising departments in Gansu Province. The result was published in March 2005. Since 2013, the SC has designated the Chinese Academy of Governance, the All-China Federation of Industry and Commerce, the Chinese Academy of Sciences and the Development Research Center of the SC to conduct third-party evaluation of the implementation of major policies, such as administrative examination and approval reform, major water conservancy projects of the SC and the policies and measures concerning drinking water safety in rural area. Since 2007, the Research Center on Public Polity of South China University of Technology has conducted third-party performance evaluations of 21 prefecture-level (or higher level) cities and 121 counties (or county-level cities and districts). The results are published on a regular basis.

In 2014, the SC designated the Development Research Center of the SC, the Chinese Academy of Sciences, the Chinese Academy of Governance and the All-China Federation of Industry and Commerce to respectively conduct third-party evaluation of "eliminating the items that require administrative review and

approval and transfer relevant power to governments at lower levels ",
"accelerating the shanty town redevelopment", "accelerating the construction
of major water conservancy projects" and "launching a batch of investment
projects to non state-owned capital". The third-party evaluation at the central
level has become normal practice.

In addition to the aforementioned models, local governments and
departments/commissions of the CG have explored several PM methods. For
example, the Ministry of Finance, the Government of Pudong New Area in
Shanghai carried out performance budget. The National Audit Office and
Kunming Municipal Government in Yunnan Province conducted performance
audit. All these practices have gained beneficial experience of PM for Chinese
governments at different levels and laid the foundation for a wider application.

### 9.1.2 Outcome of Chinese Government's PM

Up to now, almost every local government in China and most departments/
commissions of the CG have implemented PM. The understanding of PM concepts
and the construction of PM system have developed rapidly through practice. The
Chinese government has achieved remarkable outcome in this regard.

(1) More systematic and law-based PM

The Third Plenary Session of the 18th CPC Central Committee stressed in
the *Decisions of the CPC Central Committee on Several Major Questions of
Comprehensive Deepening of Reforms* that the government PM should be
strengthened, and responsibilities consolidated and corresponded with power"
. The Fourth Plenary Session brought forward the new requirement in the
*Decisions of the CPC Central Committee on Several Major Questions of the Rule of
Law* that "the law-based administration should be implemented in a profound
manner, the building of a government with rule of law accelerated". Party
Secretary General Xi Jinping also stressed for several times that "all major
reforms shall be lawful". Local governments with richer PM experience have
made their PM work more standardized and law-based. For example, Harbin
Municipal Government promulgated the first local regulation in this aspect in

2009; Hangzhou authority promulgated the PM Ordinance of Hangzhou City in 2015; local governments in Guangxi, Zhejiang, Hunan Provinces and some other cities also promulgated their own PM measures.

(2) More scientific and standardized PM

During promoting PM, local governments and departments/commissions of the CG have gained growing understanding of PM concepts and shifted priority from GDP to environmental maintenance and sustainable development. For example, the National Development and Reform Commission has introduced ecological compensation into the PA of local governments. In addition, most localities distribute their performance targets (by contracts) when promoting PM. For example, the PM Office of the Ministry of Agriculture discusses the performance targets with all departments/bureaus and signs performance agreements with heads of the departments/bureaus at the beginning of the year. The Office evaluates their performance at the end of the year according to the agreement. Beijing, Hangzhou, Qingdao, Shenzhen and other local authorities attach importance to problems found during PA, and forward them to relevant departments promptly. The departments are required to improve their performance accordingly. The PA systems of local governments and the departments/commissions of the CGs will be adjusted annually on the basis of the strategic plans. More quantitative measurements are introduced while subjective factors reduced. There are also explorations of utilizing PA's results in many aspects. The results are taken into account when it comes to promotion, appointment and awarding or punishment. In short, the government PM becomes more scientific and standardized.

(2) Wider public participation and diversified access

As long as local governments and departments that carry out PM are the public service providers, public participation is an essential component of their PA. Some departments choose the third-party appraisal in which independent research companies study how satisfied the general public is about the public service by multiple means, such as face-to-face interview, telephone call, paper questionnaire and on-line questionnaire. Some local authorities, such as

Foshan City in Guangdong Province widened the public participation in government's budget PA. In short, public participation in government's PA is widened with diversified accesses.

# 9. 2  The Development and Outcome of Administrative Accountability System

Administrative accountability refers to authorized organs' responsibility ascertainment of the administrative officials who fail to fulfill or wrongly conduct their lawful responsibilities deliberately or by mistake, and cause administrative disorder, low efficiency, delayed performance , infringement of service receiver's legitimate right, or other negative outcome. [1] All sessions of Chinese Government pay great attention to the construction of the accountability system, but the genuine administrative accountability system was started after the reform and opening-up in 1978. While China deepens the promotion of law-based administration and the construction of a law-based government, the authority continuously strengthens the restriction and supervision of the administrative power and raises the credibility and execution capability of the government by establishing scientific and effective restriction and supervision system of power execution, standardizing and completing the administrative accountability system, optimizing the correcting and accountability system, and completing the methods and procedure of accountability.

## 9. 2. 1  History of the administrative accountability system Development in China

Since 1978 when the reform and opening-up policy is adopted, the administrative accountability system development in China can be divided into two phases by the year of 2003.

---

[1]   Shen Kui & Lin Liangliang & Jiang Jiya. 2011. The Report of the Research on the administrative accountability system.

(1) Germination (before 2003)

Since the reform and opening-up, the general public has increasingly strict demand on government's accountability. This has promoted the construction of civil servants' accountability system. HR system was reformed and the establishment of civil servant system accelerated. Although new ideas about civil servants' accountability emerged at this stage, neither the concept of administrative accountability system nor a clear and systematic understanding of how a leader should shoulder the responsibility had come into shape. Leaders' responsibilities was not identified by systematic regulations but became clearer after each event.

In this phase, state-level important documents that contributed to establishing an accountability system are (1) the *Interim Regulation of Intraparty Discipline Punishment for Party Members as Leaders of Severe Misconduct of Bureaucracy and Dereliction of Duty* in 1988; (2) *the Interim Ordinance of the Appointment and Promotion of Leaders and Other Officials in CPC Committees and Governments* in 1995; (3) *the Interim Regulation of State-level Civil Servants* in 1993; (4) *the Law of Administrative Supervision approved at the 25th Meeting of the Standing Committee of the Eighth National People's Congress on May 9th* 1997; (5) *the Regulation of the Dereliction of Administrative Duties in Extremely Severe Safety Accidents* promulgated by the SC in 2001 which identifies the administrative duties in extremely serious safety accidents.

Meanwhile, the exploration of the administrative accountability system at the sub-national level can be divided into two categories: first, accountability system of officials was constructed in accord with the promotion of the administrative law-enforcement responsibility. Many local governments promulgated local laws, regulations and other regulatory documents of law-enforcement responsibility system, such as the *Measures of Implementation of the Administrative Law-enforcement Responsibility System in Henan Province and the Measures of Implementation of the Administrative Law-enforcement Responsibility System in Henan Province.* Secondly, accountability system of major safety accidents was also constructed. For example, documents, such as the Regulation of administrative accountability system of Major Safety Accidents of Beijing Municipal and the Regulation of administrative accountability system of Major Safety Accidents of the People's Government of Fujian Province, *were promulgated.* ①

(2) *Development* (*after* 2003)

*The administrative accountability system in China developed rapidly after the storm of accountability caused by the outbreak of SARS. administrative accountability system became a key component of building a law-based government and of the administration by law. On March* 22*nd* 2004, *the SC promulgated the* Implementation Outline of the Comprehensive Promotion of the Administration by Law *and raised the correspondence between duties and right. In June* 2008, *the SC promulgated the* Opinion on Enhancing the Construction of a Law-based Government *and stressed strict administrative accountability system.*

*In this phase, state-level important documents that contributed to establishing accountability system are* (1) *the Regulation of Disciplinary Punishment of CPC issued by the CPC Central Committee in December* 2003; (2) *the* Intraparty Supervision Regulation of CPC (Trial) *promulgated by the CPC Central Committee in February* 2004; (3) *the Interim Regulation of the Leaders and Other Officials of CPC* Committees and Government approved by the CPC Central Committee in April 2004. This regulation serves to be the legal substratum of administrative accountability system by listing in details nine situations in which the Leaders and Other Officials should be held responsible and resign. (4) the *Civil Servant Law of the People's Republic of China* promulgated and implemented on January 1st 2006, introducing the concepts of "being held responsible and discharged" and "being punished and dismissed" into the management system of civil servants and turning accountability ascertainment into a lawful regulation; (5) the *Punishment Ordinance of Civil*

---

① Shen Kui & Lin Liangliang & Jiang Jiya. 2011. The Report of the Research on the administrative accountability system.

*Servants in Administrative Organs* approved at the executive meeting of the SC in 2007; (6) the *Interim Regulation of the Implementation of Accountability of Leaders and Other Officials in CPC Committees and Governments*, the first lawful regulation of officials' accountability at the state-level promulgated by the central authority in July 2009, which stipulates seven situations in which officials should be held accountable; (7) the revised *Regulation of Implementing the Accountability System of Corruption-free Party Construction* promulgated by the CPC Central Committee and the SC in November 2010 which specifies the applicable situations, terms, measures, types and other components of the accountability system of the leadership and leaders of CPC committees and governments at all levels; (8) the revised *Regulation of Disciplinary Punishment of CPC* reviewed and approved at the meeting of the Political Bureau of the CPC Central Committee.

Local governments also promulgated regulations or regulatory documents of performance accountability. In July 2003, the Interim administrative accountability system Measures of Changsha Municipal Government, first of its kind in China, was promulgated. On July 1st 2004, the *Interim Accountability Measures for Executive Chiefs of Departments in Chongqing Municipal Government*, the first accountability measure document at the provincial level in China, was implemented. Afterwards, other local governments also promulgated local laws, regulations or regulatory documents and initiated the administrative accountability system. For example, the *Interim Measures of administrative accountability system of the People's Government of Tianjin Municipal* was issued in 2004, the *Temporary Measures of administrative accountability system of the People's Government of Anhui Province* in 2007 and the *Accountability Measures of Executive Chiefs in Departments of the Provincial Government and in Cities and Autonomous Prefectures by the People's Government of Yunnan Province* in 2008. In July 2011, Beijing authority issued the *administrative accountability system Measures of Beijing Municipal* which stipulated that official at all levels who commit 26 types of regulation violations or offenses, such as no fulfillment, illegal fulfillment and improper fulfillment of administrative responsibilities, will be held accountable and even dismissed. On February 15th 2012, the authority of Harbin City, Heilongjiang Province issued an administrative accountability system regulation, explicitly stipulating that officials will be held accountable in 36 situations, such as improper making of administrative polices, low efficiency, inaction, and irrational, slow, or false performance. On February 25th 2016, the administrative accountability system Measures of Hubei Province was issued and stipulated that officials in charge should be held accountable in case of collective violation of law.

In addition, governments promulgated regulations of performance accountability. For example, the People's Government of Nanhai District, Foshan City, Guangdong Province promulgated the *Interim Accountability Measures of the Usage and Performance of the Special Fiscal Fund of Nanhai District, Foshan City*①in June 2009; the authority of Chenxi County, Hunan Province promulgated the *Accountability and Appraisal Measures of the Administrative Performance of the Departments Directly under the Chenxi County Government*② in 2008; Beijing Municipal Finance Bureau issued the *Accountability Measures of Budget PM of Beijing Municipal*③ in 2011; the Ministry of Finance promulgated the *Outline of PM Work of the Budget (2012 – 2015)*④ in 2012; Sichuan Provincial Government issued the *Measures of Fault Accountability and Its Result Application under the PM System of the People's*

①   Ministry of Finance, People's Republic of China. 2009. Nanhai District, Foshan City Establish Performance Accountability System of Special Funds [ OL ] . http: //www. mof. gov. cn/pub/mof/ xinwenlianbo/guangdongcaizhengxinxilianbo/200907/t20090717 _ 182810. html. ( accessed on 17/07/ 2009)

②   Organization Department, COC Chenxi County Committee. Chenxi County Launch Evaluation Measures of Performance Accountability to Question the Working Style of Leaders and Officials [OL] . http: //www. hnredstar. gov. cn/huaihua/gbgz/t20080701_ 184843. htm. ( accessed on 01/07/2008)

③   Library of Law. Notice by Beijing Municipal Finance Bureau of Issuing the *Accountability Measures of Budget PM of Beijing Municipal (trail)* . http: //www. law-lib. com/law/law _ view. asp? id = 385230.

④   Beijing News. Budget Performance to Introduce to administrative accountability system. http: // www. bjnews. com. cn/news/2012/10/31/230728. html. ( accessed on 31/10/2012)

Government of Sichuan Province ( Trial )① in 2012; the authority of Tieling City, Liaoning Province promulgated the *Interim Measures of Work Style and Performance Accountability in Government Organs in Tieling City*② in 2013.

Moreover, new changes have occurred during implementingadministrative accountability system. Governments attach growing importance to the performance accountability when applying the PA's results. Fujian Province strictly ascertains the officials' accountability if they fulfill the responsibilities carelessly, shuffle themselves out of responsibilities, work inefficiently or with delay, or abuse their power. Xinjiang Uygur Autonomous Region takes the PA results as the basis for accountability. Heads of the departments that fall behind at the appraisal ranking will be arranged for a talk. Heads of the departments rated "disappointing" or even worse will be called up for admonition according to relevant regulations. Heads of the departments rated "disappointing" or even worse for two consecutive years will be handled by inspection departments. ③

### 9.2.2 Outcome of the administrative accountability system in China

The implementation of administrative accountability in China has accelerated the building of an accountable government, enhanced the sense of accountability and the drive to fulfill government's responsibilities, promoted officials' sense of responsibility and of duty, upgraded government's executive capability, and thus has ensured the rights to truth, of participation and of supervision and made remarkable achievements.

( 1 ) Tentative Institutional Framework of administrative accountability system

---

① chinalcn. com. Notice by the People's Government of Sichuan Province of Issuing the *Measures of Accountability for Faults and the Application of Results under the PM System of the People's Government of Sichuan Province* ( Trial ) . http: //www. china. com. cn/guoqing/gbbg/2012-08/02/content _ 26098298. htm. ( accessed on 02/08/2012 )

② Cui Bo. *Interim Measures of Accountability for the Style of Work and Performance in Governmental Organs in Tieling City* Issued. http: //www. zgtlsw. gov. cn/Article_ 1628_ 1/. ( accessed 26/02/2013 ) .

③ Xue Gang & Bao Guili & Liu Xiaokang & Yin Ynahong. 2013. Research on the Application of Performance Appraisal Results of a Service-oriented Government [ J ] . *Journal of the Chinese Academy of Governance*: Current Situation, Questions and Solutions. 2013 ( 5 ) .

There has not been any specific law or regulation of administrative accountability system but separated items in the *Law of Civil Servants*, *the Law of Administrative Supervision*, *the Punishment Regulations of Civil Servants in Administrative Departments*, *the Interim Regulation of Accountability of Leaders and Officials in CPC Committees and Governments* and other laws, regulations and intraparty regulations. On the other hand, local authorities have regulated the administrative accountability system by local laws and regulations, governmental rules, and other regulative documents. The present tentative institutional framework of administrative accountability system involves the political accountability of major faults, the moral accountability caused by personal moral conduct, and performance accountability. The sense of duty and accountability of officials at different levels, the sense of supervision of the general public and the sense of accountability of the social opinion have all been strengthened. In the political section, the public power holders who abuse the rights will be held accountable; accountability has become a normal practice and a storm of accountability occurs when there is a major incident.

(2) Accelerated Building of an Accountable Government

An accountable government should proactively meet reasonable requirements of the citizen, boldly shoulder the duties of morality, politics, administration, law and governance, and establish a full set of regulations to restrict administrative conducts. The implementation of administrative accountability system restrains officials from demanding public power and avoids the infringement of private right by excessive public power; it also enhances the sense of duty of officials who execute public power and improve their administrative conducts, establishing a good image of the government that boldly shoulder its responsibilities. More importantly, the appraisal results of government's performance serves to be the solid foundation of administrative accountability system, which strongly enhances the official's sense of responsibility and duty. The accountability mechanism based on the appraisal results adds an important component to the administrative accountability system of officials and clears up the downward channel by setting up institutional restrictions on delinquency or misconduct, creating a new way of promotion and demotion.

(3) Enhanced Efficiency of the Government

Enhancing the performance accountability raises the attention to the quality and efficiency and catches the eyes of both officials and the general public onto "how well the job is done" on the basis of specified responsibilities. The performance accountability is like the sharp blade of a guillotine over the work style of laziness and indiscipline. It encourages officials to work efficiently with quality output, assesses achievements with the actual output and promotes the pragmatic work style among governments. The PM results of an organization, personnel, projects and fiscal budgets not only expands the usage of PM results, but also enlarges the scope of responsibility ascertainment of leaders and officials, so that the problem of mediocrity and laziness could be settled and officials are encouraged to establish the administrative philosophy of "no achievements is a fault".

(4) Accelerated Building of a Service-oriented Government

Building a service-oriented government is one of the major targets during the reform of Chinese government. During the process, the government functions must evolve to create a better environment for development, provide quality and efficient public service and safeguard the fairness and justice of the society, so that the general public would be satisfied. To achieve this evolution, "the power must be caged" and exposed to people's supervision and criticism. The implementation of administrative accountability system both enhances the power restriction and the transparency of government's work. Moreover, the implementation of administrative accountability system publishes the PM results and welcomes the general public to appraise, discuss and supervise. This greatly promotes the democracy in governmental administration and builds up a platform to consolidate the rights to truth and of participation, expression and supervision. It also plays an important role in promoting the public participation in government affairs, effectively supervising government's conducts and *refreshing officials' performance.* ①

## 9.3  Current Work of Chinese Government on Performance Management and Administrative Accountability System

### 9.3.1  Current Work of Chinese Government's PM②

The report to the 18th CPC National Congress put forward the new requirement of "innovating the measures of administrative management, enhancing the credibility and executive capability of the government, and promoting the government PM". Against this backdrop, the PM of local governments in China has shifted its focus to the following work:

(1) Comprehensive Planning to Highlight Social Administration and Public Service

Local governments have to not only promote the economic development but also maintain the coordinated development among economy, society, environment, etc. At present, most governments at the provincial and municipal levels has shifted their priority from economic development to the balanced development among economy, society and public service, etc. People's livelihood has become an increasingly important topic.

(2) Scientific Reasoning to Gradually Optimize Government's PM System

During the promotion of PM work, local governments realized that advanced PM concepts had to be consolidated by an optimized PM system, as well as concreted and detailed PM steps in order to improve the executive efficiency, implementing capability and government's performance. In recent years, the government PM has been deepened. Meanwhile, local governments

---

① Liu Xutao & Du Yiguo. 2014. *Report of the Research on the Performance Accountability Based on the Government's PM.*

② Yin Yanhong. 2013. New Development Trends of the PM of Local Government, *Study Times* [N], 22/04/2013.

conducted scientific reasoning and make innovative changes during completing government's PM system and optimizing the system. For example, Beijing Municipal Government set the goal that the PM of 2011 must "enhance the basis, adhere to the regulations and seek for development". To introduce the public appraisal into the system and bridge government's work with public understanding, the Government designated academic institutions to sort out every responsibility of the government and its comprising departments, compare them with the livelihood of people and finally summarize thousands of appraisal items that are highly relevant to people's concern and personal interest, and thus easily noticed and appraised. All items comprise the data base of public appraisal, so that the index system is more scientific and specific, which standardizes government's work. Such effort showcases that local governments in China are optimizing their PM system and making the PM work more scientific and standardized.

(3) Boarder Participation to Raise the Credibility of the Government and to Lead the General Public to Supervise and Appraise the Government's Performance Effectively

The general public has participated in appraising government's performance for many years. Increasing number of governments attach greater importance to the public appraisal and its result accounts for larger proportion of the overall result. Many local governments increased the rate to over 30% and Hangzhou authority to 50%. Increasing number of people are participating in the appraisal. For example, Heshan City of Guangdong Province is home to 460 thousand permanent residents. Each year, around 12,000 people from all walks of life participate in the PA of county-level governments and its departments. The proportion rate is the highest among all county-level cities in China. The general public also enjoys more accesses to appraise, such as the Internet, telephone, letter, survey to the home, seminar of hit topics, random interviews on the street, etc. The "Three People-oriented Campaigns" run by Qingdao authority for many years will hopefully be live broadcast this year via television to reveal the process of public appraisal. The public appraisal generates great impetus for improving government's performance, diversifies the participation accesses and increases government's credibility.

(4) Enhanced and Improved Implementation of Appraisal Results

Both the experience of foreign countries and domestic pilot projects proves that the application of PA results decides whether government's PM can continue and stay effective. In recent years, local authorities tried incentives such as circulated criticism, praise, award and accountability to enhance the result application. For example, Fujian provincial authority was the first to apply the results to administrative accountability system. Until now, the results have been applied to the PM of many local governments. Some other local authority combines the PA with the evaluation of the government leadership. For example, Hangzhou municipal authority regards the appraisal results of the past four years as the evaluation basis when assigning and promoting leaders. Especially in the past two years, local governments have began to enhance the application of appraisal results in improving performance. For example, Haidian District Government of Beijing Municipal requires all departments to summit a 3000-word report of performance improvement on the basis the appraisal results. The report explicitly explains the improvement plan and will be implemented under supervision. During the two sessions of Nangong City, Hebei Province in 2012, the *Suggestions on PM Appraisal* of 25 comprising departments of the government were submitted for discussion. Further more, some local governments plans to couple the appraisal results and the fiscal budget of the department to widen the application of the results.

(5) Resource Integration to Raise the Executive Capability of the Government

The government's PM is a systematic and wide-ranging program concerning various departments and sections. To effectively leverage on it, many localities stress the integration of relevant resources. First, evaluation measures of different departments in various sectors have been unified to raise the efficiency of PM work and lighten the burden on the evaluation objects. Second, coordination mechanisms among governments at different levels or among different departments have been set up to share information and tackle problems, improving the administration efficiency and government's performance. Third, effective systems of performance information have been established to integrate the governments' PM with the on-line service office, administrative service center, public resource trade center, e-supervision platform, outbound service center, administrative review and approval system and other systems, so that the information and resource can be shared. Such effective systems can save the cost of collecting large amount of repeated information and compare the performance in a real-time manner, which promotes the dynamic supervision of the government's PM, fully utilizes the information system and greatly improves government's PM work.

### 9.3.2 Current Work of the administrative accountability system in China[①]

Since the third plenary session of the 18th CPC, to consolidate major strategic measures of comprehensive deepening the reform, the administrative accountability system in China has carried out work as follows:

(1) Great Promotion of the List of Government Rights and Liabilities and Negative List

On the basis of profound classification, elimination, adjustment, review, confirmation and procedure optimization, the government has identified items, such as government's functions, law basis, subject, responsibility and its restrictions, management process and supervision measure in the list of government rights and published to the general public. Meanwhile, a list of government liabilities, subject, method will be drafted in parallel. In addition, the universal market entry system is launched, so that various types of market subjects can equally enter any section of the market off the Negative List. The three lists draw the boundary·of the right and responsibility between the government and the market, enterprises and the society. The list of government

---

① the Program for the Implementation of Law-based Government Construction (2015 – 2020).

rights stipulates what the government can do; "everything which is not authorized by the law is prohibited". The list of government liabilities stipulates how the government should supervise the market; "the government should fulfill its responsibility stipulated by the law". The Negative List stipulates the restriction on enterprises; "everything which in not prohibited by the law is allowed". By making the three lists, the visible hands can be governed by the law, the invisible hands utilized and the hands seeking rent stopped.

(2) Strict Ascertainment of Responsibilities

The procedure system of making major administrative decisions is optimized, the subject, scope, lawful procedure and lawful responsibility identified, the procedure standardized and the rigid restriction of decision-making procedure strengthened. On the one hand, the policy-making organ assesses major administrative decisions by tracking the implementation and effect of the decisions. On the other hand, the life-long accountability system for major decision makers and the stern-to-stem ascertainment measure should be strengthened and strictly implemented. If the executive chief, responsible leaders and officials have not followed the law, have made faulty decisions or delayed making an accurate decision, and have caused major loss and terrible influence, they will be held accountable in accord with the party disciplinary, government regulation and relevant laws.

(3) Comprehensive Implementation of the Responsibility System of Administrative Enforcement of Law

The government should establish an administrative law enforcement system of authority and efficiency in which power and duty are integrated . The responsibility of law enforcement should be specified for officials at different posts of various departments and the responsibility ascertainment mechanism strengthened, improved and run a regular basis. With a universal network to supervise the administrative law enforcement, we should improve mechanisms of reporting offenses and circulating information, enhance the supervision, prevent the interference driven by the interest of departments, local protectionism and other interests and eliminate corruption.

(4) Government Affairs Published Profoundly

It is normal to publish information and exceptional not to do so. Adhering to such a principle, we should publish the decision, implementation, management, service and result. First, the publishing system of government affairs should be optimized, the channels of publishing diversified and scope and content of the information that must be published further identified. Second, the information about fiscal budget, the allocation of public resource, the approval and implementation of major construction project and the social welfare should be given the priority. Third, the system of government spokesperson and that of publishing emergency information should be optimized to response to people's concern. Fourth, the way the government publishes information should be improved by constructing an on-line service platform of government information and data for the convenience of the people. More information technologies should be applied and the publishing more unified.

(5) Optimized System of Error-correction and Accountability

Government's administrative accountability system should be standardized, systematic, specific and timely. First, measures should be strengthened to correct inaction and arbitrary conducts, tackle the laziness, incompetence and hesitation, and firmly punish delinquency and malfeasance. Second, the accountability system of constructing a clean party and a corruption-free government must be enhanced. Every mistake to be corrected, and every officials with misconduct held accountable. If localities and departments have prominent problems of formalism, bureaucratism, hedonism, and extravagance, violate regulations despite of a law-enforcement campaign, or have widespread corruption issues, the violators of regulation or law, the supervision organ and the leadership should all be held accountable.

## Reference

1. Liu X. T. (Ed) (2015) . *Case Study of the PM of Chinese Government Based on the Best Practice*. Beijing: Press of the Chinese Academy of Governance.

2. Yin Y. H. (2013, April 22) . New Development Trends of the PM of Local Government,

*Study Times.*

3. William  T. Gormley  Jr. ,  Steven  J  Balla.  ( 2007 )  . *Bureaucracy  and  Democracy-Accountability and Performance.* trans. Yu Yixuan. Shanghai: Fudan University Press.

4. Mark G. Popovich.  ( 2002 )  . *Creating High-performance Government Organizations.* Trans. Kong Xiansui & Geng Hongmin. Beijing: China Renmin University Press.

5. Liu X. T. ,  Du Y. G.  ( 2014 )  . *Report of the Research on the Performance Accountability Based on the Government's PM.*

6. Ministry of Finance, People's Republic of China.  ( 2009 )  . Nanhai District, Foshan City Establish Performance Accountability System of Special Funds. Retrieved on 17/07/2009 from http: //www. mof. gov. cn/pub/mof/xinwenlianbo/guangdongcaizhengxinxilianbo/200907/t200 90717_ 182810. html.

7. Organization  Department,  COC  Chenxi  County  Committee. Chenxi  County  Launch Evaluation Measures of Performance Accountability to Question the Working Style of Leaders  and  Officials. Retrieved  on  01/07/2008  from  http: //www. hnredstar. gov. cn/ huaihua/gbgz/t20080701_ 184843. htm.

8. Library of Law. Notice by Beijing Municipal Finance Bureau of Issuing the *Accountability Measures of Budget PM of Beijing Municipal  ( trail )* . http: //www. law-lib. com/law/ law_ view. asp? id = 385230.

9. Beijing  News. Budget  Performance  to  Introduce  to  administrative  accountability system. Retrieved on 31/10/2012 from http: //www. bjnews. com. cn/news/2012/10/31/ 230728. html.

10. chinalcn. com. Notice by the People's Government of Sichuan Province of Issuing the *Measures of Accountability for Faults and the Application of Results under the PM System of the People's Government of Sichuan Province  ( Trial )* . Retrieved on 02/08/2012 from http: //www. china. com. cn/guoqing/gbbg/2012-08/02/content_ 26098298. htm.

11. Cui B. *Interim  Measures  of  Accountability  for  the  Style  of  Work  and  Performance  in Governmental  Organs  in  Tieling  City* Issued. Retrieved on 26/02/2013 from http: // www. zgtlsw. gov. cn/Article_ 1628_ 1/.

12. Xue G. ,  Bao G, L. ,  Liu X. K. ,  Yin Y. H.  ( 2013 )  . Research on the Application of Performance Appraisal Results of a Service-oriented Government. *Journal of the Chinese Academy of Governance: Current Situation,  Questions and Solutions, 5.*

13. Shen K. ,  Lin L. L. ,  Jiang J. Y.  ( 2011 )  . The  Report  of  the  Research  on  the administrative accountability system.

14. The Program for the Implementation of Law-based Government Construction (2015 – 2020) .

(Written by: Xiaokang Liu, Director, Division of Public Administration and Policy, Department of Public Administration and Policy, Chinese Academy of Governance; Yanhong Yin, Associate Professor, Department of Public Administration and Policy, Chinese Academy of Governance)

# Chapter X

# Advancing Law-based
# Administration of Government

Rule of law, as the basic governance strategy stresses well-conceived legislation, strict law enforcement, judicial justice and national law-abiding, among which law enforcement is most significant. Whether the decisions and law enforcement of government is legitimate and appropriate appertains to people's well-being and social stability as well as the implementation of rule of law. Therefore, governance by law and establishment of law-based government are important content of fully implementing the basic strategy of rule of law and the basic principle of administration of Chinese government. The building of law-based government is crucial for rule of law and also the main target of administrative reform of modern China. Government not ruled by law isn't modern government. For many years, Chinese government has adopted a series of measures to promote government ruled by law and the guiding spirit, specific target, basic principles, requirements, main tasks and measures of Advancing Law-based Administration of Government gradually take form. Currently, the administrative authority of Chinese government at all levels has been gradually incorporated into the track of rule of law and the legal system that regulates the acquisition and operation of government authority has been initially put in place, thus law-based administration has made remarkable progress.

# 10. 1  The Choice of Advancing Law-based Administration of Government

### 10. 1. 1  Setting the Goal of Advancing Law-based Administration of Government

In 1978, Third Plenary Session of the Eleventh Central Committee of the CPC proposed the guideline that "there must be laws to go by, the laws must be observed and strictly enforced, and lawbreakers must be prosecuted", which showcased the resolution of CPC and central government to promote rule of law; in 1984, central government further clarified that " the focus should be shifted from being directed by policy to being directed by both policy and law, which implies fundamental meaning and requirement of rule of law. In 1993, working method of the State Council stipulated "law-based duty performing, law-based administration", marking the first enactment of "Law-based administration" in government report.

In 1997, the fifteenth national congress of CPC made "Governing a country according to rule of law" the guideline for CPC governance. In 1999, when the second conference of the ninth national people's congress, "administration in line with rule of law and building law-based country" was enacted in constitution as the basic strategy for governing the country; In November that year, state council put forward *Detailed Requirements for Promoting Government Based on Rule of Law in Decisions* on stepping up governing a country according to rule of law in an all-around way. To fulfill the strategic task of "governing a country based on rule of law", the sixteenth national congress of CPC set the task of "promoting administration based on rule of law" in 2002; in 2004, to meet the requirements of "governing a country based on rule of law" and "administration based on rule of law", state council promulgated "*Implementation Guidelines for Promoting Law-based Administration in an All-around way*" . It is for the first time that "*law-based administration in an all-around way and initially putting in place a government ruled by law through ten years' commitment"* was confirmed as the goal for promoting law-based administration comprehensively.

In November, 2012, the 18th national congress of CPC made " the establishment of government ruled by law " as main task of " building a moderately prosperous society in an all-around way" and at the same time set the timetable for completing this arduous task: initially putting law-based government in place by 2020. In February, 2013, the second plenary session of the 18th central committee of CPC adopted *"Plans on Institutional Reform and Function Transformation of State Council'* , which requires that government function to be separated from enterprises, government operation from capital, government functions from those of institutions and government operation from social organizations. Service-oriented government with scientific structure, better structure, efficient and clean operation and people's satisfaction should be established. In November, 2013, the third plenary session of the 18th central committee of CPC adopted *The Decision on Major Issues Concerning Comprehensively Deepening Reforms*, which made " improving and developing socialist system with Chinese character and modernizing country's administration system and governance capacity " as the overall task of comprehensively deepening reform and put forward the task of "building a law-based and service-oriented government" . In October, 2014, the forth plenary session of the 18th central committee of CPC adopted *Decision of the CPC Central Committee on Major Issues Pertaining to Comprehensively Promoting the Rule of Law*, which made arrangement on " deepening law-based administration and accelerating government ruled by law" and explicitly put forward the task of "accelerating law-based government with reasonable functions, statutory rights and responsibilities, strict law enforcement and at the same time open and honest, clean and efficient, law-abiding and faithful. In October, 2015, the fifth plenary session of the 18th central committee of CPC reviewed and adopted "suggestions on formulating the thirteenth five year plan for national economy and social development" , which posed requirements for economic development and rule of law.

In December, 2015, state council promulgated "Outlines for Advancing Law-based Administration of Government 2015 – 2020". The outline falls into three parts, which clarified the guiding thought, overall tasks, basic principles, measuring criteria and 44 actions for Advancing Law-based Administration of Government. This is an important outline for building China under rule of law in the thirteenth five-year plan period. It is both the concrete implementation of building a law-based government set by the 18th central committee of CPC and the second, third, fourth and fifth plenary session and also the systematic deployment of Advancing Law-based Administration of Government in the future five years.

### 10. 1. 2 Objective Reasons for Advancing Law-based Administration of Government

Institution is the inevitable result of social development, and the path to law-based government is in line with the law of social development.

First, the market-oriented process initiated by reform and opening up entails need for rule of law. As the deepening of marketization, traditional relationship model between acquaintanceship slacks off and people gradually get rid of the restrictions of blood relationship and geography, the range for exchange and interconnection expands, the population flows faster and requirements and reliance on regulation rise; at the same time, with the increase of labor division and personal income, the independence of individuals grows and thus pose higher demand for intellectual property protection, contract system and safety system, which directly prompts the need for "rule of law".

Second, the diversification of interests and the formation of interest groups provide the players for building law-based society. With the gradual establishment of market economy and the aggravation of interest diversification, varied interest groups are formed. Interest differentiation means the need for interest integration, and it is inevitable to encounter various legal problems while integrating interests, which promotes different interest groups to participate into the building of law-based society. As the channel for voicing the interest pursuit becomes smoother and organization becomes legitimate gradually, their cost for participating into building of law-based society becomes lower and it is easier to form a law-based society.

Third, the improvement of governance capacity provides opportunities for building law-based society. Promoting the building of law-based society has gained consensus within the party and become the primary tasks for the country development. It should become crucial state policies and actually has become the main driving force of building legal system. It plays active role in the process of attaining rule of law and thus accelerates the process of building law-based society and improves the possibility of success.

### 10.1.3 Overall Target and Criteria for Advancing Law-based Administration of Government

*Implementation of Guidelines for Advancing Law-based Administration of Government* set the overall task for Advancing Law-based Administration of Government, which is to put in place a law-based government with reasonable functions, statutory rights and responsibilities, strict law enforcement, and which is also open and fair, clean and efficient, law-abiding and honest.

How to measure the building of law-based government? The essence of law-based government is to manage government in line with law. Government is the subject of rule of law and the objects of rule of law are citizens and society. The tenets of law-based government are that government is subject to law and the only measurement for law-based government is: the nation has a sound law and regulation system and there exists such mechanism that makes this system operate in an open environment and regulate, curtail, supervise administrative activities and hold it accountable; this system and mechanism can be strictly executed and effectively operated by government, government departments and various public service institutions. Based on this, the implementation outlines for Advancing Law-based Administration of Government set seven detailed measurements for law-based government for the first time, which are full implementation of government functions according to law, comprehensive administrative system in line with law, scientific, democratic and reasonable administration decisions, strict and just implementation of constitutions and laws, transparent operation of administrative authority, effective and efficient guarantee of people's rights and the overall improvement of governing in line with law. Law-based government is initially formed if the above-mentioned tasks are completed.

## 10. 2  Main Steps and Achievements in Advancing Law - based Administration of Government

### 10. 2. 1  Build and improve administrative law and regulation system to solidify legal basis for government activities

Since the third plenary session of the 11th central committee of CPC, the landmark in China's building of legal system is the end of the situation of no law to comply with. The socialist legal system initially takes form. Law formation regarding government management and government legislation also made remarkable progress.

Up to December 31, laws enacted by national people's congress and its standing committee which are still valid are 273 cases. Among them, legislation regarding administrative management accounts for 89%. Especially the promulgation of Organic Law of the State Council of the PRC, Organic Law of the Local People's Congress and Local People's Governments of the PRC, Civil Servant Law, Law of The People's Republic of China on Administrative Punishments, Administrative License Law, Administrative Coercion Law, Administrative Procedural Law, Administrative Reconsideration Law, State Compensation Law and such main laws constitute a relatively comprehensive systematic procedures that run through administrative processes of "subject-behaviors-remedy" and lays solid foundation for Advancing Law-based Administration of Government.

Meanwhile, state council also formulated Ordinance concerning the Procedures for the Formulation of Administrative Regulations, Regulations on

Procedures for the Formulation of Rules and municipalities directly under central government also successively formulate their respective legislative procedures and rules, making government legislation have rules to follow and proceed steadily. As of February of 2016, the current effective administrative regulations enacted by state council amount to 683 pieces, local regulations 12747 pieces, rules and regulations of ministries and commissions 4926 pieces and rules of local governments 12455 pieces. These regulations and rules cover all major aspects of government administration and made more comprehensive and detailed regulations regarding government administration. On top of that, to avoid rule and regulations and regulative papers of government at all levels from violating superior laws with higher legal effect or clashing with each other, in December, 2001, state council promulgated " Ordinance on the Archivist Filing of Regulations and Government Rules" , which is to enhance the implementation of examination system of putting local rules and regulations and regulations of state council for safeguarding unification of legal system and to ensure the right implementation of rules and regulations. In March, 2007, General Office of the State council released " Notice on the Work of Clearing off Administrative Regulations and Rules" , which requires cleaning up rules and regulations in all aspects and make it more based on system.

By establishing reasonable and sound administrative rule and regulations, long-term mechanism for cleaning up, tracking and evaluation and putting on record rules and regulations, the number administrative legislation increases and its quality improves. Law basis of government activities can be consolidated.

## 10. 2. 2  Clarify the right and responsibility for government activities, improve ruling by law in the setting of administrative organizations

Currently, there are two organic laws for administrative organizations in China, namely *Local Organic Laws for Local People's Congress and Local Governments* in 1979 and *Organic Law of State Council* in 1982. Formulation of the two regulations plays an active role in law-based setting of functions of administrative organizations. But judging from the clauses, the two regulations are relatively simple, which cannot meet the realistic requirements of law-based government. In practice, the segmentation of government rights and responsibilities are achieved through "fixed system", which to some extent makes the behavior of government more regulated and authoritative.

In November, 2013, the third Plenary Session of the 18th Central Committee of CPC put it for the first time that: "promoting government at local levels and departments to have list of authorities and make the procedures of authority operation public according to law"; in October, 2014, fourth Plenary Session of the 18th Central Committee of the Communist Party of China adopted "*Decision of the CPC Central Committee on Major Issues Pertaining to Comprehensively Promoting the Rule of Law.*" which stressed again that, "implementing list system of government authority and resolutely eliminating the room for rent-seeking of power" is the major measures for fulfilling government functions and also main content for accelerating Advancing Law-based Administration of Government; in March, 2015, General Office of the CPC Central Committee and state council released "*Guiding Opinions on Promoting the List System of Departments of Government at Local Levels*", which requires the listing of administrative power of local government at all levels and its basis, execution subject and running process, corresponding responsibilities, etc, and clearly list them, make them public and receive supervision". According to this, government at all levels and government departments should promote the publicity of power list intensively. Through establishing power list and respective list of responsibilities, the limit of rights and responsibilities of local government at all levels are further clarified. Streamlining government and delegating authorities are advanced and government function system with clearly defined limit, rational division of labor, consistent right and responsibilities and efficient functions and legal guarantee and scientific and efficient mechanism for power supervision, containment and coordination are formed, which can promote law-based governance.

Besides, the law-based establishment of China's civil servant system has also made progress. In 1993, state council officially promulgated "*Provisional*

*Regulations on National Civil Servants"* , and then released a series of matching provisional regulations, such as position classification, employment, test, rewards and punishments, position promotion and demotion, position appointment and dismiss, training and exchange, salary, welfares, insurance, retirement provision that cover all links of management of civil servants; in 2005, the fifth Session of the Eleventh National People's Congress deliberated on and adopted *Civil Servant Law*, whose formulation and release marked the major breakthrough in law-based management of civil servants. Law-based management of civil servants accentuates competition and initiative mechanism and revitalizes the civil servant team and also stresses supervision and containment mechanism to regulate the behaviors of civil services.

### 10. 2. 3 Improve administrative decision mechanism; promote decision making in a scientific, democratic and law-based manner

Administrative decision making is the starting point for all administrative activities. The wrong starting point will inevitably cause behavioral mistakes. It is the basic requirement and criteria for measuring the building of law-based government to make administrative decision scientific, democratic and law-based. In 2004, *"Implementation Guidelines for Comprehensively Promoting Law-based Administration"* *of* state council made scientific, democratic and legitimate administrative decision the measuring standard for law-based government. And it clearly required that "administrative decision system is scientific, procedures are legitimate, process is open, responsibilities are clear, legitimate procedures for decision making are strictly implemented, decision making qualities are obviously improved, and decision efficiency is guaranteed ; decision against law , improper decision and delayed decision are reduced remarkably and get corrected in time; administrative decision gains increased public confidence and the capacity for decision execution is improved by large margin. "

To ensure scientific decision making, government on the one hand enhances the building of new-type think tank with Chinese characteristics and expert tank for administrative decision consultation to use external minds to improve decision quality; on the other hand the evaluation mechanism for social stability risks is implemented to improve risk evaluation.

To promote democratic decision, government lays emphasis both on the actual effect of public participation and decision making through group discussion. On the other hand, government at all levels establishes and enhances the development of platform for public participation. When it comes to items that are concerned with the economic and social development and vital interest of the masses, it is required to solicit extensive opinions, communicate fully with stake holders and feedback opinions and reasons in time. In respect to cultural education, medicine and health, resources development, environmental protection, public services and such items concerned with the wellbeing of the people, the system of opinion polls should be established. On the other hand, major decisions should be made on standing meeting of government or plenary session, leadership meeting of departments and then be determined by administrative head through group discussion.

To make administrative decision democratic, government emphasizes on improving procedural system for major administrative decisions, formulating administrative procedural rules and incorporating decision into legitimate procedures and due process; on the other hand enhancing legitimacy examination, establishing legitimacy consultant system for government to ensure that legal consultant plays active role in formulating major administrative decisions and promoting law-based administration. In addition, decision accountability system should be strengthened and evaluation and accountability system for concerned personnel after major decisions should be established and improved.

### 10. 2. 4  Vigorously promote the reform of administrative examination and approval system, promote the transformation of government functions

Influenced by highly-concentrated plan economy system, administrative examination and approval was once used extensively in many administrative areas. With the establishment and improvement of Chinese socialist market economy, existing problems in administrative approval became more and more salient and some even became institutional obstacles for the development of productivity. Therefore, it becomes the internal need for Advancing Law-based Administration of Government to reform administrative examination and approval system, regulate administrative examination, and establish power operation system with reasonable structure, scientific settings and effective procedures to ensure that power moves according to the orbit of system and rule of law.

The reform of China's administrative examination and approval system developed gradually with the deepening of reform in economic institutions, which has lasted for three decades. The third plenary session of eleventh central committee of CPC shifted the central work of the party to economic development. After that, in view of over concentration of government powers, over management and rigid management, in 1982, central government clearly put forward the idea of "decentralization of power and transfer of profits"; in 1993, to build socialist market economy, government started to raise the initiative of companies and reduce the process of examination and approval of government to companies; in 1998, departments of state Council transferred more than 280 functions to companies and social agencies; in 2001, General Office of the State Council released "*Notice on Establishing Leadership Group for Reforming Administrative Examination and Approval System of State Council*".

After that, working leadership group for reforming administrative examination and approval system of state council is established, which actively and cautiously promoted the reform of administrative examination and approval system and fully initiated reform; in 2004, after China's entry into WTO, the pace of administrative permit is remarkably accelerated, and administrative reform with slashing examination and approval items as its main content was put on agenda. In 2005, the *Administrative License Law* is promulgated, which limit the items for examination and approval and make the limit of power clear, and strengthened the supervision of administrative license activities and accountability mechanism and transfer power to people, this has far-reaching impact on right positioning of government functions.

Since the launch of reform of administrative examination and approval, State Council decided to remove and adjust all together 2374 items of administrative examination and approval in 6 installments in 2002, 2003, 2004, 2007, 2010 and 2012; since the 18th national people's congress, State Council continues to streamline governance and delegate authorities and deepen reform of administrative examination and approval. Up to February, 2016, State Council released papers for fourteen times, partially canceled, adjusted and delegated 844 items of administrative at management level, cancelled 268 items of licensing and identification of vocational qualifications, revoked 118 items of appraisal, standard reaching and recognition, cancelled three administrative charging items and changed 134 pre-licensing items for industrial and commercial administration into post-licensing items. Comprehensive cleaning-up of administrative examination and approval can reduce licensing of production and operation, narrow down the scope of examination and approval of investment projects and reduce the recognition of various institutions and its activities to the maximum extent.

Solid promotion of administrative examination and approval vigorously promotes the function transformation and innovative governance of government and facilitate the building of law-based government and create conditions for preventing and combating corruption from root.

## 10. 2. 5 Reform administrative law enforcement system, improve the efficiency of law enforcement and elevate the quality of law enforcement

Administrative law enforcement system is a vital part of government administration system. Deepening the reform in the administrative law-enforcement system is substantive content and task of deepening comprehensive reform.

The focus for reforming administrative law enforcement system is to reform the institutions for administrative law enforcement and reasonably allocate law enforcement forces. To resolve the problems of duplicate law enforcement and overlapping functions which long exist in city management and improve the level and efficiency of administrative law enforcement and lower the cost of administrative law enforcement, the government promotes comprehensive law enforcement in food and drug safety, industrial and commercial quality inspection, public sanitation, safe production, culture tourism, resource environment, agriculture, forestry, water conservancy, traffic and transportation, marine fisheries and commerce, etc. The systematic basis of comprehensive law enforcement is relatively concentrated punishment system, which dates back to *Law of the People's Republic of China on Administrative Penalty* in 1996.

In April, 1996, State Council released "Circular of the State Council Regarding the Implementation of the Law of the People's Republic of China on Administrative Penalty", which particularly stressed that all provinces, autonomous regions, and municipalities directly under the Central Government did the pilot work of relatively centralized administrative punishment; in September, 2000, the general office of State Council released "*Notice on Continuing the Pilot Work of Relatively Concentrated Administrative Punishment*" to further accelerate relatively concentrated administrative punishment. With the release of *Administrative Licensing Law* and Administrative Compulsion Law, relatively concentrated administrative licensing system and relatively concentrated coercive power system are established successively and comprehensive law enforcement system is gradually improved. Through promoting comprehensive administrative law enforcement, the team for law enforcement was integrated and the level of law enforcement was elevated. If comparing comprehensive administrative institutions with original administrative law enforcement teams, the number of law enforcement personnel is cut by large margin and law enforcement became more professional and efficient.

Another main content of administrative law enforcement reform is implementing accountability system of law enforcement. Accountability system for Administrative law enforcement is an important measure for regulating and supervising law enforcement activities of administrative institutions. In 2005, the general office of state council released "Several Opinions on Pushing Forward the Administrative Law Enforcement Responsibility System" and government at all levels made initial progress in defining responsibilities and duties of law enforcement. In practice, government at all levels and all departments actively explore all types of responsibility systems, such as making innovations in assessment system of administrative law enforcement, implementing accountability system of administrative heads, establishing and improving management system of qualification of administrative law enforcement personnel and administrative law enforcement procedural system such as the filing up of heavy punishment and hearing. Implementing accountability of law enforcement and establishing regular accountability system through setting law enforcement responsibilities for different departments and positions. The administration functions and position rights within administrative institutions are further sorted out and regulating law enforcement is guaranteed by mechanism, which greatly improves the efficiency of administration.

### 10. 2. 6 Promote the publicity of governing affairs in an all-around way; implement the internal need of building a law-based government

The publicity of government affairs is a basic work of socialist democratic rule of law and basic system for governing and also necessary for transforming government functions and establishing law-based government.

With the speeding up of rule of law in china, the system for administrative publicity is gradually promoted around the world. At present, China has initially established relatively comprehensive announcement system of national laws and regulations; hearing system as an important way of administrative publicity is explicitly provided in *Administrative Punishment Law*, *Administrative Licensing Law* and *Legislation Law*. The main way for making government affairs public is information disclosure of government and enterprise. *Regulations of the government of the People's Republic of China on Information Disclosure* implemented since May of 2008 made information disclosure an important principle in administrative practice, which vastly facilitated the building of law-based government. Departments of government at all levels adopt flexible administrative publicity forms such as "two disclosures and one supervision", government purchase, window-style service.

At the same time, the establishment of digital governance further facilitates the publicity of government affairs. In January, 1999, led by China Telecom and Economy and Information Center of National Economy and Trade Commission, more than 40 information departments of ministries, commissions, bureaus and offices coordinated to propose "the project of government affairs going public on Internet". The comprehensive launching of government affairs going public directly promoted the information process of central and local government. In October 1, 2005, portal website of central government went through test run and was open officially in January 1, 2007. Since the implementation of government affairs going public, government departments release information of government affairs to the public through internet. Most prefectural-level government set up windows on internet and formulates plans for E-government, which promote the publicity of government information in terms of technology. Administration publicity, especially digital governance promotes government at all levels to shift their role from being management-oriented to service-oriented, which greatly increase efficiency and facilitates clean government.

## 10. 2. 7 Establish efficient administrative disputes resolution mechanism to dissolve social tensions according to law in time

Resolving social tensions and disputes properly and quickly is an important link for protecting citizens' rights and interests and Advancing Law-based Administration of Government. Administrative reconsideration, administrative litigation and state compensation as main channels for solving social disputes stresses solving social tensions in a manner based on system and law.

Administrative reconsideration is channel for solving disputes within government system, which is conducive to solving administrative disputes and resolving inner tensions within the public and making the relations between government and people closer. Government at all levels correct illegal or illegitimate acts to substantively safeguard the legitimate rights of citizens, legal people and other organizations. Administrative litigation and national compensation system aim to solve administrative disputes outside government system. Since 1982, China has implemented administrative litigation system and after the Administrative Litigation Law was implemented in 1990, the system of administrative litigation is further developed and improved, which plays important role in protecting citizens, legal persons and other organizations and supervising administrative actions.

Especially since the Decision on Amending Administrative Litigation Law was deliberated and adopted in the eleventh meeting of the standing committee of twelfth national people's congress in November, 2014. Amended Administrative Litigation Law expands the scope of administrative litigation, prescribes file registration, cross-region jurisdiction system of administrative litigation cases, stresses that administrative chief should appear in the court to respond to the appeal and emphasizes the responsibility of reconsidering organs as defendants. Thus the legitimate rights of citizens, legal persons and other organizations are guaranteed and government rule of law faces higher requirements.

## 10.3  Basic experiences for Advancing Law-based Administration of Government

After 30 years of Advancing Law-based Administration of Government, Chinese government at all levels has done a lot of work in Advancing Law-based Administration of Government and made remarkable achievements and accumulated precious experiences, which mainly display in the following aspects:

### 10.3.1 The combination of party leadership, rule by people and rule of law is the prime condition for law-based government

The leadership of CPC is the fundamental feature of socialism with Chinese characteristics, which is the corner stone for socialist rule of law. The leadership of CPC and socialist rule of law is consistent: socialist rule of law complies with the leadership of CPC and leadership of party relies on socialist rule of law. Under the leadership of CPC, rule of law and rule by people are fully achieved and state and social life proceed orderly. CPC is the advocator, dominant partner and leader of socialist rule of law and rule of law follows the direction of enhancing and improving the leadership of CPC; meanwhile, as the basic way for the Modern state governance, rule of law is the choice for CPC to lead the people to great rejuvenation, and CPC leadership must rely on socialist rule of law. Rule of law is the basic strategy for the CPC to lead people to govern the country and law-based governance is the basic way for CPC to govern the country. Advancing Law-based Administration of Government is based on the basic condition of integration of CPC leadership, rule by the people and rule of law.

### 10.3.2 Comply with constitution is the fundamental guarantee for Advancing Law-based Administration of Government

Basic principles set by constitutions prescribes the fundamental system of the nation and basic rights of citizens, which show the common will and fundamental interest of people from all ethnicities. These are also fundamental principles for actions of all national organs, armed forces and all parties and social groups, and also the basis for Advancing Law-based Administration of Government. Measures for Advancing Law-based Administration of Government must be in line with constitutions.

### 10.3.3 The main direction for Advancing Law-based Administration of Government is to put economic development at center

Advancing Law-based Administration of Government is the driver and ballast for economic and social development. Comprehensive development of law-based government cannot be possible without economic development and social conditions. If too advanced, the targets and measures for Advancing Law-based Administration of Government will fail to facilitate economic and social development; if falling behind, it will impede social and economic development. So Advancing Law-based Administration of Government should center on social and economic development and make reform and development the focus for Advancing Law-based Administration of Government and insist that reform should coordinate with economic and social development, underline the status of Advancing Law-based Administration of Government in implementing rule of law and inject constant vitality into Advancing Law-based Administration of Government.

## 10.3.4    Transformation of government functions and deepening reform of administrative system is the core of Advancing Law-based Administration of Government

Advancing Law-based Administration of Government is the profound reform of old administrative model, which requires new administrative system in line with it. The building of law-based government is both the main content of and also necessary tools for transforming government functions and administrative system. During the process of society transformation, Advancing Law-based Administration of Government should progress steadily under current administrative system and match with administrative management system reform and transformation of government functions and shift the focus of government functions to economic adjustment, market supervision, society management and public service. At the same time, Advancing Law-based Administration of Government should provide enough innovation space for administrative system reform and transformation of government functions and ensure that administrative system reform and transformation of government functions can be put in place gradually.

## 10. 3. 5  Shift methodology in time drives the building of law-based government

Accelerating law-based government should be based on current achievements and gradual transformation of mentality, which relies on several transitions: first, from limitless government to limited government. Without this transition, the transformation of government functions is impossible; second, from management – oriented government to service-oriented government; management-oriented government is intent on order, mandate and penalty, while service-oriented government is intent on guidance, giving and help. The transition from management government to service government is imperative for effectively transforming government functions. Third, from traditional government to modern government; traditional government is used to managing the society, which mainly relies on campaign, conferences, slogans and leadership. Modern government requires government to meet the need of modernized governance and to ensure that government is governed by rules and thus its administration is scientific, democratic, civilized and law-based.

## 10. 3. 6  Manage officials, contain power and protect civilians' rights according to law are major tasks for Advancing Law-based Administration of Government.

The essence of law-based government is managing government in line with law. Government is the object of rule of law, while civilians and the society are the subjects. Law-based government means that government is dictated by law and government must administrate the society according to the content, aim, principles and essence of law. Government should safeguard the authority of constitution and law and provide public service and receive supervision in line with law. The focus of Advancing Law-based Administration of Government is to manage officials rather than civilians according to law; manage power rather than issues according to law. The core is protecting the rights of civilians. China's practice of Advancing Law-based Administration of Government fully shows that only through adherence to this focus and core can government administration stick to the right direction and can administrative jurisdictions be incorporated into the track of rule of law.

### 10. 3. 7    The coordination of legislation, law enforcement and supervision is the efficient way of Advancing Law-based Administration of Government

Legislation is the precondition for Advancing Law-based Administration of Government and it undertakes the responsibility of providing just and efficient rules for administrative organs; legislation is crucial for Advancing Law-based Administration of Government and is an administrative act that bears directly on the rights of the mass; supervision of administrative authority is the ballast for Advancing Law-based Administration of Government, which prevents and corrects administration going against law. The promotion of law-based government should insist on the synergy of legislation, law-enforcement, supervision and its coordination and overall progress.

### References

1. Yuan S. H. , Song G. D. . ( 2004 ) . *Readings on Law-based Administration for Officials.* Beijing: People's Publishing House.

2. Wang B. M. ( 2008 ) . *Law-based Government—Strategic Choice of Chinese Government in Rule of Law.* Beijing: Research Press.

3. Liu J. H. et al. ( 2006 ) . *Chinese Government Ruled by Law.* Beijing: Chinese Academy of Social Sciences.

4. Cao K. T. ( 2008 ) Respective and Vision of Three Decades of Building Rule of Law. Beijing: China Legal System Publishing House.

5. Literature Collection of Legislative Affairs Office of China's State Council, Chinese Academy of Governance on Strengthening the Building of Government Ruled by Law. ( 2011 ) . Beijing: Chinese Academy of Governance.

6. Supplementary Readings for *Decision of the CPC Central Committee on Major Issues Pertaining to Comprehensively Promoting the Rule of Law.* ( 2014 ) . Beijing: People's Publishing House.

7. Research Institute on Law-based Government of China University of Political Science and

Law Report on China's Law-based Government ( 2015 ) . Beijing: Social Science Literature Publishing House, 2015.

8. Wang W. H. ( 2013 ) . Procedural Approach for Advancing Law-based Administration of Government. *Jurisprudence Research*, 4.

9. Zhou H. H. ( 2014 ) . Building multi-motivation mechanism, accelerating the building of government ruled by law. *Jurisprudence Research*, 6.

10. Ma H. D. ( 2014 ) . Observation on China's Building of Law-based Government: achievements and challenges. *China's Administrative Management*, 6.

11. Research Group of Evaluating China's Government Ruled by Law. Evaluation Report on China's Law-based Government (2013) . *Administrative Jurisprudence*, 2014 (1) .

12. Ma K. ( 2011 ) . Several Questions Regarding Building China's Socialist Government Ruled by Law. *Journal of Chinese Academy of Governance*, 5.

13. Guan B. Y. ( 2015 ) . On the Connotation of Government Ruled by Law. *Nanjing Social Science*, 1.

14. Jiang M. A. ( 2015 ) . Two Questions Regarding Government Ruled by Law. *Rule of Law and Social Development*, 5.

( Written by: Jianmiao Hu, Director, Department of Law, Chinese Academy of Governance; Yan Hua, Post Doctor, Chinese Academy of Governance; Associate Professor, Law School, Fuzhou University)

# Chapter XI

# The Study of Administration in
# Contemporary China

Along with the launch of China's reform and opening-up policy and its modernization drive since 1978, reforming the government administrative system and improving administrative efficiency have become an issue that urgently needs to be emphasized. While reflecting and addressing this issue, China's public administration went through a process from advocating and restoring to studying and educating and to applying and examining. It has made a remarkable headway in academic construction, talent cultivation and social services, and has contributed its fair share to China's government reform.

## 11.1 Development and Features of the Study of Administration in Contemporary China

### 11.1.1 Development

China is a country with an abundant and enriched ideological tradition in public administration (PA). Ancient China has once created profound fine civilization achievements in practicing public administration, such as the full-fledged and distinctive governmental system, bureaucratic system, supervision system, etc. However, the research in public administration as an independent academic discipline came into being much later. At the end of the 19th century and the start of the 20th century, while the public administration system in western countries was gradually taking shape and progressing, some scholars in China began to translate and introduce influential works in this field. By the 1930s, domestic scholars have successively published some exclusive articles such as *Theories and Practices of Public Administration*, *Principles of Public Administration* and *Bureaucratic System in Europe and the United States*. Many domestic universities also opened PA courses, set up research institutions and started to impact the real administration process in the practical field. For instance, upon the resolution made by the Executive Yuan, Commission of Administrative Efficiency was established in 1934 to promote the government administrative efficiency. Gan Naiguang, then Vice Minister of Internal Affairs, was appointed as Director of the Commission. Other members include officials from various executive branches and PA professors. [1]

From 1949 to 1978, based on our national conditions and historical tasks, the Chinese government made positive explorations and great effort to improve the national status of public administration. However, due to the removal of PA from the list of academic disciplines caused by the readjustment of higher education structure in 1952, the summary of practical experiences and the scientific process of our country's public administration were extensively affected. Meanwhile, the historical accumulation and development of public administration as a discipline were also impacted. Since 1978, conducting reform on government administrative system and improving administrative efficiency have increasingly become a research topic which asks for immediate attention during the reform and opening-up as well as the modernization drive. Along with this process, China's public administration, as an independent academic discipline, went through a process from advocating and restoring to studying and educating and to applying and examining. Throughout more than 3 decades of development, it has made tremendous progress and achievements.

---

[1]  Sun Hongyun, the Administrative Efficiency Commission and the movement of administrative efficiency before the Anti-Japanese War, [J]. *Journal of Historical Science*, 2005 (2).

In early 1980s, China's veteran PA scholars including Xia Shuzhang, Huang Daqiang and Liu Yichang vehemently advocated for establishing and developing PA as an academic discipline. In 1984, General Office of the State Council and Ministry of Labor and Personnel (now Ministry of Human Resources and Social Security) hosted a "Seminar on Administrative Science" to discuss the importance of study and education in administrative science. They also suggested to establish China's public administration society. In 1985, *Chinese Public Administration*, a monthly journal, officially published its first edition, providing an important academic front for the study on administration and the reform of administrative system. In 1988, Chinese Public Administration Society (CPAS), under the charge of the General Office of the State Council, was founded in Beijing. It symbolized that since the reform and opening-up, the advocating and preparing work for restoring PA as a discipline has been completed and PA was widely accepted as an independent academic discipline in China.

After PA's academic status was established, professional education has become the "main force" for developing PA. Public administration in China has formed a relatively independent educational and scientific research system. In mid-1980s, Renmin University of China, Wuhan University, Lanzhou University, Zhengzhou University, Shanxi University and others opened PA major and schools. In 1997, Ministry of Education added Public Administration to its list of first-tier disciplines to meet the demand for inter-disciplinary talents as was required by the market economy and the modernization drive. In 1998, some universities began to cultivate PhD candidates in PA. In 2001, Master of Public Administration (MPA) education came into existence. PA education has transformed from providing indirect knowledge to providing training for practitioners so as to enable them to be decision-makers and administrators. It has greatly shortened the distance between scientific research and practical application, thus becoming an important driver for the rapid development of PA which was promoted by social practices.

In the meantime, the differentiation and integration of PA discipline and the trend of internationalization kept accelerating. Public administration is a comprehensive discipline which has a prominent feature of cross-disciplinary integration. The complexity of modern public problems makes them hard to be addressed by merely relying on the knowledge and theories of a single discipline. The research pattern of a diversified science conforms to the nature of the complex world. The development of PA as a part of social sciences is closely intertwined with the social development and is constantly differentiated and improved through practices. On the other hand, China's PA development has always walked in tandem with internationalization and has developed itself within this process. The PA academia in China attaches a great importance to draw lessons from foreign experiences. Through introducing comparative study which transcends the national border and through reflecting China's administrative practices and reform from a broader perspective, public administration in our country will be gradually brought to the international platform. Therefore, the comparative study on administrative practices and reform has gained rapid progress. In summary, PA in China has developed a very clear trajectory, the practical demand for reform and opening-up requires extensive study on PA which is in term positively affected by the international PA development.

### 11.1.2 Features

(1) Government reform and innovation have become the "major line" of PA development[1]. On the one hand, PA development in China has constructed its own system in a relatively independent manner which is in line with the disciplinary rules. On the other hand, it has conducted study on administrative theories and practices by focusing on the reform of government function and innovation in administrative pattern. Traditionally, China is an administrative country with the political power and administrative power taking dominance. Thus, in order to establish a system of the market economy, the

---

[1]   Gao Xiaoping, Process and Achievement of Administrative Management Study since China's Reform and Opening-up [J]. *Summit on Public Administration*, 2010.

prerequisite is to abolish and reduce the government's interference with micro-economic activities and to rationally define the government's economic function. In addition, enterprises shall get rid of the status as affiliated to the government so as to truly separate government from enterprises, capital and public affairs and to establish a modern enterprise system. Faced with the new situation of constant economic, social and political development, many unfitted aspects emerged in the government system including insufficient transformation of government functions, too much direct interference with micro-economic activities from the government, under-developed system of market supervision and social administration as well as a weak system of public services. The government administration itself also encountered many problems such as the deficit of public services (public services cannot meet people's need), financial deficit (it mainly refers to financial deficit in local governments, in particular governments below county-level), system deficit (there is a lack of system guarantee in many aspects of government administration), capability deficit (the government capability cannot adapt to the rapidly-changing social need), performance deficit (bureaucracy and lack of efficiency) and trust deficit (declining public trust in the government due to corruption and abuse of power). Government reform shall take scientific theories as its guidance. Government reform and innovation have become the driving force for PA development in China, thus becoming the core of PA study in China. To some extent, the latter determines the direction and component of the former, serving as a "red line" and a "major line" in PA development in China. How to establish an administrative system that is in line with social and economic development has become a requirement for PA development. Researchers in PA have conducted a series of study and exploration by focusing on hot-spot issues and difficult issues involved in government administrative reform and innovation, they have carried out an in-depth research on setting principles, organizational structure, operational process, relationship, differentiation of public affairs and rights and other major issues of government organizations under the context of reform and opening-up.

(2) Professionalization of public administration is an important driving force for its development. Government employees serve as the cornerstone and engine for the national construction, their quality and capability determine the success of national governance. In order to meet the demand for building a modern public administration, the Chinese government is in urgent need to have a team of professional government employees who have both the expertise and skills and also the righteous morality in PA. From 1980s to the present, the education and training on China's government employees have gradually become more frequent, systematic and standardized. In particular, after China adopted the system of national public servants, the development of China's government employees has become more professionalized. The professionalization of public administration lies in ensuring the professional ability and of government employees. It has become a priority for government employees to learn economic theories and management, public administration and policies and administration according to the law. The large-scale, frequent and systematic education and training for government employees has provided a good opportunity for PA development. To explore and study PA, make preparation for public positions and improve the management skills of government employees by integrating skills and management training, all these have provided a fertile soil for PA development.

(3) The problems and crisis in public sector constitute the internal driver for PA development. Public administration is in essence a science to address public problems through effective collective actions. Since the launch of the reform and opening-up, the Chinese society has undergone tremendous changes, making worldly-acknowledged achievements. However, in the social and economic sector, it has encountered many problems and confronted with many crises and challenges, the most prominent of which include problems on economic stability and sustainable development, environment pollution and ecological crisis, energy and energy security, social conflicts and social stability, food and food safety, public health, anti-poverty and unfair distribution. The problems confronting the public sector in the modern society are

highly complicated. The knowledge in public administration and policies can help us address many real social problems and the value of PA relies entirely on its ability to solve public problems. In today's society, the public attaches higher expectation on the government to tackle various social problems. They also require the government to shoulder more responsibilities which has largely transformed the nature and role of public administration. PA is no longer a mere tool for policy implementation, but a dominant force to design and carry out economic, scientific, political and social changes. In fact, it is those problems appeared in today's society that have affected the research orientation of PA and push PA researchers to look for new solutions[1].

## 11.2 Achievement of Developing Public Administration in China

### 11.2.1 Discipline construction

During the past 30 years of development, the self-awareness of the community of PA researchers has been awakened and reinforced. Meanwhile, as the reform and opening-up brought demand for public administration, the status of PA as a field for scientific research has been widely-acknowledged by the science community and the government. One result came out of the self-awareness awakening is that disciplinary development tends to be more independent and professionalized. Public administration has gradually been separated from political disciplines and other disciplines and gained its legitimate identity. It should be accredited first to the acceptance of disciplinary status by the administrative department in charge of education, second, to the demand raised by PA modernization for PA professional talents and third, to the enthusiasm of colleges and universities in expanding and developing new majors. Thanks to the rapid development of relevant schools and majors and the

---

① Zhang Chengfu, Chinese Public Administration in Transformation Era: Development and Prospects [J]. *Chinese Public Administration*, 2008 (9).

improved social status and influence of public administration, the theories and knowledge of administration have been widely disseminated. A large number of professional talents in PA· were cultivated to promote disciplinary research and development.

At present, public administration in China has established a relatively full-fledged disciplinary framework. Research on secondary disciplines has been developed successively including public management, administrative leadership, ecological analysis on administration, human resource management in public sector and study on public economy and its system. In the meantime, specialized research fields in administration have also been expanded gradually including municipal administration, educational administration, transportation administration and business administration. The research scope in PA keeps expanding and deepening and professionalized research has also been reinforced. PA research in China has been extended from all macro, meso and micro perspectives. From meso perspective, PA research has gradually expanded to study the relationship between government and market, government and society, government and enterprises and inter-government relationship. From meso perspective, more attention has been given to the formulation, implementation and evaluation of public policies and the specific policies and management in the public sector, such as public health policies and management, environment policies and management, land resource policies and management, education policies and management as well as energy policies and management. From the micro perspective, the research focused more on the scientific management of the government's internal system, such as the management of public organizations, human resource management of the public sector, public fiscal and budget management, performance management in the public sector and strategic management in the public sector. The expanded research area enables China's PA research to be adapted to China's administrative reality, focuses more on addressing public problems and utilizes multi-disciplinary knowledge to study administrative problems. There is an increasing integration among public administration and other relevant disciplines. PA has been intertwined and penetrated more with the economics, management and laws. The relevant knowledge in politics, psychology, law, economics, management science, statistics and history has provided numerous knowledge resources for PA research.

## 11. 2. 2 Talents cultivation

The study of administration in China emphasizes cultivating talents in a flexible and diversified manner. In September 1994, China National School of Administration was officially founded. It became a higher educational institution to cultivate public servants under the leadership of the State Council. Localities and governments at all levels have also established their own schools of administration. Up until now, nearly 1, 000 universities have opened undergraduate programs in Administrative Management, Public Service Management and Public Administration. More than 200 universities have opened master programs of public administration (MPA) and over 50 universities have the qualification to cultivate PhD candidates in public administration[1]. The establishment of these organizations and educational and research institutions in PA gives rise to a strong team that combines PA research, education and practices, cultivating a large number of talents for the society.

PA education emphasizes the integration of theories and practices. In order to cultivate practical and specialized talents for the government and society, the administration discipline in universities adheres to a strategy that combines "bringing in" with "going global" in the process of building the faculty team. It actively promotes the exchange and interaction among personnel who teach or study administration theories and the administrators. It also encourages universities to hire administrators with rich practical experience and theory foundation to teach there. In addition, scientific researchers and teachers from universities should go out to serve temporary positions or take part-time jobs in

---

① Lou Chengwu, Discussion on Several Issues of Public Management Development in China [J] . *China University Teaching* 2010 (5) .

governmental departments to obtain real working experiences. In terms of courses construction, equal importance should be attached to both basic knowledge and practical skills. PA curriculum aims at meeting the demand for modern administration in the transitional period and provides basic courses such as politics, management, public policy analysis, law and basic skills training. In order to improve students' comprehensive practical ability and enable PA major students to better adjust to the social development, the curriculum also add many technical courses such as administrative performance evaluation technology, public policy analysis technology, public budget and department budget planning technology, accounting technology in governmental department, auditing technology in governmental department and new technology in designing government's public image. In terms of teaching materials, emphasis has been attached to combining academic nature with applicability. Based on the need put forward by the new situation and social development, teaching materials for major PA courses were recompiled, updated and improved according to the real social development. While valuing PA theories, those materials also incorporate operational skills which is very practical and instructive. They also integrate theories with practices and coordinate the academic nature with applicability, which can effectively serve PA education and independent study.

PA education adopts a method that combines in-class education with social education, aiming at cultivating PA talents with both theoretical knowledge and practical experiences. It integrates the real need of social, political, economic and cultural construction. Through a method featuring cooperation among educational institution, scientific institution and practical departments, the professional theoretical knowledge and operational skills of the students are improved. In addition, universities also conduct collaborations with the government to create opportunities for the students to serve temporary positions or internships in grass-root administrative organizations. By going out of schools, students can contact with the social life and apply what they learned to address real problems. They can also accumulate practical experiences and deepen their understanding in the politics and administrative reality with Chinese characteristics. Thanks to the scientific system of talents cultivation, a large number of professional talents are sent to serve various areas in the government and the society each year.

### 11. 2. 3  International exchanges

As the globalization develops, PA in China is also marching towards internationalization and is having deepened and widened international exchanges.

First, arrange the translation of foreign classic works on PA. At the preliminary stage of discipline construction and theoretical research, public administration, as was imported from outside China, conducted relevant international exchanges on introducing and studying the advanced theory and practical knowledge of PA abroad. Renmin University of China, Peking University, Tsinghua University, Zhongshan University and other academic and research institutions as well as scholars have rallied relevant academic personnel to translate numerous classics and teaching materials in PA. For instance, Renmin University of China has published *Public Administration and Public Management Classics*, China National School of Administration has published *Series on Public Sector Reform Abroad* and the Commercial Press has published *Comparison of Chinese and Foreign Political Systems Series*. While the publication of these translated works has introduced the latest progress of PA theories and practices from abroad to China, it also promotes the development of PA in China.

Second, host international academic seminars. Since 1984, our government and the community of academia have hosted many large-scale international seminars on PA, such as the UN Seminar on Reforming Civil Service Systems for Development hosted in 1984, the 14th Annual Conference of East Region Organization of Public Administration held in 1991, the International Anti-Corruption Conference in 1995 and the 3rd International Institute of Administrative Sciences (IIAS) International Congress in 1996. In the meantime, Renmin University of China and American Society for Public Administration, Rutgers University, Chinese Public Administration Society, University of Electronic Science and Technology of China and University of Warwick have jointly hosted numerous international seminars on public management. Many renowned Chinese universities have also held all kinds of specific international conferences, covering topics of many major issues confronting the modern public administration, thus pushing forward the international academic exchanges of PA in China.

Third, encourage exchanges among scholars and international research cooperation. Relevant research organizations in PR have dispatched exchange scholars and students to foreign countries each year to study the latest PA theories and practical experiences. Meanwhile, many famous PA scholars have come to China to conduct regular or non-regular academic exchanges so as to learn the latest research achievements and discuss the disciplinary development. These organizations have also jointly cultivated students. Many domestic universities, research institutions and scholars have conducted joint research with international institutions ( such as the United Nations Development Program ( UNDP ), World Bank and Asian Development Bank) in many fields of common concerns ( such as government reform, environment management, governance and development and public service).

## 11. 2. 4  Contribution of China's Public Administration

Throughout several decades of research and exploration, China's public administration has made a remarkable progress, contributing a lot to our country's social science development, disciplinary development, scientific research, talents cultivation and administrative reform.

First, public administration has become a relatively independent academic discipline and has established its basic research scope and system. The professionalized research on PA has gradually been enhanced and many secondary research fields have been derived from it which include public management, public policies, public leadership, decision sciences, human resources management in the public sector, administrative psychology, public economic research and systematic analysis. In the meantime, specialized administration research areas such as municipal sciences, educational administration, health administration, transport administration and business administration have also grown steadily. In addition, PA in China has integrated China's reality and put forward theories that conform to China's national conditions. It has established a knowledge system suitable to China's administrative practices and reform, increasing the voice of China's administrative practices and reform internationally.

Second, public administration has provided a strong support for the government reform. From the central government ( the State Council) to the local level ( Provincial, municipal, country and village governments), China has elevated PA theoretical study and application to an important position which can promote administrative system reform and improve government efficiency, execution and trust. The government has actively implemented scientific administration, democratic administration and administration based on the law. It has integrated the administrative practices of civil servants with theoretical study and academic research. It has set up administration research institutions in governmental organizations and public institutions and has strengthened administrative study. The government has created conditions for administrative study by enhancing instruction, assigning tasks, spreading information and providing material support. It has supported the research work of research institutions and social groups and regarded them as "advisers" to help the government improve administration. In the process of formulating reform plans and implementing the reform, the government will listen to their opinions and suggestions and serve as "the bridge" to connect the society and unite experts and scholars, playing an important role in this regard. The academia of administration mainly studies hot-spot and difficult issues in administrative system reform, especially major topics with comprehensive, strategic and forward-looking significance. A large number of experts have conducted scientific policy research and management consultations. Over the past several decades, focusing on many important theoretical and pragmatic problems in government administration and reform such as the transformation of government function, institutional reform, personnel system reform, public fiscal reform, public service system and mechanism reform, democratic and scientific policy-making, public crisis management, reform on environmental protection system, reform on public health system and anti-corruption, scholars in public administration have provided many valuable policy suggestions. These research results has enabled PA research institutions to be important "think-tank" for the government[1].

Third, respond to the social demand and fulfill public responsibility. The extent a discipline can respond to and satisfy the demand raised by the time determines the extent it can grow and prosper. Public administration, from its first day, is an applied discipline aims at addressing public problems. The social transformation and government reform and innovation in China have put forward many questions waiting to be addressed for theoretical researchers and practitioners. Those questions include how to balance the roles of the government and the market; how to optimize the government function; how to deal with the relationship between the government and the citizen and realize democratic administration; how to optimize the public management system; how to improve government capability; how to innovate the social management system; how to realize administration according to the law and establish a government ruled by law; how to fulfill responsibilities and how to ensure enforcement and public trust. The society has attached a high expectation to the research on public administration and is expecting that scholars in this field can help tackle these questions. PA scholars have the responsibility to analyze and study various obstacles lying on the way towards a modern government, understand China's PA history and reality, interpret and explain it in the right way and provide constructive solutions and suggestions. In the process of China's PA

---

① Gao Xiaoping, Process and Achievement of Administrative Management Study since China's Reform and Opening-up [J]. *Summit on Public Administration*, 2010.

development, scholars have presented a strong sense of public responsibility which is mainly manifested in the following aspects: First, in citizen education. The scholars impart knowledge on the concept, system and mechanism of government administration as well as knowledge on public policies to university students so as to enable those students to understand China's administration reality and understand their rights, obligations and responsibilities as citizens. Second, provide education and training for public institutions and officials. No matter it is in the department of public administration of universities or in the specific educational and training institutions for officials (such as the administration schools at national or local levels and party schools), the impartment of knowledge on PA has played a very important role. The impartment enables officials to understand how to make choices more wisely, how to work more efficiently and how to provide public service more responsibly[①].

## 11. 3  Main Contents of the Study of Administration in Contemporary China

With the launch of an overhaul reform in China, public administration has taken the realistic problems in China's administration reform as the key of its research and focused on studying the rules and features of China's administration. This has strongly promoted China's administration reform and accelerated its pace. Meanwhile, PA scholars have integrated China's reality and conducted many independent thinking and explorations, yielding numerous creative results. China's PA study as a wholes engages a wide range of fields which mainly include the following areas.

---

① Zhang Chengfu, Chinese Public Administration in Transformation Era: Development and Prospects [J] . *Chinese Public Administration*, 2008 (9) .

## 11. 3. 1  The basic theoretical study on administration

First, the study on administrative philosophy. The study on administrative philosophy in China has enriched ideological roots which is able to absorb the essence from the governance practices and ideological systems of China's various dynasties. The academia of administration in China has conducted in-depth exploration in administration methods innovation, administrative culture, administrative ethics, publicness, administrative strategies and administrative development. The study content has both external tension and cohesive force. The topics of study advance step by step which transcend the quality and quantity as well as the time and space of administration, constructing the theoretical basis and core scope of administrative philosophy. The theoretical exploration and realistic study complemented and integrated with each other, providing philosophical support for the deep-rooted problems of the study on administrative system reform and innovation.

Second, the study on service-oriented government. Service-oriented government constitutes an important theoretical achievement and exerts a deep influence on China's government practices. Chinese scholars have summarized the historical process of government administration pattern which has transformed from "rule-based governance" before the contemporary times to "management-based administration" in the contemporary times and then to "service-oriented administration" in modern times. This is a dynamic and changing process in which ruling and management or management and service can have only one rises and the other falls. From the perspective of service-oriented administration, the government function lies in providing public service, correct market malfunction, provide public product, create safe, democratic and equal systematic environment, address public issues confronting the society and promote the sound social development. Purchasing public service by the government is the key to build service-oriented government which requires to tackle problems involving rules and regulations, service standard, working mechanism, social organization and supervision and evaluation. Setting up a scientific and rational evaluation standard for public service quality is the basic part of building a service-oriented government.

Third, the study on modern administration. The Chinese government has put forward to " advancing the national administration system and the modernization of administration capability" , which is also an important research topic in the academia of administration. Researchers in this field have conducted tremendous research works in this regard. The national administration system is a basic institutional system for a nation to realize national administration goals. Take China's reality as an example, it includes three areas of institutional system. The first is the national legal system. This is the basic system of a nation and a society which mainly includes the constitution, laws, administrative rules, local rules and administrative regulations. The second is the institutional system of the Party. The third is the institutional system of the society which include political consultation system and the system of grass-root autonomy. National administration capability is the actual ability for a country to realize national administration goals which showcases the ability of system implementation. In terms of China's reality, to be specific, it should include three abilities: The first is the ability of the state institutions to fulfill their duty. It mainly refers to the ability of power institutions to fulfill their lawful duties and realize national goals. The second is the ability of the general public to manage national, social, economic and cultural affairs as well as their own affairs according to law. The third is the ability to establish the national system and realize self-upgrading. It mainly refers to the ability of a nation to construct and transform the national administration system. The national administration system and the modernization of administration capability are actually a process in which the administration system and administration ability, as modern political elements, have constantly and consecutively transformed from a lower level to a higher level. In this process, the national administration system has become more full-fledged, mature and stabilized which has included a whole package of political, economic, social, cultural and ecological administration systems. And under these administration systems, the administration ability can be applied in a more effective, transparent and equitable way which includes all kinds of political, economic, social, cultural, ecological, scientific and informative approaches.

### 11.3.2 Research in administrative reform

First, reform on the administrative system. The reform on the administrative system constitutes an important part of administrative reform. Since the launch of the reform and opening-up, the Chinese government has successively launched seven rounds of large-scale system reforms which have aroused wide discussion among the academia of administration in China. The institutional basis of our country's system reform lies in the establishment of the socialist market economy and the institutionalized relationship featuring openness and cooperation that China has built with the world based on a series of institutional platforms. The core of the reform is to accommodate the need for economic and social development, readjust the structure and operation of government institutions according to the rules of economic and social development. Emphasis should be put on readjusting the relations between the government and the society, the government and the market as well as the central level and the local level. Regarding the study on government institutional reform, the discipline of administration attaches major attention on topics include how to readjust the relations between the government and the society by transforming from omnipotent government to limited government and from controlled government and service-oriented government; how to readjust the relations between the government and the market as well as the government and enterprises through government system reform; how to readjust the relations between the central level and the local level through delegating power to the local level so as to address the problem of centralization and decentralization of power.

Second, the transformation of government functions. Another important content of administrative reform is the transformation of government functions. Scholars in the field of administration have conducted research in many deep-rooted problems need to be addressed in the process of advancing the fundamental transformation of government functions. These researches mainly focus on the government, the market and the society. For instance, what are the relations among the three; what kind of power list system the government should promote; what kind of reform momentum the local government should keep; how to avoid the situation in which administrative approval falls into a digital game; how to ensure that the reform will not sink into a segmented and low-efficient circle and how to equip the various NGOs, social entities and grass-root institutions with sufficient carrying capability. Regarding these problems, scholars think that a systematic theory should be established to illustrate the relations among the government, the market and the society and among the central government and the local ones. They also think that a full-fledged and standardized system of government power list shall be formed, the internal force of reform driven by governments at various levels shall be strengthened and focus shall be attached to the quality of progress in the process of deepening the reform on administrative approval system. In addition, the management property of functions transmitted from the government to the market and the society shall be properly determined so as to identify the dimension of market supervision and enhance the supervision. Reforms on governments at various levels and locations shall be advanced in coordination with the nationwide endeavor and the absorbing ability of grass-root governments, market and the social entities shall be nurtured. It should also pragmatically strengthen the government administration and supervision throughout the whole process, provide legitimate guarantee for the reform and focus on optimizing the organizational structure and government process. Efforts should also be made to summarize the relations among different departments at different levels within the governments and realize the organic integration and coordination within the government system so as to improve the pattern to fulfill government's duties. At present, particular emphasis shall be put to streamline the administration, delegate power to the lower level, combine the decentralization of power with proper management and optimize services.

Third, the construction of a clean government ruled by the law. Building a clean government ruled by the law is the strategic goal of China's government administrative reform and is also a priority of administrative study. The core to establish a government ruled by the law is to push forward administration according to the law. Administrative study has pointed out that in order to establish a government ruled by the law and push forward administration according to the law, attention shall be attached to the following perspectives: First, law shall come first. The administrative discretion must be under control of the law. We must ensure that all kinds of administrative entities that engage in administrative management must act according to the law and strictly fulfill their lawful duties. Those administrative entities and personnel violating the law must bear relevant legal liabilities. Any violation such as the abuse of administrative power, law enforcement overstepping its due boundary and administrative inaction must be investigated. Second, the process must be efficient, reasonable and appropriate in its procedures. The essence of administration according to the law does not only require act according to the law, but also emphasizes the efficiency and rightfulness of administrative management in handling specific affairs. The priority is to provide highly-efficient administrative activities and high-quality public service, ensure the initiative and enthusiasm of administrators and gain good service profit with a relatively low cost. Third, we must equalize rights with obligations. Administrative entities at various levels and their staff enjoy administrative rights and obligations. Here, "obligations" refers to both administrative obligations and administrative responsibilities. Administrative entities and their staff must bear legal responsibilities for their act violating the law. The academia of administration has put forward the criteria for a clean government which is as follows: the government officials shall have the integrity in performing their official duties; government agencies, public departments and other legal entities are abide by the law; the acquisition and application of the public power and public resources are selfless and legitimate; the jurisdiction and law enforcement are just an impartial and legal policies are all for the people. Building a clean government requires to establish a power operational mechanism with checks and balances, promote the modernization of government administration, build a comprehensive and sound anti-corruption system and a strong law-enforcement agency against the corruption and forge a powerful and dynamic citizen society.

### 11. 3. 3  Research in government management innovation

Innovation in government management patterns is an important area of major concern of administration. Government management innovation is an enduring theme of government development and administration study. The modern administration mainly studies the following issues:

First, enhance openness and transparency of the government. Under the strong push of experts in the academia of administration and other disciplines, China has made a great progress in its legislation on information disclosure. The mechanism of government information disclosure has been gradually improved with a constantly expanded scope which has ensured people's right to know, participate and supervise. Improving government's openness could promote the establishment of scientific and democratic decision-making mechanism of the government, such as establishing a decision-making mechanism that combines people's participation with experts' analysis and government's decision. The scholars have conducted extensive and in-depth discussion on " government reform and innovation in the big-data era" . The advent of the big-data era has brought a strike to the national governance status leaded by the state featuring the tripartite co-governance of " state-society-market" . The full expression of discourses, participation and interaction, consensus building and rules integration constitute the main resources and opportunities that the big-data era has granted to the national governance. " Consultative governance" might become a great opportunity to utilize these resources maximally. While the application of big-data technology has improved the precision of the administrative management, the data openness has granted people the right to analyze and use data, making " data democracy" a possibility. The general public could check the resolution process of relevant legislations and public policies, gradually reveal the " black box" of decision-making in the past and express their political interests and appeals on various platforms. Some scholars have introduced these new things into the research on public service. The "Mobile government" has provided a highly-efficient and all-round platform of public service to improve government work[1].

Second, how to build the government emergency management system. The modern China is undergoing a profound social transformation, displaying many features of a risk society. The increasingly frequent emergence of public crisis events have threatened the social peace and stability. In recent years, the study on public crisis management has attracted much attention from the scholars. The academia of administration has paid timely attention and responded to social risks, promote government to initially establish an emergency management system featuring the response pursuant to different classifications, localized management, information sharing and collaboration based on the division of labor.

Third, improve execution and public trust of the government. The administration research in China discusses major tools to improve execution and public trust of the government. 1. Performance management. The overall performance of the government has received more and more attention. Some local governments and departments have begun to conduct positive exploration in government performance evaluation, playing a conducive role in enhancing responsibility, improving service, raising efficiency, deepening openness, improving the reward and punishment mechanism and strengthening implementation. 2. Provide feedback through supervision. The governmental supervision department shall obtain information through conducting supervision and inspection, find problems in the process of government execution and correct them timely so as to manage things well and put everything under control. A strong supervision and inspection will play a constructive role to improve the implementation of various government projects. 3. Initiate cultural

---

① Xu Kaiyi, Review on China's Administration Research in 2015 [J] . *The Journal of Yunnan Administration College*, 2016 (1) .

construction work. It should advocate the culture of government execution and form a culture of government execution featuring "immediate response and action". It should take improving execution as the basic criteria in examining governmental agencies, government officials and civil servants. It should also nurture a kind of government execution culture with the core of the concept of "immediate response". 4. Process reengineering. Many local governments have initiated government process reengineering guided by government's public need. It aims at optimizing examining and approving procedures, rationalizing working relations, addressing function duplication and improving technical methods in order to reduce government hierarchy, streamline administrative procedures, realize the cross-functional process and intensive management as well as improve administrative efficiency and government execution. 5. Advance government quality management. It has integrated the basic concept, working principle and operational pattern of quality management into administrative management so as to ensure the overall quality and efficiency of government departments' work, providing high-quality public goods and services. The goal is to obtain customer satisfaction and people's satisfaction of public services and their trust in the public sector constitute the main criteria for examining the performance of the public sector. Quality stands at the center and participation by all serves as the foundation. It emphasizes the coordination and collaboration among each individuals and departments and also between individuals and departments. It regards other individuals or departments as its customers and strives to establish government organizations that are full of vigor and vitality.

## References

1. Bai G. (1996) . *General History of the Chinese Political System* (*Volume* 1), People's Publishing House.

2. Yu X'A. (2011) . Did Liang Qichao really say that "China's officials shall all study public administration"?, *Chinese Public Administration*, *Edition*, 2.

3. Mao G. R. (2011) . On the formation of the concept of "administration" and "public administration" —a response to Mr. Yu Xing'an, *Chinese Public Administration*, 10.

4. Gao X. P. (2010) . Process and achievement of the study on administrative management since China's reform and opening-up policy, Summit on Public Administration.

5. Zhang C. F. ( 2008 ) . China's Public Administration in the transformative era: development and prospect, *Chinese Public Administration*, 9.

6. Lou C. W. ( 2000 ) . Discussions on several issues regarding the current academic development of China's public management, *China University Teaching*, 5.

7. Zhou Z. R. ( 2012 ) . Integration between Internationalization and Localization: An Overview of Public Administration Development in China over the Past 30 Years and Beyond. *Journal of Public Administration*, *1*, 10 – 15.

8. Liu P. ( 2013 ) . China's Public Administration Discipline: A Critical Thinking towards Localization. *Journal of Renmin University of China*, *3*, 98 – 107.

9. He Y. L. ( 2007 ) . What Kind of Research We are Doing: An Evaluation of Chinese Public Administration Research. *Public Administration Research.*

10. Liu X. R. ( 2002 ) . Service-oriented Government: Target of the Reform of Chinese Government under the Background of Economic Globalization. *Chinese Public Administration*, *7*, 5 – 7.

11. Chi F. L. ( 2006 ) . Comprehensively Understand the Meaning of the Public Service-Oriented Government. *People's Tribune*, *5*, 14 – 15.

12. Chinese Public Administration Society research project group ( 2006 ) . Definition and Essence of Service-oriented Government. *Journal of Theoretical Reference*, *6*: 29.

13. Jay D. White, Making sense with diversity: The context of research, theory, and knowledge development in public administration. Review of Research in Public Administration: Reflections on Theory and Practice . Beijing: *Tsinghua University Press.*

14. He Y. ( 2005 ) . Evaluation on the Methodology in Public Administration Research and its Future Development. *Chinese Public Administration*, *10*.

( Written by: Jie Liu, Deputy Director, Liaison Department, Chinese Public Administration Society )